DISMISSAL LAW
IN THE
REPUBLIC OF IRELAND

by

Mary Redmond, B.C.L., LL.M. (N.U.I.), Ph.D. (Cantab.), Solicitor,
Fellow and Tutor of Christ's College, Cambridge

Published in 1982 by
The Incorporated Law Society of Ireland
and printed by
The Leinster Leader Limited, Naas, Co. Kildare
ISBN 0 902027 22 0

Cover design by Bill Hastings

TO MY PARENTS

INTRODUCTORY NOTE

The Incorporated Law Society of Ireland established a committee in 1969 to promote the publication of text-books and commentaries on the law in Ireland. The Society has since sponsored the publication of the following:

Cole, J. S. R., *Irish Cases on Evidence* (1972) (published by the Society).

Cole, J. S. R., *Irish Cases on Criminal Law* (1975) (published by the Society).

Wylie, J. C. W., *Irish Land Law* (1975) (published by Professional Books Ltd.).

Johnston, R. W. R., *Wealth Tax* (1976) (published by the Society).

Wylie, J. C. W., *Irish Conveyancing Law* (1978) (published by Professional Books Ltd.).

Nowlan, K. I., *A Guide to the Planning Acts* (1978) (published by the Society).

Walsh, E. M., *Planning and Development Law* (1979) (published by the Society).

O'Reilly & Redmond, *Cases and Materials on the Irish Constitution* (1980) (published by the Society).

Williams, A. G., *Principles of Corporation Tax in the Republic of Ireland* (1981) (published by the Society).

The Garda Síochána Guide. Fifth edition (1981) (published by the Society).

Cole, J. S. R., *Irish Cases on Evidence*. Second edition (1982) (published by the Society).

Keane, R., *The Law of Local Government in the Republic of Ireland* (1982) (published by the Society).

Grants from the Arthur Cox Foundation were made available to assist the publication of several of the above books.

Preface

Since the Unfair Dismissals Act, 1977, came into force in the Republic of Ireland hundreds of employers have been called upon to appear and to defend their decisions before the Rights Commissioners or the Employment Appeals Tribunal. The Act provides a charter of rights for over one million employees. Alongside the vibrance of the Act's jurisdiction, the Constitution and the common law provide further sources of redress.

The picture which confronts one is exhilarating, but it is also depressing. To borrow Lord Tennyson's words, the law — above all, unfair dismissal law — appears as a 'codeless myriad of precedent, [a] wilderness of single instances'. In this most essential area, there is no textbook, no monograph, there is not even a pamphlet setting out the rudiments of unfair dismissal law. An abbreviated version of twenty-seven cases appeared in 1981, entitled *Reports of Important Decisions by the Employment Appeals Tribunal under the Unfair Dismissals Act 1977: Years 1977 and 1978.* There is nothing besides.

Nor is the subject explained in a wider setting. There is (yet) no textbook on Irish labour law. At the present time, when it comes to source material for the law on termination of employment, the lawyer (not to mention the individual worker, employer or trade unionist) must find his or her way around Law Reports and indices, statutes and statutory regulations. Daunting as this task may be, it is as nothing compared to the 'lawlessness' of the statutory jurisdiction. Recommendations of the Rights Commissioners are not available to the public. Determinations of the EAT are issued selectively.

The present work attempts to prevent the wilderness of Irish dismissal law from becoming altogether unmanageable. It seeks to place the law in a field of legal, if not of logical, consistency. All three jurisdictions, constitutional, common law and statutory, are concerned. The analysis, it is hoped, is one of timeliness. In June, 1982, the Minister for Labour indicated his intention to improve the Unfair Dismissals Act, 1977, in the course of his speech on the Department's Estimate in Dáil Éireann. The law is as of January, 1982.

I owe an inestimable debt of gratitude to many people but to none more than to Dr. Patrick Elias, Fellow of Pembroke College, Cambridge. He has been unfailing in his assistance and encouragement particularly during the time when an earlier version of this work was being prepared for submission as a doctoral thesis to the University of Cambridge. I am grateful to the British Council for a one-year Research Scholarship which enabled me, in 1978, to commence research on Irish dismissal law as a graduate student at Christ's College, Cambridge. I remain ever grateful to Christ's College for having appointed me a Research Scholar in 1979-80 and for having assisted so generously during that time in helping to defray research costs. My thanks are also due to the Stationery Office, Dublin, for permission to reproduce the text of the Unfair Dismissals Act, 1977, and of the statutory regulations which appear in the appendices to this book.

Responsibility for errors remains squarely my own.

Mary Redmond

Christ's College, Cambridge.
1 July, 1982.

Foreword

The word "dismissal", stemming as it does from the Latin for "sending away", conjures up for an employee the situation of being thrown out of work, perhaps unjustly, perhaps also unexpectedly. In whatever way it is communicated, the word has the harsh ring of finality, in some ways not dissimilar to a prison sentence. The status quo has been radically altered, even destroyed. If the "sentence" of dismissal is known in advance or even apprehended, the waiting period will often give rise to mounting anxiety, possibly resulting in fright or despair when the axe eventually falls. This is because the event can develop into an alarming social catastrophe for the dismissed employee, who may have reason to apprehend long or even permanent unemployment, collapse of family plans, poverty and even ill-health and tragedy.

To an employer, the notion of "dismissal" means disturbing reflections on the unpleasantness involved in having to let a long standing employee go, as well as such possible consequences as worsening industrial relations with retained staff, the problem of compensation, the possibility of having to appear publicly before a Court or Tribunal, and possibly be judged to have acted unfairly, with the added possibility of being forced to reinstate the dismissed one.

From the very nature of the concept of "dismissal" it is only to be expected that, even as far back as the primitive beginning of human work relationships, the termination of such relationships should have given rise to an endless number of confrontations, grievances and disputes, inevitably claiming the attention of sociologists, politicians, legislators, lawyers, trade unions and employers' organisations.

It goes without saying that the subject provides a difficult although rich field of scholarly endeavour for a legal author. Dr. Mary Redmond has given us a truly magnificent book, dealing with the social as well as the legal and constitutional ramifications of the subject with particular reference to the Irish context. All interested people owe her a debt of gratitude for expending her exceptional talents and her valuable time on the compiling and writing of this book. As well as having all the signs of authentic scholarly research the book is extremely well written. Dr. Redmond has applied in a clear and logical way her very highly developed powers of comparison and legal analysis. Her work takes due account of a vast amount of previously published work on the subject, beginning with Mr. Matthew Dutton's book, published in 1723, entitled *The Law of Masters and Servants in Ireland*. She includes a valuable bibliography. She relishes concepts that are changing or new, such as compensation for mental distress or injured feelings, and loss of job satisfaction. What she has written about the impact of the Irish

Constitution on the law of dismissal is, in my opinion, first class and it indicates a penetrating insight into the philosophy of the Constitution and the evolution of its legal implications.

She has dealt extensively with Irish case law. In this connection she has the courage to point out any unsoundness of reasoning she sees in some of the controversial judgments. At the same time I must say that I cannot recall any instance where she has taken a debatable viewpoint, where she has not fairly set out the opposing viewpoint which she rejects. I commend the attention of our legislators to her suggestions on amendments to the Unfair Dismissals Act.

I have learned a lot from this stimulating book, and I welcome it, and feel honoured to have been asked to write the foreword.

John Gleeson

12 Shrewsbury Road,
Dublin 4.
26 May, 1982.

TABLE OF CONTENTS

Introductory Note vi

Preface vii

Foreword ix

Summary of Contents xii

Table of Irish Cases xviii

Table of British and other Cases xxviii

Tables of Statutes xxxvii

Table of Statutory Instruments xli

Abbreviations xlii

Dismissal Law in the Republic of
Ireland 1

Appendix I 233

Appendix II 256

Appendix III 260

Appendix IV 264

Appendix V 267

Appendix VI 272

Appendix VII 273

Bibliography 274

Articles 278

Official Publications 284

Index 285

SUMMARY OF CONTENTS

Chapter One

HISTORICAL DEVELOPMENT OF THE LAW'S PROTECTION AGAINST WRONGFUL TERMINATION OF EMPLOYMENT

Introduction: The nature of the work 1

A. Historical Evolution of Statute and of Common Law on Termination of Employment in Ireland 4

   (1) Statute law 4

   (2) The relationship of master and servant at common law 18

   (3) The common law action for wrongful dismissal 23

B. Individual Employment Rights and Organised Activity in Ireland 25

Chapter Two

THE IRISH CONSTITUTION AND DISMISSAL

Introduction: Stages of Constitutional Development in Ireland 28

A. Infringement of Constitutional Provisions and Dismissal 32

B. Remedies under the Constitution 40

Chapter Three

DISMISSAL AT COMMON LAW—TERMINATION BY THE PARTIES

Introduction: The Importance of Contract 45

A. Identifying the Nature of Employment 46

   (1) Employees 46

   (2) Office-holders 47

   (3) Persons whose employment is regulated by statute ... 50

B. Lawful Dismissal 51

   (1) Due notice of termination 52

      (i) At common law 52

      (ii) Contracts apparently incapable of termination by notice 54

      (iii) Statutory notice 56

(2) Lawful summary dismissal 57

   (i) Grounds existing at time of dismissal 57

   (ii) Grounds discovered subsequent to dismissal 61

C. Wrongful Dismissal 62

(1) Ordinary employees 62

   (i) Breach of procedural limitations 63

   (ii) Breach of an implied term of fairness 64

   (iii) Breach of substantive limitations 66

(2) Office-holders and special category employees 67

   (i) *Audi alteram partem* 69

      (a) Employees governed by statute 70

      (b) Offices held at will or pleasure 74

      (c) The scope of *audi alteram partem* 76

   (ii) *Nemo judex in re sua* 78

D. The effect of Breach of the Employment Contract on the
Concept of Termination at Common Law 81

Chapter Four

REMEDIES FOR WRONGFUL DISMISSAL

A. Ordinary Employees 87

(1) Equitable remedies 87

(2) Damages 91

   (i) General principles on which damages are awarded
for wrongful dismissal 91

   (ii) Specific cases 94

      (a) Breach of substantive limitations 94

      (b) Breach of procedural limitations 94

      (c) Damages and the elective theory of repudiatory
breach 95

   (iii) Specific application of principles relating to
damages for wrongful dismissal 98

   (iv) Other forms of pecuniary loss and deductions:
pensions and perquisites 101

   (v) Liability to income tax 104

(vi) Social Welfare benefits 107

(vii) The mitigation of loss 107

B. Office-holders and Public Employees 109

(1) Declaratory relief 109

(2) Damages as an alternative remedy 110

(3) Damages as an additional remedy 111

Chapter Five

STATUTORY UNFAIR DISMISSAL

A. The Need for Legislation concerning Dismissal: Background
Influences 116

B. The Unfair Dismissals Act 120

(1) Basic principles 120

(2) Enforcing authorities under the Act 121

(3) The winds of change? 128

C. Preliminary Requirements in the Act 128

(1) Qualifications and exclusions 128

(2) Time-limit for presentation of claims and appeals 133

(3) Fact of dismissal 134

(i) Termination, repudiatory breach and unfair
dismissal 136

(ii) The 'fact' of constructive dismissal: criteria
involved in its establishment 140

(iii) Doubt as to facts surrounding dismissal 142

(4) Date of dismissal 143

Chapter Six

REASONABLENESS AND THE EMPLOYER'S ROLE UNDER THE UNFAIR DISMISSALS ACT

A. The Employer's Reason for Dismissal 145

(1) Identifying the employer's reason 145

(i) Dismissals deemed not be unfair 147

(a) Capability, competence or qualifications 148

(b) Conduct 149

(c) Redundancy 150

(d) Other substantial grounds 153

(ii) Dismissals deemed to be unfair 154

(2) Evidence of the employer's reason 156

B. Reasonableness of the Employer's Decision to Dismiss ... 158

(1) The nature of the employer's enquiry 160

(i) Warnings 162

(ii) Adequate hearings 164

(2) Reasonableness of employer's conclusion in the light of all the circumstances 166

C. Constructive Dismissal: the Reason therefor 169

Chapter Seven

REMEDIES FOR UNFAIR DISMISSAL

Introduction: *Proprietas* in Employment 175

A. Primary Remedies under the Act 176

(1) The Constitution 176

(2) Reinstatement and re-engagement defined 178

(3) No right to primary remedies 181

B. Compensation 184

(1) Broad approach of the EAT 184

(2) Compensation described 186

(i) Actual loss 188

(ii) Deductions 191

(iii) Liability to income tax 192

(iv) Prospective loss 192

(v) Superannuation 195

(vi) Contributory action by complainant or by employer 197

(vii) The duty to mitigate 199

(viii) *Ex gratia* or severance payments 201

Chapter Eight

COLLECTIVE ASPECTS OF UNFAIR DISMISSAL

A. The Individualisation of Collective Issues in the Act 203
B. The Trade Disputes Act and Dismissal 205
C. Express Limitations on Managerial Prerogative in the Act   206
   (1) Trade union activities 207
   (2) Unfair selection for redundancy 209
   (3) Dismissal for participating in strike or other industrial
      action 212

Chapter Nine

A FINAL DRAWING TOGETHER OF STRANDS AND TRENDS

A. Three Jurisdictions Contrasted 220
   (1) Trends in EAT practice since 1977 223
      (i) Resort to the EAT 223
      (ii) Number of dismissals adjudged unfair 224
      (iii) Legal representation 224
      (iv) Withdrawal of claims 225
      (v) The parties 225
   (2) The EAT: consistency or finality? 226
B. Whither the Contract Model? 227

Appendix I

Unfair Dismissals Act, 1977 (No. 10 of 1977) 233

Appendix II

Unfair Dismissals (Claims and Appeals) Regulations,
1977 (S.I. No. 286 of 1977) 256

Appendix III

Unfair Dismissals (Calculation of Weekly Remuneration)
Regulations, 1977 (S.I. No. 287 of 1977) 260

Appendix IV

Extracts from Redundancy (Redundancy Appeals Tribunal) Regulations, 1968 (S.I. No. 24 of 1968): Regulations 10 to 17 (2), 19-20 A, 23, 24 264
(See also Appendix II, S.I. No. 286 of 1977, Regulation 10.)

Appendix V

Claimant's originating application to the Employment Appeals Tribunal 267

Appendix VI

Distribution of Compensation awarded by the EAT in determinations of Unfair Dismissal in 1980 272

Appendix VII

Representation at Sittings of the EAT in 1980 273

TABLE OF IRISH CASES

Ahern v. Ahern Fabrics Ltd. UD 74/1977 .... 193n, 195n
A La Francaise Ltd. v. Monaghan UD 13/1977 .... 188n, 208n
Allen v. Wellman Int. Ltd. UD 152/1979 .... 163n
Ardmore Studios (Ireland) Ltd. v. Lynch and Others [1965] IR 1 .... 26n
Arklow Pottery Ltd. v. O'Reilly UD 241/1979 .... 157n

Barr v. Marley Extrusions (Ire.) Ltd. UD 78/1978 .... 197n
Bartlett v. Kerry County Council UD 178/1979 .... 130n
Bartley v. Royal Dublin Golf Club UD 151/1978 .... 163n, 175n
Bastow v. Anderson Co. UD 314/1978 .... 167n
Becton Dickinson Ltd. v. Lee [1973] IR 1 .... 35n, 38n, 206n, 215n
Belford v. Doyle UD 286/1978 .... 163n
Bennett v. Byrne & Sons Ltd. UD 173/1980 .... 148n
Bevan v. Daydream Ltd. UD 31/1978 .... 148n
Boland v. Dublin Corporation [1946] IR 88 .... 61n
Boyd v. Fitt (1863) 14 1CLR 43 .... 92n
Branigan v. Collins (Godolfin Gallery) UD 28/1977 .... 191n, 193n
Breen v. Cooper IR 3 CL 621 .... 24, 98n
Breslin v. Dublin Board of Assistance (1956) 90 ILTR 158 ..... 50n, 52n, 55n
Breslin & McKeever v. Gilchrist & Co. (1903) 37 ILTR 99 20
Brewster v. Burke and Minister for Labour (High Court,
  unreported, 8 February 1978) 59n
British & Irish Steampacket Co. Ltd. v. Branigan [1958] IR 128 .... 205n
Brown v. McInerney Construction Ltd. UD 117/1981 .... 209n
Buckley v. Disabled Artists Ltd. UD 3/1978 .... 191n, 193n
Burke v. Garvey (High Court, unreported, April 1977) 51n
Burke & O'Reilly v. Burke and Quail [1951] IR 216 .... 30n
Bux v. Toohey & Co. Ltd. UD 137/1978 .... 158n, 167n, 193
Byrne v. Allied Transport Ltd. UD 11/1979 .... 161n
Byrne v. Bradden Design Centre Ltd. UD 176/1978 .... 163n, 189n
Byrne v. Clayton Inns Ltd. UD 21/1978 .... 134n
Byrne v. Ireland [1972] IR 241 44
Byrne v. Limerick Steamship Co. [1946] IR 138 .... 53n, 87n, 103n
Byrne v. North Strand Furniture Ltd. UD 12/1980 .... 163n
Byrne v. P. J. Hegarty & Sons Ltd. UD 126/1978 .... 152n, 195n
Byrne v. R. H. M. Foods Ltd. UD 69/1979 .... 171n

Caffin, deceased, Re [1971] IR 123 .... 30n
Cahill v. Sutton (Supreme Court, unreported, 9 July 1980) 31n
Callaghan v. CIE UD 278/1981 .... 155n
Callanan v. Thomas & Edward McWilliams UD 299/1978 .... 157n
Canavan v. K. A. Burke (Carriers) Supplies Ltd. UD 15/1977 .... 168n
Cannon v. John Bolton Motors Ltd. UD 58/1979 .... 168n
Carroll v. Bird 3 Esp. 201 .... 14n
Carroll v. Condons Cash & Carry Ltd. UD 160/1979 .... 152n
Carroll v. Peter Lyons Ltd. UD 229/1979 .... 173n
Carvill v. Irish Industrial Bank [1968] IR 325 .... 48n
                           54n, 58, 58n, 61, 62, 105, 197n
Cassidy v. Connolly UD 75/1977 .... 202n
Caulfield v. Campbell Catering Ltd. UD 341/1979 .... 129n
Challoner v. Irish Meat Producers Ltd. UD 56/1977 .... 168n
Cherubini v. J. Downes & Son Ltd. UD 22/1978 .... 134n

Chevalier v. Herve Mahe, Ty Ar Mor Restaurant UD 60/1977 .... 188n
Clark v. CIE UD 104/1978 .... 158n, 169n, 183n
Clarke v. P. J. Hegarty & Sons Ltd. UD 36/1978 .... 211n
Clarke v. Hogan UD 135/1978 .... 179n
Clehane v. Gouldings Chemicals Ltd. UD 280/1978 .... 211n
Clifford v. Galvins Hardware Ltd. UD 1/1978 .... 191n
Coates v. Ryan UD 51/1979 .... 180n
Condon v. Rowntree Mackintosh Ltd. UD 195/1979 .... 165n, 199n
Conlon v. PMPA Farm Machines Ltd. UD 173/1978 .... 150n
Connolly v. Midland Tarmacadam Ltd. UD 19/1979 .... 163n
Cook v. Carroll [1945] IR 515 .... 30n
Corcoran v. Central Remedial Clinic UD 7/1978 .... 172n
Corcoran v. Kelly & Barry & Associates UD 174/1978 .... 163n, 193n
Corcoran v. Weatherglaze Ltd. UD 20/1981 .... 155n
Cork & Bandon Rly Co. v. Goode 13 CB 826 .... 112n
Corrigan v. Rowntree Mackintosh (Ireland) Ltd. UD 39/1978 .... 142n
Corry v. NUVGATA [1950] IR 315 .... 58n, 206n
Costello v. Kellys Carpetdrome UD 78/1980 .... 152n
Cotter v. Ahern (High Court, unreported, 25
    February 1977) 36n, 37n, 107n, 113
Coughlan v. Contract Cleaners Ltd. DEE 1/1978; EE3/1978 .... 190n
Cox v. ESB [1943] IR 94 .... 52n, 111
Cox v. ESB [1944] IR 81, 89 .... 103n
Cox v. ESB [1945] Ir. Jur. Rep. 58 .... 76n
Cox v. Industrial Contract Engineers Ltd. UD 133/1978 .... 168n
Criminal Law (Jurisdiction) Bill 1975, In Re, (1976) 110 ILTR 69 .... 3n
Crowley v. Cleary [1968] IR 261 .... 36n
Crowley & Others v. Ireland, INTO and Others (Supreme
    Court, unreported, 1 October 1979) 33n, 34n, 212-13n
Cullen v. Keal Ltd. UD 324/1979 .... 154n
Cuneen v. Prenderville (Waterville Lake Hotel) UD 19/1980 .... 202n

Darley v. The Queen (1846) 12 Cl. & F. 520 .... 74n
Deaton v. A.G. [1973] IR 170 .... 29n
De Burca & Anderson v. A.G. [1976] IR 38 .... 29n
Deegan v. Chums Ltd. UD 103/1979 .... 150n
Delaney v. Garvey (High Court, unreported, 12 August 1977) 109n
Delaney v. Mather & Platt (Irl.) Ltd. UD 73/1978 .... 211n
Devlin v. Player & Wills (Ire.) Ltd. UD 90/1978 .... 149n, 158n, 165, 169n
Doheny v. Allplast Ltd. UD 120/1979 .... 190n, 191n
Donnelly v. Minister for Defence (High Court, unreported,
    8 October 1979) 51n
Doran v. Lennon and O'Kelly [1945] IR 315 .... 206n
Dowling v. W. B. Peat & Co. Ltd. UD 93/1978 .... 201n
Doyle v. J. J. Carron & Co Ltd. UD 236/1978 .... 149n
Doyle v. Nitrigin Eireann Teo UD 148/1978 .... 132n, 182n
Doyle v. Pierce (Wexford) Ltd. UD 50/1979 .... 202n
Du Bois v. Meic Teo Hydromarine International UD 222/1978 .... 146n
Duffy v. Sutton [1955] IR 248 .... 92n
Dunne v. Duignan UD 261/1979 .... 193n
Dunne (B.) Ltd. v. Fitzpatrick [1958] IR 29 .... 205n, 212n
Dunne v. Harrington UD 166/1979 .... 158n, 159-60, 160n
Durnin v. Building & Engineering Co. Ltd. UD 159/1978 .... 168n
Dwan (W.J.) Ltd. v. Tynan UD 120/1980 .... 164n

East Donegal Cooperative Livestock Marts Ltd. v. A.G.
[1971] IR 317 .... 30*n*, 31*n*, 68*n*, 72*n*, 74*n*
Eate v. Semperit (Ireland) Ltd. UD 46/1977 .. 121*n*, 189*n*, 195*n*, 201*n*, 202*n*
Educational Co. Ltd. v. Fitzpatrick [1961] IR 345 .... 18*n*,
30, 35-6, 41, 43, 205*n*, 209*n*, 212*n*
Ennis v. Donabate Golf Club Ltd. UD 118/1978 .... 165, 191*n*, 193*n*
Esplanade Pharmacy Ltd. v. Larkin [1975] IR 285 .... 206*n*
Evode Industries Ltd. v. Hearst and Others UD 396-8/1979 .... 188*n*

Farrell v. Rotunda Hospital UD 35/1978 .... 167*n*, 191*n*
Fay v. The Order of Hospitalers of St. John of God
UD 92/1980 .... 191*n*, 199*n*
Ferenka Ltd. v. Lewis UD 26/1977 .... 182*n*
Ferodo Ltd. v. Clusker UD 139/1979 .... 168*n*
Fitzgerald v. St. Patrick's College UD 244/1978 .... 135*n*
Fitzgerald v. Williams Transport Ltd. UD 151/1978;
UD 165/1978 .... 129*n*, 168*n*
Fitzpatrick v. Nolan (1851) 1 ICR 671 .... 21*n*
Fitzpatrick v. Wymes (High Court, unreported, 17 May 1973) 51*n*
Flaherty v. Minister for Local Government and Public
Health and another [1941] IR 587 .... 50*n*
Flanagan v. Collen Bros. (Dublin) Ltd. UD 72/1980 .... 210*n*
Flanagan v. Magnier UD 365/1979 .... 130*n*
Fleming v. Athlone Manufacturing Co. Ltd. UD 140/1978 .... 132*n*
Floody v. Chas. Dougherty & Co. Ltd. UD 46/1980 .... 168*n*
Flynn v. Brendan L. Brophy Ltd. 329/1979 .... 150*n*
Flynn v. GNR Co. (Ire.) Ltd. (1955) 89 ILTR 46 .... 32*n*,
62*n*, 52*n*-53*n*, 58, 76-7, 79-80, 107
Foley v. Mahon R. McPhillips Ltd. UD 267/1979 .... 181*n*
Forgan v. Burke (1861) CP 12 CL (Ir.) 495 22
Fox v. Ashling Hotel Ltd. UD 108/1978 .... 196*n*
Freeman v. O'Flaherty UD 9/1978 .... 142*n*
Friel v. John Sisk & Son Ltd. UD 71/1978 .... 150*n*, 209*n*
Fullam v. Curragh Knitwear Ltd. UD 76/1978 .... 134*n*, 149*n*, 163*n*, 168*n*

G. v. An Bord Uchtála (1979) 113 ILTR 25 .... 38*n*
Gaffney v. Hughes UD 269/1978 .... 191*n*
Gaffney v. Press Knives Ltd. UD 304/1978 .... 163*n*
Gahon v. Lawlor UD 326/1979 .... 181*n*
Gallagher v. Linson Ltd. UD 87/1979 .... 157*n*
Gallivan v. Irish Commercial Society Ltd. UD 319/1979 .... 152*n*
Galway Crystal Ltd. v. McMorrow UD 1/1977 .... 168*n*
Gardiner v. Kildare Co. Council (1952) 86 ILTR 148 .... 50*n*, 52*n*, 55*n*
Gannett v. Botany Weaving Mill Ltd. UD 355/1979 .... 152*n*
Garrett v. CIE UD 177/1980 .... 165*n*
Garvey v. Ireland and Others [1981] IR 75 ..... 2*n*, 40*n*, 51*n*, 75-6, 75*n*, 110
Garvey v. Ireland and Others (High Court, unreported,
19 December 1979) 101,113-115
Geraghty v. Abouds Pages Ltd. UD 46/1978 .... 195*n*
Glass v. Lissadell Towels Ltd. UD 320/1979 .... 142*n*
Gleeson v. Minister for Defence [1976] IR 280 .... 51*n*
Gleeson v. Sheehan UD 14/1979 .... 155*n*
Glover v. BLN Ltd. [1973] IR 338 .... 40, 43-4, 48, 49,
59-61, 62, 64-7, 68*n*, 77, 92*n*, 93, 102-3, 103*n*, 104-6, 112, 161*n*

Goggin v. AnCO UD 344/1979 .... 159n
Gould v. O'Shea's Ltd. UD 323/1978 .... 150n, 210n
Gouldings Chemicals Ltd. v. Bolger [1977] IR 211 .... 26n, 205n
Grant v. Wm. Grant & Sons (1916) 50 ILTR 189 .... 20n
Grassick v. T. P. O'Connor & Sons Ltd. UD 114/1979 .... 208n
Greeley v. Baker UD 96/1978, UD 130/1978 .... 189n
Greeley v. Handcraft Lampshades UD 96/1978 .... 134n

Halpin v. Aemec Engineering Ltd. UD 333/1979 .... 191n
Hamilton v. Magill (1883) 12 LR Ir. 186 24-5
Hamlin v. Gt. Northern Rly. I H. & N. 408 .... 98n
Handley v. Moffat (1873) 7 ILTR 9; (1873) IR 7 CL 104 .... 14, 14n
Hanratty v. Minister for Industry & Commerce [1931] IR 189 .... 55n
Harrington v. Gleeson (1897) 31 ILT 429 .... 58n
Harris v. P. V. Doyle Hotels UD 150/1978 164
Harrison v. Alan Gay Ltd. UD 58/1978 .... 148n, 157n
Hartery and Welltrade (Middle East) Ltd. v. Hurley
    (High Court, unreported, 15 March 1978) 59n
Hassett v. Leonard TV Consultants (Limerick) Ltd.
    UD 76/1977 .... 201n
Haughey, P., *in re* [1971] IR 217 .... 39, 40, 65
Hayes & Caffrey v. B. & I. Line UD 192/1979 .... 131n, 133n
Hayes v. Sean Curtin & Sons Ltd. UD 137/1979 .... 209n
Hayes v. Dexter 13 ICLR 22 .... 55n
Haynes v. Duggan Bros. Contractors Ltd. UD 50/1981 .... 209n
Healy v. Cormeen Construction Ltd. UD 98/1978 .... 163n, 189n, 193n, 194n
Healy v. Joseph Brennan Bakeries Ltd. UD 622/1980 .... 181n
Hennessy v. McCann Nurseries Ltd. UD 7/1979 .... 197n
Hennessy v. Read & Write Shop Ltd. UD 192/1978 .... 158n, 159, 161n
Hennessy v. SAFA (Ireland) Ltd. UD 57/1978 .... 211n
Herman v. Owners of S.S. Vicia [1942] IR 305 107
Hertz Rent A Car Ltd. v. Hughes UD 10/1980 .... 164n
Hevey v. Dublin Port & Docks Board UD 161/1978 169
Higgins v. Donnelly Mirrors Ltd. UD 104/1979 .... 133n, 172n
Hilton v. Carrigaline Pottery Co. Ltd. UD 153/1979 .... 146n
Hogan v. Minister for Justice, Garvey v. Others
    (High Court, unreported, 17 May 1973) 51n, 73-4
Hogan, Farrell and Dolan v. Cantrell & Cochrane
    Ltd. UD 41-3/1979 .... 168n
Humphries v. Weartex UD 89/1979 .... 211n
Hunt v. Gordon & Thompson Ltd. UD 34/1977 .... 193n
Hutton v. Major George Philippi UD 291/1980 .... 130n
Hyland v. Balmoral Dublin Ltd. UD 63/1978 .... 142n
Hynes v. Conlon [1939] Ir. Jur. Rep. 49 .... 26n, 32n
Hynes v. Frederick Inns Ltd. UD 172/1978 .... 160n, 161n
Hynes v. Garvey [1978] IR 174 .... 51n, 109n

Irvine v. Midland Gt. W. Rly. (Ir.) Co. (1879) 6 LR Ir. 55 .... 92n, 107n

Jackson v. D. J. McCarthy & Co. Ltd. UD 297/1978 .... 158n
James v. Western Contractors Ltd. UD 132/1980 .... 210n
Johnson v. Longleat Properties (Dublin) Ltd.
    (High Court, unreported, 19 May 1976) 100

Kavanagh v. Weartex Ltd. UD 256/1979 .... 209n
Kean v. Fitzgerald (1894) 28 ILT 620 .... 59n
Kearney v. Midland Health Board UD 247/1979 .... 130n
Kearney v. Standard (1938) Ltd. UD 138/1978 .... 200n, 210n
Keen v. Dymo Ltd. [1977] IRLR 118 .... 146n
Keenan v. Raheny and District Credit Union Ltd. UD 111/1980 .... 171n
Kelly v. CIE UD 28/1978 .... 165-6, 179n
Kelly v. Steward & Son Ltd. UD 320/1978 .... 164n
Kenealy v. The Mayor, Aldermen and Burgesses of the
    Borough of Kilkenny [1905] 2 IR 167 .... 76n
Kenneally v. Ballinahina Dairies UD 254/1978 .... 153n
Kennedy v. Cappincur Joinery Ltd. UD 38/1977 .... 152n
Kennedy v. Dataproducts (Dublin) Ltd. UD 12/1981 .... 127n
Kennedy v. J. & L. Goodbody Ltd. UD 8/1978 .... 151n, 201n
Keon v. Hart (1867) C.P. 2 C.L. 138 22
Kerr v. Marley Extrusions (Ireland) Ltd. UD 78/1978 .... 189n
Kerr v. Tower Hotel Group Ltd. UD 12/1977 .... 163n,
                                            189n, 191n, 193n, 197n, 199n
Kingston v. Irish Dunlop Co. Ltd. [1969] IR 323 .... 90n
Kinlan v. Ulster Bank Ltd. [1928] IR 171 98
Kinsella v. D. L. Rafter UD 312/1978 .... 211n
Kirwan v. Dart Industries Ltd. & Leahy UD 1/1980 .... 47, 129n
Kirwan v. Northside Motors Ltd. UD 12/1979 .... 157n

Lamb Bros. (Dublin) Ltd. v. Davidson (High Court,
    unreported, 4 December 1979) 47
Landers v. A.G. (1973) 109 ILTR 1 .... 37n
Lavery v. Irish Silver Ltd. UD 68/1977 .... 169n, 182n
Lawler v. Linden (1876) C. P. 10 C.L. 188 .... 22n
Ledwidge v. Peter Mark Ltd. UD 70/1978 .... 166n, 168n, 189n, 200n
Limerick Health Authority v. Ryan [1969] IR 194 .... 130n
Lint v. Johnston (1893) 28 ILTR 16 14
Lissadel Towels Ltd. v. O'Halloran UD 203/1978 .... 201n
Loughran v. Bearcroft Caterers UD 61/1978 .... 193n
Loughran v. Bellwood Ltd. UD 206/1978 .... 157n
Lynch v. Palgrave Murphy [1962] IR 150 .... 46n
Lyons v. O'Meara Camping (Ireland) Ltd. UD 188/1978 .... 202n

Macauley v. Minister for P & T [1966] IR 345 .... 126n
McBride v. Midland Electrical Co. UD 37/1979 .... 175n, 181n
McCabe v. Lisney & Son UD 5/1977; (High Court, unreported,
    16 March 1981) 123n, 152n, 197, 197n, 197-8, 201n, 222n
McCarthy v. Irish Shipping Ltd. UD 100/1978 .... 165n, 191n, 193n
McCormac v. P. H. Ross Ltd. UD 206/1979 .... 208n
McCoy v. AET Ltd. UD 60/1979 .... 153n
McDonald v. Bord na gCon [1965] IR 217 .... 68, 71
McDonnell v. Minister for Education [1940] IR 316 54
McElvany and McPhillips v. Irish Joinery Monaghan Ltd.
    UD 26/1980 .... 209n
M'Eniry v. The Waterford & Kilkenny Rly Co.
    (1858) 8 C.L. (Ir) 312 .... 23n
McGee v. A.G. and The Revenue Commissioners
    [1974] IR 284 .... 2n, 28n, 40n
McGibbon v. Mark Royce Ltd. UD 90/1978 .... 163n
McGowan v. Kelleher Public Works Ltd. UD 9/1980 .... 168n

McGrath v. C. A. Jenkins & Sons Ltd. UD 227/1978 .... 129*n*, 172*n*
McGrath v. Short UD 315/1978 .... 167*n*
McGrath and O'Ruairc v. The Trustees of the College of
  Maynooth (Supreme Court, unreported, 1 November 1979) 34*n*, 80
McGrory v. Campbell UD 49/1979 .... 172*n*
McGuigan v. The Guardians of the Poor of the Belfast Union
  (1885) 18 LR Ir 89 .... 20*n*
Macken v. Irish Equestrian Federation (High Court, unreported,
  20 July 1978); (Supreme Court, unreported, 31 May 1979) 37*n*
McLeish v. Ten Pin Bowling Co. of Ireland UD 94/1978 .... 158*n*
McLoughlin v. Cappincur Joinery Ltd. UD 36-7/1977 .... 191*n*, 210*n*
McLoughlin v. GSR Co. (1944) 78 ILTR 74 .... 52*n*
McMahon v. Cootehill Livestock Sales Ltd. UD 102/1980 .... 179*n*
M'Mahon v. Leonard 6 HLC 870 .... 55*n*
McSweeney v. OK Garages Ltd. UD 107/1978 .... 158*n*
McSweeney v. Sunbeam Ltd. UD 62/1978 .... 181*n*, 182*n*, 189*n*, 191*n*, 195*n*
Madigan v. Yvonne Models Ltd. UD 295/1978 .... 195*n*
Maher v. B. & I Line UD 271/1978 .... 129*n*
Maher v. Beirne and Others (1959) 93 ILTR 101 .... 206*n*
Maguire v. Dunnes Stores (Drogheda) Ltd. UD 19/1978 .... 169*n*
Maguire v. Ofrex Group (Ireland) Ltd. UD 90/1980 .... 196*n*
Mallon v. McKone Estates Ltd. UD 76/1979 ....209*n*
Malone v. Lewicki Microelectronics Ltd. UD 249/1979 ....147*n*
Marsh v. UCD UD 27/1977 .... 166*n*, 181*n*, 182*n*
Martin v. Weldon Ltd. UD 30/1978 .... 191*n*, 200*n*
Martyn v. Stewart and Others 1907, unreported 79
Maunsell v. Minister for Education and the Very Rev.
  Canon Breen [1940] IR 213 70
Mayo-Perrott v. Mayo-Perrott [1958] IR 336 .... 30*n*
Meade v. Talbot Ireland Ltd. UD 69/1980 .... 211*n*
Meath Co. Council v. Creighton UD 11/1977 .... 161, 164*n*
Merchants of Waterford Case YB 2 Ric. 3, f. 12;
  1 Hen. 7, f. 2 .... 18*n*
Meskell v CIE [1973] IR 121 .... 32, 32*n*, 36, 38*n*, 42, 44, 177*n*
Mid-Western Health Board v. Ponnampalam (Circuit
  Court, unreported, 26 March 1980) 127*n*
Miller v. P. Faulkner & Sons Ltd. UD 200/1978 ....202*n*
Minister for Industry & Commerce v. Healy [1941] IR 545 .... 46*n*
Moloney v. J. & L. Goodbody Ltd. UD 6/1978 .... 151*n*, 210*n*
Mooney v. Collen Bros. UD 73/1980 .... 209*n*
Moran v. A.G. [1976] IR 400 .... 37*n*
Moran v. Bailey Gibson Ltd. UD 69/1977 .... 165*n*
Moran v. Collen Bros. UD 71/1980 .... 209*n*
Morrissey v. Morton UD 115/1980 .... 169*n*
Moynihan v. Greensmyth [1977] IR 55 .... 127*n*
Mulcahy v. O'Sullivan and Walsh [1944] IR 336 .... 103*n*
Mulcahy v. Seaborn Ltd. UD 157/1978 .... 158*n*
Mullen v. Linenhall (1972) Ltd. UD 94/1980 .... 168*n*
Mullins v. Standard Shoe Co. Ltd. UD 134/1979 .... 155*n*, 193*n*
Mulloy v. The Minister for Education [1975] IR 88 .... 34*n*
Murphy v. Binchy & Sons Ltd. UD 243/1978 .... 143*n*
Murphy v. Pollock & Pollock (1863) 15 C.L. (Exch.) 224 .... 23*n*
Murphy v. Stewart [1973] IR 97; (1973) 107 ILTR 117 .... 36*n*, 37
Murphy v. Sweeney UD 216/1978 .... 130*n*
Murphy v. Valley (Investment) Ltd. UD 112/1980 .... 200*n*

Murray v. Antolec Ltd. UD 51/1980 .... 129n
Murray v. CTV Services Ltd. UD 109/1978 .... 189n, 191n
Murray v. Meath Co. Council UD 43/1978 .... 159n, 165n, 199n
Murray v. Reilly UD 3/1978 .... 189n
Murtagh v. O'Connor & Breen Ltd. UD 186/1978 .... 189n, 194n
Murtagh Properties Ltd. v. Cleary [1972] IR 330 .... 3n, 30n, 36n, 37n

NEETU v. McConnell (High Court, unreported, 20 June 1977) 110, 111n
National Union of Railwaymen v. Sullivan [1947] IR 77 .... 177n
Nicholson v. An Bord Uchtála [1966] IR 667 .... 31n
Nolan v. Brooks Thomas Ltd. UD 179/1979 .... 148n
Nolan v. Steel & Engineering Supplies Ltd. UD 34/1981 .... 168n

Oakes v. Lynch UD 214/1978 .... 129n
O'Brien v. Keogh [1972] IR 144 .... 127n
O'Brien v. Manufacturing Engineering Ltd. [1973] IR 334 .... 127n
O'Brien v. Murphy Plastics (Dublin) Ltd. UD 142-4/1980 .... 140n
O'Byrne v. Orchard Insurance Ltd. UD 172/1979 .... 152n
O'Callaghan v. Cork Corporation UD 309/1978 .... 132n
O'Callaghan v. Denis Mahony Ltd. UD 117/1979 .... 132n
O'Callaghan v. Quinnsworth UD 68/1978 .... 193n
O'Cearnaigh v. ITGWU UD 383/1979 .... 129n
O'Connaill v. The Gaelic Echo Ltd. (1958) 92 ILTR 156 .... 52n
O'Connell v. Listowel UDC (1957) Ir. Jur. Rep. 43 .... 93n
O'Connor v. Galco Ltd. UD 208/1979 .... 153n
O'Connor v. Heat Recovery Ltd. UD 105/1980 .... 175n
O'Connor v. Marley Extrusions (Irl.) Ltd. UD 135/1979 .... 162n, 199n
O'Connor and O'Connor v. Guiry UD 65/1978 .... 142n
O'Cruadhlaoich v. Minister for Finance (1934) 68 ILTR 174 .... 48n, 52n
O'Donovan v. A.G. [1961] IR 114 .... 29n
O'Donovan v. Gillen UD 101/1978 .... 126, 191n
O'Dowd v. Collis Lee Ire. Ltd. UD 170/1979 .... 152n
O'Farrell (F.) Ltd. v. Nugent UD 120/1978 .... 168n, 188n, 194n
Oglesby v. McKone Estates Ltd. UD 61/1979 .... 150n
O'Grady v. Cornelscourt Shopping Centre Ltd. UD 210/1979 .... 172n
O'Hare v. The Curtain Centre Ltd. UD 149/1978 .... 158n, 189n
O'Leary v. Cranehire Ltd. UD 167/1979 .... 172n
O'Leary v. Tracy Shoes (Douglas) Ltd. UD 350/1979 .... 158n, 159n
O'Loughlin v. Minister for Social Welfare [1958] IR 1 .... 131n
O'Mahoney v. Arklow UDC and Minister for Local Government
    [1965] IR 710 .... 50n, 52n
O'Neill v. Breffni Proteins Ltd. UD 78/1981 .... 130n
O'Neill v. Flynns Garage UD 122/1981 .... 172n
O'Neill v. Furlong & Sons Ltd. UD 75/1978 .... 164n
O'Neill v. Murphy UD 122/1980 .... 152n
O'Neill and O'Connor v. PMPA Ins. Co. Ltd.
    UD 124, 130/1980 .... 196n
O'Reilly v. Dodder Management UD 311/1978 .... 162-3, 163n
O'Reilly v. Furlong & Sons Ltd. UD 75/1978 .... 163n
O'Reilly v. The Irish Press (1937) 71 ILTR 194 .... 52n
O'Reilly v. Pullman Kellog Ltd. UD 340/1979 143
O'Riain v. Independent Newspapers UD 134/1978 .... 47n
O'Rourke v. E. M. Halpin & Co. Ltd. UD 45/1977 .... 153n
O'Rourke v. Ryans Meat Market UD 112/1978 .... 194n, 195n
O'Shea v. P. J. Cullen & Sons UD 17/1977 .... 168n, 189n, 193n

O'Sullivan v. Western Health Board UD 131/1979 .... 131*n*
Owens v. Ramsbottom UD 103/1980 .... 170*n*

Parker v. Cathcart (1866) 17 ICLR 778 .... 92*n*, 98*n*
Pattison v. Institute for Industrial Research and Standards
(High Court, unreported, 31 May 1979) 26*n*
Phipps v. Laffin UD 18/1979 .... 129*n*, 163*n*
Ponnampalam v. Mid-Western Health Board UD 300/1979; (Circuit Court,
unreported, 26 March 1980) 131*n*, 132*n*, 147*n*
Potts v. Plunkett (1859) 9 C.L. (Ir.) 290 .... 21*n*
Power v. Binchy and Others (1929) 64 ILTR 35 .... 57*n*, 58
Power and Others v. National Corrugated Products
UD 336/1980 .... 217, 218

Qu. (The Commrs. of the Town of Boyle and T. Wynne) v.
M. Cunningham (1885) 16 L.R. Ir. 206 .... 20*n*
Quigley v. Beirne and Others [1955] IR 62 .... 206*n*
Quigley v. Western Health Board UD 114/1978 .... 130*n*, 132*n*
Quinn v. Ken David Ltd. UD 264/1979 .... 132*n*
Quinn v. Quality Homes (High Court, unreported, 21
November 1977 .... 100*n*
Quinns Supermarket Ltd. v. A.G. [1972] IR 1 .... 34*n*

R. (Fitzmaurice) v. Neligan (1884) 14 L R Ir. 149 .... 74*n*
R. (Jacob) v. Blaney [1901] 2 IR 93 .... 74*n*
R. (McMorrow) v. Fitzpatrick [1918] 2 IR 103 .... 74*n*
R. (Riall) v. Bayly [1898] 2 IR 335 .... 74*n*
Reardon v. St. Vincent's Hospital UD 74/1979 .... 148*n*
Reddington v. Duffy's Bakery UD 153/1978 .... 170*m*
Redland Purple Ltd. v. O'Halloran UD 51/1978 .... 164*n*
Redmond v. Royal Marine Hotel UD 196/1978 .... 163*n*
Reid v. H. B. Prosser Ltd. UD 185/1978 .... 202*n*
Reid v. Sharkey UD 132/1978 .... 130*n*
Richardson v. H. Williams & Co. Ltd. UD 17/1979 .... 163*n*
Riddell v. Mid/West Metals Ltd. UD 687/1980 .... 170*n*
Riordan v. Butler [1940] IR 347 .... 206*n*
Riordan v. Dairy Disposal Co. Ltd. UD 55/1979 .... 152*n*
Riordans Travel Ltd. v. Acres Co. Ltd. (High Court,
unreported, 17 January 1979) 201*n*
Roche v. Kelly & Co. Ltd. [1969] IR 100 46
Rodgers v. ITGWU (High Court, unreported,
15 March 1978) 36*n*, 38*n*
Rossiter v. Sisters of La Sagesse UD 92/1978 .... 182*n*, 194*n*
Ryan v. A.G. [1963] IR 294 31-2
Ryan v. Solus Teoranta UD 106/1977 .... 153*n*
Ryan v. Tender Meats Ltd. UD 42/1978 .... 164*n*
Ryder & Byrne v. Commissioners of Irish Lights, UD 31;
82/1977; (High Court, unreported, 16 April 1980) ....123*n*, 130*n*, 148*n*.

Savage v. Ruaine UD 59/1978 .... 202*n*
Sheehan v. Cork Fruit Co. Ltd. UD 187/1978 .... 153*n*
Shiel, *In Re* Trusts of Will of S., (Supreme Court,
unreported, 23 November 1977) 105*n*
Shiels v. Bonner Engineering Ltd. UD 67/1977; 18/1978 .... 164*n*, 188*n*
Shiels v. Clery & Co. (1941) Ltd. (High Court, unreported,
13 October 1979) 88, 109*n*

Silver Tassie Co. Ltd. v. Cleary and Others and Same v. Beirne and
  Others (1959) 93 ILTR 101 .... 206n
Sinclair v. Armstrong Autoparts (Ire.) Ltd. UD 225/1978 .... 153n, 211n
Sloan & Co. Ltd. v. Dunne UD 69/1978 .... 164n, 169n
Smith v. Beirne (1955) 89 ILTR 24 .... 205n
Smith v. de Jong UD 207/1978 .... 158n
Smyth v. Irish Board Mills Ltd. UD 9/1979 .... 209n
Stakelum v. Canning [1976] IR 314 .... 48n
Stamp v. A. N. Stamp Ltd. UD 11/1978 .... 168n
State (Burke) v. Lennon and A.G. [1940] IR 136 .... 2n
State (Curtin) v. Minister for Health [1953] IR 93 .... 50n, 52n
State (Duffy) v. Minister for Defence (Supreme Court,
  unreported, 9 May 1979) 72n
State (Gleeson) v. Minister for Defence [1976] IR 280 .... 57n,
                                                      68-9, 72-3, 109, 111n
State (Healy) v. Donoghue [1976] IR 325 .... 2n, 39n
State (Killian) v. Minister for Justice [1954] IR 207 .... 79n
State (McGarrity) v. The Deputy Commissioner of the
  Garda Siochana (High Court, unreported, 10 August 1977) 109n, 111n
  August 1977) 109n, 111n
State (Quinn) v. Ryan [1965] IR 642 .... 30n, 126n
State (Ryan & Others) v. Lennon & Others [1935] IR 170 .... 29n
State (Sheehan) v. McMahon and Others (Supreme Court,
  unreported, 25 October 1977) 81, 111n
Stenson v. Fluid Dynamics UD 251/1978 .... 130n
Stevens v. Mid-Western Health Board UD 67/1979 .... 147n
Stevenson v. Dalton Secondary & Preparatory Schools
  UD 10/1978 .... 132n

Talbot (Ireland) Ltd. v. ICTU, Merrigan and Others
  (Supreme Court, unreported, 1 May 1981) 206n, 212n, 213n
Tara Mines Ltd. v. Duffy UD 50/1980 .... 213n
Tierney v. ASW [1959] IR 254 .... 38n
Tilson, infants, *in re* [1951] IR 1 .... 30n
Timmins v. Munster Simms Hardware Ltd. M 384/1980 .... 202n
Tormey v. Display Development Ltd. UD 2/1977 .... 153n, 200n
Trans Irish Lines Ltd. v. Delaney UD 6/1977 .... 191n, 193n
Transport Salaried Staffs Association v. CIE
  [1965] IR 180 42

Wachuku v. Redmond UD 102/1979 .... 153n
Walsh v. J. D. Carr & Co. UD 91/1978 .... 153n
Walsh v. The Dublin Health Authority (1964)
  98 ILTR 82 .... 50n, 54-5
Walsh v. F. N. Woolworth & Co. Ltd. UD 296/1978 .... 168n
Walsh v. Smiths (Portlaoise) Ltd. UD 164/1978 .... 163n
Ward v. Spivack Ltd. [1957] IR 40 .... 103n
Warner-Lambert Ltd. v. Tormey and Hegarty
  UD 255/1978 .... 160n, 164n, 168n
Warren v. Cross Channel Carriers Ltd. UD 44/1977 .... 188n
Waters v. Kentredder (Ire.) Ltd. UD 3/1977 .... 149n, 153n,
Watson v. Dept. of P. & T. UD 220/1979 .... 131n
Watson v. Flanagan UD 209/1978 .... 210n
Wheatley v. Ulster Bank Ltd. UD 18/1977 .... 188n
Whelan v. Hartley & Synden (Tube Investment) Ltd. UD 49/1978 .... 150n
White v. Fry-Cadbury (Irl.) Ltd. UD 44/1979 .... 160n, 169n, 199n

White v. Scotts Foods Ltd. UD 29/1979 .... 153n
Williams Transport Group Ltd. v. McCafferty UD 152/1978 .... 169n
Wilson v. Brereton (1843) 5 LR Ir 466 .... 22n
Woodhouse v. The RIAM (1908) 2 IR 357 .... 24n
Woods v. Apollo Shopfitting Ltd. UD 202/1979 .... 152n

Zambra v. F. G. Duffy UD 154/1978 .... 158n, 166n, 201n

Abernethy v. Mott Hay & Anderson [1974] IRLR 213 146
Abrahams v. Herbert Reiach Ltd. [1922] 1 KB 477 .... 94n
Acklam v. Sentinel Insurance Co. Ltd. [1959] 2 Lloyd's Rep. 683 .... 67n
Adderley v. Dixon (1824) 1 Simons & Stuart 607 .... 88n
Addis v. Gramophone Co. Ltd. [1909] AC 488 .... 98, 101, 114, 115
African Association Ltd. and Allen, re [1910] 1 KB 396 .... 53n
Archbold Freightage Ltd. v. Wilson [1974] IRLR 10 .... 201n
Associated Tyre Specialists (Eastern) Ltd. v. Waterhouse
  [1976] IRLR 386 .... 173n
Ayanlowo v. IRC [1975] IRLR 253 .... 165n

Ball v. Coggs (1710) 1 Bro. Parl. Cas. 140 .... 21n, 88n
Banco de Portugal v. Waterlow & Sons [1932] AC 452 108
Banerjee v. City & East London Area Health Authority
  [1979] IRLR 147 .... 153n
Barber v. Manchester Regional Hospital Board [1958] 1 All ER 322 ..... 67n,
                                                                                    90n
Bariamis v. John Stephen of London Ltd. [1975] IRLR 237 .... 173n
Barthorpe v. Exeter Diocesan Board of Finance [1979] ICR 900 .... 49n
Basnett v. J. & A. Jackson Ltd. [1976] ICR 63 103-04
Bateman v. British Leyland UK Ltd. [1974] IRLR 101 .... 183n
Bates Farms & Dairy Ltd. v. Scott [1976] IRLR 214 .... 157n
Bauman v. Hulton Press Ltd. [1952] 2 All ER 1121 .... 103n
Beach v. Reed Corrugated Cases Ltd. [1956] 1 WLR 807 .... 102n, 105n
Beattie v. Parmenter (1889) 5 TLR 396 .... 57n
Beckham v. Drake (1849) 2 HLC 579 .... 107n
Beeston v. Collyer (1827) 2 C & P 607; 4 Bing. 309 53
Bendall v. Pain & Betteridge [1973] IRLR 44 .... 164n
Bessenden Properties Ltd. v. Corness [1974] IRLR 338 .... 199n, 210
Bex v. Securicor Transport Ltd. [1972] IRLR 68 .... 174n
Bivens v. Six Unknown Naval Agents of the
  Federal Bureau of Narcotics (1969) 409F (2d. Cir. 1969) 41n
Blackman v. P.O. [1974] IRLR 46 .... 160n
Blackwell v. G.E.C. Elliott Process Automation Ltd.
  (1976) 11 ITR 103 .... 189n
Boast v. Firth (1868) LR 4 CP 1 .... 52n
Bold v. Brough, Nicholson & Hall Ltd. [1964] 1 WLR 201 .... 101n,
                                                                                 102n, 105n
Boston Deep Sea Fishing and Ice Co. Ltd. v. Ansell
  (1888) 39 Ch. D. 399 .... 60n, 61, 61n
Bowie v. British Leyland (UK) Ltd. [1976] IRLR 48 .... 199n
Brace v. Calder [1895] 2 QB 253 .... 108n
Bracey (A.G.) Ltd. v. Iles [1973] IRLR 210 .... 197n, 199-200
Breach (F.T.) v. Epsylon Industries Ltd. [1976] IRLR 180 .... 173n
Brear v. W. Wright Hudson Ltd. [1977] IRLR 287 .... 155n
Brennan & Ging v. Ellward (Lancs.) Ltd. [1976] IRLR 378 .... 207n
Briggs v. Imperial Chemical Industries (1968) 3 ITR 276 .... 174n
Bristol Garage (Brighton) Ltd. v. Lowen [1979] IRLR 86 .... 172n
British Aircraft Corporation v. Austin [1978] IRLR 332 .... 172, 172n
British Broadcasting Corporation v. Dixon [1979] 2 All ER 112 .... 55n
British Broadcasting Corporation v. Ioannou [1975] ICR 167 .... 55n, 135
British Guiana Corporation v. Da Silva [1965] 1 WLR 248 .... 94n, 99
British Homes Stores Ltd. v. Burchell [1978] ITR 560 .... 159n

British Labour pump v. Byrne [1979] ICR 347 .... 162n
British Transport Commission v. Gourley [1956] AC 185 ...... 104, 105, 106
Brittains Arborfield v. Van Uden [1977] ICR 211 .... 190n
Broome v. Cassel & Co. [1972] 2 WLR 645 115
Brown v. Southall & Knight [1980] IRLR 130 137-8
Burdekin v. Dolan Corrugated Containers Ltd. EAT 5376/72 .... 179n
Byrne v. Kinematograph Renters Society [1958] 1 WLR 762 .... 65n

Calvin v. Carr [1979] 2 All ER 440 81
Capel v. Child 2 C & J 558 .... 70n
Carr v. Alexander Russell Ltd. [1976] IRLR 220 .... 161n
Casteldine v. Rothwell Engineering Ltd. [1973] IRLR 99 .... 158n
Chant v. Aquaboats [1978] ICR 643 .... 207n
Chappell v. Times Newspapers Ltd. [1975] ICR 145 .... 89n
Chriss v. John Lichfield [1975] IRLR 28 .... 158n
Chrystie v. Rolls Royce (1971) Ltd. [1976] IRLR 336 .... 199n
City of Birmingham v. Beyer [1977] IRLR 211 .... 207n
Clarkson Int. Tools Ltd. v. Short [1973] ICR 191 .... 211n
Clayton v. Oliver [1930] AC 209 99
Cockburn v. Alexander (1848) 6 CB 791 .... 93n
Collier v. Sunday Referee Publishing Co. [1940] 2 KB 647 .... 100n
Connolly v. Robinson (1946/72) 200n
Cook v. Thomas Linnell & Sons Ltd. [1977] ICR 770 .... 148n
Coombe v. Coombe [1951] 2 KB 215; [1951] 1 All ER 767 .... 202n
Cooper v. Wandsworth Board of Works (1863) 14 CB (NS) 180 .... 71n
Copson v. Eversure Accessories Ltd. [1974] ICR 636 .... 195n
Cort (R) & Son Ltd. v. Charman
   The Times Law Report 3 August 1981 144
Cottle v. Cottle [1939] 2 All ER 535 .....:...................................... 79n
Courtaulds Northern Textiles Ltd. v. Andrew [1977] IRLR 84 .... 171n
Cox v. Phillips Industries Ltd. [1976] 3 All ER 161 .... 100,101, 114
Crampton v. Dacorum Motors Ltd. [1975] IRLR 169 .... 201n
Crouch v. P.O. [1973] 3 All ER 225 .... 207n
Cruikshank v. Hobbs [1977] ICR 725 217-18
Curtis v. Paterson (Darlington) Ltd. [1974] IRLR 88 .... 179n, 201n
Cussons v. Skinner 11 M & W 161 .... 61n

Dacres v. Walls Meat Co. Ltd. [1976] IRLR 20 .... 165n
Daily Office Cleaning Contractors Ltd. v. Shefford
   [1977] RTR 361 .... 108n
Davis v. Marshall (1861) 4 LT 216 .... 54n, 93n
Davson v. France (1959) 109 LJ 526 .... 52n
Davy v. J. A. Sollins (Builders) Ltd. [1974] IRLR 324 .... 173n
Dawkin v. Antrobus 17 Ch. D. 115 77
Day v. Savadge [1615] Hob. 85 .... 78n
Decro-Wall Practitioners Int. S.A. v. Practitioners in Marketing Ltd. [1971]
   1 WLR 361; 1971 2 All ER 216 .... 82, 83
Deegan v. Norman & Sons Ltd. [1976] IRLR 139 .... 199n
De Francesco v. Barnum (1890) 45 Ch. D. 430 .... 88n
Delanair v. Mead [1976] ICR 552 .... 152n
Denmark Productions Ltd. v. Boscobel Productions Ltd.
   [1969] 1 QB 699 .... 83n
Derving v. Kilvington [1973] 8 ITR 266 .... 216n
De Stempel v. Dunkels [1938] 1 All E.R. 238 53
Devis (W) & Sons Ltd. v. Atkins
   [1977] AC 931 .... 61n, 137n, 157n, 162n, 197n, 198

Devonald v. Rosser & Sons [1906] 2 KB 728 .... 94n
Diesan v. Samsan [1971] SLT 49 .... 100n
Dixon v. BBC [1979] QB 546 135
Dobson & Heather v. K.P. Moritt Ltd. [1972] IRLR 101 .... 179n, 201n
Donovan v. Invicta Airways [1969] 2 Lloyd's Rep. 413 .... 171n
Dowsett Engineering Construction Ltd. v. Fowler
  (1977) EAT 425/76 .... 174n
Dunk v. Geo. Waller & Son Ltd. [1970] 2 QB 163 .... 99n

Earl v. Slater Wheeler (Airlyne) Ltd. [1972] IRLR 115;
  [1973] 1 All ER 145 .... 157n, 162n
East India Co. v. Vincent (1740) 2 Atkyns 83 .... 21n, 88n
Edwards (Inspector of Taxes) v. Clinch [1980]
  STC 438 .... 48n, 49n, 50n
Edwards v. Skyways Ltd. [1964] 1 WLR 349 .... 26n
Egg Stores (Stanford Hill) v. Leibovici [1976] ITR 289 .... 148n
Emmens v. Elderton (1853) 13 CB 495 23
Everwear Candlewick Ltd. v. Isaac [1974] ICR 525 .... 189n

Fairman v. Oakford (1860) 5 H & N 635 .... 53n
Fanshaw v. Robinsons & Sons Ltd. [1975] IRLR 165 .... 173n
Farthing v. Midland Household Stores Ltd. [1974] IRLR 354 .... 181n
Ferguson v. Dawson Ltd. [1976] 3 All ER 817 .... 47n
Field v. Leslie & Goodwin Ltd. [1972] IRLR 12 .... 191n
Fillieul v. Armstrong (1837) 7 Ad. & E. 557 .... 58n
Finnerty v. Devro Ltd. [1976] IRLR 84 .... 171n
Fisher v. W.B. Dick & Co. Ltd. [1938] 4 All ER 467 .... 53n
Fletcher v. Photo Precision Ltd. [1973] IRLR 169 .... 201n
Ford v. Milthorn Ltd. [1980] IRLR 30 .... 173n
Ford Motor Co. Ltd. v. AUEFW [1969] 2 QB 303 .... 26n
Ford Motor Co. Ltd. v. Hudson [1978] IRLR 66 .... 158n
Foxall v. International Land Credit Co. (1867) 16 LT 637 .... 52n
Francis v. Kuala Lumpur Councillors
  [1962] 1 WLR 1411 .... 83n, 90n, 109-10, 111
Fray v. Voules (1859) 1 E & E 839 .... 87n
Fybe & McGrouther Ltd. v. Byrne [1977] IRLR 29 .... 172n

GKN (Cwmbran) Ltd. v. Lloyd [1972] ITR 160 .... 83n
Gannon v. Firth [1976] IRLR 415 .... 138n, 139
Gardner v. Beresford [1978] IRLR 63 .... 173n, 174n
Gardner v. Peeks Retail Ltd. [1975] IRLR 244 .... 207n
Gargrave v. Hotel and Catering Industrial
  Training Board [1974] IRLR 85 .... 151n
George v. Beecham Group [1977] IRLR 43 .... 155n
George v. Davies [1911] 2 K.B. 445 .... 52n
George Edwardes (Daly's Theatre) Ltd. v. Comber
  (1926) 42 TLR 247 .... 52n
General Medical Council v. Spackman [1943] AC 627 .... 77n
Gilbert & Goldstone [1976] IRLR 257 .... 173n
Giles (C.H.) & Co. Ltd. v. Morris [1972] 1 WLR 307 88-9
Gillies v. R. Daniels & Co. Ltd. [1980] IRLR 457 .... 172n
Glynn v. Keele University [1971] 1 WLR 487 .... 77n
Golomb & William Porter & Co. Ltd.'s Arbitration, re (1931)
  144 LT 583 .... 93n, 100n
Goodbody v. British Railways Board [1977] IRLR 84 .... 183n

Gordon v. Potter (1859) 1 F. & F. 644 .... 103n
Grace v. Northgate Group Ltd. [1972] IRLR 53 .... 171n
Great Western Railway Co. v. Bater [1920] 3 KB 266 48
Green v. Wright (1876) 1 CPD 591 .... 53n
Griswold v. Connecticut (1965) 381 US 479 .... 32n
Grundy v. Sun Printing and Publishing Association (1916) 33 TLR 77 .... 52n
Guaranty Trust Co. of New York v. Hannay & Co. [1915] 2 KB 536 ... 90n
Gunton v. London Borough of Richmond-upon-Thames
 [1970] IRLR 321 .... 63, 83-4, 85, 86, 90n, 95, 96, 135-6

Hackwood v. Seal (Marine) Ltd. [1973] IRLR 17 .... 179n
Hadjioannou v. Coral Casinos Ltd. [1981] IRLR 352 .... 164n
Hadley v. Baxendale (1854) 9 Exch. 341 .... 24, 92
Hallam v. Baguley & Co. Ltd. (355/73) 179n
Hamlin v. Gt. Northern Rly 1 H. & N. 408 .... 98n
Hamm v. Edwards [1972] IRLR 102 .... 154n
Harbutts Plasticine Ltd. v. Wayne Tank & Pump Ltd.
 [1970] 1 QB 447 .... 139n
Hare v. Murphy Bros. [1974] 3 All ER 940 .... 139n, 169n
Hart v. A. R. Marshall & Sons [1978] 2 All ER 413 .... 148n
Haughton Main Collieries Co., in re [1956] 1 WLR 1219 .... 105n
Hazells Offset Ltd. v. Luckett [1977] IRLR 430 .... 158n
Heath v. Longman Ltd. [1973] 2 All ER 1228 .... 214n
Hemmings v. International Computers Ltd. [1976] IRLR 37 .... 173n
Heywood v. Wellers [1976] 1 All ER 300 100
Hill v. AUEF (1973) Ind. Tribunal 1509/73 190
Hill v. C.A. Parsons Ltd. [1975] 1 Ch. 305 .... 83n, 89, 90n, 93
Hilti (Great Britain) Ltd. v. Windridge [1974] ICR 352 .... 189n
Hitchcock v. The Post Office [1980] IRLR 100 .... 49n
Horsley Smith & Sherry Ltd. v. Dutton [1977] IRLR 1972 .... 147n
How v. Tesco Stores Ltd. [1974] IRLR 194 .... 201n
Hughes-Jones v. St. John's College, Cambridge [1979] ICR 848 .... 49n
Hunt v. British Railways Board [1979] IRLR 379 .... 170n

Industrial Rubber Products v. Gillon [1977] IRLR 389 .... 172n
Isle of Wight Tourist Board v. Coombes [1976] IRLR 413 .... 173n

Jackson v. Hayes, Candy & Co. Ltd. [1938] 4 All ER 587 .... 108n
Jackson v. Horizon Holidays Ltd. [1975] 3 All ER 92 .... 100n
Jamieson v. Aberdeen County Co. [1975] IRLR 348 .... 199n
Jarvis v. Swan's Tours Ltd. [1973] 1 All ER 71............................... 100n
John v. Rees [1969] 2 WLR 1294 78
Joines v. B. & S. (Burknale) Ltd. [1977] IRLR 83 .... 146n
Jones Bros. (Huntstanton) Ltd. v. Stevens [1955] 1 QB 275 .... 6n
Judd v. Hammersmith Hospital Board of Governors [1960] 1 WLR 328   101n

Kallinos v. London Electric Wire [1980] IRLR 11 .... 138n
Kemp v. Shipton Automation Ltd. [1976] IRLR 305 ....198n
Kendrick v. Aerduct Productions [1974] IRLR 322 .... 201n
Keys v. Shoefayre Ltd. [1978] IRLR 476 .... 172n
Khanum v. mid-Glamorgan Area Health Authority [1978] IRLR 215 .... 165n
King v. University of Saskatchewan [1969] 6 DLR (31) 120 .... 80n
Kingston v. Preston (1773) 2 Doug. 689; 99 ER 436 229
Knight v. AG [1979] ICR 194 .... 49n

Knighton v. Rhodes [1974] IRLR 71 .... 171*n*
Kyle Stewart Contractors v. Stainrod (1977) EAT 406/77 .... 210*n*

Laird v. Pim (1841) 7 M & W 474; 151 ER 852 229
Langston v. AUEW [1974] ICR 180 .... 38*n*
Langston v. AUEW (No. 2) [1974] ICR 510 .... 38*n*
Lavarack v. Woods of Colchester Ltd. [1976] 1 QB 278 .... 102*n*, 103*n*
Law v. Chartered Institute of Patent Agents [1919] 2 Ch. 276 .... 79*n*
Laws v. London Chronicle (Indicator Newspapers) Ltd.
  [1959] 1 WLR 698 .... 57-8, 82*n*
Leary v. NUVB [1971] Ch. 34 81
Leeson v. GNC (1889) 43 Ch. D. 366 .... 79*n*
Leonard (Cyril) & Co. v. Simo Securities Trust Ltd. [1972] 1 WLR 80 .. 61*n*
Lindsay v. Queens Hotel Ltd. [1919] 1 KB 212 .... 103*n*
Little v. Charterhouse Magna Assurance Co.
  [1980] IRLR 19 .... 172*n*
Lloyd v. Standard Pulverised Fuel Co.
  [1976] IRLR 115 .... 201*n*
Logabox v. Titherley [1977] IRLR 97 .... 172*n*
London Borough of Camden v. Pedersen
  [1979] IRLR 377 .... 172*n*
London Transport Executive v. Clarke
  [1981] IRLR 166 139
Lowndes v. Specialist Heavy Engineering Ltd.
  [1976] IRLR 246 .... 162*n*
Luckhurst v. Kent Litho Co. Ltd.
  [1976] EAT 302/76 .... 171*n*
Lyon v. St. James Press Ltd. [1976] IRLR 215 .... 207*n*

McCabe v. Chicpack Ltd. [1976] IRLR 38 .... 173*n*
McClelland v. N.I. General Health Services Board
  [1957] 1 WLR 594 .... 54, 55, 67*n*
McGrath v. de Soissons (1962) 112 LJ 60 .... 103*n*
McInnes v. Onslow-Fane [1978] 3 All ER 211 .... 38*n*
McKendry v. Avery Hardoll [1977] IRLR (369/77 EAT) 207*n*
McKenzie (D. & J.) Ltd. v. Smith [1976] IRLR 345 .... 173*n*
McLaren v. Chalet Club (1951) 1 CLC 2508 .... 99*n*
McMorn v. Exquisite Knitwear (1975) COIT 346/226 .... 208*n*
MacNeilage v. Arthur Roye (Turf Accountants) Ltd.
  [1976] IRLR 88 .... 173*n*
Maddison v. Council of Engineering Institutions
  [1977] ICR 30 .... 202*n*
Malloch v. Aberdeen Corporation
  [1971] 2 All ER 1278 .... 67, 67*n*, 70*n*, 71
Managers (Holborn) Ltd. v. Hohne
  [1977] IRLR 230 .... 171*n*
Mansfield Hosiery Mills Ltd. v. Bromley
  [1977] IRLR 301 .... 162*n*
Manubens v. Leon [1919] 1 KB 208 .... 103*n*
Marbé v. Geo. Edwardes [1928] 1 KB 269 99
Market Investigations Ltd. v. Minister of Social
  Security [1969] 2 QB 173 .... 47*n*
Marley Tile Co. v. Shaw [1978] IRLR 238 .... 208*n*
Marriott v. Oxford & District Co-op. Soc.
  [1970] 1 QB 186 .... 171*n*

Marsden v. Fairey Stainless Ltd.
[1979] IRLR 103 .... 138*n*, 218*n*
Marshall v. Harland & Wolff Ltd. [1972] 7 ITR 150 .... 148*n*
Marshall (Thomas) Exports Ltd. v. Guinle [1978] IRLR 173 .... 83, 84
Marzetti v. Williams (1830) 1 B. & Ad. 415 .... 87*n*
Mason v. The Post Office [1973] IRLR 51 .... 181*n*
Massey v. Crown Life Insurance Co. [1978] ICR 594 .... 47*n*
Meade v. London Borough of Haringay [1979] 1 WLR 637 .... 34*n*
Merchandise Transport Ltd. v. BTC [1962] 2 QB 173 .... 226*n*
Meridian Ltd. v. Gomersall [1977] ICR 597 .... 181*n*
Metropolitan Properties v. Lannon [1969] 1 QB 577 .... 79*n*
Miller v. Rafique [1975] IRLR 70 .... 207*n*, 208*n*
Milthorn Toleman Ltd. v. Ford [1978] IRLR 306 .... 172*n*
Modern Injection Moulds Ltd. v. Price
[1976] ICR 370 .... 211*n*
Moore v. Der Ltd. [1971] 1 WLR 1476 .... 201*n*
Moreton v. Selby Protective Clothing Co. Ltd.
[1974] IRLR 269 .... 171*n*
Morgan v. Fry [1968] 2 QB 710 .... 215*n*
Morris v. C.H. Bailey Ltd.
[1969] 2 Lloyd's Rep. 215 109
Morris v. Gestetner Ltd. [1973] 1 WLR 1378 .... 180*n*
Moss v.Chesham UDC (1945) 172 LT 301 100

Nagle v. Fielden [1966] 2 QB 633 .... 38*n*
Newell v. Canadian Pacific Airlines (1977)
14 OR 752 .... 100*n*
Newman v. T.H. White Motors Ltd. [1972] IRLR 49 .... 163*n*
Nicoll v. Greaves (1864) 17CB (N.S.) 27 .... 52*n*
Normansell (Robert) (Birmingham) (Ltd.) ITO v. Barfield
(1973) 8 ITR 171 .... 190*n*
Norris v. Southampton City Council
The Times (3 February 1982) 169*n*
Northman v. London Borough of Barnet (no. 2) [1980] IRLR 65 .... 179*n*
Norton Tool Co. Ltd. v. Tewson
[1973] 1 All E.R. 183; [1972] ICR 501 .... 185*n*-186*n*, 190*n*, 194*n*

O'Brien v. Int. Harvester Co. of Great Britain
[1976] IRLR 374 .... 158*n*
O'Hare v. Rotaprint Ltd. [1980] ICR 44 .... 152*n*
Oliso-Emosingoit v. Inner London Magistrates
Courts Services EAT 139/77 .... 181*n*
Osman v. Saville Sportswear Ltd. [1960] 1 WLR 1055 .... 97*n*
Overseas School of English v. Hartley
[1977] EAT 86/77 .... 174*n*

Pagano v. HGS [1976] IRLR 9... 200*n*
Page One Records Ltd. v. Britton [1968] 1 WLR 157 .... 88*n*, 90*n*
Palmanor Ltd. v. Cedron [1978] IRLR 303 .... 173*n*
Parry v. Cleaver [1970] AC 1 .... 105*n*
Parsons v. BNM Laboratories Ltd.
[1964] 1 QB 95 .... 105*n*, 107
Payzu Ltd. v. Hannaford [1918] 2 KB 348 .... 54*n*
Payzu Ltd. v. Saunders [1919] 2 KB 581 .... 108*n*

Pearlberg v. Varty [1972] 2 All ER 6 .... 71n
Pedersen v. London Borough of Camden
  [1981] IRLR 173 .... 140n
Photo Productions Ltd. v. Securicor Ltd.
  [1980] 2 WLR 283; [1980] 1 All ER 556 .... 84-6, 139n, 231
Post Office v. UPOW [1974] 1 All ER 229 .... 208n
Poussand v. Spiers (1876) 1 QBD 410 .... 52n
Powrmatic Ltd. v. Bull [1977] ICR 469 .... 196n
Price v. Gourley Bros. Ltd. [1973] IRLR 11 .... 158n
Price v. Guest Keen and Nettlefolds
  [1918] AC 760 .... 52n

R v. Barnsley Licensing JJ.
  [1960] 2 QB 167 .... 79n
R v. Darlington School Governors (1844)
  6 QB 682 .... 74n
R v. Gt. Bowden (Inhabitants) (1827) 7 B & C
  219; 108 ER 716 .... 21n
R v. Jennings (1966) 57 DLR (2nd) 644 106
R V. Liverpool Taxi Operators Association
  [1972] 2 QB 299 .... 71n
R. v. P.O., *ex p.* Byrne [1975] ICR 221 .... 111n
R v. St. Peter's in Dorchester (Inhabitants)
  (1973) Burr. S.C. 515; 95 ER 25 .... 22n
R. S. Components Ltd. v. Irwin [1973] ICR 535 .... 171n
Rank Xerox (UK) Ltd. v. Goodchild
  [1979] IRLR 185 .... 165n
Rasool & Others v. Hepworth Pipe Co. Ltd. [1980] IRLR 80 138-9
Raynor v. Remploy Ltd. [1973] IRLR 3 .... 158n, 190n
Ready Mixed Concrete (South East) Ltd. v. Minister of Pensions
  [1968] 2 QB 497 .... 46n
Reilly v. The King [1934] AC 176 .... 48n
Ridge v. Baldwin [1964] AC 40 .... 43n, 49, 65, 74n, 77-8
Ridgway v. Hungerford Market Co. (1885) Ad. & El. 171 .... 61n
Rigby v. British Steel Corporation [1973] ITR 191 .... 211n
Robinson v. Crompton Parkinson Ltd. [1979] IRLR 61 .... 172n
Robinson v. Flitwick Frames Ltd. [1975] IRLR 261 .... 171n
Robinson v. Hindman (1800) 3 Esp. 235 .... 23n
Robson (J.B.) v. Cambrian Electric Products Ltd. [1976] IRLR 109 ...... 173n
Rookes v. Barnard [1964] 2 WLR 269 .... 115, 215n
Royal Naval School v. Hughes [1979] IRLR 383 .... 130n, 159n
Rumsey v. Owen White and Catlin (1978) 245 EG 225 .... 108n
Ryan v. Jenkinson (1855) 25 LJ (NS) QB 11 .... 54n
Ryan v. Mutual Tontine Association [1893] 1 Ch. 116 .... 88n
Ryan v. Shipboard Maintenance Ltd. [1980] ICR 88 .... 132n

Salt v. Power Plant Co. Ltd. [1936] 3 All ER 322 .... 54n
Sanders v. Ernest A. Neale Ltd. [1974] ITR 395 .... 83, 89
Sarvents v. Central Electricity Board [1976]
  IRLR 66 .... 183n
Saunders v. Scottish National Camps [1980]
  IRLR 174 .... 160n
Savage v. J. Sainsbury Ltd. [1980] IRLR 109 .... 143n
Scott v. Aveling Barford Ltd. [1977] IRLR 419 .... 170n, 172n

Scottish Co. Op. Ltd. v. Lloyd [1973] ICR
137 .... 186n, 194n, 195n
Sealey & Others v. Avon Aluminium Co. Ltd.
[1978] IRLR 285 .... 139n
Sheet Metal Components Ltd. v. Plumridge
[1974] IRLR 86 .... 171n
Shindler v. Northern Raincoat Co. Ltd. [1960]
1 WLR 1038 .... 108n
Simmons v. Hoover Ltd. [1977] ICR 61 .... 216n, 219
Simpson v. Roneo Ltd. [1972] IRLR 5 .... 151n
Sloan v. General Medical Council [1970]
1 WLR 1130 .... 76n
Smith v. Arana Bakeries Ltd. [1979]
IRLR 423 .... 138n
Smith v. Hayle Town Council [1978] ICR 996 .... 208n
Smith v. The Queen (1878) LR 3 App Cas 614 .... 70n
Smith v. Thompson (1849) 8 CB 44 .... 93n
Smith & Tickell v. Cornwall CC COIT 803/182 .... 171n
Smithson v. Sydney Chambers & Co. Ltd. [1976]
IRLR 13 .... 171n
102 Social Club and Institute Ltd. v. Bickerton
[1977] ICR 911 .... 48n
Stepek Ltd. v. Hough (1973) 8 ITR 516 .... 189n
Stevenson v. United Road Transport Union [1977]
ICR 893 .... 50, 66, 91, 110n
Stevenson, Jordan and Harrison Ltd. v. McDonald
and Evans [1952] 1 TLR 101 .... 46n
Stewart v Glentaggart Ltd. [1963] SLT 119 .... 106n
Stock v. Frank Jones (Tipton) Ltd. [1978] ICR 347 217
Stocks v. Magna Merchants Ltd. [1973] ICR 530 .... 103n
Storey v. Fulham Steel Work Co. (1907) 24 TLR 89 ..... 52n
Stratford v. Lindley [1965] AC 307 .... 215n
Sutton & Gates (Luton) Ltd. v. Boxall [1978]
IRLR 486 .... 148n
Sycamore v. Myer & Co. Ltd. [1976] IRLR 84 .... 171n

Tarnesby v. Kensington and Chelsea and Westminster Area
Health Authority (Teaching) [1981] IRLR 369 .... 148n
Taylor v. Furness Withy Ltd. (1969) 6 KIR 488 .... 50n
Taylor v. National Union of Seamen [1967]
1 WLR 532 .... 90n, 95n, 114n
Theedom v. British Railways Board [1976] IRLR 137 ... 173n
Thomas & Betts Manufacturing Co. Ltd. v. Harding
[1978] IRLR 213 .... 185n
Thompson v. Eaton Ltd. [1976] 3 All ER 383 .... 138n, 214n, 216n, 218n
Thornton v Champion Association Weavers Ltd [1977]
IRLR 385 .... 199n
Tippett v. Int. Typographical Union Local 226
(1977) 71 DLR (3rd) 146 .... 100n
Todd v. N.E. Electricity Board [1975] IRLR 130 .... 183n
Tolnay v. Criterion Films [1936] 2 All ER 1625 99
Tomlinson v. The London Midland & Scott. Rly. Co.
[1944] 1 All ER 537 .... 63n
Tradewinds Airways Ltd. v. Fletcher [1981] IRLR 272 .. 189n

Trust Houses Forte Leisure Ltd. v. Aquilar [1976]
  IRLR 251 .... 157n
Turner v. London Transport Executive [1977] IRLR 441 .... 172n
Turner v. Mason (1845) 14 M & W 112 57

Vaughan v. Weighpack Ltd. [1974] ICR 261 .... 189n, 190
Vidyodaya University of Ceylon v. Silva [1964]
  3 All ER 865 .... 67n, 70n
Vine v. NDLB [1956] 3 All ER 944; [1957]
  AC 500 .... 49, 83n, 90n, 109, 110
Vokes Ltd. v. Bear [1973] ICR 1 .... 166-7, 211n

Warburton v. Co-Op Wholesale Society Ltd. [1917] 1 KB 663 .... 53n
Ward v. British Domestic Appliances [1972] IRLR 8 .... 191n
Wares v. Caithness Leather Products [1974] IRLR 162 .... 173n
Warner v. Barbers Stores [1978] IRLR 109 .... 173n
Warner Bros. Pictures Inc. v. Nelson [1937] 1 KB 209 .... 89n
Warren v. Super Drug Markets Ltd. (1965) 54 DLR
  (2d.) 183 .... 53n
Watling & Co. Ltd. v. Richardson (1978) EAT 774/77 .... 211n
Wells v. Derwent Plastics Ltd. [1978] ICR 424 .... 199n
Wells v. E. & A. West Ltd. [1975] IRLR 269 .... 199n
Western Excavating (ECC) Ltd. v. Sharp [1978]
  ICR 221 .... 140, 141n, 170n, 172n
Wetherall (Bond St.) v. Lynn [1977] IRLR 333 .... 172n, 173n
White and Carter (Councils Ltd.) v. McGregor [1962]
  AC 413 97
Whitwood Chemical Co. v. Hardman [1891] 2 Ch. 416 .... 87n
Wicks v. Smethurst Ltd. (1973) COIT 251/83 .... 154n
Wigan Borough Council v. Davies [1979] IRLR 127 .... 172n
Wilkins & Others v. Cantrell & Cochrane (Great Britain) Ltd.
  [1978] IRLR 483 .... 172n, 218-19
Williams v. Lloyds Retailers Ltd. [1973] IRLR 262 .... 179n, 201n
Wilson v. Leslie Blass Ltd. [1975] IRLR 75 .... 171n
Wimpey (G.) & Co. Ltd. v. Cooper [1977] IRLR 205 .... 172n
Winnet v. Seamark Bros. Ltd. [1978] ICR 1240 .... 216n
Witham v. Hills Shopfitters Ltd. (1976) IT 17091/76/B 173n
Withers v. General Theatre Corporation [1933] 2 KB
  536 .... 99n
Wood v. Woad LR 9 Ex. 190 .... 70n
Woods v. Olympic Aluminium Co. Ltd. [1975] IRLR 356 .... 147n
Woods v. WM Car Services (Peterborough) Ltd. [1981]
  IRLR 347 .... 140n
Wynes v. South-Repps Hall Broiler Farm Ltd. [1968]
  ITR 407 175-6

Yates v. British Leyland [1974] IRLR 367 .... 158n
Yetton v. Eastwoods Froy Ltd. [1967] 1 WLR 104 .... 108n
Yorkshire Engineering & Welding Co. v. Burnham
  [1974] ICR 77 .... 103n
Young & Woods Ltd. v. West [1980] IRLR 201 .... 47, 47n
Young, James & Webster v. British Rail, The Times
  13 August 1981 .... 35n
Young's of Gosport Ltd. v. Kendell [1977] ICR 907 .... 193n

TABLES OF STATUTES

1. Statutes of Saorstát Éireann and the Oireachtas (1922-1981)
2. Statutes of the Parliament of Ireland (to 1800)
3. Statutes of the Parliament of England, Great Britain and the United Kingdom (1349-1980)

1. Statutes of Saorstát Éireann and the Oireachtas

1924	Railways Act (No. 29) s. 55	42n
1925	Police Forces (Amalgam.) Act (No. 7)	75-6, 113
	s. 14	73
1926	Local Authorities (Officers and Employees) Act (No. 39)	111
1927	Electricity (Supply) Act (No. 27)	217n
	s. 3(9)	112n
1935	Criminal Justice (amendment) Act (No. 6)	40n
1939	Offences against the State Act (No. 13)	217n
1941	Trade Union Act (No. 22)	64n, 207, 210
	s. 11	18n, 205n
	Part III	34
1946	Industrial Relations Act (No. 26)	118n, 204n
	s. 21(2)	125n
1954	Defence Act (No. 18) s. 73	72n
1956	Civil Service Commissioners Act (No. 45), Schedule	131n
1956	Civil Service Regulation Act (No. 46), ss. 5, 6, 17	51
1957	Statute of Limitations (No. 6)	114n
	s. 11	87n, 202
1962	Statute Law Revision (Pre-Union Irish Statutes) Act (No. 29)	14
1964	Finance Act (No. 15) ss. 8, 9	105
1967	Income Tax Act (No. 6)	192
	s. 114	105
	s. 115	105, 192n
1967	Redundancy Payments Act (No. 21)	118n, 124, 194
	s. 7(2)	151n
	s. 16	129n
	s. 31(2)	125n
	s. 39(17)	125n
	Sched. 3	194n
1969	Industrial Relations Act (No. 14)	27, 119, 124
	s. 13	124n, 127
1971	Redundancy Payments Act (No. 20)	118n
	ss. 4, 10	151n
1971	Trade Union Act (No. 33)	64n, 207, 210
1973	Minimum Notice and Terms of Employment Act (no. 4)	56-7, 63, 103, 118n, 180, 188-9, 194
	s. 2	129n
	s. 3	57n
	s. 4	56
	s. 8	57n
	s. 9	64

   s. 11 .... 57*n*
   Sched. 1, rule 6 .... 180*n*
1974 Anti-Discrimination (Pay) Act (No. 15) 27, 186*n*
1977 Social Welfare Act (No. 3) s. 13(2) 130*n*
1977 Protection of Employment Act (No. 7) 118, 211*n*
1977 Unfair Dismissals Act (No. 10)
    2, 27, 45, 86, 103, 119, 120-219 *passim,* 221-7 *passim,* 231

   Text of Act 233

   s. 1 .... 134, 135, 136, 143, 145*n,* 215, 216, 217
   s. 2 .... 222*n*
    (1) 130-1, 131*n*-32*n*
    (2) 135
    (4) 180*n*
   s. 5 .... 154, 206, 212-19, 222*n*
    (2) 212-18
   s. 6 (1) 120, 154, 207, 209, 214, 215
    (2) 130*n,* 154, 206, 207-09, 209-11
    (3) 150-3, 154, 206, 209-10, 211*n*
    (4) 147, 148, 150
    (6) 147, 153, 156
    (7) 208
   s. 7 .... 178-202, 222*n*
    (1)(c) 183, 185-8, 197*n,* 198, 222*n*
    (2) 183, 187, 198, 201
     (a) 197-9
     (b) 197-9, 222*n*
     (c) 199-201
     (d) 187*n,* 199, 203*n*
    (3) 198
    (4)(c) 182*n*
   s. 8 .... 126, 222*n*
    (2) 133
    (5) 134*n*
    (6) 121*n*
    (9) 125*n*
    (10) 127
   s. 9(2) 134*n*
   s. 10(1) 122*n,* 134*n*
    (3) 122*n*
    (4) 122*n,* 134*n*
   s. 13 .... 121, 142*n,* 202, 202*n*
   s. 14(3) 187, 199
    (4) 146
   s. 15 127
    (2) 126*n,* 127*n*
   s. 16 .... 183*n*
   s. 17 .... 124, 186
   s. 18 124
   s. 19 183
   s. 20 .... 129*n*
1977 Employment Equality Act (No. 16) 27, 186*n*
1979 Redundancy Payments Act (No. 7) 124, 125*n*
1979 Garda Síochána Act (No. 16) 75*n*

1980   Finance Act (No. 14), s. 10 .... 105, 192*n*
1981   Social Welfare (Consolidation) Act (No. 1) 107
1981   Maternity Protection of
      Employees Act (No. 2) 27, 156
      s. 1 .... 55*n*
      s. 24 133
      s. 25 .... 130, 133

2. Statutes of the Parliament of Ireland (To 1800)

1366   Statutes of Kilkenny 7*n*
1447   Sons of Labourers and Travailers on the
      Ground (25 Henry VI c. 7) 7-8
1494   Poynings Law (10 Hen. VII c. 22) 7*n*, 8
1542   Act for Servants Wages (33 Hen. VIII c. 9) 11
1569   Act for Servants Wages (11 Eliz. c. 5 sess. 1) 11*n*
1707   Act for Servants Wages (6 Anne c. 13) 11-12
1715   Servants Act (2 Geo. 1 c. 17) 12-15
1720   Declaratory Act (6 Geo. 1 c. 5) 7*n*
1751   Wages and Servants Act (25 Geo. 11 c. 8) s. 2 14

3. Statutes of the Parliament of England, Great Britain and the United Kingdom

1349   Statute of Labourers (23 Edw. III c. 1) 6-7, 11, 12*n*
1350   Statute of Labourers (25 Edw. III c. 1) 11
1562   Statute of Artificers (5 Eliz. c. 4) 8, 11, 12
1604   Statute of Labourers (1 Ja. 1 c. 6) 11*n*
1609   Statute of Apprentices (7 Ja. 1 c. 3) 11*n*
1679   Habeas Corpus Act (31 Car. 2 c. 2) 28*n*
1799   Combination Act (39 Geo. III c. 81) 18*n*
1800   Act of Union of Great Britain and Ireland
      (39 & 40 Geor. III c. 67) 1*n*, 15
1800   Combination Act (39 & 40 Geo. III c. 106) 18*n*
1803   Unlawful Combinations (Ireland) Act (43 Geo. III c. 86) 18*n*
1824   Combination Laws Repeal Act (5 Geo. IV c. 95) 18*n*
1856   Statute Law Revision Act (19 & 20 Vict. c. 64) 11*n*
1858   Chancery Amendment Act (21 & 22 Vict. c. 27) 41
1863   Statute Law Revision Act (26 & 27 Vict. c. 95) 11*n*
1867   Master and Servant Act (30 & 31 Vict. c. 141) 15-16
1875   Conspiracy and Protection of Property Act
      (38 & 39 Vict. c. 86) 18, 217*n*
      s. 17 .... 11*n*
1906   Trade Disputes Act (6 Edw. 7 c. 48) 18, 205-06, 213*n*
      s. 1 18

	s. 2	18, 35, 205*n*
	s. 3	18, 205*n*
	s. 4	18, 205*n*
	s. 5	18, 205-06
1963	Contracts of Employment Act (c. 49)	56*n*
1971	Industrial Relations Act (c. 7)	2, 89, 216*n*
	s. 24(1)(b)	160*n*
	s. 116	185*n*
	Sched. 6, para 5	178*n*
1974	Health and Safety at Work Act (c. 37)	147*n*
1974	Trade Union and Labour Relations Act (TULRA) (c. 52) 141*n*, 216*n*	
	Sched. 1	178*n*, 180*n*, 217
1975	Employment Protection Act (c. 71)	178*n*
1978	Employment Protection (Consolidation) Act	
	(EPCA) (c. 44) 2, 56*n*, 123*n*, 178*n*, 185-6	
	s. 1	63
	s. 13(9)	150*n*
	s. 42(1)	132
	s. 53(4)	146*n*
	s. 55 .... 137, 140, 144	
	s. 57(2)	147*n*
	(3)	148*n*
	s. 58	207*n*, 208*n*
	s. 59	150*n*, 210
	s. 62 .... 213*n*, 214-15, 214*n*-15*n*, 216*n*, 217*n*	
	s. 64(3)	208*n*
	s. 68	178*n*
	s. 69	178*n*
	s. 70(7)	181
	s. 71	123*n*, 179*n*
	s. 72	185*n*
	s. 73	185*n*
	s. 74	185*n*
1980	Employment Act (c. 42)	2
	s. 5	145*n*
	s. 6	187*n*
	s. 7	208*n*
	s. 8	132*n*
	s. 9	185*n*

TABLE OF STATUTORY INSTRUMENTS

Ireland:

1932   Rules and Regulations for National Schools 70*n*
1968   Redundancy (Redundancy Appeals Tribunal) Regulations
      (S.I. No. 24 of 1968) 190*n*
      Extracts from text of Regulations 264
1969   Redundancy (Redundancy Appeals Tribunal)
      (Amendment) Regulations (S.I. No. 26 of 1969) 124
1971   Garda Síochána (Discipline) Regulations
      (S.I. No. 316 of 1971) 73-4
1972   Factories (Ionising Radiations) Regulations (S.I. Nos. 17 and 249
      of 1972) 155*n*
1977   Unfair Dismissals (Claims and Appeals) Regulations
      (S.I. No. 286 of 1977) 133, 134
      Text of Regulations 256
1977   Unfair Dismissals (Calculation of Weekly Remuneration)
      Regulations (S.I. No. 287 of 1977) 186*n*, 188*n*, 189*n*
      Text of Regulations 260
1979   Circuit Court Rules (S.I. No. 10 of 1979) 123*n*

Britain:

1947   Industrial Tribunals (Labour Relations) Regulations 190*n*
1977   Employment Protection (Recoupment of Unemployment Benefit
      and Supplementary Benefit) Regulations (1977 S.I. No. 674) 191
1979   Unfair Dismissal (Variation of Qualifying Period)
      Order (1979 S.I. No. 1723) 185*n*
1980   Industrial Tribunals (Rules of Procedure)
      Regulations (1980 S.I. No. 884) 190*n*, 225*n*
1980   Employment Protection (Variation of Limits)
      Order (1980 S.I. No. 2019) 179*n*, 185*n*
1982   Unfair Dismissal (Increase of Compensation Limit) Order
      (1982 S.I. No. 76) 179*n*
1982   Employment Protection (Variation of Limits) Order
      (1982 S.I. No. 77) 179*n*

ABBREVIATIONS

All ER	All England Law Reports
COIT	Central Office of the Industrial Tribunals
EAT	Employment Appeals Tribunal (Ireland)
	Employment Appeal Tribunal (Britain)
EA	Employment Act 1980
EE	Equal Pay decisions
EPA	Employment Protection Act 1975
EPCA	Employment Protection (Consolidation) Act 1978
FUE	Federated Union of Employers
ICR	Industrial Court Reports 1972-74
	Industrial Cases Reports 1975-to-date
ICTU	Irish Congress of Trade Unions
ILO	International Labour Organisation
ILTR	Irish Law Times Reports
ILTSJ	Irish Law Times and Solicitors Journal
Ir Jur R	Irish Jurist Reports
IR	Irish Reports
IRLR	Industrial Relations Law Reports
ITR	Industrial Tribunal Reports
NIRC	National Industrial Relations Court
TULRA	Trade Union and Labour Relations Act 1974
UD	Determinations of the (Irish) EAT under the Unfair Dismissals Act 1977
WLR	Weekly Law Reports

CHAPTER ONE

Historical Development of the Law's Protection Against Wrongful Termination of Employment

Introduction: The Nature of the Present Work

'You may find it in the fragments of Gregorius and Hermogene's codes, and in all the codes of Justinian's down to the codes of Louis and Des Eaux — that the sweat of a man's brows, and the exudations of a man's brains, are as much a man's own property, as the breeches upon his backside.'

— Laurence Sterne: *Tristram Shandy*
Vol. III ch. 34.

The field of interest of the present work spans the Constitution, common and statute law. It has taken a long time for law codes anywhere to recognise that a man's work is akin to his property. Ireland and Britain are among those jurisdictions where a limited degree of recognition is found but, in general, the work-property concept is seen as through a glass darkly. Its theory remains undeveloped, its practical implications unexplored.

This study is essentially comparative. The law on termination of employment in Ireland cannot be analysed in isolation from British law because the relationship between Ireland and Britain for eight hundred years was a very important element in establishing the nature and characteristics of the Irish legal and social systems. Until the independence of Saorstát Éireann in 1922, legislation passed by the Westminster Parliament in such matters as trade union law, trade disputes, social security and industrial accidents was frequently applied to Ireland as well.[1] Apart from legislative influences, the British system of labour relations affected the growth of labour practices in Ireland because of factors such as geographical contiguity, the free movement of labour, and the operation of British unions and companies in Ireland. As the British House of Lords was the final judicial court of appeal before 1922, a common jurisprudence was established throughout the islands. Decisions of

1. Before the Act of Union of Great Britain and Ireland, in 1800, the precise application in Ireland of statutes passed at Westminster was not free of controversy. At the same time, the Parliament of Ireland was legislating for that jurisdiction. See fn. 15 *post*.

1

the House of Lords are still highly persuasive for the courts in Ireland.

Since 1922, there have been significant divergences in Irish labour law. These have occurred at common law, under statute and by virtue of the enactment in 1937 of the Constitution of Ireland (*Bunreacht na hÉireann*) — yet the assumptions and structures of the systems in the two jurisdictions remain similar. In both, essential elements of the tradition continue in spite of the nature of specific legal provisions. For instance, Ireland's Unfair Dismissals Act, 1977, is similar to Britain's statutory provisions concerning dismissal first enacted in the Industrial Relations Act, 1971, and, following a series of statutory adventures, now found in the Employment Protection (Consolidation) Act, 1978, as amended by the Employment Act, 1980. But any assumptions that the intentions and aspirations of the legislature in either jurisdiction are fully and accurately reflected in subsequent behaviour and events would be highly misleading. Between the intentions of the Oireachtas and of Westminster respectively, and the phenomena at which they are directed, there mediate many contingencies which impede, refract or distort the former in terms of their impact on the latter. These include the interpretations applied by the courts, tribunals, administrators, managers and the rank and file, the effectiveness of enforcement and the priorities and general vigilance of those affected by the measures concerned. It is instructive to compare the outcome where these contingencies have operated or operate differently in the two systems. The Irish Act is not on all fours with the Employment Protection (Consolidation) Act. In accordance with its usual custom, the Oireachtas modelled its Act on the corresponding British legislation but tailored it to take account of specific features in Irish industrial relations. Where the statutory provisions are noticeably dissimilar between the two jurisdictions, they merit particular examination.

The most important divergence from British law took place when the Constitution of Ireland was adopted following a plebiscite in 1937. The Constitution introduces a fundamentally different dimension into Irish law. It is not only a written document, but also a basic code delimiting the area of legislative competence. It provides for judicial review of legislation and lays down a list of human rights which are protected by the courts. The Preamble, which is cited from time to time by judges as a guide when interpreting legislation,[2] refers to the promotion of

2. See *The State (Burke)* v. *Lennon and A-G* [1940] I.R. 136, 155; recent examples are *McGee* v. *A-G and the Revenue Commissioners* [1974] I.R. 284, 310, 318-'9; *State (Healy)* v. *Donoghue* [1976] I.R. 325, 347; *Garvey* v. *Ireland and Others* [1981] I.R. 75.

'. . . the common good, with due observance of Prudence, Justice and Charity, so that the dignity and freedom of the individual may be assured, [and] true social order attained . . .'

Article 45 lays down Directive Principles of Social Policy.[3] They contain an undertaking that the State will direct its policy towards securing, for example,

'That the citizens (all of whom, men and women, equally have the right to an adequate means of livelihood) may through their occupations find the means of making reasonable provisions for their domestic needs'

Again the State

'. . . pledges itself to safeguard with especial care the economic interests of the weaker sections of the community, and, where necessary, to contribute to the support of the infirm, the widow, the orphan and the aged'

And

'The State shall endeavour to ensure that the strength and health of workers, men and women, and the tender age of children shall not be abused and that citizens shall not be forced by economic necessity to enter avocations unsuited to their sex, age or strength'.

These Principles evidence the view that a constitution expresses 'not only legal norms but basic doctrines of political and social theory'.[4] They lie at the very core of unfair dismissal law. The most important fundamental rights in relation to the employment relationship are set out in Article 40 (see chap. two below). Here, as in general, the Constitution has been neither an unqualified triumph nor merely an

3. The Directive Principles are borrowed from the Spanish Republican Constitution of 1937. As stated, they are of a vague and generalised nature and cannot be described as identifying the kind of social and economic rights laid down, for example, in the European Social Charter.

4. *In re Criminal Law (Jurisdiction) Bill 1975* (1976) Vol. 110 ILTR 69, 76 *per* O'Higgins C.J. Any of the Principles cited in the text could arise for consideration in regard to labour legislation. It is generally held that they are no more than noble-sounding exhortations. Article 45 declares that the Principles are 'intended for the general guidance of the Oireachtas. The application of those Principles in the making of laws shall be the care of the Oireachtas exclusively, and shall not be cognisable by any Court under any of the provisions of this Constitution'. But, in the High Court case of *Murtagh Properties Ltd.* v. *Cleary* [1972] I.R. 330, Judge Kenny ascribed a limited usefulness to Article 45. From his *dicta*, (335-'6) it seems the Principles may be looked to for the enumeration of personal rights under Article 40.3.1. See chapter two *post*, p. 31. This may only be done where the allegedly unconstitutional activity takes place *inter partes*, i.e., where there is no involvement on the part of the State.

obeisance towards conventional constitutional formularies.[5] How far the relevant fundamental rights it enshrines have been effective can be discovered only from the experience of the period of forty years or so that has elapsed since it came into force. A constitutional philosophy in relation to dismissal has slowly unfolded over the last decade against a background of judicial interpretation which lays (perhaps undue) stress on the rights of the individual. The relationship between the employer and the individual worker is regarded as crucial and the activities of the worker as part of a collectivity are scarcely perceived as worthy of consideration. In chapter two, the supreme position of the Constitution in the hierarchy of legal values in Ireland appears as a highly significant feature of the law in relation to termination of employment. Throughout the work, it will be demonstrated how much the influence of the Constitution is brought to bear on every aspect of the law. At times this influence is subtle, at others it is dynamic. To understand the slow and often cumbersome evolution of dismissal law, it is necessary to go back in time. In this chapter, two broad areas are examined:

A. The historical development of statute and of common law in Ireland at a time when that country and Britain shared the same, or broadly the same, legal system; and

B. The effectiveness of the trade union movement in relation to individual employment rights and the deficiencies of collective bargaining.

These influences reveal something of dismissal as a social phenomenon although their testimony is far from comprehensive. Historical records are lacking. Often one is grasping at statutory straws. Historical sources of Irish law on termination of employment are minefields for the unwary, but to omit them altogether would effect greater incomprehension.

A. **Historical Evolution of Statute and of Common Law on Termination of Employment in Ireland**

(1) *Statute Law*

The law on termination of employment is rooted within the contract model but the circumstances which gave rise to this model (involving the so-called progression from status to contract) differed

5. In general, see J. M. Kelly: *The Irish Constitution*; also R. F. V. Heuston: 'Personal Rights under the Irish Constitution' (1976) Vol. XI *The Irish Jurist* 205; J. Temple Lang: 'Private Law Aspects of the Irish Constitution' (1971) Vol. VI *The Irish Jurist* 237; M. Crowe: 'Human Rights, the Irish Constitution and the Courts' (1971) 47 *Notre Dame Lawyer* 281; A.G. Donaldson: *Some Comparative Aspects of Irish Law* (Duke University Press, Durham 1957); Messineo: 'La Nuova Constituzione Irlandese' 88 *Civiltà Cattolica* 239, 246; H. Franzen: 'Irland und Grossbrittanien seit 1919' in *Jahrbuch des offentlichen Rechts* (1938) 280-375.

as between Ireland and England. Until the nineteenth century, the contract of employment was hidden under the cloak of service as a status. The move from status to contract is just one label to describe the historical changes which took place before the end of that century. The classic statement, of course, is that of Sir Henry Maine.[6] The idea underpinning his concept was principally one of a social move from family to individual. Maine equated family to the traditional law of Persons and thereby to Status. His account emphasises an important feature of pre-capitalist law, namely, that master and servant relations were treated by lawyers up to the eighteenth century as a branch of the law of persons, more specifically, the law of domestic relations.[7] They were rooted in a society where subordination to legitimate authority was accepted as natural.[8]

The difficulties experienced in England of adapting the pattern of unfree serf labour to a new contractual relationship were not acutely felt in Ireland where political instability and endemic warfare continually hampered the country. In the 14th and 15th centuries, there was no Irish manufacture of importance. Agriculture was backward by contemporary English standards. The social and intellectual developments that were linked with industrial and mercantile expansion in other parts of Western Europe had little effect on mediaeval Ireland.[9] Likewise during the 16th and 17th centuries, and in the centuries that followed, many historic events affected the country.[10] Alongside the poverty and isolation in Ireland, social and

6. 'The movement of the progressive societies has been uniform in the one respect. Through all its course it has been distinguished by the gradual dissolution of family dependency and the growth of individual obligation in its place. The individual is steadily substituted for the Family, as the unit of which civil laws take account . . . Nor is it difficult to see what is the tie between man and man which replaces by degrees those forms of reciprocity in rights and duties which have their origin in the Family. It is Contract . . . Thus the status of the slave has disappeared — it has been superseded by the contractual relation of the servant to his master': Sir Henry Maine: *Ancient Law: Its Connection with the Early History of Society and its Relation to Modern Ideas* (1912) 99-100.

7. See O. Kahn-Freund: 'Blackstone's Neglected Child' (1977) 93 L.Q.R. 508, 510.

8. This acceptance runs through Dutton's treatise, see page 8 *post*. Further, the developing concept of individual obligation lay beneath the contract model. There is a clear link between the rise of individualism and contract.

9. J. C. Beckett: *The Making of Modern Ireland 1603-1923*, 16.

10. The 16th and 17th centuries saw, e.g., the Reformation, the Cromwellian interlude, the Restoration, the Bloodless Revolution, the accession of the Hanoverians. In addition there was a gradual extension of English administration throughout the country, the settlement of English and Scottish planters in Ulster, the rising in 1641 and the Williamite wars. The Penal laws had the most pernicious effects on Irish society. They fostered the worst vices of ascendancy on the one side and slavery on the other; and they exacerbated divisions which sprang from

economic developments were taking place in England. These were ultimately of the greater importance for Irish law.

The legislative developments discussed here concern persons standing in what Blackstone called 'private economic relations'.[11] In earliest times, the contractual basis of the master-servant relation did not form part of the legal definition. For instance, a labourer's duty to serve, as will be seen, was based on legal compulsion imposed by magistrates or Justices of the Peace under statute. A person employed under the Poor Law was liable to serve a master with whom he never entered into a contract. The duty to work for another was the essence of the relationship: it could arise simply from the condition of 'having no visible effects' and being therefore liable to be directed by the Justices to compulsory work, or from the condition of being a son of a labourer or 'travailer upon the ground'.

Although the word 'status' is much misused in law,[12] the early master-servant relation was based on status, not on contract. Very early on, in 1349, the Statute of Labourers[13] introduced a system of compulsory labour. The Act was passed to combat the scarcity of labour and the inflationary situation following upon the Black Death. It controlled the increasing number of landless labourers working for a money wage by a system of forced labour. 'The object of this legislation' wrote Fitzjames Stephen, 'was to provide a kind of substitute for the system of villainage and serfdom which was then breaking down'.[14] Under the Act any landless person under sixty could be compelled to work for whichever master required his services. This was reinforced by a penalty of imprisonment for any servant departing his service. Whether the Act applied in Ireland at the time is a

---

differences of religious faith. In addition, during the period 1600-1800, the great mass of Irishmen were subject to galling restrictions on their economic freedom. For example, a ruinous export duty was imposed on Irish woollen goods: 10 Wm. III c. 5(1), see Chart, fn. 23 *post,* chap. 62, for an account of the woollen and linen industries between 1600-1800. The matter is also treated in Murray *op. cit.*, fn. 23 *post, passim.*

11. *Commentaries,* cited O. Kahn-Freund, *art. cit.,* fn. 7 *ante,* 511. The chief relations in private life, according to Blackstone, were Master and Servant, Husband and Wife, Parent and Child, Guardian and Ward.

12. O. Kahn-Freund: 'A Note on Status and Contract in British Labour Law' (1967) 30 MLR 635.

13. 23 Edw. III c. 1; in that year Parliament, though called, did not meet on account of the Plague. The statute begins: 'Whereas late against the Malice of Servants, which were idle, and not willing to serve after the Pestilence, without taking excessive Wages. . . .'

14. *History of the Criminal Law of England,* Vol. III, p. 204, see also 274; cf. also *Jones Bros. (Hunstanton) Ltd. v. Stevens* [1955] 1 Q.B. 275, judgment of Lord Goddard.

matter of constitutional controversy.[15] Whatever about theoretical considerations, however, and the later impact of Poyning's Law,[16] if an English Act were then to be applied in Ireland, the steady practice was that it had to be enacted by the Parliament of Ireland.[17] The extent of application of Acts passed by the Parliament of Ireland was in turn limited to the King's subjects living within the jurisdiction of the Crown.[18] (This restriction lasted until 1541 when, under Henry VIII, Ireland passed from being a Lordship to a Kingdom.)[19]

The Parliament of Ireland, which began to be summoned regularly from the middle of the thirteenth century,[20] frequently enacted legislation for that jurisdiction. In 1447, compulsory labour was effected by an Irish Act entitled the 'Sons of Labourers and Travailers of the Ground'.[21] It laid down that they

> 'shall be labourers and travailers upon the ground as they were in old time and in all other works and labours lawful and honest'.

15. For an authoritative summary of the material relating to the mediaeval Irish parliament see Richardson & Sayles: *The Irish Parliament in the Middle Ages*; see, too, G. J. Hand: *English Law in Ireland 1290-1324* — although the period he covers serves only as an introduction for present purposes. A useful historical picture of the relationship between Westminster and the Parliament of Ireland is found in B. Kiernan: *History of the Financial Administration of Ireland to 1817*. Ball's *Irish Legislative Systems* is enlightening, as is F. H. Newark's 'Notes on Irish Legal History' (1947) 7 NILQ 121. The most concise treatment of this highly controversial subject is in A. G. Donaldson: *Some Comparative Aspects of Irish Law*. Poyning's Law, 1494 (10 Hen. VII c. 22) was a general confirmation of English Acts by the Irish Parliament (see B. Bradshaw: *The Irish Constitutional Revolution of the Sixteenth Century*). The Declaratory Act in 1720 (the 'Sixth of George the First'), *inter alia*, asserted the legislative supremacy of the British Parliament over Ireland. The power of Westminster to legislate for Ireland was a highly contentious issue within Ireland and was frequently denied. In practice unless the Parliament of Ireland re-enacted Westminster legislation the latter did not apply in Ireland. Whatever about the theoretical extension of English Acts, many limitations existed on their effectiveness. First, the area of Anglo-Norman influence waxed and waned considerably until the beginning of the 17th century. As a result there was not always machinery to enforce the legislation. Secondly, the native Irish living in the jurisdiction of the royal courts did not always have access to these courts (see S. Gwynn: *The History of Ireland*, 116).

16. See footnote 1 *ante*.

17. Note that Dutton, p. 8 *post*, refers to the Statute of Labourers as being of force in Ireland by Poyning's Law (at 1). He also notes (at 3) that no action had been brought 'in this age under the Statute'.

18. Statutes of Kilkenny, 1366.

19. Confirmed by Parliament in 1612-'13 when an Act was passed retrospectively declaring that all laws were applicable to all people.

20. See Donaldson, *op. cit.*, footnote 15 *ante*, 39.

21. XXV Hen. VI, c. 7.

The Statute was enacted as the 'Sons' were allegedly becoming

> 'kearnes,[22] evil-doers, wasters, idle men, and destructioners of the king our sovereign lord's liege-people, to the great decay of the . . . commons, and impoverishment of the state'.

In the absence of records, it is not possible to gauge either the practical necessity[23] or the effectiveness of master and servant legislation in Ireland. Nonetheless some degree of practical need may be inferred from the fact that a textbook on *The Law of Masters and Servants in Ireland* was published in Dublin in 1723[24] (surely the first on the topic in the English-speaking common law world). The author, Matthew Dutton, affirms in the Preface that

> '. . . no English books can be of much service to us here, without reading and making use of them with a great deal of caution and wariness; for . . . as to Servants, Artificers and Labourers, the old statutes made in England (and of force here by Poyning's Law[25]) concerning them, many things therein are now grown obsolete . . .'[26]

He continues

> '. . . And as for English books, of the Office of Justices of the Peace, they treat of diverse Statutes not of force in this Kingdom, and especially that branch of their Office, that relates to Masters, Artificers, Apprentices, Servants and Labourers is taken up (in those Books) with the Statute of *5 Eliz. cap. 4* and some few subsequent statutes, and the Judgments and Resolutions of the Judges grounded upon them . . . all other statutes before that time made (though many of them are still in force here by Poyning's Law) are there repealed by that Statute, but it don't extend to Ireland'.[27]

22. A 'kearne' is a lightly armed infantryman.
23. See D. A. Chart: *The Economic History of Ireland,* 44, quoting from Sir W. Petty's *Economic Writings*. The entire population in the middle of the 17th century was estimated at 1,100,000. Of these Petty reckoned that 780,000 could be considered old enough to be capable of work. The tillage of 500,000 acres of corn employed c. 100,000 workers; the working of wool and making up of cloth another 75,000; while 12,000 were engaged in the tending of cattle and sheep. See, for useful background information, three works by G. O'Brien: *Economic History of Ireland from the Union to the Famine; The Economic History of Ireland in the Eighteenth Century; The Economic History of Ireland in the Seventeenth Century.* Further see A. Murray: *Commercial Relations between England and Ireland; W. Lecky: History of Ireland in the Eighteenth Century.*
24. Talbot Press.
25. 10 Hen. 7, c. 22 (as it is cited in the printed versions of the Irish statutes; though it was originally c. 39). See fn. 15 *ante*.
26. At vi.
27. At viii.

So, 'modern' books written in England could not be of sufficient authority for Justices of the Peace in Ireland. Where, however, no express direction or authority was given by any law in force in Ireland,

> 'it seems (according to Sir Richard Bolton[28]) that the English statutes may serve for some direction to them . . .'[29]

Dutton defines the term 'servant' in the Preface.[30] He was such person

> 'as, by agreement and retainer, oweth duty and service, to another, who therefore is called his Master.'

Among servants, some were ordinary, menial and familiar, that is, they were constantly in the house or family and attending on their master's business; and

> 'these are either for a less time, as, such as are hired or retained by the year, half or quarter of a year, or such as are for a longer time, and retained by Indenture and Covenant in writing, as Apprentices, which are generally for seven, and sometimes for eight or more years, and others are extraordinary, and upon occasion only, some of which are sometimes dwelling with their Masters and others are not, and are hired by the day, week or month, such as Artificers and Labourers.'

Dutton's definition of 'servant' may be contrasted with that of Sir William Blackstone in the First Book of his *Commentaries*.[31] The *Commentaries* were published over four decades later, in 1765 (and a comparison between the first edition and the 18th, published in 1821, shows that the text is substantially the same). For Blackstone the master-servant relation is

> 'founded in convenience, whereby a man is directed to call in the assistance of others, where his own skill and labour will not be sufficient to answer the cares incumbent upon him.'

The duty to serve is the essence of the employment relationship. Blackstone's myopic view of the contractual element in the service

---

28. Bolt. *Just. Lib.* 2, 13.
29. Fn. 24 at ix.
30. At i.
31. Bk. 1, 1st edition (18th ed., 485).

relation was identified by the late Professor Kahn-Freund as a major stultifying factor in the development of a contractual basis in the English law of employment relations.[32] Dutton, on the contrary, was aware of a contractual element as the reference to 'agreement' in his definition illustrates. This is noteworthy notwithstanding that in his subsequent treatment of the master-servant relation, he regards the agreement or contract as an *accidentale,* not an *essentiale,* of the relation. Dutton makes it clear that the master and servant had a work-wages relationship — but, once more, he refers to an agreement *inter partes* —

> 'the general rule of Law, is that according as the retainer and agreement is, so the Servant, Artificer, and Labourer must do his work, and so the Master must pay his wages; and if either of them fail, they may have reciprocal remedy against each other . . .'[33]

In Ireland, therefore, the contractual element was accorded a degree of recognition from the early 18th century onwards. This recognition may have resided in theory alone but it is none the less remarkable. The contractual element is very important in individual employment law.

Dutton's analysis of master and servant law in early eighteenth century Ireland is not, unfortunately, comprehensive. One does not know what sort of people were 'servants' at the time. His account relates to a certain segment of society, a fact borne out even by the most elementary insight into economic and social history. We do not hear about the skilled craftsman who, having served his apprenticeship as a mason or a carpenter or a tailor, then entered employment in his trade. We hear nothing about those employed in shipping, distilling, tanning, or the linen or woollen industries.[34] These industries were conducted on the basis of employed labour. True, in Ireland their development in Dutton's day was subject to commercial restrictions imposed by Westminster. True, too, an Industrial Revolution (as such) never took place in Ireland (and it had not yet begun in England) but by the early 18th century, an important minority of Irish men and women were employed in industry. There were also

---

32. *Art. cit.,* fn. 7 *ante, passim.*
33. Page 1.
34. See, e.g., Chart *op. cit.,* fn. 23 *ante,* Chap. IV, 62 (also Murray, O'Brien, etc., fn. 23). An interesting picture of the state of Ireland's external commerce is given in Petty's 'Treatise of Ireland' (*Economic Writings,* 592) where Irish exports for 1685 are given in detail. The most prominent items are beet, butter, corn, lamb and rabbit skins, hides (salted and tanned), wool (exported to England only), frieze, woollen cloth, linen cloth, linen yarn, beer and whiskey.

persons engaged in the world of commerce such as Agents; there were Stewards, Bailiffs and Receivers, but Dutton expressly excuses the striking out of these particular categories from his textbook because (o happy and familiar fault)

> 'what concerns [the above-named servants] hath swell'd the Book bigger than I at first intended it.'

Dutton claimed that the categories of 'other servants' were adequately dealt with in the common law of England (a disputable fact). The chief value of Dutton's work lies in his remarks throughout the text, asides which are not directly related to master and servant legislation. They serve as an important if limited barometer concerning the problems and status of servants in early 18th century Ireland.[35]

Dutton provides a useful catalogue as to how the relation of master and servant is established and terminated and of the sources of the obligations to which it gives rise. His caution in relation to the Statute of Artificers (*5 Eliz. cap. 4*) p. 8 *supra,* is particularly interesting as that Act is commonly believed to have applied in Ireland. (The Elizabethan Statute of 1562 was an elaboration of the two Statutes of Labourers passed by Edward III in 1349 and 1350.[36]) In fact, part of the subject-matter of that Act was dealt with by the Parliament of Ireland twenty-one years beforehand, when the Act for Servants Wages, 1542,[37] enabled Justices of the Peace to proclaim the wages of artificers and labourers (who were paid by the day) and of servants at husbandry (who were paid by the year).[38] Although not in the same form, the remainder of the Statute of Elizabeth was embodied in an Act of the Parliament of Ireland in 1707,[39] during the reign of Queen Anne. That Act dealt with matters such as the testimonial required

35. See, in particular, chapters VII and VIII.

36. It must be read in conjunction with subsequent legislation especially (but not only) the Jacobean Statute of Labourers, 1604, 1 Ja. 1, c. 6, and the Statute of Apprentices, 1609, 7 Ja. 1, c. 3. The statute of 1562 was repealed by the Conspiracy and Protection of Property Act, 1875, s. 17; the Jacobean statutes by the Statute Law Revision Acts, 1856 and 1863.

37. XXXIII Hen. VIII c. 9; revived and continued by 11 Eliz. 5, Sess. 1 (1569).

38. 'But such rating and limiting of wages of Servants, Artificers and Labourers is not much minded of late, either in England or Ireland, though there are also Acts of Parliament in England for that purpose (e.g., 5 Eliz. c. 4, 1 Jac. 1 c. 6). I have seen some such rates made heretofore in England, but I have not met with any made in this kingdom, therefore can't satisfie the curiosity of my Reader by setting down any such rates at any time made here' (Dutton, *op. cit.* fn. 24 *ante,* 182): Sir Richard Bolton (*Bolt. Just.,* fn. 28 *ante,* 135) very much complained of the neglect of justices in rating wages in his time.

39. VI Anne c. 13; see *The Journals of the House of Commons of the Kingdom of Ireland* (A. 1707, 510, 512).

from a master before a servant could be discharged or put away.[40] No master or mistress could hire a servant without a discharge from his previous service.[41] The Act was re-enacted in similar form in the Servants Act, 1715,[42] a statute which resembles, but is by no means identical to, *5 Eliz. cap. 4.*

The Servants Act shows that still in theory, if to a declining extent in practice, the law of master and servant was the law of the status of those liable to be directed to work at wages fixed without their concurrence and liable to be punished for not accepting work on demand and for not doing it in accordance with the direction. The Irish legislation was hard and oppressive and imposed obligations on the servant alone. The corresponding English Act in some respects protected the servant. For example, that Act provided against termination of the relationship before the end of the agreed term except 'for some reasonable cause or matter' and with the consent of a Justice of the Peace or Mayor and through a provision for one quarter's notice (ss. 5 and 6). Moreover, the English Act imposed obligations on masters as well as on servants. Under the Irish Act, if a servant departed his service without consent within the time for which he was obliged to serve, the master could complain upon oath before a Justice of the Peace or Chief Magistrate in the City or Town where the master lived and the civil authority was empowered to issue a warrant for bringing the servant before him. Following examination and due proof upon oath of the offence, the Justice or Chief Magistrate could put the servant in the stocks for a time not exceeding six hours or send him to the House of Correction of the County to be kept at hard labour for a period not longer than ten days. Afterwards, if the master desired the servant to return to his service, this could be ordered by the Justice or Chief Magistrate. If the servant refused to return to his master, he could again be committed to hard labour and corporally punished. Alternatively the master could discharge the servant.[43]

Under the same Act, no servant could hire or offer himself to be hired into any service while actually in service, and before the time for

40. Para. V.
41. Para. IX. The form was: 'MEMORANDUM, That A. B. the Bearer hereof, was retained by me, C. D., of Etc. as a menial Servant for the space of one year ending the   day of this instant   during which time he behaved himself very expertly, honestly and faithfully [or such character as the Master thought fit] and I do hereby discharge the said A. B. from my said service. Witness my hand this day of Anno Dom. (Dutton, 27-'8).
42. 2 Geo. 1, c. 17; note that the Statute of Labourers was not repealed by the Servants Act and so both Acts laid down punishments concerning the departure of servants (see Dutton, 51). See *The Journals of the House of Commons of the Kingdom of Ireland* (A, 1715, 79).
43. See Dutton, 78.

which he had contracted or hired himself had expired, without a licence from his master 'unless such servant [did] first give one month's notice' to his master. If the servant contravened this provision he could be committed to the House of Correction for any time not exceeding ten days or put in the stocks for no longer than six hours. A master had three months within which to complain and all determinations by the Justice or Chief Magistrate were conclusive between the parties. Because there are no appellate records, the extent of invocation of the Act cannot be known.

Under the Servants Act, idle and disorderly servants could not only be punished but masters could also part with them. If servants were drunkards, idle or otherwise disorderly[44] in their services, a Justice or Chief Magistrate could put them in the stocks or send them to a House of Correction. If the Master desired the servant to return to his service after the punishment, the justice was empowered to order him to do so.

Termination of the master-servant relationship depended on the Servant's being duly discharged. If he was, this was a good bar of any action taken by the master for departing his service.[45] The master could discharge his servant by word. If put away by his master, the servant was entitled to wages for the time served. If, on the other hand, the servant agreed to being put away he had no action to recover any part of his wages (but he could seek the help of a Justice of the Peace if his wages were within the Act of 1715). If a servant left of his own accord before his time had expired he lost all his wages.[46] Where the master discharged his servant, saying he should serve him no longer, the servant could not serve against the master's will (compare the modern refusal to grant specific performance of contracts of service). At the same time the view was expressed by one writer,[47] and endorsed by Dutton, that unilateral termination of the relationship would be invalid: the master could not discharge his servant within the term except the servant agreed thereto. Conversely the servant could not depart from his master without the master's licence or agreement[48] (an interesting foreshadow of the contractual principle of mutuality).

44. 'Those words are very extensive, wherefore Servants can't now be guilty of any offences, but they may be exemplarily punished by this Statute, in case the Justice don't think the complaint against them to be frivolous and vexatious' (Dutton, footnote at 129).
45. Dutton 73; *Bro. Lab.* 22.
46. *Ibid.,* 73, citing *Dalt. Just.* 129, and *Bro. Lab.* 30, 38, 40, 48.
47. *Bro. Lab.* 27.
48. If a servant retained for a year happened within the time of service to fall sick, or to be hurt or lamed, or otherwise became *non potens in corpore* by act of God, or in doing his Master's business, it seems the master could not put the servant away, nor abate any part of his wages for such time: *Dalt. Just.* 129; cited Dutton, 80.

Section IV of the Servants Act, 1715, dealt with the master's obligation to give a certificate of discharge. If a master refused to discharge his servant, a Justice of the Peace or Chief Magistrate could look into the cause. If, after five days, he received no answer, or if the reply was not sufficient, he could issue a certificate of discharge without fee. There was no recognition of anything akin to a servant's right to work. Although a master's refusal to discharge a servant prevented the latter from obtaining other employment, the common law allowed no action for damages by the servant against the master for refusing to give a certificate of character: *Lint v. Johnston*.[49] Although the Servants Act is by now obsolete in Ireland, it remains on the statute-book. Curiously, very minor deletions were effected by the Statute Law Revision Act, 1962.[50]

The punishment of putting a servant in the stocks as a form of discipline disappeared in a later Wages and Servants Act passed by the Parliament of Ireland in 1751.[51] Section 2 of that Act provided that Justices, upon complaint on oath by a master or employer against a servant or labourer, for 'misdeameanour, miscarriage or ill-behaviour in such his or her service or employment' could examine and punish a servant by House of Correction for one month, by abating wages, or by discharging. Likewise, Justices could hear complaints of ill-treatment by servants and, on satisfactory proof of same, discharge the servant from service.

Cases on these Acts were extremely rare. In *Handley v. Moffat*,[52] which concerned breach of the statutory duty imposed on masters to give a discharge under the Servants Act, 1715, (s. 4), Monaghan C.J. observed that

49. (1893) 28 ILTR 16. L. had been compelled to issue a summons to recover her wages after she left her employment but her employer refused to give up her certificate or to give her a discharge so as to enable her to get other employment. As she had been prevented from obtaining other employment she claimed £5 compensation for breach of the contract. The justices awarded £2.00 compensation and 50p costs but, on appeal, the Recorder held no action of the kind could be maintained at common law. The only remedy available to a servant was that provided by the statute, para. 4 (see, too, *Handley v. Moffat* 7 ILTR 9; *Carroll v. Bird* 3 Esp. 201).

50. The Statute Law Revision (Pre-Union Irish Statutes) Act, 1962 (no. 29), Schedule. Very minor deletions were made from sections 3, 6 and 7, and section 19 was repealed *in toto*. Although, e.g., the Jacobean statutes were repealed by Statute Law Revision Acts (fn. 36 *ante*) the purposes of the latter Acts seem to be viewed differently in the two jurisdictions.

51. XXV Geo. II c. 8. (The Act also concerned Recovery of Wages). It was in force for 2 years and continued in several amendments by 29 Geo. 2, c. 8 and 1 Geo. 3, c. 17; it was made perpetual by 5 Geo. 3, c. 15, para 32 (1765). Under s. 2, servants could complain against their masters for ill-treatment, etc.

52. (1873) IR 7 CL 104.

'. . . from the time of the passing of the Act to the present day,
over 150 years, no . . . action appears to have been brought
[under s. 4]'[53]

In time, the system of compulsory labour became intertwined with
the Poor Law under which parishes were responsible for providing
the able-bodied industrious pauper with either employment or relief.
In 1838, a public system of poor relief was established in Ireland.[54] It
was apparently not easy to improvise useful works for the able-bodied
without, *inter alia*, a careful organisation of labour. The Government fell back on the workhouse system and from 1838 onwards
employment for the able-bodied was found only within the walls of
the workhouse. Gradually it extended beyond these as well.

In 1800, following the Act of Union of Great Britain and Ireland,
a series of statutes was passed at Westminster dealing with master
and servant law. The last Master and Servant Act (so styled) was
passed in 1867.[55] Its major purpose was to inject a measure of
equality into the law by affording the same statutory remedies to both
master and servant.[56] Redress in Ireland was limited to those persons
within the jurisdiction of the Metropolitan Police District of Dublin.
Section 4 provided that where 'the Employer or Employed' should
neglect or refuse to fulfil any contract of service, or the Employed
should neglect or refuse to enter or commence his service according
to the contract, or absent himself from service, the aggrieved party
could complain before one of the Divisional Magistrates. The latter
was empowered to award compensation for breach or non-
performance of the contract of service. He could also direct the fulfil-
ment of the contract of service, or annul the contract and discharge
the parties from its obligations. Alternatively he could impose a fine
not exceeding £20 on the offending party (section 9). The same
procedure was available in the event of any dispute as to the rights
and liabilities of either of the parties, or where there were allegations of
misusage, misdemeanour, misconduct, ill-treatment or injury to the
person or property of either of the parties under any contract of
service.

The Act of 1867 gave separate treatment to aggravated mis-

53. At 108.
54. Chart, *op. cit.*, fn. 23 *ante*, 101; see, too, J. E. Bichens: *Ireland, and its
Economy*, Chap. VI 'On Poor Laws'; for Marx's account of the Poor Law System in
England see *Capital I*, chap. XXVIII.
55. *30 & 31 Vict.*, c. CXLI, cf. W. A. Hunter: 'The Master and Servant Act,
1867, and the first report of the Royal Commission, 1874'; D. Simon: 'Master and
Servant' in *Democracy and the Labour Movement*; J. Ed. Davis: 'The Master and
Servant Act, 1867; with an introduction, notes and forms, and tables of offences'.
56. See Anon: 'Master and Servant' (1866-'7) S.J. 11, 327.

conduct, misdemeanour or ill-treatment. Where the alleged misconduct was not committed in the *bona fide* exercise of a legal right, either existing or *bona fide* or reasonably supposed to exist, and where pecuniary compensation or any other remedy under the Act was not appropriate, a convicted party could be committed at the Magistrate's discretion to the Common Gaol or House of Correction for a period not greater than 3 months with or without hard labour (section 14). Where proceedings had not been instituted under the Act, parties to the contract of employment could enforce their rights by action or by suit in the ordinary courts of law or equity. In England, in contradistinction to Ireland, there are many reported cases under the Master and Servant Acts.[57] Part of the explanation for the absence of Irish cases lies in the limited application of these Acts. A more important explanation may lie in the political history of Ireland during the 19th century. It consisted largely of a recurrent struggle by the majority of the Irish people to regain their civil and religious liberties. In 1846-'7, the Great Famine imposed a new pattern of society and of politics. The economic position of the country deteriorated drastically. A huge and growing proportion of an increasing population lived on the land or, more specifically, on the potato crops which they raised from their plots of ground. Agriculture in the true sense was almost unknown. Industries, with the exception of the linen trade, were in decline.[58] It was not until the beginning of the 20th century that Ireland began to advance in a long cycle of growing world prosperity and expanding trade.[59]

The statistics reproduced below say something about the dominant trends in employment during the latter half of the 19th century in Ireland. They show a decline in agriculture; a sharp decline in manufactures; a slow but steady increase in weight of the building and transport industries and of the public and professional service; and a notable increase in domestic service (truly suggesting that

57. See M. R. Freedland: *The Contract of Employment,* 137; C. M. Smith on *Master and Servant.*

58. See the works cited earlier, fn 23 *ante,* and J. Meenan: *The Irish Economy Since 1922,* 10; J. J. Clancy: *Ireland: As she is, As she has been, and As she ought to be,* Chapter VII; R. D. Collison Black: *Economic Thought and the Irish Question 1817-1870;* J. N. Murphy: *Ireland, Industrial, Political and Social.*

59. All agricultural products, except the (by then) neglected wheat, were selling well; cattle prices in particular were buoyant. Traditional Irish industries profited also from worldwide prosperity. The linen trade continued to expand its markets. Shipyards and other industries shared in the advance. Brewing and distilling prospered: whiskey, mineral waters and biscuits enjoyed a seemingly secure prestige. The movement in support of Irish industries, which began about the beginning of the century, helped other forms of production, notably woollens and hosiery which had been depressed: Meenan, *op. cit.,* fn. 58 *ante,* 10.

'servants are more numerous where poverty makes service cheap'[60]).
Simple gross statistics suggest little about individuals' experiences but
they do prescribe the economic limits within which these experiences
occur.

Employment of the People of Ireland 1851-81 as % of occupied population				
	1851	1861	1871	1881
Agriculture	48.4%	49.9%	40.7%	41.1%
Fishing	0.4%	0.3%	0.4%	0.5%
Mining	0.4%	0.4%	0.3%	0.4%
Building	2.0%	2.4%	2.2%	2.4%
Manufacture	22.8%	20.7%	19.5%	16.0%
Transport	1.4%	1.8%	2.1%	2.2%
'Dealing' (i.e., Shops etc.)	3.6%	4.1%	4.6%	4.8%
Public and Professional service	2.2%	3.7%	4.3%	5.0%
Domestic service	10.4%	13.3%	15.2%	18.0%

Source: G. Best, *Mid-Victorian Britain, 1851-'70*, 99.

Nineteenth century England witnessed economic changes which
effected a revolution in legal forms and institutions.[61] Industrialisation, the capitalist mode of production and the rise of wage-labour
transformed the economic structure and society of that country.
Nothing underwent as revolutionary a change there as the working
population. With this development may be linked the atrophy of the
contract of employment in the statute law of 19th century England
(and, it may be added, Ireland).[62] The bulk of labour law, and
especially the bulk of legislation for the protection of workers,
developed until well into the 20th century outside the framework of
the contract of employment. Only comparatively recently (see pages
26-27 below) did legislation begin to confer on workers contractual
rights which could not be abrogated to their detriment. The wage
fixing provisions of earlier statutes passed into a limbo before the end
of the Napoleonic war and with it an important basis of the old
doctrine of master and servant. Before the middle of the 19th
century, employment in Ireland, no less than in England, in industry
and trade, in agriculture and in domestic service, rested on a contrac

60. As the astonished Charles Booth remarked, cited G. Best: *Mid-Victorian
Britain 1851-'70*, 98.
61. This is explored in Ken Foster's paper, fn. 72 *post*, p. 29.
62. O. Kahn-Freund: *art. cit.* fn. 7 *ante*, 524.

tual basis. The repeal of the Combination Acts[63] confirmed this. The freedom of workmen to combine in order to improve their wages, hours and other conditions of employment implicitly presupposed that these conditions were based on contract and not on status. It was not until 1875 that a manual worker and his employer were made equal contracting parties in the eyes of the law: the Conspiracy and Protection of Property Act, 1875, abolished the rule whereby it was a criminal offence for the worker, but not for the employer, to break the contract. In 1906, the Trade Disputes Act was passed which excluded the new tort of 'simple' civil conspiracy[64] in respect of acts done 'in contemplation or furtherance of a trade dispute' (s. 1), permitted peaceful picketing in trade disputes (s. 2), excluded the torts of inducing breach of employment contracts or interference with business in trade disputes (s. 3) and gave complete immunity in actions in tort to trade unions (s. 4). This Act, as amended,[65] and to the extent that it is not inconsistent with the Constitution,[66] is still in force in Ireland. It defined 'trade dispute' for the first time (s. 5) and the definition has been held to cover a dispute in relation to termination of employment.[67]

The remedies which existed at common law are now considered. As will be seen, they were slow in moving into focus.

(2) *The Relationship of Master and Servant at Common Law*

Developments taking place at common law in England, in turn closely linked to changing economic circumstances, had a marked impact on the master-servant relation in Ireland.[68] When eventually

63. In theory the English Combination Acts of 1799 and 1800 applied to Ireland as well, but in 1803, Westminster passed a separate Act, the Unlawful Combinations (Ireland) Act (43 Geo. 3 c. 86) which declared in its preamble that previous anti-combination laws in Ireland had 'been found to be inadequate to the suppression thereof' and put into effect provisions which would outlaw all such combinations. The 1803 Act was repealed by the Combination Laws Repeal Act, 1924 (5 Geo. IV, c. 95).

64. See by the author: 'The Tort of Conspiracy in Irish Labour Law'(1973), vol. 8, *The Irish Jurist* 252.

65. Trade Union Act 1941, s. 11; on the Act in general, see M. Abrahamson: 'Trade Disputes Act – Strict Interpretation in Ireland' (1961) 24 MLR 596.

66. *Educational Co. Ltd. v. Fitzpatrick* [1961] IR 345.

67. See Chapter eight, page 205.

68. Occasionally a discrepancy is to be found between English judgments and the practical political views expressed in Ireland at the time: e.g., the case of the *Merchants of Waterford* (Y.B. 2 Ric. 3, f. 12; 1 Hen. 7, f. 2) in which English judges were first of opinion that Ireland was not bound by an English statute, but later held that English statutes bound persons living in Ireland. Against this may be set an Irish parliamentary view, for in 1460 the Irish parliament asserted that, although Ireland was subject to the same 'obedience' as England, nevertheless it was bound only by statutes made by Irish parliaments or great councils: Donaldson, *op. cit.*, fn. 15 *ante*, 41.

contract doctrine began to be applied to the employment relation, it was never applied in its pure form. That would have given both parties full discretion to define the scope of authority.[69] It would have borne a damaging double edge. As Fox puts it

> '[It] would have suggested implications alarming to property owners ... The damaging implications of pure contract doctrine for the employer would have been that it could not allow him to be the sole judge of whether his rules were arbitrary or exceeded the scope of his authority.'[70]

Pure contract theory would have given the employer the power to make rules by express or implied agreement or by custom. It also carried with it the less attractive notion of a right of appeal to an external adjudicator on whether or not those rules or alleged breaches thereof were consistent with the contractual power. Consequently

> 'these needs were met by infusing the employment contract with the traditional law of master and servant ... in the very heyday of contract the evolving modern law of employment was drawing heavily on the old master servant law by incorporating the traditional subordination of the workman'.[71]

Thus, the contract of employment acquired the dual feature of equality and domination.[72] In terms of doctrinal development at common law this can be traced through the implied terms of fidelity, the employee's duty to obey orders, the employer's right to control the conditions of work, and the employer's power to discipline. The alliance of master and servant law with the contract of employment meant the incorporation of implied terms, reserving full authority and control to the employer. At the same time, his authority was stripped of any personal duty, commitment or responsibility.

The common law on wrongful dismissal cannot be understood without an awareness of this feature of the contract of employment. In addition, the structure of the contract needs to be properly understood. Moreover, although it has been argued that the contract of employment is not a contract but a continuing implied renewal of

69. Selznick: *Law, Society and Industrial Justice*, 122-'37.
70. *Beyond Contract, Work Power and Trust Relations*, 183. Further, see, P. Atiyah: *The Rise and Fall of Freedom of Contract*, 523.
71. *Ibid.*, 188.
72. See this theme, *passim*, in K. Foster's 'From Status to Contract: Legal Form and Work Relations 1750-1850' *Warwick Law Working Papers*, Vol. 3, no. 1 (My. 1979).

contracts at every minute and hour,[73] the converse and better approach, which is borne out by the caselaw, treats the contract of employment as a single contract. In allowing the employee an action for wrongful dismissal, the common law recognised an employee's interest in the continuance of his employment and gave a particular legal expression to that interest.[74] It was well into the nineteenth century, as will be seen, before English courts recognised the implications of this approach.[75]

Irish caselaw in the 19th century illustrates many of the rules which flow from the master-servant contract model. The master had a general authority to discipline, command and control the servant in the operation of the enterprise and in the servant's private life. This was especially true of apprentices and of indentured and living-in servants. In *Breslin & M'Keever v. Gilchrist & Co.*[76] Overend J. declared that

> '. . . if an apprentice misbehaves the master has the power of correcting him by personal chastisement, provided it be moderate, and the whole control as regards his morals is also with the master.'[77]

Moreover, at common law, the master and servant relation was not terminable during its currency. This was exemplified in various ways — many of the rules in this respect derived from statute rather than common law. For instance

(a) there was a presumption of yearly hiring;
(b) apprentices and indentured servants were taken on for a term of years;

---

73. J. R. Commons: *Legal Foundations of Capitalism* 285. First published 1924.

74. M. R. Freedland: *The Contract of Employment* 20-'1. If the contract were regarded as a mere work-wages bargain, a question would arise as to whether the contract is terminable at will or whether it is terminable, expressly or implicitly, by notice. See in this respect *M'Guigan v. The Guardians of the Poor of the Belfast Union* (1885) 18 LR Ir. 89; *Grant v. Wm. Grant & Sons* (1916) 50 ILTR 189; but see *The Qu. (The Commissioners of the Town of Boyle and T. Wynne) v. M. Cunningham* (1885) 16 L.R. Ir. 206.

75. See Foster *art. cit.*, fn 72 *ante*, 8.

76. (1903) 37 ILTR 99, 99. (Co. Ct.).

77. However, it was 'old and settled' law that in the absence of an express agreement in the contract of apprenticeship the master cannot dismiss the apprentice for anything but the most serious misconduct, such as felony, or being a habitual thief' (*ibid.*, 99). In this case, the apprentice had been dismissed for insubordination towards his master's housekeeper for which he refused to apologise when called upon to do so; he succeeded in an action for breach of the contract of apprenticeship and was awarded the return of his deposit. (*Semble*, he had no right to damages.)

(c) there was no requirement of notice: the only notice which
     could be given to terminate was one which expired on the
     final day of the agreement;
(d) servants needed testimonials from their previous master
     declaring they had been discharged from service.[78]

The policy behind yearly hirings was to avoid seasonal unemployment. This was very much in the interests of the ratepayer who had to
finance the application of the Poor Law. Although the risk of
seasonal unemployment hit agricultural labourers but not domestic
servants, the presumption of yearly hiring was very early extended far
beyond agricultural work to conditions which it did not fit at all.
From the point of view of the common law there were two central
questions: when could a year's hiring be presumed and what was
meant by a yearly hiring if there had been absences or premature
termination? These questions had important implications for the law
relating to termination of employment as yearly hirings were non-
terminable and meant

'. . . the parties are [not] at liberty to separate when they please;
on the contrary . . . one is bound to service, and the other
bound to employ, for a year.'[79]

---

78. Other rules deriving from the master and servant model were (i) the master
had a reciprocal duty of care and a duty for the general welfare of the servant. But
'. . . mischievous would it be, were the principle sustainable, that an employer must
warrant the safety of those employed by him' as C. J. Lefroy observed in *Potts v.
Plunkett* (1859) 9 C.L. (Ir.) 290, 301 (Q.B.D.). The master's duty of care did not
extend to responsibility for injuries occurring to the servant in the course of employment, although resulting from that employment. The servant was supposed to undertake the service subject to all the risks which might occur during its continuance.
Where the servant was engaged on work of a dangerous nature, the law required the
existence of negligence on the part of the master *and* the absence of rashness on the
part of the servant; (ii) the master had a proprietary interest in the servant — he was
liable to third parties for his servant's misconduct and could sue third parties for loss
of his services; (iii) specific performance of the contract was available as a remedy.
Early cases (e.g., *Ball v. Coggs* (1710) 1 Bro. Parl. Cas. 140; *E. India Co. v. Vincent*
(1740) 2 Atkyns 83; see M. R. Freedland *op. cit.*, fn. 74 *ante*, 272-'3) show
it was not until the 19th century that objections to such an order were operative. When they were operative, it was in procedural rather than substantive terms. A
rare exception based on substantive objections is *Fitzpatrick v. Nolan* (1851) 1 ICR
671 in which it was held that a suit could not be sustained which sought to enforce
an agreement for the continuance of the plaintiff's duties or personal services, to the
defendant, inasmuch as those services might be rendered in a manner productive of
injury rather than benefit to the latter. *Semble*, also, the employer could not have
maintained a suit to oblige the other party to discharge his duty according to the
agreement.
79. *R. v. Gt. Bowden (Inhabitants)* (1827) 7 B & C 219; 108 ER 716.

The old statutory rule under the Servants legislation that hirings were for a year led to judicial interpretation that all indefinite hirings were for one year.[80] Chief Justice Monaghan observed, in *Keon v. Hart,*[81] that

> 'There is no doubt that a general hiring is a yearly hiring, though in cases of menial servants ... the contract is terminable by paying a month's salary, but that is only the rule when there is nothing in the document to show a different intention of the parties.'[82]

From the nineteenth century on, the courts began to reject the notion of an annual hiring as an automatic implication. Indefinite or general hirings were still presumed to be annual hirings but this was subject to a contrary intention being expressed or implied. In *Forgan v. Burke,*[83] Chief Justice Monaghan described the law —

> 'Where the hiring is under a special agreement, the terms of that agreement are of course to be observed. If there be no special agreement, but the hiring is a general one, without mention of time, it is to be considered to be for a year certain. If the servant continues in employment beyond that year, a contract for a second year is implied, and so on; and, though a hiring in general words is *prima facie* presumed to be for a year, even though the master and servant may have thought that they could separate within the year, and though the circumstances of the servant leaving in the middle of the year, or having previously served for a shorter time than a year, will not prevent the usual interpretation from taking place, yet this

80. Cf. Lord Mansfield in *R. v. St. Peters in Dorchester (Inhabitants)* (1763) Burr S.C. 515; 95 E.R. 25: 'Hirings in general and indefinitely give a presumption of hiring for a year'.

81. (1867) C.P. 2 C.L. 138, 141.

82. Many cases concerned menial servants. One, *Lawler v. Linden* (1876) C.P. 10 C.L. 188 ran to the absurd length of a disquisition as to the derivation of *moenia.* Counsel argued as to its Saxon, Greek or Latin origin. Mr. Justice Lawson opined that *moenia* had nothing at all to do with 'menial'; he regarded the word as deriving from the Saxon *meiny* which occurs in Chaucer and Shakespeare.

83. (1861) CP 12 CL (Ir) 495; citing Smith's *Mercantile Law* (6th ed. c. 8, 425). In the case before him the plaintiff had agreed with the defendant in the following terms: 'I agree to serve Major B. as steward from My. 31, 1858, for £80 per annum ... three months notice required on each side'. He was wrongfully dismissed from employment during a current year without any previous notice. The C.J. held the hiring was a yearly one, which could be determined by either party giving to the other 3 months notice before the end of the current year. Damages were assessed on that principle. The plaintiff's contract, fortunately for him, was a special one (see an earlier example of a special contract: *Wilson v. Brereton* (1843) 5 LR Ir 466).

presumption, arising from the use of general words, is capable of being rebutted. Thus, a general hiring, at weekly wages, is but a weekly hiring, if there be no other circumstance whence the intended duration of the contract can be collected; e.g., a hiring at so much per week, for so long a time as the master and servant shall agree, are weekly hirings; but, if there be any circumstance to show that a yearly hiring was intended, a reservation of wages payable at shorter intervals will not control it; as, where the contract was to serve "for four shillings and ninepence a week", or "at the rate of four shillings a week", the parties having liberty of parting at a month's notice from either, this was held to be a hiring for a year; for the mention of a month showed that the stipulation for a weekly payment of wages was not intended to limit the duration of the contract. But an indefinite hiring by piece-work, or a hiring to do a certain quantity of work, cannot be considered a yearly hiring.'

Once automatic hirings for a year began to be rejected, judicial questions arose about the period of hire and the length of notice.[84] One of the reasons why judicial change occurred was the move to a contractual framework. Although an annual hiring could be implied from the parties' presumed intention, in the final analysis its relation with concepts of non-terminability and compulsory labour was essentially non-contractual. A free contract model required that parties could enter and leave employment freely.

(3) *The Common Law Action for Wrongful Dismissal*

Wrongful dismissal constituted the most important type of breach of contract. By 1800 an action for this breach was specifically recognised by the courts.[85] Different analyses were tried and rejected in the caselaw of the nineteenth century. Judges experimented with an approach which analysed the employment relationship as one of mere 'service and pay' whereby the employer was under no continuing obligation to employ but only to pay remuneration accrued due. In the English case of *Emmens v. Elderton*[86] (1853), the 'service and pay' theory was rejected and the principle established that wrongful termination of the contract of employment gives rise to

---

84. Problems of vicarious liability and common employment also began to loom large: see *M'Eniry v. The Waterford & Kilkenny Rly. Co.* (1858) 8 C.L. (Ir) 312; *Murphy v. Pollock & Pollock* (1863) 15 C.L. (Exch.) 224. On the question of notice, see chapter 3, pages 52-56.

85. *Robinson v. Hindman* (1800) 3 Esp. 235.

86. (1853) 13 CB 495; see Freedland, *op. cit.*, fn. 74 *ante*, 22-'3.

an action for breach of an implied undertaking by the employer to maintain the employment relationship. In *Breen v. Cooper*,[87] a domestic servant was expelled late at night from the defendant's house in the country without her necessary clothes and without money. She brought an action for wrongful dismissal upon a contract of service providing for dismissal without notice. The jury found in her favour and awarded her £20 damages, i.e., 50p wages due and £19.50 general damages for injury suffered under the circumstances of dismissal. On appeal by her employer, Baron Fitzgerald held for the Court of Exchequer that there was no sum owing to the plaintiff save wages due, but he also made an award in respect of the servant's implied notice period:

> 'I think the Plaintiff was entitled to be put, so far as pecuniary compensation could put her, in the same position as she would have been if at the time of her dismissal she had been paid the wages due to her, together with an additional fortnight's wages; and she could not recover as special damages in respect of any matters, save such as would not have happened to her had the contract been fulfilled by payment of those moneys at the time of her dismissal. I can find no evidence of any damage in this case which would not equally have happened, though the contract had been fulfilled in the respect complained of, by payment of those moneys at the time of dismissal.'[88]

A further indication as to the Irish courts' attitude towards the action for wrongful dismissal may be gleaned from their ready endorsement of the principle of *Hadley v. Baxendale*.[89] According to this principle, damages may be awarded for breach of contract in respect of loss flowing naturally from the breach or where loss arises from special circumstances within the contemplation of the parties. The courts in Ireland gave a very narrow interpretation to the second limb of this rule.[90] Up to the decision in *Hamilton v. Magill* (1883), Irish judges were unlikely to have contemplated an award of damages for wrongful dismissal in respect of loss flowing from breach of an implied term to maintain the work relationship. In *Hamilton's* case, however, Chief Baron Palles came close to recognising an implied term of this sort when he restated the principle to allow for the fact that the parties to a contract usually contemplate its performance rather than its breach:

---

87. (1869) IR 3 CL 621 (Exch.).
88. At 624-'5. See, too, *Woodhouse v. The RIAM* (1908) 2 IR 357, 368.
89. (1854) 9 Exch. 341. See further, chapter 4 *post*.
90. It must be remembered, however, that most cases concerned office-holders and not employees or servants whose only remedy lay in a suit for damages.

'The damages recoverable [are] such as might arise naturally (i.e. according to the usual course of things) from such breach of contract itself, or from such breach committed under circumstances in the contemplation of both parties at the time of the contract.'[91]

This approach has been developed in the caselaw of the twentieth century.

B. Individual Employment Rights and Organised Activity in Ireland

By the nineteenth century, there was an abundance of labour legislation but there was no smoothness or logic about the way it had developed. Moreover, the legislation had a patchwork design, its effectiveness was far from assured, and the range of topics covered by protective statutes remained narrow. In dismissal and other vital areas of individual employment law there were no statutory protections at all. The view gradually became steadfast that these fell more appropriately and more effectively within free collective bargaining rather than regulatory legislation.

Other historical considerations peculiar to Ireland may be mentioned. At the time of the second world war, the Irish worker inherited a century old legacy of stagnation – mainly attributable to poor economic decision-making – (whether by politicians, civil servants, or businessmen). He was 'the residuary legatee of the mediocrity of the ruling élite in Irish society'.[92] An important consequence of stagnation in the context of termination of employment was that Ireland had no work ethic or morality of work. This was reinforced by the small scale of Irish society, by the importance of personal relationships and by the frequency of face to face situations. The merit of the individual as a worker took second place to other criteria in assessing the rewards of work. Moreover, the degree of industrialisation was still slight. This had implications for the wider work ethic: issues such as dismissal did not weigh heavily on the industrial relations consciousness. By and large Irish workers were not able to draw on the moral, intellectual, financial or political resources of a flourishing working class culture – there was virtually no working class in the normal Western European sense. Southern Ireland was predominantly agricultural until after the second world war. As late as 1946, agriculture accounted for 47% of total employment, services for 36% and industry for only 17%. (The last included building and construction.) There were few big factories outside the

---

91. (1883) 12 LR Ir. 186, 202.
92. J. Lee: 'The Role of the Worker in Irish Society since 1945' in *Trade Unions and Change in Irish Society* (ed. D. Nevin), page 11.

public service. As late as 1958, only 40 concerns employed more than 500 people.[93] In 1965, there was still over 30% of the work-force employed in agriculture.[94] The collective need for legislation regulating individual employment was not strongly felt.

Further, a political dimension of working class culture — so important in Britain, for example — was almost wholly lacking in Ireland. The worker was left to fall back on his trade union. Because of the stagnant society in Ireland, and the lack of any larger vision, the function of the trade unions for most groups except the most unskilled was to preserve their differentials against all comers, not least other workers. Differentials became the main bargaining point between employers and employees.

Until fairly recently, collective agreements reflected the cautious and conservative policy of regulating only those matters such as wages which traditionally formed the *raison d'être* of trade unions. Of late, discipline and dismissal procedures have been included in some collective agreements. The significance of this development has yet to be fully appreciated. In a long line of cases, Irish judges have assumed, without argument or discussion, that collective agreements are contractually binding between the parties.[95] Whether the parties to a collective agreement intend to enter into legal relations,[96] or whether the theory of contractual effect conforms to social expediency, the legal enforceability of collective agreements is potentially of great significance in dismissal law. Trade unions can include detailed, carefully drafted, procedural and substantive provisions concerning discipline and dismissal in collective agreements, and these are capable of being enforced before the ordinary courts, independently of a dismissed employee's rights at common law. At the present time, however, trade unions seem oblivious to the legal ramifications of this and where collective bargaining does cover such matters as discipline and dismissal, it is

93. See Meenan, *op. cit.,* fn. 58 *ante,* in partic. chap. 2; GJT Clampett: 'The Economic Life of Ireland' (1928) *JIBI* 139, 228, 241; W. P. Coyne (ed.) *Ireland: Industrial and Agricultural* (Dub. 1902); R. C. Geary: 'Irish Economic Development since the Treaty' (1951) *Studies* 399; G. O'Brien: 'The Economic Progress of Ireland 1912-'62' (1962) *Studies* 9; D. O'Mahony: 'Economic Theory and the Irish Economy' (1960) *JIBI* 251; same: *The Irish Economy* (Cork 1967).

94. In 1978 this figure was less than 20% — still very high by EEC standards (average 8%); see 'Ireland seeks the High Road' *The Economist* (Nov. 24, 1979).

95. *Hynes v. Conlon* (1939) *Ir. Jur. R.* 49; *Ardmore Studios (Ireland) Ltd. v. Lynch and Others* [1965] I.R. 1; *Gouldings Chemicals Ltd. v. Bolger* [1977] I.R. 211; *Pattison v. Institute for Industrial Research and Standards* (High Court unreported, 31 May 1979).

96. A collective agreement is, after all, 'a business-like document': *Gouldings* case, fn. 95, at 231 *per* O'Higgins C.J. The Supreme Court expressly rejected the British case of *Ford Motor Co. Ltd. v. AUEFW* [1969] 2 Q.B. 303 in favour of *Edwards v. Skyways Ltd.* [1964] 1 WLR 349.

very often defective in procedural and substantive terms.

This last point was recognised by the Sub-Committee of the Employer/Labour Conference set up in 1972 to consider Codes of Fair Employment and Dismissal Procedures.[97] In their *Report* the sub-committee drew on corroborative information from the Central Statistics Office regarding sources of disputes between employers and trade unions. The facts bear out the many problems which arose at the time in relation to dismissal.[98] The *Report* suggested a detailed format for dismissal and disciplinary procedures suitable to every form of enterprise. As a general principle, it recommended that there should be no breach of rule to which the penalty of instant dismissal attached. However, it recognised that pending investigation which could lead to dismissal, summary action in the form of immediate suspension should attach to alleged breaches of the most serious rule. The sub-committee recommended that their procedure be implemented through incorporation into employer-trade union agreements when these came up for renewal. Unfortunately, this has not been done on any real scale.

The last decade or so in Ireland has seen the development (prompted by international influences) of a series of protective statutes which provide individual workers with a statutory floor of rights. In part, these remedy the deficiencies of collective bargaining. The floor may be improved upon by collective bargaining but it cannot be taken away or diminished. A system of Rights Commissioners was established under the Industrial Relations Act, 1969. The system embodied a form of voluntary arbitration to deal with individual grievances in employment. Roughly half the cases dealt with each year by the Commissioners concerned dismissal. The need for legislation to deal with termination of employment was obvious. The Unfair Dismissals Act, enacted in 1977, attempted to fill this need. It is the most noteworthy extension of regulatory legislation in Ireland. Provisions concerning dismissal are also found in the Anti-Discrimination (Pay) Act, 1974, and the Employment Equality Act, 1977.[99] Very recently, the scope of the Unfair Dismissals Act was further increased by The Maternity Protection of Employees Act, 1981.

97. The Irish National Productivity Centre were requested to undertake a research project in the area when the Employer/Labour Conference decided that a study on Codes of Fair Employment and Dismissal Procedures should be initiated. The sub-committee consisted of 3 employer and 3 Congress representatives.

98. In 1963, '65 and '71, disputes as to engagement and dismissal of workers were more frequent than disputes arising from any other single source, while in other years (between 1963-'71) frequency of disputes in this regard was, in the main, second only to disputes arising from disagreements as to wage settlements: *Report*, 3. See below, chapter 8, p. 203-4.

99. See chapter 7, p. 186.

CHAPTER TWO

The Irish Constitution and Dismissal

Introduction: Stages of Constitutional Development in Ireland

Ireland's legal system belongs to the common law as opposed to the continental tradition. In the past half-century, important developments have taken place to affect the law in Ireland and to introduce into it the conception of limitation upon legislative competence.[1] The Constitutions of 1922 and of 1937 represent landmarks in these developments. A revolutionary feature of the Constitution of the Irish Free State, 1922, was the inclusion of fundamental rights.[2] These had little effect, however, as during the whole period of its operation the

1. Contrast the British position. Lord Shawcross, former British Attorney General, expressed the idea of parliamentary sovereignty dramatically in a remark that has been widely quoted: 'Parliament is sovereign; it can make any laws. It could ordain that all blue-eyed babies should be destroyed at birth; but it has been recognised that it is no good passing laws unless you can be reasonably sure that, in the eventualities which they contemplate, those laws will be supported and can be enforced.' This is, doubtless, a deformation of the genuine conception of the common law, but it is clearly accepted as part, and an important part, of the (unwritten) constitution of Britain.

2. In no other Constitution in the Empire, with the exception of a single clause in the British North America Act, was any attempt made to fetter the discretion of parliaments by imposing juristic limitations on their legislative capacity: J. Morgan: *The Constitution a Commentary,* p. 17, cited M. Crowe: 'Human Rights, the Irish Constitution and the Courts' (1971) 47 *Notre Dame Lawyer* 281, at 284, footnote 8. The English tradition was not to have abstract formulations of human rights, but rather pragmatic guarantees such as the Magna Carta or the Habeas Corpus Act of 1679 or, in more general terms, the concept of 'the rule of law' and judicial precedent. In Ireland, a distrust of such guarantees was engendered down the years due for instance to the many suspensions of the Habeas Corpus Act. Hence the decision of the framers of the Free State Constitution to insert provisions concerning fundamental rights is very understandable. On the Free State Constitution see: Denis Gwynn: *The Irish Free State Constitution 1922-27,* Chap. III, 38; Nicholas Mansergh: *The Irish Free State Constitution; its Government and Politics,* Chap. IV, 50; J. G. Swift MacNeill: *Studies in the Constitution of the Irish Free State*; Darrell Figgis: *The Irish Constitution explained*; Leo Kohn: *The Constitution of the Irish Free State*; B. Farrell: 'The Drafting of the Irish Free State Constitution' (1970), Vol. 5 *Irish Jurist* 115, at 118.

The most remarkable contribution of the Constitution of the United States to the Irish Free State Constitution was the conception of a judiciary empowered to decide the question of the validity of any law having regard to the provisions of the Constitution (Articles 65 and 66). In the last decade or so, it has become common practice for Irish judges to refer to U.S. Supreme Court decisions when determining rights issues under the Irish Constitution. E.g., *McGee v. Attorney General and the Revenue Commissioners* [1974] I.R. 284 *passim*.

Constitution could be amended like any ordinary piece of legislation.[3] The draft of a new constitution was debated in Dáil Éireann and submitted to the people by way of plebiscite in July, 1937. It came into force the following December and is still the Constitution of Ireland.[4] The Preamble to the Constitution and the Directive Principles of Social Policy (Article 45) were encountered in chapter one. The fundamental rights provisions (Articles 40-44) are of the greatest importance in relation to dismissal.

Although in 1937 the superior courts' work was less daring and innovatory than one might have expected,[5] judicial review of legislation and of acts *inter partes* has grown in importance in the last fifteen years. The development of a constitutional jurisprudence has been aided by the fact that in 1965 the Supreme Court rejected the

3. A further difficulty resided in the fact that Irish judges by virtue of their training and experience were not accustomed to deciding cases which involved constitutional guarantees of human rights. See in general A. G. Donaldson: *Some Comparative Aspects of Irish Law.* One remarkable exception is: *The State (Ryan & Others) v. Lennon & Others* [1935] I.R. 170, 204-'5 (Chief Justice, diss.).

4. The Constitution is a rigid one recognising the doctrine of the separation of powers. It establishes a bicameral legislature (the Oireachtas); an executive responsible to the lower House of Parliament (Dáil Éireann) on the traditional lines of the British Constitution; and a judiciary composed at the highest levels of a High Court and a Supreme Court. According to a survey the Irish judiciary is predominantly middle-class in origin and liberal/centrist in politics: P. Bartholomew: *The Irish Judiciary*, chap. 3. For a most interesting discussion as to whether Irish judges are class biased in the context of labour law see Charles McCarthy: *Trade Unions in Ireland 1894-1960*, chap. 12.

Article 15, s. 4, sub-s. 1 specifically prohibits the Oireachtas from enacting any law which is in any respect repugnant to the Constitution or to any provision thereof. This prohibition is general: if the law in question is in any respect repugnant to any provision of the Constitution the court must hold that part of it unconstitutional: *O'Donovan v. A-G* [1961] I.R. 114, 217. The impugned section remains intact except for the deletion of the offending words: *Deaton v. A-G* [1963] I.R. 170, 184.

The power of judicial review is given by Articles 34, s. 3, sub-s. 2 and 34, s. 4, sub-s. 4. The former provides that 'Save as otherwise provided by this Article, the jurisdiction of the High Court shall extend to the question of the validity of any law having regard to the provisions of this Constitution, and no such question shall be raised (whether by pleading, argument or otherwise) in any Court established under this or any other Article of this Constitution other than the High Court or the Supreme Court.' The latter provision runs: 'No law shall be enacted excepting from the appellate jurisdiction of the Supreme Court cases which involve questions as to the validity of any law having regard to the provisions of this Constitution.'

There is a presumption of constitutionality in favour of Acts of the Oireachtas, but the Supreme Court has emphasised that there is a difference between laws passed before and after the 1937 Constitution came into force. Laws passed between 1922 and 1937 are presumed not to be in conflict with the Free State Constitution of 1922 but enjoy no such presumption in respect of the 1937 Constitution: *de Búrca v. A-G* [1976] I.R. 38, 58. See further R. F. V. Heuston: 'Personal Rights under the Irish Constitution' (1976) Vol. XI *Irish Jurist* 205, 205-'7.

5. McWhinney: The Courts and the Constitution in Catholic Ireland (1954) 29 *Tul. L. Rev.* 69.

rigid application of the rule of *stare decisis*. In two cases, it refused to be bound by its own precedents and in fact reversed decisions already given. *Stare decisis* is now regarded as a matter of policy rather than as an unalterably binding rule.[6]

Constitutional actions inter partes

The Constitution expressly protects the rights or freedoms of individuals from violation by the State. But, partly as a result of its abstract language, it has private law aspects as well.[7]

In *Educational Company of Ire. Ltd. v. Fitzpatrick*[8] Mr. Justice Budd observed that, if an established right in law exists, a citizen has a right to assert it and it is the duty of the courts to aid and to assist him in the assertion of his right:

> 'Obedience to the law is required of every citizen, and it follows that if one citizen has a right under the Constitution there exists a correlative duty on the part of other citizens to respect that right and not to interfere with it.'

To say otherwise, the judge pointed out, would be tantamount to saying that a citizen can set the Constitution at nought and that a right solemnly given by fundamental law is valueless:

> 'It follows that the courts will not so act as to permit any body of citizens to deprive another of his constitutional rights and will in any proceedings before them see that these rights are protected, whether they be assailed under the guise of a statutory right or otherwise . . . If the Oireachtas cannot achieve this end, so much the less can any unauthorised body of citizens.'[9]

6. *The State (Quinn) v. Ryan* [1965] I.R. 642. See J. M. Kelly: *The Irish Constitution*, 266.

7. See J. Temple Lang: 'Private Law Aspects of the Irish Constitution' (1971) Vol. VI *The Irish Jurist*, 237, 243. The Irish Constitution has been held to affect the rights of citizens against one another in the areas of, e.g., family law, succession, privilege in the law of evidence. See, for example, *In re Tilson, infants* [1951] I.R. 1; *Burke and O'Reilly v. Burke and Quail* [1951] I.R. 216; *Mayo-Perrott v. Mayo-Perrott* [1958] I.R. 336; *Re Caffin decd.* [1971] I.R. 123; *Cook v. Carroll* [1945] I.R. 515.

8. [1961] I.R. 345, 368-'9.

9. This was reinforced in 1971 by Walsh J. in the Supreme Court in *East Donegal Livestock Mart v. A.G.* [1971] IR 317, 338, which reaffirmed that rights guaranteed by the Constitution are intended to be protected by the provisions of the Constitution. To afford proper protection, the provisions must enable the person invoking them not merely to redress a wrong resulting from the infringement of the guarantee, but also to prevent the threatened or apprehended infringement of the guarantees and to put to the test an apprehended infringement of these guarantees. The judge obviously envisaged proceedings akin to *quia timet* proceedings in injunction cases. One of the first cases involving a so-called private constitutional action was *Murtagh Properties Ltd. v. Cleary* [1972] IR 330.

The question of *locus standi* under the Constitution may be relevant. Although the Constitution refers to 'citizens' in almost every instance, the test of citizenship is not applied in individual cases.[10] In 1980, the Supreme Court unanimously held[11] that a plaintiff must show he had been personally affected injuriously by an impugned statute [or, one may add, action] or that he is in imminent danger of being the victim of it. The Court reserved the right to waive or relax this rule if there are 'weighty countervailing considerations justifying a departure from the rule'.

Unspecified Personal Rights

Most important from the point of view of the interpretation of fundamental rights is the judgment given in the High Court in *Ryan v. A.G.*[12] (1963) by Mr. Justice Kenny. The Court was called upon to interpret Article 40, s. 3, sub-s. 1, under which the State guarantees to protect the 'personal rights' of the citizen (see below). In the course of his judgment, which was upheld by the Supreme Court, Kenny J. held that

'The personal rights which may be invoked to invalidate legislation are not confined to those specified in Article 40 but include all those rights which result from the Christian and democratic nature of the State.'[13]

Judge Kenny conceded that this view imposes on the High and the Supreme Court a difficult and responsible duty to ascertain and declare the guaranteed personal rights of the citizen:

'In modern times, it would seem to be a function of the legislative rather than the judicial power, but it was done by the courts in the formative period of the Common Law, and there is no reason why they should not do it now.'[14]

The Supreme Court likewise took the view that the enumeration of 'personal rights' in Article 40, s. 3, sub-s. 2, of the Constitution relating to 'life, person, good name and property' was not exhaustive and admitted that to attempt to make a list of all the rights which may

10. *Nicolaou v. An Bórd Uchtála* [1966] IR 667.
11. *Cahill v. Sutton* (Supreme Court unreported, 9 July 1980). See, also, *East Donegal Co-Op. Livestock Mart Ltd. v. A.G.* [1970] IR 317, 388.
12. [1963] IR 294.
13. At 312. See, in this context, Mr. Justice B. Walsh in J. O'Reilly and M. Redmond: *Cases and Materials on the Irish Constitution* (Foreword).
14. At 313.

properly fall within the category of personal rights would be difficult.[15] Acknowledgment of implied or 'undisclosed' human or personal rights in Article 40, s. 3, sub-s. 1 has encouraged a great deal of judicial creativity[16] — not least in the area of labour law. The Constitution makes no reference, e.g., to the right to work, nor the right to strike — yet both have been enumerated by judges.[17] Part A of this chapter contains a discussion of constitutional rights which may be violated by dismissal. The question of remedies for breach of express or implied rights is critical. This is explored in Part B.

A. Infringement of Constitutional Provisions and Dismissal

In 1972, the law was described by Walsh J. in the Supreme Court in *Meskell v. CIE*.[18] One of the questions argued in detail before the Court was the effect of a constitutional right (in this case the right to form an association) as against the ordinary common law rights of an employer to engage or dismiss his workers, when, in so doing, he was not in breach of contract. Mr. Justice Walsh was categorical that, if an employer threatens an employee with dismissal should he join a trade union, the employer is putting pressure on the employee to abandon the exercise of a constitutional right and is interfering with the employee's constitutional rights:

'If the employer dismisses the worker because of the latter's insistence upon exercising his constitutional right, the fact that the form or notice of dismissal is good at common law does not in any way lessen the infringement of the right involved or mitigate the damage which the worker may suffer by reason of his insistence upon exercising his constitutional right.'

15. At 344, 345.
16. It is interesting to note the curious coincidence that on almost the same date the Supreme Court of the US in *Griswold v. Connecticut* (1965) 381 US 479 held that there exists in the US Constitution a residue or penumbra of personal rights.
17. Personal rights may be distinguished from property rights. The aggregate of a man's property rights constitutes his estate, his assets or his property in one of the many senses of that most equivocal of legal terms. The sum total of a man's personal rights, on the other hand, constitutes his status or personal condition, as opposed to his estate. The former are the elements of a man's wealth; the latter elements in his well-being. A citizen may of course have a personal right to own property. See: J. M. Kelly, *op. cit.*, fn. 6 *ante*, 360; R. V. F. Heuston: 'Personal Rights under the Irish Constitution (1976), Vol. XI, Part 2 *Irish Jurist*, 205; J. Temple Lang, *art. cit.*, fn. 7 *ante*, 253; D. Costello: 'Aspects of a Judicially Developed Jurisprudence of Human Rights in Ireland' in *Understanding Human Rights* (ed. A. D. Falconer), 148; B. Chubb: *The Constitution and Constitutional Change*, Part III.
18. [1973] IR 121, 135. Contrast *Flynn v. G.N.R.Co. (Ire.) Ltd.* (1955) 89 ILTR 46. The earlier High Court decision in *Hynes v. Conlon and Others* [1939] *Ir. Jur. Rep.* 49 cannot stand in the light of *Meskell*.

The judge was unequivocal that

> 'To exercise what may be loosely called a common-law right of
> dismissal as a method of compelling a person to abandon a
> constitutional right, or as a penalty for his not doing so, must
> necessarily be regarded as an abuse of the common-law right
> because it is an infringement, and an abuse, of the Constitution
> which is superior to the common law and which must prevail if
> there is a conflict between the two.'

The same considerations, in Judge Walsh's view, apply where a
person is dismissed or penalised because of his insistence upon, or his
refusal to waive, the right to dissociate.

Likewise, constitutional rights must not be exercised in such a way
as to frustrate, infringe or destroy the constitutional rights of others.
Once it is sought to exercise these rights without regard to the rights
of others, or without regard to the harm that may be done to others,
what is taking place is an abuse and not the lawful exercise of a right
given by the Constitution. Such abuse ranks equally with infringement of the rights of others and is condemned by the Courts.[19]

In relation to unconstitutional dismissal, the most important
express rights[20] are:

> 'All citizens shall, as human persons, be held equal before the
> law. This shall not be held to mean that the State shall not in its
> enactments have due regard to differences of capacity, physical
> and moral, and of social function.'
> —Art. 40, s. 1.

19. *Crowley v. Ireland, INTO and Others* (Supreme Court unreported, 1 October
1979), *per* O'Higgins C.J.
20. Arts. 40-44 provide a comprehensive list of rights, and jurists and others
interested in legal and constitutional philosophy have found much of interest in the
terminology and the qualifications used in the formulation of the various rights. The
framers of the constitution had the experience of the 18th and 19th centuries to guide
them, from Rousseau's *Contrat Social* and the French *Declaration des droits de
l'homme et du citoyen*, John Locke's *Treatise of Civil Government* and the American
Declaration of Independence to the many constitutions and declarations of rights
that, in the 19th and 20th centuries, were inspired by these documents. See
Messineo: 'La Nuova Costituzione Irlandese', 88 *Civiltà Cattolica* 239 at 246.
That writer failed to do justice to the sources of inspiration of the constitution. 'As
well as the influence of the political teaching of St. Thomas Acquinas and the Papal
Encyclicals, which affects everything in it, there is also the philosophical influence of
the tradition of liberal democracy, as well as the impact of the practical turn of mind
of the English constitutional lawyers, whose work has so profoundly coloured Irish
thinking': J. Newman: *Studies in Political Morality* (1962) 421 cited M. Crowe *art.
cit.*, fn. 2 *ante*.

'The State guarantees in its laws to respect, and, as far as practicable, by its laws to defend and vindicate the personal rights of the citizen.'

—Art. 40, s. 3, sub-s. 1.

'The State guarantees liberty for the exercise of the following rights, subject to public order and morality: . . . The right of the citizens to form associations and unions.

'Laws, however, may be enacted for the regulation and control in the public interest of the exercise of the foregoing right.'

—Art. 40, s. 6, sub-s. 1(iii)

'The State shall not impose any disabilities or make any discrimination on the ground of religious profession, belief or status.'

—Art. 44, s. 2, sub-s. 3.

These rights may be violated directly[21] or indirectly[22] by dismissal. By far the most important express right in this context is freedom of association.[23] Although the adjective 'trade' does not appear before the word 'union' in Article 40, s. 6, sub-s. 1(iii), the sub-section clearly includes the right of citizens to form trade unions.

Freedom of association has been considered in a number of Irish cases. From the earliest of these, it has been strictly construed in favour of individual interests. In 1947 the Supreme Court held unconstitutional a statutory attempt in the Trade Union Act, 1941, to confer on specified unions the right to organise and to represent workers in a specific union, to the exclusion of other unions: *NUR v. Sullivan*.[24] In the opinion of the Court, any attempt to prescribe which unions workers were entitled to join was not an attempt to regulate or control the right to form unions but an attempt altogether to abolish the exercise of that right.[25] The tight legalism of the

21. *McGrath and Ó Ruairc v. The Trustees of the College of Maynooth* (Supreme Court unreported, 1 November 1979) where Art. 44, s. 2, sub-s. 3 was unsuccessfully invoked. Further on this sub-s. 3 see *Quinns Supermarket Ltd. v. A-G* [1972] IR 1; and *Mulloy v. The Minister for Education* [1975] IR 88.

22. The right, e.g., to free primary education could be indirectly affected if a purported dismissal had the consequence of depriving third parties thereof; see a discussion of the right in circumstances of industrial action in *Crowley's case,* fn. 19 *ante.* Contrast *Meade v. London Borough of Haringay* [1979] 1 WLR 637.

23. See J. P. Casey: 'Some Implications of Freedom of Association in Labour Law: a comparative study with special reference to Ireland' (1972) 21 I. & C.L.Q. 699.

24. [1947] I.R. 77 in which Murnaghan J. for the Supreme Court declared *ultra vires* Part III of the Trade Union Act, 1941. See J. M. Kelly *op. cit.,* fn. 6 *ante,* 469.

25. The decision has been regarded as a body-blow by the trade union movement ever since. See *Report of the Committee on the Constitution* (1967), paras. 116-122 inclusive; Charles MacCarthy, *op. cit.,* fn. 4 *ante,* 486.

Supreme Court in this case was later sustained in *Educational Co. of Ireland Ltd. v. Fitzpatrick*.[26] Here, the Supreme Court decided by a majority of 3:2 that picketing was contrary to the law when its purpose was to compel employers to dismiss those in their employment who were not members of a particular union.[27] The company had been asked by the union to compel certain employees to join. When they refused, strike action began and the company's premises were picketed. In the circumstances, picketing was held to be *ultra vires* and to lie outside the protection of section 2 of the Trade Disputes Act, 1906.[28] To the extent that it authorised or facilitated an unconstitutionality, the Act was held to be inconsistent, *pro tanto*, with Article 50 of the Constitution.[29]

The *Educational Co.* case established the principle that a freedom or right to associate necessarily included a correlative right not to join. In effect the judgment destroyed the legality, in the sense of the enforceability, of closed shop or union security arrangements.[30] The right of dissociation followed by implication. According to Kingsmill Moore J.:

'I think a guarantee of a right to form associations and unions is only intelligible where there is an implicit right to abstain from joining such associations or unions'.[31]

26. [1961] I.R. 345. See J. M. Kelly, *op. cit.*, fn. 6 *ante*, 472; Chas. MacCarthy, *op. cit.*, fn. 4 *ante*, 512; and R. V. F. Heuston: 'Trade Unions and the Law', *Irish Jurist* (1969), Vol. IV (NS) 10.

27. Two separate *rationes decidendi* can be found in the case: J. P. Casey, *art. cit.*, fn. 25 *ante*, 704. See Chas. MacCarthy, *op. cit.*, fn. 4 *ante*, chapter 12 and at 517 a particularly pertinent comment . . . 'the whole purpose of legalism, the attainment of objective equity, was turned on its head by the very operation of legalism itself, which left cases to be construed almost in the manner of a lottery'.

28. [1961] I.R. 345, 398, *per* Ó Dálaigh J. (as he then was).

29. Article 50 reads: 'Subject to this Constitution and to the extent to which they are not inconsistent therewith, the laws in force in Saorstát Éireann immediately prior to the date of the coming into operation of this Constitution shall continue to be of full force and effect until the same or any of them, shall have been repealed or amended by enactment of the Oireachtas'.

30. Note, however, highly important *dicta* in the dissenting judgment of Judge Henchy in *Becton Dickinson Ltd. v. Lee* [1973] I.R. 1, 47-'8 (Supreme Court). The judge suggested that where a prospective employee was required to join a particular union 'the matter is one of contract and there is no compulsion or coercion, and no interference with the citizen's free choice. . . . Not alone is it not in derogation of his constitutional right, it is in exercise of that very right'. See in this context E. P. de Blaghd: 'How closed can my shop be?' (1972) 106 I.L.T.S.J. 67.

31. At 395. See J. P. Casey, *art. cit.*, fn. 25 *ante*, 707-'8. Contrast Article 11 of the European Convention on Human Rights and Fundamental Freedoms (which is not part of Irish domestic law under Article 29.3) where freedom of dissociation is not protected as a concomitant of the protection of freedom of association. In spite of this see the wide interpretation of the European Court of Human Rights in *Young, James & Webster v. BR* (*The Times*, 13 August 1981).

The right of dissociation is now entrenched in Irish law.[32] For example, in *Meskell v. CIE*,[33] Meskell was dismissed by CIE where he had worked as a bus conductor for fifteen years. At all times during his employment he had been a member in good standing of a trade union. Four trade unions had members in the employment of CIE. They were dissatisfied with the level of union membership among employees, and were trying to reduce the number of employees in arrears with union dues. The relevant unions tried to compel the defendants to withhold certain benefits from some employees. The defendants refused to do so. Instead they agreed to terminate the contracts of employment of all employees and to offer each one immediate re-employment under the same general terms as theretofore if he agreed, as a special and additional condition of employment, to the special condition. At the date of his dismissal, Meskell was a member of one of the four unions and had paid all his union dues. When first employed by CIE, union membership had not been a term of his contract of service. He sued the defendants for damages in the High Court and claimed a declaration that his dismissal by CIE was a violation of his rights under Article 40, s. 6, sub-s. 1(iii). He also claimed damages for conspiracy. The claims were dismissed by Teevan J. in the High Court and the plaintiff appealed to the Supreme Court. The Court held Meskell was entitled to a declaration that his dismissal was a denial and a violation of, and an unlawful interference with, his constitutional rights,[34] and that the

---

32. The logical consequences of the decision seem very wide indeed as Maguire C.J. observed in his dissenting judgment: 'It is a strange feature of this case that the plaintiffs hesitate to press their argument to its logical conclusion. If the contention is right that action which aims at persuading non-union men to join a union is a denial of the right given by Art. 40.6 (iii) [sic] it would seem to me that each step taken with this end in view is an infringement of the Article. The demands upon the employers that men shall be dismissed if they do not join the union, the threat of a strike to support this demand and, above all, the strike itself would seem to me just as much a derogation of the right of the non-union workmen as the placing of a picket on the premises. Yet it is conceded that none of these steps does violence to the constitutional rights of all the non-union workmen or of their empoyers.' At pp. 381-'2. Kingsmill Moore J. was at pains to discount these possibilities. He suggested that strike action would be legitimate. But his *dicta* do not answer Maguire C.J.'s query. The case was followed by the High Court in *Crowley v. Cleary* [1968] IR 261; and *Murtagh Properties Ltd. v. Cleary* [1972] IR 330. Article 40, s. 6, sub-s. 1(iii) has become a source of new rights: see further *Rodgers v. Irish Transport and General Workers Union* (High Court unreported, 15 March 1978, Finlay P.).

33. [1973] IR. 121. See, too, *Cotter v. Ahern* (High Court unreported, 25 February 1977). That there is a limit in practice on the right of association and dissociation in the trade union context appears from *Murphy v. Stewart* [1973] IR 97; 107 ILTR 117.

34. An extract of Walsh J.'s judgment in the Supreme Court on this point is given earlier, pp. 32-3.

agreement between CIE and the four unions to procure or cause that dismissal was an actionable conspiracy[35] because the means employed constituted a breach or infringement of the plaintiff's constitutional rights. The plaintiff was also held entitled to damages.[36]

It is clear that, as against an employer, a union membership agreement cannot be legally enforced in Ireland. In practice, however, closed shop agreements are entered into by unions and employers. This can generate further problems concerning the rights of individual workers against one or both of the collective parties. For instance, a trade union exercising a monopoly may refuse to accept a particular applicant into membership. If a post-entry closed shop is in operation, so that as a result of such refusal, an employer has no option but to dismiss an employee-applicant, it seems an employee may proceed against the trade union or unions concerned claiming breach or infringement of his constitutional right to work.[37] (There is no reason in principle why he might not also institute proceedings against the employer.) The Supreme Court discussed the question, *obiter*, in *Murphy v. Stewart*[38]

> 'It has been submitted in this Court on behalf of the plaintiff and not really contested by the defendants that among the unspecified personal rights guaranteed by the Constitution is the right to work; I accept that proposition.[39] The question of

35. See by the author: 'The Tort of Conspiracy in Irish Labour Law' (1973), Vol. VIII, *Irish Jurist*, 252, and see *Cotter v. Ahern*, fn. 33 *ante*.

36. See page 42 *post*.

37. The right to work has not yet formed the *ratio decidendi* of any Irish case. It has been invoked most often in the context of abuse of trade union or collective power. Apart from the example given in the text, see *Murtagh Properties Ltd. v. Cleary* [1972] IR 330 (which more correctly involved the right in relation to equal access to employment for men and women workers); *Macken v. Irish Equestrian Federation* (High Court unreported, 20 July 1978). In *Landers v. AG* (1973) 109 ILTR 1, legislation was attempted]y impugned; and in *Moran v. AG* [1976] IR 400 the right arose in relation to the appropriate body charged with the power of withdrawing a taxi-driver's licence.

38. [1973] I.R. 97, at 117 *per* Walsh J.

39. See Walsh J. speaking extra-judicially at a Symposium on 'Human Rights and the Churches' organised by the Irish School of Ecumenics, 2-3 December 1978: '. . . the undoubted human right to work . . . places upon the State an obligation to so order the economic resources of the country and the organisation of industry and labour that persons will not find themselves denied the opportunity to work. In this context the right to work involves work of a nature and subject to such conditions, including a just wage, which will not be incompatible with the dignity of the person involved. It also means that organisations, whether they be of employers or workers, shall not be permitted to operate in a way which denies other persons the opportunity to exercise their fundamental right to work.' And see B. Hepple: "A Right to Work?" (1981) ILJ 65; J. Jackson: 'The Right to Work' (1959), Vol. 13, *Christus Rex*, 203.

The 'right to work' according to Lord Denning in 1973 means 'that a man should

whether that right is being infringed or not must depend upon
the particular circumstances of any given case; if the right to
work was reserved exclusively to members of a trade union
which held a monopoly in this field and the trade union was
abusing the monopoly in such a way as to effectively prevent
the exercise of a person's constitutional right to work, the
question of compelling that union to accept the person concerned into membership (or indeed of breaking the monopoly)
would fail to be considered for the purpose of vindicating the
right to work.'[40]

Outside of a closed shop situation there is no constitutional right to
join the union of one's choice.[41]

If a trade union monopoly takes the form of a pre-entry closed
shop, there is judicial authority to the effect that an individual's
acceptance of employment in such circumstances may amount to a
waiver of his constitutional rights under Article 40, s. 6, sub-s. 1(iii).[42]
Hence a subsequent dismissal because an individual refused to join
the pre-specified union once employed, or because an employee left
the union having been accepted by it, would not be unconstitutional.
That constitutional rights may be waived where there is full
knowledge as to the nature of the act and full consent thereto is now
settled.[43] However, since constitutional rights lie at the apex of rights

---

be given the opportunity of doing his work where it is available and he is ready and
willing to do it': *Langston v. Amalgamated Union of Engineering Workers* [1974]
I.C.R. 180, 190 (Court of Appeal). The case was remitted to the NIRC for
consideration of an alternative cause of action. Sir John Donaldson said '. . . there is
no doubt that over the years there has been an increasing acceptance of the proposition that everyone has a right to work, in the same sense as he has a right to eat and
a right to be housed. . . . But it is a general right, not a right to work for any particular employer or in any particular place. The right is based on public policy':
Langston v. A.U.E.W. (No. 2) [1974] I.C.R. 510, 521 (NIRC). See, earlier, *Nagle
v. Fielden* [1966] 2 QB 633, 646-'7 (CA *per* Denning M.R.) and see some of the
jurisprudential difficulties inherent in the right, exposed in *McInnes v. Onslow-Fane*
[1978] 3 All E.R. 211, 217 (*per* Megarry V-C).

40. See Walsh J. foreshadowing these *dicta* in *Meskell v. CIE* [1973] IR 121,
136. And see Roscoe Pound: *Jurisprudence* (chapter 14, 160) '. . . closed shop and
closed union are incompatible with the "right to work" '. It will be crucial to
establish that a trade union is abusing monopolistic power. There will be no case to
meet where the union is simply pursuing *bona fide* objectives such as the provision of
job opportunities for younger persons in a particular employment by means of a
compulsory retirement age: *Rodgers v. ITGWU*, fn. 32 *ante*.

41. See *Tierney v. Amalgamated Society of Woodworkers* [1959] IR 254.

42. *Becton Dickinson Ltd. v. Lee* [1973] IR 1, 47-'8 *per* Henchy J. See fn. 30
ante.

43. *G. v. An Bord Uchtála* (1979) ILTR 25. See, by the author: 'Waiver of
Constitutional Rights' (1979-'80) DULR 104.

in Ireland's legal system, the courts will not readily infer waiver. It is likely to be particularly difficult to establish the consent necessary for waiver in relation to a pre-entry closed shop where workers may be obliged to join the particular union under threat of economic deprivation. Moreover, if the pre-entry closed shop agreement requires a person not only to become but to remain at all times a member of a particular union, it is doubtful whether the courts would uphold this wider longterm commitment as being consistent with the Constitution.

In addition to the right to work, the other most important right which has been identified as latent in the guarantees of Article 40, s. 3, and which affects the law on termination of employment, is the right to basic fairness of procedures. This right is regarded as essential in the interests of justice. The late Chief Justice, Cearbhall Ó Dálaigh, described Article 40, s. 3 of the Constitution as a guarantee to the citizen of basic fairness of procedures: *In re Pádraig Haughey*[44]

> 'The Constitution guarantees such fairness and it is the duty of the Court to underline that the words of Article 40, section 3, are not political shibboleths but provide a positive protection for the citizen . . .'

The use of fairness is significant. In Britain, this concept is becoming more familiar in relation to natural justice cases.[45] The right to basic fairness of procedures is capable of a wide application in both private and public law

> '. . . in proceedings before any tribunal where a party to the proceedings is on risk of having his good name or his person or property, or any of his personal rights jeopardised, the proceedings may be correctly classed as proceedings which may affect his rights, and the State, either by its enactments or through the courts, must, in compliance with the Constitution, outlaw any procedures which will restrict or prevent the party concerned from vindicating these rights.'[46]

It is difficult to imagine proceedings where a person is on greater risk of having his good name or his property jeopardised than disciplinary or dismissal proceedings. The Supreme Court decision necessitates

44. [1971] I.R. 217, 263. See, too, *The State (Healy) v. Donoghue* [1976] I.R. 325, 110 ILTR 9.
45. A single test of fairness has been welcomed enthusiastically in that jurisdiction: Paul Jackson: *Natural Justice*, 11-13.
46. At 264 *per* Ó Dálaigh C.J.

extensive and far-reaching changes in the procedures of many Irish administrative tribunals, and probably also of trade unions, employers, and employers' organisations – even those not exercising judicial or quasi-judicial[47] functions.

By far the most important legacy of *Haughey's* case is the constitutionally inspired term of fairness which the Supreme Court implied in the contract of employment of a company director in *Glover v. B.L.N. Ltd.*,[48] see further page 64 below, chapter three. The Irish courts are willing to graft an implied term of fairness onto terms already in an employee's contract of employment, at least where there are already procedural or substantive limitations on the employer's power to dismiss. Where appropriate, the term imports more than the two well known established tenets of natural justice, *nemo judex sit in causa sua* and *audi alteram partem*.[49]

B. Remedies under the Constitution

By constitutional remedies is meant remedies available as a matter of constitutional right for the redress of constitutional wrongs. The Irish Constitution is almost completely silent concerning the remedies to be employed for its implementation. Constitutional remedies may be defensive in character where they re-assert the *status quo ante,* e.g., if natural justice has not been observed or if evidence is deemed inadmissible on account of a deliberate and conscious violation of constitutional rights. Or they may be affirmative in character where they predicate a particular result. Conceptual difficulties can arise where conduct in violation of the Constitution is not of a kind that would be actionable at common law. In such cases implemental remedies are accorded which take their tenor from the Constitution itself.[50] Where, however, conduct is normally actionable at common law, doubt may arise as to the propriety of implementing a constitutional right. But the general (and surely more correct) view in Ireland

47. See J. Temple Lang: 'Private Law Aspects of the Irish Constitution' (1971), Vol. VI *Irish Jurist*, 237, 241. The Fifth Amendment of the US Constitution reads '. . . nor shall any person be subject for the same offence to be twice put in jeopardy of life or limb; nor shall he be compelled in any criminal case to be a witness against himself, *nor be deprived of life, liberty or property without due process of law'* [emphasis added]. The Fourteenth Amendment reads '. . . nor shall any State deprive any person of life, liberty or property, *without due process of law* . . . [emphasis added]'.
48. [1973] I.R. 388. See chapter 4.
49. *Garvey v. Ireland and Others* [1981] I.R. 75 *per* Henchy J. at 100.
50. E.g. *McGee v. Revenue Commissioners and A-G* [1974] I.R. 284: Supreme Court held legislative prohibition on importation of contraceptives in Criminal Justice (Amendment) Act, 1935, contrary to right of marital privacy.

is that a constitutional right will not be deemed lost because the same is or might be actionable at common law. An apparent dichotomy between constitutional and common law remedies could be misleading, it is submitted, in a legal system where the Constitution is supreme. The common law is applied in Ireland only to the extent that it has been received under Article 50 of the Constitution.[51] The Constitution controls the common law: although in part it is implemented in accordance with the common law, the latter comes peculiarly within the province of the Constitution.

It is unfortunate, perhaps, that the drafters of the Constitution did not contemplate or give any attention to a species of constitutional remedy.[52] In the *Educational Co.* case,[53] Budd J. made it clear that

'If an established right in law exists a citizen has the right to assert it and it is the duty of the courts to aid and assist him in the assertion of his right. The courts will therefore assist and uphold a citizen's constitutional rights.'

The manner in which the courts will carry out this task has never been analysed.[54] In many cases, the remedy sought for a violation of the Constitution will be a declaration that breach has taken place. Or an injunction restraining unconstitutional action may be sought. Since Lord Cairns Act (Chancery Amendment Act, 1858)[55] the courts may award damages as well as, or instead of, an injunction whenever an injunction may be awarded. The first case in which an award of

51. See fn. 29 *ante*.
52. Contrast US where constitutional remedies are not fully accepted. In *Bivens v. Six Unknown Named Agents of the Federal Bureau of Narcotics* (1969) 409 F 2d 718 (2d Cir. 1969), the Court of Appeals for the Second Circuit analysed damages for breach of constitutional right more closely than it had been analysed before, from a judicial point of view. The Court held that an action in damages for conduct violative of the 4th Amendment does not lie in a federal matter. The grounds for this decision were (1) the framers of the Constitution had contemplated such relief would be accorded by the common law; (2) the creation of such a remedy was properly the subject of congressional action; only a strong showing of necessity, not made in *Bivens*, would justify its creation by the judiciary; (3) the burden of developing 'policy' rules concerning, e.g., computation of damages once the basic cause of action is recognised counselled judicial restraint. See A. Hill: 'Constitutional Remedies' (1969) 69 *Col. L. Rev.* 1109; A. Katz: 'The Jurisprudence of Remedies: Constitutional Legality and the Law of Torts in Bell v. Hood' (1968) 117 *U. Penn. L. Rev.* 1; (Note) 'State Remedies for Federally-Created Rights' (1963) *47 Minn. L. Rev.*; H. M. Hart and H. Wechsler: 'The Federal Courts and the Federal System' (1954) 54 *Col. L. Rev.* 650; H. M. Hart: 'The Relations between State and Federal Law' (1954) 54 *Col. L. Rev.* 489, 523-'24, 528.
53. [1961] I.R. 345, 368-'9.
54. J. Temple Lang *art. cit.*, fn. 7 *ante*, 247.
55. 21 & 22 Vict. c. 27.

damages was made for breach of a constitutional right was *Meskell v. CIE*,[56] the facts of which are set out at page 36, above. Walsh J. gave it as his view that 'the plaintiff is entitled to such damages as may, upon inquiry, be proved to have been sustained by him'.[57] He referred to the case of *Transport Salaried Staffs Association v. CIE*[58] which established that those who have an interest in enforcing a statutory duty[59] have a right of action even where the statute itself provides no penalty for breach of the obligations imposed by it and does not indicate any way in which the duty is to be enforced:

> '*A fortiori*, a person whose constitutional rights have been infringed may sue to enforce them or he may sue for damages suffered by reason of the infringement.'[60]

Damages were settled out of court by agreement between the Board of Directors of CIE and Meskell. As a result, the basis of their computation is unknown.[61] On first principles, constitutional and common law rights ought not to be equated when it comes to computing damages for their breach. The precise quantum of damages for breach of a constitutional right lies outside our present compass, but it is suggested that the normal principle on which damages are awarded, namely, that the victim should be placed in the same position as he was in before he suffered the wrong, should not be the criterion. Damages for breach of a constitutional right should be not only compensatory or consequential: they should relate to the breach *per se*. In the latter sense, something akin to punitive or exemplary damages would be appropriate, to 'punish' and make an example of the defendant and to deter others from acting in a similar manner.

Many remedies for breach of a constitutional right are as yet uncharted. In 1971, Temple Lang suggested that those Articles in the Constitution which are intended to protect individuals' rights should give rise to an action for whatever remedy was 'appropriate in the circumstances'.[62] In 1972, Casey proposed, on the basis of the

56. [1973] I.R. 121.
57. At 136.
58. [1965] I.R. 180.
59. The case involved s. 55 of the Railways Act, 1924, which provides, *inter alia*: '(i) From and after the passing of this Act the rates of pay, hours of duty and other conditions of service of railway employees shall be regulated in accordance with agreements made or to be made from time to time between the trade unions representative of such employees of the one part and the railway companies and other persons by whom they are respectively employed of the other part'.
60. [1973] I.R. 121, 138.
61. Society of Young Solicitors Lecture 101, April 1977, 32 (J. O'Driscoll).
62. *Art. cit.*, fn. 7 *ante*, 246.

reasoning in the *Educational Company* case, that for an employer's breach of the duty to respect constitutional rights, a person dismissed would surely be entitled to a remedy, 'if not reinstatement . . . then damages'.[63] Nor could the argument be rebutted, he wrote, by saying that although a worker had a particular constitutional right he had no right to be employed by his employer:

> 'The reasoning would be as follows; the citizen has a right to work; if he is in employment that right is good against the employer. It is not an absolute right and therefore dismissal for good cause would be competent. However, dismissal for exercising a constitutional right could not be dismissal for good cause; the power to terminate employment is abused when this end is achieved . . .

> 'it is suggested that the courts will have to modify common law rules on dismissal to protect the right guaranteed by Art. 40.6.1° (iii) [and, one may add, by other Articles]. This reshaping of the common law has been carried out by the Irish courts before and there seems no reason why it should not be done again where this is necessary to reinforce constitutional rights.'[64]

Before Casey wrote in 1972, the remedy of reinstatement was hinted at in a judicial context. In *Glover v. B.L.N. Ltd.*,[65] Judge Walsh commented on the following passage from Lord Reid in *Ridge v. Baldwin*[66] which Judge Kenny had cited with approval in the High Court:

> 'The law regarding master and servant is not in doubt. There cannot be specific performance of a contract of service, and the master can terminate the contract with his servant at any time and for any reason or for none. But if he does so in a manner not warranted by the contract, he must pay damages for breach of contract.'

The particular point did not arise for decision in *Glover*, but Judge Walsh nonetheless expressly reserved his opinion on the correctness of this statement in *Ridge*:

---

63. J. P. Casey, *art. cit.*, fn. 25 *ante*, 714.
64. Casey adds a salutary reminder: 'The French courts came to abandon received notions of the employer's unfettered discretion and they did so without any test to build upon': *ibid.*, 714-'15.
65. [1973] I.R. 388, 427.
66. [1964] A.C. 40, 65.

'If it is intended to convey that a court cannot make a declaration which would have the effect of reinstating a person wrongfully dismissed.'

Judge Walsh took up a similar theme in *Meskell v. CIE*.[67] He recalled the many occasions[68] on which the Supreme Court had said that a right guaranteed by the Constitution or granted by the Constitution could be protected by action

'or enforced by action even though such action may not fit into any of the ordinary forms of action in either common law or equity and that the constitutional right carries within it its own right to a remedy or for the enforcement of it.'[69]

'Enforcement' of the implied right to basic fairness of procedures could mean only reinstatement or re-engagement. It is particularly significant that Walsh J. regarded it as irrelevant whether an action brought for protection or enforcement of a constitutional right should fit into any of the ordinary forms of action at common law or in equity. The judge awarded damages, but his concluding remarks are telling

'As there is no claim in the present case for reinstatement, I do not need to consider that matter'.[70]

Professor Heuston describes *Meskell* as a 'remarkable decision'.[71] Whether it will encourage the disappearance of nominate torts and certain contractual claims and their replacement by an innominate claim for infringement of personal rights is uncertain (and perhaps improbable). The importance of *Meskell* is that it leaves no doubt that the Constitution superimposes a font of law on statute and on common law. At the same time it comprises a separate jurisdiction in its own right, capable of conferring whatever remedy is appropriate in the circumstances, including reinstatement in the face of unconstitutional dismissal. Later chapters illustrate how the Constitution, both in letter and in spirit, extends beyond the provision of a separate juridical system safeguarding individual rights. It operates as a screen through which all common and statute law must pass.

---

67. [1973] I.R. 121.
68. Notably *Byrne v. Ireland* [1972] I.R. 241.
69. At 135.
70. At 135.
71. 'Personal Rights under the Constitution' (1976) Vol. XI *Ir. Jur.* 205, 221.

CHAPTER THREE

Dismissal at Common Law — Termination by the Parties

The Importance of Contract

Under the Unfair Dismissals Act, 1977, a dismissing employer must prove not only the reason or reasons for dismissal, he must also satisfy the EAT that he has acted reasonably in all the circum stances. Due recognition is given to managerial prerogative and the Tribunal is astute not to be seen to support anything in the nature of undesirable curbs on employer prerogative. At common law, the position is quite different. Unless constitutional considerations are involved, the matter is essentially one of contract and the contract of employment, as chapter one outlined, embodies a dual feature of equality and domination. Managerial prerogative receives little or no scrutiny. Wrongful dismissal, most simply stated, is dismissal in breach of contract. An employee cannot challenge his dismissal unless it has taken place in breach of contract or in violation of his constitutional rights. Similarly, an employer's only line of defence resides in the cluster of terms in the employment contract. If he has terminated the contract in accordance with its terms, and is not guilty of an unconstitutionality, irrespective of his motives or of the arbitrary nature of his action, an employee's claim for wrongful dismissal will not succeed.

Most persons at work in the main branches of economic activity in Ireland,[1] in agriculture, industry and services,[2] are governed by the

1. The most recent indicator of the number of persons employed is provided by the Labour Force Survey, 1979; for the estimated labour force and number of persons at work in the main branches of economic activity at mid-April 1974 to 1980 see *Economic Review and Outlook,* Summer 1980 (Stationery Office, Dublin, Prl. 8967).
2. The following figures are of interest in that they show a pattern of decline in agricultural and a rise in industrial and service employment, a pattern typical of a country in the process of industrialisation:

| | Employment by Sector (thousands) | | | |
	1974	1958	1976	1981 (est.)
Agriculture	554	407	243	219
Industry	241	243	304	358
Services	435	418	488	532
Total	1230	1068	1035	1109

—*C.I.I. Newsletter,* 2 September 1980.

contract of employment.[3] The common law distinguishes ordinary employees from office-holders, or persons whose employment is public or is regulated by statute. The distinction relates not only to the rights of these workers but also, and most importantly, to their remedies (as to which, see chapter five). This chapter begins by identifying briefly the criteria applied by the courts in determining the existence of the various categories of worker. It will become apparent that there is no consistent or uniform definition of 'employee' or of 'office-holder' at common law.

A. Identifying the Nature of Employment

(1) *Employees*

In order to discover the identifying mark or marks of ordinary employees, it is helpful to distinguish between employees and self-employed persons. An employee essentially works under a contract of service but it is not always easy to define the status of a worker in this way. In Ireland the criterion applied by the civil courts to determine the relationship of employee is that of control, whereby the subordinate nature of the relationship is regarded as central to the contract of employment: *Roche v. Kelly & Co. Ltd.*[4] In Britain, as large sections of industry became more skilled and more technological, the 'control test' gave way to the so-called 'integration test' which asked 'Did the alleged servant form part of the alleged master's organisation?'[5] but this likewise failed to provide a clear answer[6] and a 'mixed test' has more recently been developed.[7] It may be applied in two stages. The first question to ask is whether there is control. This is a necessary but not a sufficient test. It must then be determined whether the provisions of the contract are consistent with its being a contract of service. There may be indications, for example, that a worker is an entrepreneur rather than an employee. In this event the

3. About one in four persons at work in Ireland is employed in the public sector. See *Trade Union Information* Summer 1978 (ICTU Dublin).
4. [1969] I.R. 100; see the earlier unsatisfactory approach of Hanna J. in *Minister for Industry and Commerce v. Healy* [1941] IR 545, 553. See, too, *re* control, *Lynch v. Palgrave Murphy* [1962] IR 150.
5. (1951) 14 MLR 504, at 505-'6. Lord Denning developed the test in *Stevenson, Jordan and Harrison Ltd. v. MacDonald and Evans* [1952] 1 T.L.R. 101.
6. Rideout suggests that its variable content may have provided an insufficient disguise for a decision reached by far less explicable paths of reasoning: *Principles of Labour Law*, p. 9.
7. In *Ready Mixed Concrete (South East) Ltd. v. Minister of Pensions* [1968] 2 Q.B. 497 (McKenna J.); See R. Townshend-Smith: 'Recognising a Contract of Employment' (1979) 129 NLJ 993; Freedland provides a descriptive definition in *The Contract of Employment*, 8. Elsewhere he hints at an analytical definition.

fundamental test to be applied is whether the person who has engaged himself to perform particular services is in business on his own account.[8] Where this business is already well established that will be a significant, though not a decisive, factor. The process of classification is regarded as an issue of law, not fact: *Young and Woods Ltd. v. West*.[9] The Irish EAT recently applied the mixed test in a case concerning statutory unfair dismissal: *Kirwan v. Dart Industries Ltd. & Leahy*.[10]

The term 'self-employed person' is generally used to distinguish a person who may be said to work for an employer but does so as an independent contractor. He is bound by a contract 'for services', i.e., his obligation is to do a certain job or jobs as distinct from the more general obligation to serve in any required aspect of the description of services which he has undertaken. Until recently judges were willing to leave the decision as to the type of contract under which labour is supplied to the parties themselves. They were not prepared, in Wedderburn's phrase, to 'pierce the veil' of self-employment. But both British[11] and Irish cases have now departed from this approach. In *Lamb Bros. (Dublin) Ltd. v. Davidson*,[12] Costello J. in the High Court sought to uncover 'the reality of the employment relationship'. At the same time, however, he accorded considerable importance to 'the clear intention of the parties', but only in so far as this was not inconsistent with the reality of their relationship.

(2) *Office-holders*

It is no easier to define an 'office-holder' than an employee.[13] The term is sometimes used to describe those in positions of authority in a variety of public and private institutions. Although the distinction between office-holders and ordinary employees has a long historical basis, there has been little or no attempt to distinguish between these

8. *Market Investigations Ltd. v. Minister of Social Security* [1969] 2 Q.B. 173 (Q.B.D.). See Hepple & O'Higgins: *Individual Employment Law*, 59.
9. [1980] IRLR 201; (1981) ILJ 124 (note).
10. UD I/1980.
11. E.gg., *Ferguson v. Dawson Ltd.* [1976] 3 All ER 817; *Massey v. Crown Life Insurance Co.* [1978] ICR 594; *Young and Woods Ltd. v. West* fn. 9 *ante*.
12. High Court unreported, 4 December 1979. Compare EAT's determination that claimant was an independent contractor in *O Riain v. Independent Newspapers* UD 134/1978.
13. The distinction has a long historical basis. Office-holders were public office-holders, with duties concerning the public, most of which were treated by the Crown. These offices were included in the class of freeholds. They could be bought and sold and were subject to the law of property. Both public and private offices were protected by the common law. See B. Napier: *The Contract of Service: The Concept and its Application* unpublished doctoral thesis for the University of Cambridge, 1976.

workers at common law. There is much overlap between the two categories. In *Glover v. B.L.N. Ltd.*[14] Judge Kenny described the characteristic features of an office:

> 'it is created by Act of the National Parliament,[15] charter, statutory regulation, articles of association of a company or of a body corporate formed under the authority of a statute, deed of trust, grant or by prescription, and . . . the holder of it may be removed if the instrument creating the office authorises this.'[16]

The judge made no distinction between office-holders as the term has been traditionally understood and persons whose employment is, e.g., regulated by statute or established under the articles of association of a company. Yet different principles of law may apply to each category. Judge Kenny's definition is less helpful, it is suggested, than the classic exposition of 'office-holder' given by Rowlett J. in *Great Western Railway Co. v. Bater*.[17] This is what the term connoted:

> 'a subsisting, permanent, substantive position, which had an existence independent of the person who filled it, which went on and was filled by successive holders . . . a substantive thing that existed apart from the holders.'

In *Glover*, it was emphasised that as the holder of an office may hold such office under contract, the presence or absence of a contract cannot be the feature which distinguishes an office from employment so far as the principles of natural justice are concerned. It followed, according to Kenny J., that someone such as the plaintiff, who was appointed a company director under a fixed-term contract, could successfully invoke natural justice

> 'if his position under the contract resembles that of the holder of an office.'[18]

14. [1973] IR 383. See too *Carvill v. Irish Industrial Bank Ltd.*]1968] I.R. 325; *Stakelum v. Canning* [1976] IR 314.

15. The holder of an office under an Act of the Oireachtas may be removed if the office itself is abolished under statute: *Ó Cruadhlaoich v. Minister for Finance* (1934) 68 I.L.T.R. 174. See, too, *Reilly v. The King* [1934] A.C. 176.

16. At 414. Contrast *102 Social Club and Institute Ltd. v. Bickerton* [1977] ICR 911, 919-'20.

17. [1920] 3 K.B. 266 at 273-4; subsequently approved by the House of Lords, [1922] 2 AC 1; recently approved by the Court of Appeal in *Edwards (Inspector of Taxes) v. Clinch* [1980] *Simon's Tax Cases* 438; [1980] 3 All E.R. 278. On *Edwards* see (1981) ILJ 52 (note).

18. *Per* Kenny J. at 415.

In *Ridge v. Baldwin*,[19] Lord Reid spoke about the kind of case which can resemble dismissal from an office

> 'where the body employing the man is under some statutory or other restriction as to the kind of contract which it can make with its servants, or the grounds on which it can dismiss them.'[20]

Judge Kenny adopted this criterion. Glover could not be validly dismissed for serious misconduct without its being the unanimous view of the directors of the holding company that the misconduct had a defined effect. He was therefore held to be the holder of an office.

Kenny J. was correct to point out that 'office' and 'contract of employment' are not mutually exclusive.[21] But the High Court judgment is unsatisfactory inasmuch as it implies that a person employed under a contract of employment which contains substantive limitations as to dismissal may be equated, for the purposes of remedies, with an office-holder. The latter's position is obviously the more favoured at common law but this does not justify extending the category of office-holder in an unprincipled way. In *Glover* the only justification advanced for the High Court's decision was a rather dubious interpretation of *obiter dicta* in *Ridge v. Baldwin*, above.[22] It is not surprising that, on appeal, the Supreme Court chose a different route to arrive at its decision (in outcome the Court's finding was similar to that in the lower Court).

The concept of office-holder has considerably widened in recent times, to include persons whose employment involves a special status. The class of status-holder has itself increased so much that the classification of occupations covered is a task matched in difficulty only by that of formulating principles to justify their special treatment. In the British case of *Vine v. National Dock Labour Board*,[23]

19. [1964] AC 40, 65.
20. See the fascinating comment on these *dicta* by S. A. de Smith in *Administrative Law*, 231, fn. 11, which, if correct, suggests that Judge Kenny incorrectly construed the passage.
21. The view clearly does not stand in the light of decisions such as *Barthorpe v. Exeter Diocesan Board of Finance* [1979] ICR 900 *per* Slynn J. at 904 and it was decisively rejected in *Edwards*, fn. 17, *ante*, per Buckley L.J. at 281 (All E.R.). It does not follow that an office-holder who is 'employed' is so under a contract of employment. He may work under a contract to execute work or labour: *Hugh-Jones v. St. John's College, Cambridge* [1979] ICR 848 *per* Slynn J. at 852, or indeed under a contract *sui generis*. See *Hitchcock v. The Post Office* [1980] IRLR 100. Further, there will be some office holders who do not have a contractual relationship at all with the person or body which appoints them: cf. *Knight v. A-G* [1979] ICR 194 *per* Slynn J. at 199.
22. See fn. 19 *ante*.
23. [1956] 3 All E.R. 944, 948; [1957] AC 500, 508-9.

for instance, Viscount Kilmuir L.C., dealing with a registered dock worker, said that the situation was entirely different from the ordinary master and servant cases and referred to the docker's status as a registered worker which he was entitled to have supported by statute. The employment concerned in another British case of considerable importance, *Stevenson v. United Road Transport Association*,[24] was neither public nor coloured by statute. The plaintiff was a regional officer employed by a trade union. He was dismissed without a fair warning or time to prepare his case. The Court of Appeal held that his dismissal was void, placing much reliance on the fact that the executive committee's power to dismiss on behalf of the union was circumscribed by the rules of the union and that dismissal would put an ex-officer in a bad light before his colleagues, union members. It would seem from his case that the courts in Britain will discover a status not only from the fact that an employer is a public or quasi-public body whose decisions are open to judicial scrutiny but also from the consequences a dismissal may have on a man's reputation and career within an organisation, particularly a trade union.

(3) *Persons whose employment is regulated by statute*

There are two types of employment to consider. First, the *vires* of a particular body in regard to dismissal may be defined by statute. For example, a local government,[25] local authority,[26] or statutory body cannot employ or dismiss servants except under statutory authority. Their powers are derived from statute and must be exercised in accordance with the statute (and with the Constitution). Secondly, dismissal may be in breach of a prohibition upon termination of employment, imposed by statute or by regulation.[27] This type of case is distinguishable from the first as there may be a statutory prohibition upon dismissal in cases of private employment where the employer is not a statutory authority.[28]

---

24. [1976] 3 All E.R. 29. See S. A. de Smith *op. cit.*, fn. 20 *ante*, 230. Contrast *Edwards* case, fn. 17 *ante*.
    25. See *Breslin v. Dublin Board of Assistance* (1956) 90 I.L.T.R. 158; *The State (Curtin) v. Minister for Health* [1953] I.R. 93; *Gardiner v. Kildare Co. Council* (1952) 86 I.L.T.R. 148.
    26. See *O'Mahony v. Arklow U.D.C. and Minister for Local Government* [1965] I.R. 710; *Walsh v. The Dublin Health Authority* (1964) 98 I.L.T.R. 82; *Flaherty v. Minister for Local Government and Public Health and another* [1941] I.R. 587.
    27. Both types of statutory regulation may be present.
    28. Cf. *Taylor v. Furness Withy Ltd.* (1969) 6 KIR 488.

Garda[29] and army officers[30] are relatively straightforward examples of office-holders whose employment is regulated by statute. Persons working in the civil service enjoy considerable security of tenure although it is unsettled in law whether a civil servant is an office-holder or has a contract of employment.[31] As already noted, these alternatives need not be mutually exclusive. In Ireland the predominant view is that civil servants are 'office-holders'. But although the word 'office' is used in the relevant legislation, in most cases it would be more accurate to regard civil servants as persons whose employment is regulated by statute. The principal Act governing their employment is the Civil Service Regulation Act, 1956. s. 5 of which states that 'established' (i.e.) permanent civil servants:

'hold office at the will and pleasure of the Government'

Section 6 refers to 'unestablished' or temporary officers and states that

'the appropriate authority may terminate the services of a civil servant who is not an established civil servant'

Other conditions of employment of civil servants, established or otherwise, are not detailed but are fixed by the Minister for the Public Service in whom general regulatory and control functions are vested under s. 17 of the Act.

B. Lawful Dismissal

Lawful dismissal is dismissal in accordance with an employee's contract of employment. Most commonly it occurs where an employee is given due notice of termination — although what constitutes due notice is not always free of difficulty. An employee may also be summarily dismissed in accordance with his contract of employment. Both forms of lawful dismissal are considered here. Most (though not all) of what follows in Sections (1) and (2) is exclusively referable to ordinary employees.

29. See *Garvey v. Ireland and Others* [1981] I.R. 75; *Hynes v. Garvey* [1978] I.R. 174; *Burke v. Garvey* (High Court unreported, April 1977); *Hogan v. Minister for Justice, Garvey and Others* (High Court unreported, September 1976); *Fitzpatrick v. Wymes and Others* (High Court unreported, 17 May 1973).

30. See *Donnelly v. Minister for Defence* (High Court unreported, February 1977); *Gleeson v. Minister for Defence* [1976] I.R. 280.

31. See S. A. de Smith: *Constitutional and Administrative Law*, 180, 192-196; W. G. Friedmann: *Government Enterprise*, Chap. 16; Leo Blair: 'The Civil Servant — A Status Relationship?' 21 M.L.R. 265.

(1) *Due notice of termination*

(i) *At common law*

The contract of employment is subject to an implied term allowing it to be terminated by the unilateral act of giving notice. If an employer gives notice of the length which the contract requires, or the minimum statutory notice which the law requires, if that is greater (see *post*), the contract is lawfully terminated. Generally, in the absence of an express term in the contract,[32] or a statutory provision concerning dismissal,[33] or custom and practice[34] or where there is no contract, the law requires that reasonable notice is given.[35] The

32. *Flynn v. G.N.R.Co. (Ire.) Ltd.* (1955), 89 I.L.T.R. 46, 53.

33. E.gg., *Cox v. E.S.B.* [1943] I.R. 94, 109, 231, 233; 1945 *Ir. Jur. Rep.* 58 (local government office); *McLoughlin v. G.S.R. Co.* (1944) 78 I.L.T.R. 74 (agreed scheme as to conditions of service of railway employees pursuant to s. 55 Railways Act, 1924); *Gardiner v. Kildare Co. Council* (1952) 86 I.L.T.R. 148 (local government office); *The State (Curtin) v. Minister for Health* [1953] I.R. 93 (local government office); *Flynn v. G.N.R. Co. (Ire.) Ltd.* fn. 32 *ante* (case concerned *inter alia* whether Flynn was an 'excepted person' for purposes of Unemployment Insurance Acts, 1920-'21); *Breslin v. Dublin Board of Assistance* (1956) 90 I.L.T.R. 158 (local government office); *O'Mahony v. Arklow U.D.C. and Minister for Local Government* [1965] I.R. 710 (local government office).

34. Two cases involving the newspaper world and custom as to notice are *O'Reilly v. The Irish Press* (1937) 71 I.L.T.R. 194 (High Court) (chief sub-editor of daily paper failed to prove usage or custom entitling him to 6 months' notice); and *Ó Conaill v. The Gaelic Echo Ltd.* (1958) 92 I.L.T.R. 156 (member of editorial staff of monthly magazine held entitled to at least 1 month's notice). Contrast the British case of *Grundy v. Sun Printing and Publishing Association* (1916) 33 T.L.R. 77. See, further, *Nicoll v. Greaves* (1864) 17 C.B. (N.S.) 27 at 84; *Foxall v. International Land Credit Co.* (1867) 16 L.T. 637; *George v. Davies* [1911] 2 K.B. 445; *George Edwardes (Daly's Theatre) Ltd. v. Comber* (1926) 42 T.L.R. 247; *Davson v. France* (1959) 109 L.J. 526.

35. Termination with correct notice is sometimes erroneously thought to be necessary where the contract of employment is frustrated. It is not always easy to determine whether there has been such a change in circumstances as to frustrate the contract. If legislation renders further performance of a contract impossible it is clear that the contract will be discharged: *Ó Cruadhlaoich v. Minister for Finance* (1934) 68 I.L.T.R. 174 (High Court). But the coastline is far less obvious in cases involving illness or incapacity. If it is permanent, illness or incapacity will frustrate the contract, e.g., *Boast v. Firth* (1868) LR 4CP 1. If of so prolonged a nature as to prevent the employer from getting substantially what he has bargained for, it is most probable that illness or incapacity will have the same effect. From case-law, it seems illness or incapacity will determine the contract of employment if it is of such a nature as to frustrate the business object of the engagement. In *Flynn v. Great Northern Railway Co. (Ire.) Ltd.* (1955) 89 I.L.T.R. 46, Mr. Justice Budd in the High Court recited various British authorities such as *Poussard v. Spiers* (1876) 1 QBD 410 and *Storey v. Fulham Steel Work Co.* (1907) 24 T.L.R. 89, which illustrate the difficulty of determining whether a contract has been frustrated or not. In the latter, Alverstone L.J. seemed to indicate the necessity of the master's giving notice before the contract is terminated. (This was further implied, although it was not an issue in *Price v. Guest Keen and Nettlefolds* [1918] AC 760.) In *Flynn's* case,

principle of termination by reasonable notice was first accepted in *Beeston v. Collyer*,[36] but the basic concept was of a contract impliedly for a year.[37] With time, examples of an implied yearly hiring declined (see chapter one above) and the notion of an implied term as to notice to terminate gained ground.[38] In *De Stempel v. Dunkels*,[39] Lord Justice Greer used the ordinary contractual rules for the implication of terms to conclude that the parties to a contract would not have intended otherwise than that the contract should be terminable by notice. But the notice must be reasonable and

> 'The question, what is reasonable notice, depends upon the capacity in which the employee is engaged, the general standing in the community of the class of persons, having regard to the profession to which the employee belongs, the probable facility or difficulty the employee would have in procuring other employment in the case of dismissal, having regard to the demand for persons of that profession, and the general character of the services which the engagement contemplates.'[40]

Budd J. took the view that notice of termination was not necessary. He cited with approval Lord Justice Scrutton in *Warburton v. Co-Operative Wholesale Society Ltd.* [1917] 1 KB 663 where he said that, under decided cases, a servant incapacitated by illness and in the absence of notice does not cease to be employed unless the illness is such as to interfere seriously with or to frustrate the business purpose of the contract. In *Byrne v. Limerick Steamship Co.* [1946] IR 138, Overend J. was of the same opinion. He described frustration as operating automatically to determine the entire contract; it did not depend upon the volition of the parties nor even upon their knowledge. Accordingly, in *Flynn's* case, Budd J. asserted that

> 'If frustration is the test, there does not in principle seem to be any reason why a Master should have to give notice to terminate a contract, already frustrated, and my view therefore is that notice is unnecessary.'

In the case before him, the employee was permanently incapacitated to perform his duties as a fireman on the footplate. His incapacity was held to frustrate the business object of the engagement.

36. (1827) 2 C. & P. 607; 4 Bing. 309.

37. Early cases dealt with the question whether the contract automatically terminated at the end of that year or whether notice in advance of the date of expiry was required. Other decisions recognised that there might be special implied exceptions to the presumption of a yearly hiring, e.g., *Green v. Wright* (1876) 1 C.P.D. 591. In *Fairman v. Oakford* (1860) 5 H. & N. 635, Pollock C.B. expressed the opinion, *obiter*, that the indefinite hiring of a clerk was not impliedly for a year but was determinable by 3 months notice.

38. By 1910, Lord Alverstone C.J. said: 'The general principle applicable to contracts of service is that, in the absence of misconduct or of grounds specified in the contract, the engagement can only be terminated after reasonable notice': *Re African Association Ltd. and Allen* [1910] 1 K.B. 396.

39. [1938] 1 All E.R. 238; see, too, *Fisher v. W. B. Dick & Co. Ltd.* [1938] 4 All E.R. 467.

40. *Warren v. Super Drug Markets Ltd.* (1965) 54 D.L.R. (2d.) 183.

Earlier cases held that the period of notice should be the same as that governing the payment of wages[41] but they were largely concerned with avoidance of the presumption of a yearly hiring. There is no authority to support the general proposition of a presumption that the period of notice is the same as that governing the payment of wages. Today the matter depends upon status more than anything else. For instance, a year's notice has been held appropriate for the managing director of a company.[42]

Whether notice should terminate at a particular time was discussed in *McDonnell v. Minister for Education and Another*,[43] where a teacher was given 3 months notice to terminate at the end of July. O'Byrne J. took the view that the only reasonable time at which the particular employment should terminate was at the end of the school year; any notice of less than 6 months terminating at the end of the school year would be neither reasonable nor sufficient to terminate the plaintiff's employment. On appeal the Supreme Court did not disturb the trial judge's finding in relation to length of notice but the Court disagreed that notice should terminate at any particular time other than that which may be express or implied in the contract of employment.

(ii) *Contracts apparently incapable of termination by notice*

Parties to a contract of employment may make a contract which is apparently incapable of termination by notice.[44] In *McClelland v. Northern Ireland General Health Services Board*[45] applications were invited for posts which 'subject to a probationary period . . . will be permanent and pensionable'. The House of Lords left no doubt that the word 'permanent' did not preclude the right to give notice. Rather, it indicated the attachment of fringe benefits, such as pension rights, which normally accompany 'permanence'. In *Walsh v. The*

41. *Davis v. Marshall* (1861) 4 L.T. 216, 217; *Payzu v. Hannaford* [1918] 2 K.B. 348.

42. *Carvill v. Irish Industrial Bank Ltd.* [1968] I.R. 325; and see O'Keeffe J.'s comments at 344.

43. [1940] I.R. 316: See 'Notice of Termination of a Contract of Service' (1941) 75 ILT & SJ 59. See, too, *Ryan v. Jenkinson* (1855) 25 LJ (NS) QB 11.

44. A case in point is *Salt v. Power Plant Co. Ltd.* [1936] 3 All E.R. 322, in which the engagement was stated to be for a minimum of 3 years, subject to right of cancellation in the event of wilful default. Thereafter there was to be a right to terminate by 6 months notice prior to the ensuing December 31, and in the absence of such notice the engagement was to be 'permanent'. Notice to terminate the contract was eventually given 11 years after its commencement but it was held that the provision for permanency after 4 years meant that the contract was for the life of the employee, subject only to an express provision that the performance of the employee's duties should be to the satisfaction of the directors.

45. [1957] 1 W.L.R. 594. See a note on this case in 73 L.Q.R. 281.

Dublin Health Board,[46] Mr. Justice Budd discussed the meaning of 'permanence'. In the case of a contract of service, a person may be said to be 'permanently' employed when he is employed for an indefinite period on the regular staff of a particular employer, as distinct from persons taken on casually for a temporary or defined period. That did not necessarily mean that such a person has a contract of employment for life. On the other hand, a person may be given 'permanent' and pensionable employment where, under his contract, he holds employment for life or for life subject to the right of an employer to dismiss him for misconduct, neglect of duty or unfitness. This may mean employment is to last until the employee reaches full pensionable age, subject to the rights of the employer just mentioned.

> 'As to what is meant, and should be implied as being in the contemplation of the parties, depends upon the true construction of the whole contract viewed in the light of the surrounding circumstances and all relevant matters.'[47]

Mr. Justice Budd expressly followed the reasoning of the House of Lords in *McClelland's* case that an offer of permanent and pensionable employment without more should be properly construed as a hiring for an indefinite period terminable on reasonable notice.[48]

Parties may of course end the contract of employment by mutual consent. Often, such consent exists from the time of their initial agreement to enter into the employment relationship. When the fixed term is over, the contract automatically comes to an end. Likewise an agreement may relate to a particular job and, upon completion thereof, the contract will come to an end. But contracts which stipulate that an agreement is to last for a certain period only may enable one or both of the parties to terminate it before that time, e.g., by giving notice of a particular length.[49] The legal significance between these two types of contract is considerably important.

46. 98 I.L.T.R. 82, 86. On the presumption of permanence see *Gardiner v. Kildare Co. Council* (1952) I.L.T.R. 148; *Hanratty v. Minister for Industry and Commerce and Others* [1931] IR 189; *M'Mahon v. Leonard* 6 HLC 870; *Hayes v. Dexter* 13 ICLR 22; contrast *Breslin v. Dublin Board of Assistance* (1956) 90 ILTR 158.

47. 98 ILTR 82, 86. The Maternity Protection of Employees Act, 1981, s. 1, in its definition of 'employer' invokes the notion of 'permanence' in the first sense described by Budd J.

48. At 88.

49. This is still a 'fixed term' contract: see *BBC v. Dixon* [1979] 2 All ER 112, (cf. (1978) 7 I.L.J. 131) refusing to follow *BBC v. Ioannou* [1975] ICR 167 on which there is a note in (1975) 4 I.L.J. 245. See V. Jeffers: 'Fixed-Term Contracts' (1978) 128 N.L.J. 180; A. E. Norris: 'Fixed Term Contracts: The Continuing Problems' (1979) 129 N.L.J. 1195.

(iii) *Statutory notice*

In manual and blue-collar employment, the implied period of notice was scarcely reasonable by any social or economic standard (it was frequently one week; it is surely an oddity of the common law that yearly hiring should have given way to such notice). Inadequate periods of notice of dismissal could no longer be overlooked when they occurred in situations of mass redundancy and often, too, in areas of high unemployment. In 1973, the Oireachtas attempted to remedy this deficiency by enacting the Minimum Notice and Terms of Employment Act, a statute foreshadowing much more extensive provision for job security.[50] The Act lays down minimum periods of notice for every employee as defined therein.[51] The definition excludes self-employed persons and ex-employees. Section 4 provides that where the employee has been employed for at least 13 weeks, the employer is required to give him notice of dismissal which satisfies certain minimum requirements:

Period of continuous service	Notice required
13 weeks to 2 years	Not less than 1 week
2 years to 5 years	2 weeks
5 years to 10 years	4 weeks
10 years to 15 years	6 weeks
15 years and over	8 weeks

According to section 4 of the Act, the minimum period of notice required of an employee to terminate his contract of employment is, in all cases, not less than one week, provided the employee has been in continuous service for not less than 13 weeks. This represents a welcome attack on the old contractual principle of mutuality, hallowed by the common law, under which an employer and employee respectively are required to give identical periods of notice to terminate the contract of employment. The statutory periods replace any shorter ones specified in the contract but may be displaced by an express contractual requirement of a longer period of notice. Equally, custom and practice, or any other method of

50. In Britain, similar legislation was first passed in 1963 with the Contracts of Employment Act; see now EPCA 1978, s. 49. On the Act of 1963, see F. White: 'Terminating the Contract of Employment' (1964) J.B.L. 314.

51. 'Employee' means an individual who has entered into or works under a contract with an employer, whether the contract be for manual labour, clerical work or otherwise, whether it be expressed or implied, oral or in writing, and whether it be a contract of service or of apprenticeship or otherwise: s. 1 of the Act of 1973.

implying better terms may suffice.[52] Common law implications apply during the first 13 weeks of employment. They also apply to office-holders such as established civil servants, members of the Garda Síochána and of the Defence Forces, and to certain other groups (e.g., sailors, fishermen) expressly excepted under the Act.[53]

(2) *Lawful summary dismissal*

(i) *Grounds existing at the time of dismissal*

The right to terminate the contract of employment with reasonable notice is quite separate from the right to terminate the contract summarily, i.e., without notice, in the case of breach by the other side where the 'grounds for dismissal during the term contracted for must be such that they amounted to a repudiation of the contract on the part of the employee'.[54] Termination of employment without notice will constitute a lawful dismissal only where there are grounds which the law regards as sufficient to justify the dismissal. If these grounds do not exist, an employer will be held to be in breach of contract and liable to pay damages for wrongful dismissal.[55]

The test of breach of contract at an early stage of development was based on status rather than on the particular contractual obligations of an employee.[56] As early as *Turner v. Mason*,[57] however, the courts relied on a strict contractual approach. This approach has characterised the common law ever since. In *Laws v. London*

---

52. See Dix and Crump: *Contracts of Employment*, 133.

53. Section 3. Disputes under the Act of 1973 may be referred to the EAT (section 11) and the same section provides that there is a right of appeal from the Tribunal to the High Court on a point of law. Section 8 preserves the right of any employer or employee to terminate a contract of employment without notice because of misconduct by the other party.

54. *Power v. Binchy and Others* (1929) 64 ILTR 35, 39 *per* Meredith J.

55. If either party to the contract of employment is aware of a breach by the other side of such seriousness as to justify summary dismissal or summary termination by the employee, but the reason is not invoked within a reasonable period, he will lose the right to terminate the contract and be left only with the remedy of damages: *Beattie v. Parmenter* (1889) 5 TLR 396. See, too, *State (Gleeson) v. Minister for Defence* [1976] IR 280.

56. Cronin and Grime: *Labour Law*, 86-87; see, too, Hepple & O'Higgins *Employment Law*, para. 551.

57. (1845) 14 M & W 112. The defendant's maid had asked for permission to absent herself from work until the next day so that she could visit her mother, whom she had heard was dying. Permission was refused; the maid went nonetheless and was dismissed without notice. According to the court, the plaintiff could not be permitted to place her moral duty to another before her contractual duty to her employer.

Chronicle (Indicator Newspapers) Ltd.,[58] Lord Evershed, M.R. affirmed that

> 'It is, no doubt . . . generally true that wilful disobedience of an order will justify summary dismissal since wilful disobedience of a lawful and reasonable order shows a disregard — a complete disregard — of a condition essential to the contract of service, namely, the condition that the servant must obey the proper orders of the master, and that unless he does so the relationship is, so to speak, struck at fundamentally.'

It is impossible to define the reason or reasons which will be regarded as sufficient to justify summary dismissal. Grounds which entitle an employer not to enter into a contract to employ and those which justify dismissal of an employee already employed must be distinguished: *Power v. Binchy.*[59] Here Meredith J. held that, as a rule, mere non-attendance of an employee at his post on one occasion is not a ground for dismissal.[60] Further, an employee's absence from a meeting with his employers to which he is summoned to answer charges against him does not constitute an aggravation of his offence such as would justify dismissal on otherwise inadequate grounds. Depending on the position of responsibility held, absence on one occasion may constitute misconduct, as in *Flynn v. G.N.R. Co. (Ire.) Ltd.*[61] where the plaintiff, a fireman, failed to report for duty. In the circumstances, this was held to be a serious matter.[62]

Mr. Justice Kenny attempted an exposition of the law in the earliest of the two most important Irish cases concerning wrongful dismissal, *Carvill v. Irish Industrial Bank Ltd.,*[63] where he said that the grounds relied on, to justify dismissal without notice of an employee, must be actions or omissions by the employee which are inconsistent with the performance of the express or implied terms of his contract of service:[64]

> 'One of these implied terms is that the employee will have that degree of competence[65] which he has represented himself as

58. [1959] 1 W.L.R. 698. See J. C. Woods: 'The Disobedient Servant' (1959) 22 M.L.R. 526.

59. Fn. 54 *ante.*

60. See *Fillieul v. Armstrong* (1837) 7 Ad. & El. 557.

61. Fn. 32 *ante.*

62. At 58. See too, *Carvill v. Irish Industrial Bank Ltd.,* fn. 42 *ante,* where an isolated incident by a company director was deemed sufficient by Kenny J. in the High Court (although not by the Supreme Court) to justify summary dismissal.

63. Fn. 42 *ante.*

64. At 335.

65. E.g., *Corry v. NUVGATA* [1950] I.R. 315. Incompetence was regarded as breach of an implied term in the early case of *Harrington v. Gleeson* (1897) 31 ILT & SJ 429.

having at the time when he was originally employed; another term is that the employee will conduct his employer's business with reasonable competence. The incompetence relied on to justify summary dismissal must, however, be judged by reasonable standards, and the employer must establish that an error was caused by incompetence and not by mistaken judgment or human error. An error relied on to justify summary dismissal must be judged by the standards which prevail among people in Ireland who are engaged in business.'

Those who are in business have sometimes to take risks but, in judging the behaviour of commercial men, the judge had to bear in mind that they often take calculated risks.

'Another implied term of the contract of service between an employer and an employee is that the employee will act honestly towards his employer and that the employee will not take or misuse the employer's property or divert to himself profits or property which belong to the employer.'

In the second important Irish decision, *Glover v. B.L.N. Ltd.*,[66] several serious charges were made against the plaintiff, who was the technical director of four companies. His contract of appointment provided that he could be dismissed without compensation if guilty of any serious misconduct or serious neglect in the performance of his duties which, in the unanimous opinion of the board of directors of the holding company, affected injuriously the business or property of the holding company or of any of its subsidiaries. The main charges of serious misconduct related to the sale of capital equipment and goods to the operating company by another company. Glover was a shareholder in this latter company and it was managed by his son. Initially, Glover did not disclose his interest in the company to his co-directors, although after a time all the directors of the operating company were informed by Glover that he had this interest. There was no evidence before the High Court to establish that the operating company suffered any loss from the various transactions with which Glover was involved. The directors of the holding company could not reasonably have concluded that the dealings with the other company injuriously affected the property or business of the operat-

66. [1973] IR 388, 405 *per* Kenny J. See (1968) 3 *Ir. Jur.* (NS) 322 and (1973) 8 *Ir. Jur.* 297 (Notes). Further on misconduct, see *Hartery and Welltrade (Middle East) Ltd. v. Hurley (High Court unreported, 15 March 1978); Brewster v. Burke and Minister for Labour* (High Court unreported, 8 February 1978); see the early case of *Kean v. Fitzgerald* (1894) 28 ILT & SJ 620 (Ex.) in which a general descrioption of misconduct was given.

ing company.[67] It was not misconduct, Judge Kenny said, to put oneself in a position where duty and interest might clash: it was a counsel of prudence not to do so. Rather, misconduct lay in failing to reveal the position to those likely to be affected by it, so that they could not decide whether the performance of the duty would be influenced by the competing interest.[68]

The argument relating to the main charge of misconduct against Glover failed because the directors could not reasonably conclude that the contracts injuriously affected the business, property or management of any of the companies. There was one charge of serious misconduct which Judge Kenny was prepared to accept, however: it related to work done by employees of the operating company for Glover during hours when they were employed by it and for which no charge was ever made:

> 'If the operating company had been a small private company in which nearly all the shares were owned by one person I would not have regarded what happened as being serious misconduct because the difference between a small private company and a privately-owned business is one which is understood by few. But the operating company was wholly owned by a public company whose shares were quoted on the stock exchange and which employed about 640 people. After much consideration, I have come to the conclusion that it was serious misconduct.'[69]

The trial judge's assessment of the facts and his conclusion that the plaintiff was guilty of serious neglect of duty and of serious

---

67. Counsel for Glover cited the following passage from the judgment of Cotton L.J. in *Boston Deep Sea Fishing and Ice Co. Ltd. v. Ansell* (1883) 39 Ch. D. 339 at 357: 'If a servant or a managing director, or any person who is authorised to act, and is acting, for another in the matter of any contract, receives, as regards the contract, any sum, whether by way of percentage or otherwise, from the person with whom he is dealing on behalf of his principal, he is committing a breach of duty. It is not an honest act, and, in my opinion, it is a sufficient act to shew that he cannot be trusted to perform the duties which he has undertaken as servant or agent. He puts himself in such a position that he has a temptation not faithfully to perform his duty to his employer. He has a temptation, especially where he is getting a percentage on expenditure, not to cut down the expenditure but to let it be increased, so that his percentage may be larger'. Kenny J. did not accept this as a correct statement of the law (at 406).

68. The modern view of the position of directors of companies is to be found in the Companies Act, 1963 (s. 194), in Article 84 of the model articles for public companies and in Article 7 of those for private companies in Table A to that Act. These show that when a conflict between duty and interest arises, a director is bound to disclose the nature of his interest to his co-directors. In Judge Kenny's opinion, the same rule applied to those employed (at 407).

69. At 412.

misconduct were not challenged when the case went on appeal to the Supreme Court (see further, page 64, below).[70]

(ii) *Grounds discovered subsequent to dismissal*

In Britain, for purposes of the law of wrongful but not unfair dismissal, an employer who has dismissed an employee for, e.g., serious neglect of his duties, may rely on grounds discovered subsequent to the actual date of dismissal: *Boston Deep Sea Fishing and Ice Co. v. Ansell*.[71] This view was emphatically rejected by the Irish Supreme Court in *Carvill v. Irish Industrial Bank Ltd.*,[72] where there was no evidence that at the time of dismissal any of the matters complained of subsequently were within the knowledge of the defendants. The defendants relied upon the principle that it is not necessary that an employer, dismissing an employee for good cause, should state the ground for such dismissal and, provided good ground existed in fact, it is immaterial whether or not it was known to the employer at the time of the dismissal. O'Keeffe J., for the Supreme Court, found it difficult to understand how an act could be relied on to justify dismissal unless it was known at the time of dismissal. He recognised that there can be some breaches of contract so fundamental as to show that the contract is entirely repudiated by the party committing them, and that such an act might be relied upon in an action for wrongful dismissal. These would not justify a particular dismissal, according to Mr. Justice O'Keeffe, but they would support the plea that a dismissed servant had himself put an end to the contract:

> 'Where the act is not of so fundamental a character but would warrant the dismissal of the servant at the option of the employer, it appears to me to be quite illogical to say that an employer may be heard to say he dismissed his servant on a ground unknown to him at the actual time of dismissal'.[73]

---

70. *W. Devis & Sons Ltd. v. Atkins* [1977] AC 931; [1977] ICR 662; [1977] 3 All ER 40; [1977] IRLR 314 (HL).

71. (1888) 39 Ch.D. 339. And see *Ridgway v. Hungerford Market Co.* (1885) Ad. & El, 171 — corporation clerk entered protest of his own in the minute book at what he regarded as the injustice of his dismissal: this was regarded as an adequate ground for same. These common law rules were approved by the Court of Appeal in *Cyril Leonard & Co. v. Simo Securities Trust Ltd.* [1972] 1 W.L.R. 80, at 82, 86. The *Boston* case was impliedly approved by Black J. in *Boland v. Dublin Corporation* [1946] IR 88, 103-'4.

72. [1968] I.R. 325.

73. At 345-'6. This is in fact the reasoning of Lord Abinger C.B. in *Cussons v. Skinner* 11 M. & W. 161, 168.

An employer is not without rights, however, in respect of subsequent misconduct. He can probably rely on it as a ground for reduction of damages and, in an appropriate case, it may reduce the damages to the point of extinction.

In *Glover*[74] the board of directors acted with great haste in dismissing the plaintiff. They relied on a report which did not contain complaints or allegations of misconduct set out with the particularity with which they were set out subsequently in the reply to the plaintiff's notice for particulars. Judge Walsh added a further gloss to the principles enunciated in *Carvill*:

> '. . . that the misconduct, if known but not in fact used as a ground for dismissal at the time, cannot be relied upon afterwards in an effort to justify the dismissal'.[75]

C. Wrongful Dismissal[76]

(1) *Ordinary employees*

In relation both to procedural safeguards, and to the remedies available to challenge dismissal, the protection which ordinary employees enjoy is more limited than that which applies to office-holders and to persons whose employment is public or is regulated by statute. To a certain extent, the Constitution has eased the harsh results which flow from these distinctions but, constitutional considerations apart, the crucial difference remains that an ordinary employee's redress in the event of dismissal depends upon the terms of his contract of employment. Wrongful dismissal, as noted earlier, is dismissal in breach of contract. If a worker is an ordinary employee, first and foremost wrongful dismissal may take the form of dismissal with inadequate notice. Secondly it may comprise unlawful summary dismissal where the employer is unable to justify his decision to dismiss summarily, i.e., where there has been a repudiatory breach on the employee's part but it is not sufficiently serious to exonerate the employer's action. Both types of dismissal have been dealt with above. There are at least three other ways in which an employee may be wrongfully dismissed in breach of contract,

---

74. Fn. 66 *ante*.
75. At 426. But see pp. 64, 65 *post*.
76. See 'Wrongful Dismissal' (1919) 53 ILT & SJ 75; 'Dismissal — Wrongful or Otherwise' (1959) 93 ILT & SJ 213; A. Samuels: 'Summary or instant dismissal of an employee' (1967) 111 Sol. J., 709; S. Weisbard: 'Termination of contract of service' (1968) 118 N.L.J. 412; H. L. Fridman: 'Termination of the Contract of Employment' (1966) 116 N.L.J. 551, 660; H. M. Levy: 'The Role of the Law in the U.S. and England in Protecting the Worker from Discharge and Discrimination' 18 I. & C.L.Q. 558; E. Herz: 'The Protection of Employees on the Termination of Contracts of Employment' 69 *Int. L. R.*, 215.

namely, where dismissal is in breach of express procedural limitations in the contract of employment, or of an implied term of fairness, or of express substantive limitations. These will be considered *seriatim.*

(i) *Breach of procedural limitations*

The parties to a contract of employment may have expressly incorporated procedural safeguards into the contract.[77] Because these safeguards assume the status of contractual terms, breach will give rise to an action at common law.

In *Gunton v. London Borough of Richmond-upon-Thames*[78] the employee was a college registrar, his contract being terminable by one month's notice in writing on either side. In addition he was subject to a disciplinary procedure which allowed for appeals and which, if followed properly, would take over one month to run its course. A majority in the Court of Appeal held that the effect of the disciplinary code was to render it wrongful to dismiss the plaintiff on disciplinary grounds ('inefficiency, misconduct or indiscipline') without following the agreed procedure but that it would not have affected a dismissal for other reasons, e.g., redundancy. In the event, Gunton's dismissal was recommended 'on the ground of his conduct being wholly inconsistent with the terms of his contract' but the procedure was not followed precisely, some of the initial stages being missed out. Nevertheless, Gunton implemented the appeal procedure on the merits of the recommendation rather than on the failure to adhere to the terms of the code. His appeal was rejected and he was given one month's notice. His purported dismissal was held to be wrongful as being in breach of contract but the appeal to the Court of Appeal turned on whether he had been dismissed effectively, albeit wrongfully, and on the measure of damages (pages 83, 84 *post*).

In Ireland there is little evidence as to any significant development in the adoption of disciplinary or dismissal procedures. The Minimum Notice and Terms of Employment Act, 1973, for the first time placed employers under a statutory obligation to furnish employees on request with a written statement as to terms of employment (cf. EPCA, s. 1). Originally the statement was not required to include any reference to disciplinary or dismissal procedures, but now the Unfair Dismissals Act (s. 14(1)) requires an employer, whether requested to or not, to give to an employee, not later than 28 days after he enters

---

77. Or procedural safeguards may be implied from other written sources such as collective agreements: *Tomlinson v. The London Midland & Scott. Rly. Co.* [1944] 1 All E.R. 537. See, in general, 'Dismissal Procedures; A Comparative Study' 81 *Int. L. R.*, 403.

78. [1970] IRLR 321; see (1981) ILJ 50; [1981] CLJ 33 (notes).

into a contract of employment, a notice in writing setting out the procedure[79] he will observe before and for the purpose of dismissing the employee. To an increasing extent, employers are incorporating dismissal procedures into the written terms they are required to give under s. 9 of the Act of 1973, but it should be emphasised that these terms are not binding on an employer unless they have been incorporated into an individual employee's contract of employment.

(ii) *Breach of an implied term of fairness*

The preceding section dealt with the effect of express procedural limitations in the contract of employment on an employer's power to dismiss. In Ireland, the parties' stated intention in the matter of disciplinary or dismissal procedures is not conclusive. Guided by the Constitution, the courts are willing to imply a term of procedural fairness and have done so where an employer was subject both to express procedural and substantive limitations in relation to dismissal: *Glover v. B.L.N. Ltd.*[80] The facts in *Glover* and the judgment of the High Court are detailed at page 59 above. In spite of the fact that Glover was adjudged guilty of misconduct within the terms of his contract of employment, as an office-holder, he was held to be entitled to invoke natural justice. Because the plaintiff had not been given prior notice of the charges against him, Judge Kenny held that his dismissal was invalid and that he was entitled to 'damages'.[81]

When *Glover* was appealed, the Supreme Court nimbly sidestepped the need to distinguish between office-holders and ordinary employees in relation to procedural due process. The fact that Glover held his employment under a service agreement was not seen as an obstacle. Clause 12(c) of the service agreement provided that the plaintiff could not be validly dismissed for misconduct unless it was serious misconduct and was of a kind which, in the unanimous opinion of the board of directors of the holding company present and voting at the meeting, injuriously affected the reputation, business or property of either that company or of the subsidiary companies. The operation of the clause necessarily involved the ascertainment of the facts alleged to constitute serious misconduct; the determination that they did in fact constitute serious misconduct; and that the members of the board present and voting should be unanimously of opinion that the serious misconduct injuriously affected the reputation,

79. 'Procedure' is one that has been agreed upon by or on behalf of the employer concerned and by the employee concerned or a trade union, or an excepted body under the Trade Union Acts, 1941 and 1971, representing him or has been established by the custom and practice of the employment concerned: s. 14(3).

80. Fn. 66 *ante.*

81. Concerning the granting of an award of damages and a declaration as to invalidity of dismissal see page 111 below.

business or property of the holding company or of the subsidiary companies. The Supreme Court was able to base its decision squarely on contractual considerations. It held that it was necessarily an implied term of the contract in question that the inquiry and determination should be fairly conducted. In doing so, the Court derived support from its earlier decision in *In re Haughey*[82] that a guarantee of fair procedures was among a citizen's personal rights under Article 40, s. 3 of the Constitution. Walsh J. declared that

> '... public policy and the dictates of constitutional justice required that statutes, regulations or *agreements* setting up machinery for the taking of decisions which may affect rights or impose liabilities should be construed as providing for fair procedures.'[83]

The Court distinguished *Ridge v. Baldwin*[84] which Kenny J. had relied upon at first instance. Unlike the case before the Court, the facts there were not governed by the terms of a contract. The existence of a contract was crucial and

> '... once the matter is governed by the terms of a contract between the parties, it is immaterial whether the employee concerned is deemed to be a servant or an officer in so far as the distinction may be of relevance depending on whether the contract is a contract for services or a contract of service.'[85]

In the case of express procedural limitations, the purpose and effect of implying a term of fairness will be to inject a greater degree of efficacy into these stipulations. Where the limitations are substantive, the implied term will ensure that natural justice is observed. The position following *Glover* is that ordinary employees whose dismissal is limited by express contract terms are entitled to the same procedural safeguards as office-holders. The overriding principle of fairness embraces both categories of worker. Even if there had been no pre-existing contractual relationship, Walsh J. suggested, *obiter*, that a contract between the plaintiff and the defendants would probably have been implied.[86] His *dicta* suggest that fairness might be implied in a contract whether or not it contained substantive or

---

82. [1971] I.R. 217, chapter two, pages 39-40 *ante*.
83. At 425, emphasis added.
84. [1964] A.C. 40.
85. At 427 *per* Walsh J.
86. At 428. As Harman J. held in *Byrne v. Kinematograph Renters Society* [1958] 1 WLR 762.

procedural limitations. From a constitutional perspective, this is unobjectionable. Even more, however, Walsh J. could be interpreted as saying that the courts might be willing to infer the existence of a contract for the purposes, effectively, of implying a term of fairness. But this would be to go too far, it is submitted. To 'ratiocinate' backwards would involve a dangerous and unwelcome departure from common law principles. The application of *Glover* should not require such a stretch of the contractual imagination.

In Britain, the position relating to procedural fairness for ordinary employees is far less secure. The following *dicta* of Buckley L.J. in *Stevenson v. United Road Transport Union*[87] may be contrasted with the stark policy of the common law:

> 'In our judgment, a useful test can be formulated in this way. Where one party has a discretionary power to terminate the tenure or enjoyment by another of an employment or an office or a post or a privilege, is that power conditional on the party invested with the power being first satisfied on a particular point which involves investigating some matter on which the other party ought in fairness to be heard or to be allowed to give his explanation or put his case? If the answer to the question is Yes, then unless, before the power purports to have been exercised, the condition has been satisfied after the other party has been given a fair opportunity of being heard or of giving his explanation or putting his case, the power will not have been well exercised.'

These *dicta*, it has been suggested, exhibit a greater judicial willingness to imply the basic element of natural justice now than formerly, at least where dismissal can be on specific grounds only.[88] But such comments are speculative and in the absence, e.g., of a specific reference to procedures in the dismissed worker's contract of employment, one suspects they may be tilting at windmills.

(iii) *Breach of substantive limitations*

Finally, a contract of employment may contain substantive limitations on an employer's power to dismiss, i.e. dismissal may be restricted to specified grounds having a defined effect, as in *Glover's* case. The Supreme Court[89] there endorsed the opinion of the High Court that, because of the express provisions in cl. 12(c) of Glover's service agreement, page 64 above, no implied term could be read into

---

87. [1977] 2 All E.R. 941; [1977] ICR 893.
88. Harvey on *Industrial Relations and Employment Law* (ed. P. Elias) 7.
89. Fn. 66 *ante*, at 424.

the contract that the plaintiff might be summarily dismissed for misconduct. On the contrary, the clause expressly provided that the plaintiff could not be validly dismissed for misconduct unless it was 'serious misconduct' of the kind set out. *Sed quaere.* Substantive limitations will affect an employer's initiative as to the grounds upon which he can dismiss but they cannot, it is submitted, affect his response by way of dismissal where the initiative to terminate, so to speak, comes from the employee, i.e., where the latter is guilty of repudiatory breach. In other words, if an employee is appointed, say, for life dismissible only for misconduct, there should be a presumption against his dismissal for any other reason, such as redundancy. But, whatever substantive limitations are found in his contract, if an employee behaves in a way that is seriously inconsistent with the contract, if he is guilty, e.g., of gross misconduct, he should not be able to complain if his employer reacts by summarily dismissing him and the courts would be highly unlikely to treat an employer as having restricted that fundamental power. The general principle may be stated thus: if dismissal can be justified only on impermissible substantive grounds, and is not otherwise a lawful summary dismissal, an ordinary employee will be entitled to claim damages for breach.[90]

(2) *Office-holders and special category employees*

Subject to what has been said in relation to an implied term of constitutional fairness, office-holders and persons whose employment is public or is regulated by statute enjoy greater legal protection than ordinary employees[91] against wrongful termination of employment. Above all, the distinction is relevant to the application of natural justice. Lord Wilberforce observed in *Malloch v. Aberdeen Corporation*[92]

'One may accept that if there are relationships in which all requirements of the observance of rules of natural justice are

90. *Acklam v. Sentinel Insurance Co. Ltd.* [1959] 2 *Lloyd's Rep.* 683, 689. An interesting case in this regard is *McClelland v. N.I. General Health Services Board* [1957] 1 WLR 594 which involved employment of a public rather than a private nature. It represents a significant extension of the scope of such cases from procedural to substantive questions.

91. Contrast the position of office-holders, etc., under the Unfair Dismissals Act, 1977 (s. 1) which is far less secure.

92. [1971] 2 All E.R. 1278 at 1294. See S. A. de Smith, *op. cit.,* fn. 20 *ante,* 228. Contrast *Vidyodaya University of Ceylon v. Silva* [1964] 3 All E.R. 865 (P.C.) which Lord Wilberforce in *Malloch* said would not be followed for purposes of English or Scottish law; and *Barber v. Manchester Regional Hospital Board* [1958] 1 All E.R. 322.

excluded (and I do not wish to assume that this is inevitably so) these must be confined to what have been called "pure master and servant" cases, which I take to mean cases in which there is no element of public employment or service, no support by statute, nothing in the nature of an office or a status which is capable of protection. If any of these elements exist, then, in my opinion, whatever the terminology used, and even though in some *inter partes* aspects the relationship may be called that of master and servant, there may be essential procedural requirements to be observed, and failure to observe them may result in dismissal being declared to be void.'

Natural and Constitutional Justice

In Ireland the idea became popular over the last decade that natural justice was subsumed under a broader heading of 'constitutional justice'. Superficially it was an attractive notion, not least because it applied to all workers irrespective of their status. In time, however, the concept has been shown to offer nothing that a normal interpretation of the Constitution does not already provide. Constitutional justice was first mooted by Walsh J. in *McDonald v. Bord na gCon*[93] where he gave it as his view that

'In the context of the Constitution, natural justice might be more appropriately termed constitutional justice, and must be understood to import more than the two well-established principles that no man shall be a judge in his own cause and *audi alteram partem.*'

There has to be a constitutional context before constitutional justice becomes applicable. It is precisely this requirement which has given the quietus to 'constitutional justice'. In *The State (Gleeson) v. Minister for Defence*[94] Henchy and Kenny JJ. (Supreme Court) sought to distinguish between natural and constitutional justice. Because of the wide scope of constitutional guarantees, whatever value 'constitutional justice' may have as a term of generic connotation, Judge Henchy looked upon a plea of a denial of constitutional justice as lacking the concreteness and particularity necessary to identify and bring into focus the precise constitutional issue being raised.[95] The necessary implementation of express or implied constitutional guarantees meant that decisional acts or procedures might be

93. [1965] IR 217, 242. See, also, *East Donegal Coop. Ltd. v. A-G* [1970] IR 317, 104 ITLR 81 and *Glover v. BLN Ltd.* [1973] IR 388.
94. [1976] IR 280.
95. At 295.

impugned for a wide variety of reasons depending on the circumstances of the case. Henchy J pointed out that to plead a denial of constitutional justice it was necessary to prove

> '(1) the application in the circumstances of the case of a specified constitutional right, either express or implied; (2) that the decision or decisional process in question has infringed that right; and (3) that the plaintiff stands aggrieved by that infringement.'[96]

Kenny J. rejected counsel's use of 'natural' and 'constitutional' justice as though they were synonymous. He too stressed the need for a constitutional context before constitutional justice may apply. In recent cases, the courts have tended to rely on natural justice to the exclusion of constitutional justice. The latter has not been pleaded in its own right. Inasmuch as the various components of the plea of lack of constitutional justice are already well established (there is no difference, e.g., between alleging breach of a specific constitutional right and denial of constitutional justice as outlined by Henchy J.) the concept appears to be redundant.[97] The two basic tenets of natural justice and their scope will now be examined.

(i) *Audi alteram partem*

The maxim[98] implies that no judicial or quasi-judicial decision may be taken without giving the party affected an opportunity of stating his case and of being heard in his own defence. A right to be heard and to defend oneself is illusory without time to prepare a defence and knowledge of the case to be met. What is sufficient notice will vary with the facts as will the detail which must be given of the case to be met. Usually a party claiming he has been denied natural justice will rely on the inadequacy of the notice he has received, whether as to the details of the case he is to answer, or as to time, so that he is unable to prepare his defence satisfactorily. The tendency of the courts today is to extend rather than restrict the application of the rule. An infringement or threatened infringement of some known right, constitutional, proprietary, contractual or personal, is always a *sine qua non* for the application of the rule. Most Irish cases concern workers whose employment is regulated by statute. These will be examined first.

96. *Ibid.*
97. See J. M. Kelly: *The Irish Constitution,* 190.
98. As to its origins in the common law see J. M. Kelly: 'Audi Alteram Partem' (1964) 9 *Natural Law Forum* 103. For application of natural justice in broad sphere of administration, where an administrative organ is bound to act judicially, see J. M. Kelly: *op. cit. supra,* 186.

(a) *Employees governed by statute*

'Elementary justice' requires that a person be given express notice of a tribunal about to sit, to one's knowledge, to determine whether or not to put an end to one's career, as Mr. Justice Gavan Duffy sagely remarked in *Maunsell v. Minister for Education and the Very Rev. Canon Breen.*[99] The principle applied even where the person affected had no merits; more significantly, it applied even though a statutory enactment did not seem to have contemplated notice and it applied to everybody having authority to adjudicate upon matters involving civil consequences to individuals.[100] In *Maunsell's* case, the plaintiff brought an action against the Minister for Education and the manager of his school as his salary had been withdrawn after a certain date because of a fall in the average attendance of pupils below a prescribed minimum.[101] On a construction of the relevant statutory regulation, he succeeded in getting a declaration that his salary had not been lawfully withdrawn. He had never been told by or on behalf of the Department of Education that he had a case to meet upon specific grounds, nor that the Department wished to have his answer to that case, if he had any answer to make, before coming to a decision.

Later cases have made it abundantly clear that, where employment is regulated by statute, strict adherence to the express terms of the Act is not necessarily sufficient. In Britain, not every employee whose terms are regulated by statute can enjoy the benefit of natural justice and it is difficult to predict the category into which a worker will be placed.[102] Sometimes, a worker is better off if his position is not spelled out in the statute because, among other things:

---

99. [1940] IR 213, 234.

100. The leading English cases at the time were cited by Gavan Duffy J. as representing a law equally well settled in Ireland, viz., *Capel v. Child* 2 C & J 558, 577; *Wood v. Woad* L.R. 9 Ex. 190, 196; *Smith v. The Queen* 3 A.C. 614. The principle, according to the judge, could not be more tersely expressed than in the lines of Seneca:

> *Quicunque aliquid statuerit, parte inauditâ alterâ,*
> *Aequum licet statuerit, haud aequus fuerit.*

> (*Medea* 199-200)

> 'Whosoever would determine anything, without having
>   heard the other of the two sides,
> Even though he might give a just determination, would
>   still not be just'.

See, too, the later case of *Malloch v. Aberdeen Corporation* [1971] 2 All E.R. 1278.

101. Contrary to Rule 82, subrule 1, of the Rules and Regulations for National Schools under the Department of Education, 1932.

102. See, e.g., *Vidyodaya University of Ceylon v. Silva,* fn. 92 *ante.*

'. . . the courts will not fly in the face of a clearly evinced parliamentary intention to exclude the operation of |natural justice|'.[103]

Moreover, where there is room for manoeuvre because a statute is ambiguously silent on the question of natural justice, the courts will generally show circumspection before insisting on the interpolation of judicial-type procedures.[104] Paradoxically, therefore, where there are no positive words in a statute requiring that a party shall be heard, this may leave more scope for the implication of fairness and

'. . . the justice of the common law shall supply the omission of the legislature.'[105]

Much will depend on the judge or judges concerned. In *Malloch, supra,* the House of Lords by a Celtic majority of 3:2[106] implied that natural justice should be observed in a statutory context where it was not specifically required, because the statutory form of protection invoked by the dismissed employee would have been less effective if it did not carry with it a right to be heard.

In Ireland the Constitution is responsible for moulding this area of the law. The courts operate a presumption of constitutionality in relation to legislation and, under the so-called 'double construction rule', where two constructions of an Act are possible, one which is constitutional, the other unconstitutional, the courts presume that the Oireachtas intended the constitutional construction to prevail: *McDonald v. Bord na gCon.*[107] Of considerable significance to the application of natural justice is the fact that

'. . . the presumption of constitutionality is not only the presumption that the constitutional interpretation or construction is the one intended by the Oireachtas but also that the Oireachtas intended that proceedings, procedures, discretions and adjudications which are permitted, provided for, or

---

103. *Op. cit.,* fn. 20 *ante,* 179.

104. *Ibid.* For a stimulating and informative account of some contexts in which judicial procedures would be inappropriate see G. Ganz: *Administrative Procedures.*

105. *Cooper v. Wandsworth Board of Works* (1863) 14 CB (NS) 180, 194 (*per* Byles J.); see *Pearlberg v. Varty* [1972] 2 All E.R. 6; *R. v. Liverpool Corp., ex p. Liverpool Taxi Operators Association* [1972] 2 Q.B. 299.

106. Reid, Wilberforce L.JJ. and Lord Simon of Glaisdale; Lord Morris of Borth-y-Gest and Lord Guest dissenting.

107. [1965] I.R. 217; see further, J. O'Reilly and M. Redmond: *Cases and Materials on the Irish Constitution,* 237.

prescribed by Act of the Oireachtas are to be conducted in accordance with the principles of constitutional justice.'[108]

Where, therefore, substantive grounds for dismissal are laid down in legislation, a person cannot be discharged on the basis of any of these without first having been notified of the reason or reasons for the intended dismissal and being allowed to speak in his own defence: *The State (Gleeson) v. Minister for Defence.*[109] Gleeson, a member of the Defence Forces, who had been enlisted for a statutory period of 3 years, was sent a certificate of discharge which gave 'His services being no longer required' as the reason for his discharge. His military conduct was categorised as 'unsatisfactory'. Later it was conceded this should have read 'fair'. The discharge of a man from the permanent Defence Forces is allowed for 'prescribed reasons'.[110] There are twenty-four such reasons set out in the Defence Forces Regulations.[111] One of these, used in Gleeson's case, applied to 'a man whose discharge is clearly desirable in the interests of the services and in whose case no other reason for discharge is applicable.[112] The Supreme Court held that Gleeson's discharge was invalid because there had been a breach of natural justice. He should have been given an opportunity of being heard before being discharged. The plaintiff

'was never informed of the reason for his discharge until after he had actually been discharged; and he was given no information as to the facts or findings relied on to support that reason until the affidavits made on behalf of the respondent Minister were filed in the . . . proceedings.'[113]

The Court issued a salutary reminder that the rules of natural justice are not absolute. 'Other cases', said Judge Henchy,

'will depend on their own circumstances, including whether the

---

108. *East Donegal Co-Op. Livestock Mart Ltd. v. A-G* [1970] I.R. 317, 341 *per* Walsh J.

109. [1976] I.R. 280, distinguished in *The State (Duffy) v. Minister for Defence (Supreme Court unreported, 9 May 1979).*

110. Section 73 of the Defence Act, 1954.

111. Article 10, para. 58.

112. Para. 58(r): the sub-par. provides that before a person's commanding officer could validly have directed his discharge for this reason, it was necessary that the prosecutor's discharge should be clearly desirable in the interests of the service, and that none of the other twenty-three reasons could be said to be applicable. The other twenty-three reasons cover a wide variety.

113. At 295-'6.

person discharged has, by delay, acquiescence or other conduct, lost his right to relief".[114]

Where discretionary powers as to dismissal are laid down under statute, their exercise must conform to the standards of fairness and of natural justice. For instance, the Garda Síochána Disciplinary Regulations 1971[115] made by the Minister for Justice pursuant to the Police Forces (Amalgam.) Act, 1925, s. 14, provide that, notwithstanding anything in the Regulations, the Commissioner of the Garda Síochána may dismiss any member, not higher than the rank of Inspector, whom he considers unfit for retention in the Force. Dismissal under Regulation 34 requires the consent of the Minister for Justice and may be exercised only in certain cases.[116] An opportunity of advancing reasons to the Commissioner against the proposed dismissal is provided by the same Regulation. In *Hogan v. Minister for Justice, Garvey and Others*[117] the plaintiff was purportedly dismissed pursuant to the Regulations of 1971. He had allegedly committed a breach of discipline by reason of his attendance at and taking part in a demonstration organised by Sinn Féin, Kevin Street. Hogan was suspended prior to dismissal under Regulation 34 of the Disciplinary Regulations. The Commissioner of the Garda Síochána sent a note to the plaintiff stating that he considered him unfit for retention in the Force and that he proposed, subject to the consent of the Minister for Justice, to dismiss him. He went on to tell the plaintiff that he intended to set up a Special Inquiry to give him an opportunity of advancing reasons against his proposed dismissal. Hogan submitted, *inter alia,* that Regulation 34 was repugnant to the Constitution because it failed to respect his personal rights and his rights under natural justice. In the High Court, Hamilton J. held that the plaintiff did not, under the Constitution or by statute, have the right to remain in office as a member of the

114. At 297.
115. Garda Síochána (Discipline) Regulations, 1971 (S.I. no. 316 of 1971). Regulations 8 to 12 of these Regulations deal with investigation of alleged breaches of discipline by members of the Garda Síochána, the manner in which it is to be conducted, the information to be given to the member concerned, the procedure to be followed at the Board of Inquiry, the submission of a report to the Commissioner, the powers of the Commissioner; they also provide for the right of appeal to the Board constituted in accordance with the provisions of the said Regulations.
116. Where the Commissioner is not in any doubt as to the material facts and (a) the relevant breach of discipline is of such gravity that the Commissioner has decided the facts and breach merit a dismissal and that the holding of an inquiry could not affect his decision; (b) where the disclosure of facts relating to the breach of discipline would, in the opinion of the Commissioner, be liable to affect the security of the State or to do serious and unjustifiable damage to the rights of some other person or to have other similar grave consequences.
117. High Court unreported, 8 September 1976.

Garda Síochána. He could remain in such office, however, until it was terminated in accordance with the relevant Regulations, statutory procedures and the rules of natural justice. The power given to the Commissioner under Regulation 34 was not absolute, unqualified or arbitrary. It could only be exercised by the Commissioner in specified instances, fairly, judicially, and in accordance with the principles of natural justice.[118] The judge carefully considered the alleged notice of dismissal. Taking it as a whole, he concluded that it did not in fact purport to dismiss the plaintiff from the Force:

> 'It is a badly drafted document designed to comply with Regulation 34 and to start in motion the procedure which might ultimately lead to the exercise of [the Commissioner's] powers under the said Regulation'.[119]

As the notice did not give Hogan the essential or any facts or findings alleged to constitute the reason for his proposed discharge, Hamilton J. held that Hogan had not been given a reasonable opportunity of presenting a response.[120]

(b) *Offices held at will or pleasure*

In Britain, if an office is held at the will and pleasure of the Crown, it appears that a person who holds such office is not entitled to natural justice before being removed.[121] Older judicial authorities in the main exemplify or are derived from the concept in British constitutional theory that the King can do no wrong and that offices held at royal pleasure are outside the reach of natural justice. Irish cases in the nineteenth and early twentieth century endorsed this view.[122] However, the Supreme Court recently emphasised that:

> 'Judicial precedents resting on [a theory of immunity and of executive absolutism] are of little value today, particularly in a State such as this where constitutional guarantees compel the

118. At 23. See *East Donegal Co-Op. Livestock Mart Co. Ltd. v. A-G.* [1970] I.R. 344, p. 72 above, fn. 108.

119. At 25.

120. The judge held that Hogan, before the special inquiry, was entitled to be given (a) full notice of the grounds upon which the Commissioner considered him unfit for retention as a member of the Garda Síochána; (b) full notice of the essential facts and findings alleged to constitute the reason for so considering and (c) particulars of the alleged breach of discipline.

121. *R. v. Darlington School Governors* (1844) 6 QB 682, *Ridge v. Baldwin* [1963] AC 40.

122. See, e.g., *Darley v. The Queen* (1846) 12 C1 & F 520: *Reg (Fitzmaurice) v. Neligan* (1884) 14 L.R. Ir. 149: *Reg (Riall) v. Bayly* [1898] 2 I.R. 335: *R (Jacob) v. Blaney* [1901] 2 I.R. 93: *R (McMorrow) v. Fitzpatrick* [1918] 2 I.R. 103.

recognition of personal fundamental rights which prior to the Constitution could have been overborne by theories of executive prerogative or public policy. It has to be remembered also that the pre-Constitution common law, like the pre-Constitution statute law, survives only to the extent that it is consistent with constitutional requirements; and to satisfy that test it must, where necessary, be modified or adapted in such a way as will fit it into the constitutional scheme of things.'[123]

The Constitution enters any inquiry as to whether, under the common law as it is understood today, the holder of an office at will or pleasure may claim he is entitled to natural justice before being removed. The courts will not deny to citizens the shield against injustice which constitutional guarantees are intended to provide. *Garvey v. Ireland and Others*[124] illustrates the extent to which this principle applies even where state security and matters of the gravest national interest may be concerned.

In January, 1978, Garvey, the Commissioner of the Garda Síochána, was called upon to resign by the Government. He declined to do so, whereupon the Government purported to remove him the same day without notice. The Commissioner brought proceedings for wrongful dismissal. In its defence the Government relied on the Police Forces (Amalgam.) Act, 1925, which provides that the Commissioner of the Garda Síochána may be removed at any time by the Executive Council (now the Government).[125] By a 4:1 majority,[126] the Supreme Court held that the Police Forces (Amalgam.) Act, 1925, did not empower the Government to terminate the office of Commissioner of the Garda Síochána at any time without giving reasons

123. *Garvey v. Ireland and Others* [1981] I.R. 75, 99 *per* Henchy J. In general on 'Dismissal at Pleasure' see G. Ganz: 'Public Law Principles Applicable to Dismissal from Employment' (1967) 30 MLR 288, 292.

124. *Supra.*

125. The Act was first employed in 1925, when Superintendent Bill Geary of Kilrush, Co. Clare, was dismissed by the Government after allegations that he had passed information to the local I.R.A. commander, Mr. T. J. Ryan. The Act was again invoked in 1933, when the de Valera administration decided to dismiss the then Commissioner, Gen. Eoin O'Duffy, and to replace him with Colonel Eamonn Broy. When questioned in Dáil Éireann about the dismissal, Mr. de Valera said he was not obliged to give any explanation. It was the prerogative of the Government to dismiss any Government Commissioner in whom they did not have full confidence. He was pressed by Mr. W. T. Cosgrave as to whether the new Commissioner had any quality which O'Duffy lacked. Mr. de Valera replied simply: 'Yes. He was not Commissioner of Police under the previous Government'. After the Supreme Court decision in *Garvey,* the Oireachtas passed the Garda Síochána Act, 1979, validating retrospectively every act done by Mr. Garvey's appointed successor in office, from the date of his appointment to 14 May, 1979, the date of the former Commissioner's resignation.

126. O'Higgins C.J., Henchy, Parke, Griffin JJ., Kenny J. diss.

and affording him an opportunity of making representations. The Chief Justice emphasised that the position of Commissioner was not an office tenable merely at pleasure. The Act of 1925 was continued in force in 1937, the date of the new Constitution, only to the extent that it was not inconsistent with the Constitution. Under Article 40, s. 3, sub-s. 1, fair and just procedures must be extended to all whose rights are affected by the decisions of others. According to Judge Henchy:

> 'An office such as this, which provides its holder with his livelihood, and in which he may reasonably hope to qualify for honourable retirement, is such an integral part of what goes to make up his dignity and freedom, that his removal from it should have attached to it at least the justification of a stated and examinable reason.'

The reason for a proposed dismissal, in Judge Henchy's view, need not always be specific or particularised.[127] It will usually be sufficient if an indication is given in general terms as to the ground upon which the Government proposes to exercise its discretion, for example, because of the Commissioner's ill-health, to improve the efficiency of the Force, or because the Commissioner has lost the confidence of the Government. If the given reason is specific misconduct, the Commissioner should be accorded an opportunity of dealing adequately with the complaint. Judge Henchy did not agree that a general reason would be of little or no use. It would enable the Commissioner to know the area of dissatisfaction and accordingly to address representations to the Government.

The principles enunciated by the Supreme Court in *Garvey* are not confined, it is clear, to those who hold office at the will or pleasure of the Government but extend to all office-holders whose employment may be terminated at pleasure.

(c) *The scope of audi alteram partem*

The law regarding the hearing of charges before domestic tribunals was summarised by Budd J. in *Flynn's* case:[128]

> 'The person accused must be informed clearly of that with which he is charged. He must then get a fair hearing. This does

127. Contrast *Sloan v. General Medical Council* [1970] 1 W.L.R. 1130. It is clear, that although the reason given at the time of dismissal need not be the real reason, an employer must have been aware of its existence at the time: *Cox v. E.S.B.* (1945) *Ir. Jur. Rep.* 58. See, too, *Kenealy v. The Mayor, Aldermen and Burgesses of the Borough of Kilkenny* [1905] 2 I.R. 167.

128. (1955) 89 ILTR 46.

not mean necessarily such a hearing as he would get in a court of law. It means that he will be treated fairly according to our ordinary standards of fair play. He must get a fair opportunity of refuting the charge. When I speak of a fair hearing I mean a hearing that is fair having regard to the nature of any agreement or contract which he may have entered into as regards the nature of the hearing. He may, for example, have agreed that the charge shall be determined on written submissions. If so, he cannot complain of any unfairness if the Tribunal does not hear oral evidence.'

With regard to the hearing before a tribunal, and the procedure to be adopted, if there are rules and regulations the court will see that these have been observed. If these rules and regulations appear to involve a contracting out of the requirements of natural justice, the courts will apply the usual tests as to waiver.[129] Apart from that, the tribunal is master of its own procedure and is not bound by the rules of evidence:

'The court will not, as a general rule, interfere with [a tribunal's] decision unless it be one where the decision is one come to *mala fide*; see *Dawkin v. Antrobus*.[130] It does not matter in the least that the court would have come to a different decision so long as the decision is honest.'[131]

It may be contended in particular circumstances that a hearing would make no difference to the plaintiff's case. In *Glover v. B.L.N. Ltd.*,[132] Judge Walsh unreservedly rejected this proposition:

'The obligation to give a fair hearing to the guilty is just as great as the obligation to give a fair hearing to the innocent.'[133]

Perhaps the most tempting situation in which to deny a right to a hearing is where it seems there is no answer to a charge because the alleged wrongdoer was caught in *flagrante delicto*. In the British case of *Ridge v. Baldwin*,[134] Streatfield J. succumbed to this temptation at

129. See page 38, chapter two *ante*.
130. 17 Ch. D. 115.
131. Budd J. recommended the judgment of Lord Wright in *General Medical Council v. Spackman* [1943] A.C. 627 where he ably summarises the case law on domestic tribunals up to the date of that case.
132. [1973] I.R. 388. See, too, *Glynn v. Keele University* [1971] 1 WLR 487, and D. H. Clarke: 'Natural Justice — Shadow or Substance' (1975) *Public Law* 20.
133. At 429.
134. [1961] 2 W.L.R. 1054. See A. L. Goodhart: 'Ridge v. Baldwin: Administration and Natural Justice' (1964) 80 L.Q.R. 105.

first instance when he held a chief constable had no right to be heard by his watch committee since at the Central Criminal Court for the purposes of his trial he had convicted himself of unfitness to hold the office of Chief Constable. He had been dismissed without a hearing by his watch committee after his conduct had been the subject of adverse comment by a judge in the course of a trial which concluded with the conviction of a number of members of his force on charges of corruption. He himself had been acquitted of the charges against him. The House of Lords heard the final appeal and held that even if the Chief Constable could not have hoped in the disciplinary proceedings to persuade the watch committee that he ought to be allowed to continue in his position the committee had a number of courses open to it. They might have followed the most lenient course if they had heard the Chief Constable. The justification for not excluding the right to a hearing was given by Megarry J. in *John v. Rees:*[135]

> ' "When something is obvious" (it may be said), "why force everybody to go through the tiresome waste of time involved in framing charges and giving an opportunity to be heard? The result is obvious from the start." Those who take this view do not, I think, do themselves justice. As everybody who has anything to do with the law well knows, the path of the law is strewn with examples of open and shut cases which, somehow, were not; of unanswerable charges which, in the event, were completely answered; of inexplicable conduct which was fully explained; of fixed and unalterable determinations that, by discussion, suffered a change. Nor are those with any knowledge of human nature who pause to think for a moment likely to underestimate the feelings of resentment of those who find that a decision against them had been made without their being afforded any opportunity to influence the course of events.'

(ii) *Nemo judex in re sua*

An important argument with regard to the constitution and nature of a tribunal is that its personnel should not include persons who are in effect prosecutors or who might be suspected of bias.[136] The *nemo*

---

135. [1969] 2 W.L.R. 1294, 1335.
136. The importance of this principle could hardly be more clearly illustrated than by the *dictum* in *Day v. Savadge* [1615] Hob. 85, 87: 'Even an Act of Parliament made against natural equity as to make a man judge in his own cause is void in itself for *iura naturae sunt immutabilia* and they are *leges legum.*' The common law distinguishes between two types of bias, that arising from financial interests and that arising from such causes as relationship to a party or witness. The

judex rule is very rarely invoked in the context of individual employment law largely because an important exception to the rule, namely,
the principle of necessity, is likely to apply. On the basis of this principle, a person who is *prima facie* disqualified for interest or bias may
be held competent and obliged to adjudicate if no other duly qualified
person is available or no other duly qualified tribunal can be constituted. Parties to a contract, or the members of an organisation may
agree, for example, that the power to dismiss shall be committed to a
person or an authority interested in the result. Even judges may be
obliged to hear a case in which they have an interest — although in
the famous case of *Martyn v. Stewart and Others*[137] where the
plaintiff complained of wrongful expulsion from his club, the judges
who heard the action comprised only those who were not themselves
members of the same club.[138] The principle of necessity will not be
mechanically applied if injustice would result, and in all cases the
courts are likely to scrutinise the actual proceedings being challenged.
The principle was applied in *Flynn v. G.N. Rly. Co. (Ire.) Ltd.*[139]
where the prosecutor reported to an official of the company, and
excused his absence from work on grounds of illness. He did not
produce a medical certificate. He was given one month's notice of
dismissal for failure to report on duty without prior notification. The
prosecutor's appeal against this notice was heard by another official
who affirmed the company's decision. He alleged that the case should
not have been heard by the first official as he had charged him and
could not be expected to act impartially in dismissing him. According
to Mr. Justice Budd, however, it would fly

---

latter type is relevant here. It has often been described as a challenge to favour. See,
Cottle v. Cottle [1939] 2 All E.R. 535; *Law v. Chartered Institute of Patent Agents*
[1919] 2 Ch. 276; *Leeson v. G.N.C.* (1889) 43 Ch. D. 366. British authorities on
the question of bias are few. They suggest that some judges believe there are different
tests laid down and that it is necessary to choose the correct one. In *R v. Barnsley
Licensing JJ.* [1960] 2 QB 167, 187 (see, too, *Metropolitan Properties v. Lannon*
[1969] 1 QB 577) Lord Devlin seemed to recognise the existence of two tests — (i)
that of a reasonable suspicion of bias and (ii) that of a real likelihood of bias, a test
which imposes a heavier burden of proof on the person making the allegation. In that
jurisdiction, all turns in the end on the view the court takes of the facts. The judge
who says there is no real likelihood of bias will just as likely say there was no
reasonable suspicion of bias; a judge who is prepared to find a reasonable suspicion
of bias is hardly likely to deny a real likelihood of bias.

137. 1907, unreported.

138. Again, in *The State (Killian) v. Minister for Justice* [1954] IR 207, where
the validity of the appointment of judges since 1937 was in issue, the Court which
heard the case was specially composed of judges who had been appointed before that
date.

139. Fn. 128 *ante*.

'in the teeth of the machinery of the negotiation rules to suggest that [the same man] could not hear the charge.'

The rules provided that the charge should be heard by an 'appropriate officer' and he was satisfied the first official was such an officer. He must act impartially and without bias, but the judge saw no reason for thinking he was in any way biased in an unfair sense:

'Of course he knew of the plaintiff's record, but so must any master, and I am satisfied he did not allow that to blind his judgment in the matter at issue.'[140]

One of the very few occasions on which the rule against bias was discussed in its more general application was *McGrath and Ó Ruairc v. The Trustees of the College of Maynooth.*[141] The plaintiffs, while Roman Catholic priests, had been appointed to teach in Maynooth College (which is a National Seminary). On becoming laicised, they were dismissed. One limb of their argument was that the decisions to remove them from office were arrived at by the Trustees of the College (seventeen Bishops) long before the meeting of the Trustees at which the actual resolutions were passed. Some items of evidence allegedly indicated a predetermination by the defendants, before the plaintiffs were either charged or heard, to remove them from Maynooth. It was contended that the entire proceedings against the plaintiffs were contrary to the principles of natural justice and therefore invalid. In the Chief Justice's view, this submission, 'even if factually correct' did not entitle the plaintiffs to succeed:

'A preconceived view as to what action should be taken or as to what the result ought to be, does not invalidate administrative action of the kind, provided the body concerned is willing to hear what may be said by the party charged and affords to him a full and real opportunity of making his defence.'

It is unfortunate that the distinction was not made between having a crystallised point of view about certain issues and appearing to have judged the facts or merits of a particular case prior to a scheduled hearing. The distinction is one between administrative expertise and prejudgment. The latter, it is suggested, should always be a fatal flaw in any decision.

A final point, which applies to both tenets of natural justice, relates

---

140. At 55. *King v. University of Saskatchewan* [1969] 6 DLR (31) 120 shows the courts taking a sympathetic and realistic approach to the difficulties of institutions in organising appeal procedures.

141. Supreme Court unreported, 1 October 1979, see chapter two, page 34, fn. 21 *ante*.

to procedures allowing for appeal. If a two-tier procedure is laid down by regulations, and an error occurs in the second tier, that of review, the entire proceedings are not thereby invalidated. The decision reached upon the first tier of investigation will stand: *The State (Sheehan) v. McMahon and Others.*[142] The Supreme Court affirmed that:

> 'There is no reason why the error of the Appeal Tribunal in thinking that they had no jurisdiction to review should be held to invalidate what had gone before.'[143]

A liter, of course, if an error occurs at the first stage of the procedure: see *Leary v. National Union of Vehicle Builders*[144] where it was held that a failure to comply with the rules of natural justice at the initial hearing cannot be remedied by a proper hearing or appeal. While the Privy Council recently decided that this is not necessarily the case with every organisation, it suggested the principle should apply to trade unions: *Calvin v. Carr.*[145]

D. The Effect of Breach of the Employment Contract on the Concept of Termination at Common Law

The various ways in which an employment contract may be breached by an employer have been described in Parts B and C of this chapter. A crucial question remains. What is the precise effect of an employer's repudiatory breach on the contract of employment? Wrongful dismissal, as noted, constitutes dismissal in breach of contract. It involves a termination of the contract as well as of the relationship of employment. Does an employer's repudiatory conduct automatically terminate the contract, or if not, or if only on occasion, is termination dependent upon some further act or election by the injured party? These issues are complex but at the same time they are fundamental to an understanding of wrongful dismissal. Not only do they reveal much about the nature of the law's protection, and the principles upon which remedies for wrongful dismissal are based, they also highlight many of the inadequacies which bedevil the so-called contract model of employment. More than anything, they are

142. Supreme Court unreported, 25 October 1977.
143. The Supreme Court thought it scarcely conceivable, having regard to the admitted facts and the lightness of the penalty, that the Appeal Tribunal would do other than affirm the disciplinary action that had been taken. At the end of the day, therefore, Sheehan's limited success in his certiorari proceedings was likely to prove Pyrrhic.
144. [1971] Ch. 34.
145. [1979] 2 All E.R. 440.

significant in relation to statutory unfair dismissal. The latter is not treated as a concept with a special meaning but as one which stems from the ordinary common law of contract. The effect of contract doctrine on statutory unfair dimissal is fully discussed in chapter five below. The focus here is solely on termination at common law.

A basic problem arises because contractual repudiation cannot be clearly or consistently defined. Its meaning was explored in *Decro-Wall Practitioners Int. S.A. v. Practitioners in Marketing Ltd.*[146] wherein Sachs L.J. 'at the risk of being dubbed old-fashioned' said that, to constitute repudiation, the breach of contract must go 'to the root of the contract.'[147] Repudiation is frequently described in such terms. The employment is 'struck at fundamentally'[148] or there is a deliberate flouting of essential contractual conditions. It is a serious matter, not lightly to be inferred. Cheshire and Fifoot refer to the summary dismissal of an employee, founded upon his alleged breach, as affording an illustration of repudiation.[149] It is precisely where repudiation takes the form either of walking out or of dismissing that contention has arisen. There is little difficulty where, e.g., an employer wishing to continue the relationship of employment unilaterally insists upon a change in the terms of employment to which he is not contractually entitled. An employee then may either stay or go. If he decides to go, the contract is terminated as and when he leaves. Termination is elective. There is no question of the repudiatory breach itself automatically terminating the employment relationship. This, indeed, represents general contract theory. In the event of breach at common law, an injured party has the option of treating the contract as continuing or of regarding himself as discharged from any further obligations under the contract. But problems are manifold where repudiatory breach in the specific contract of employment takes the form of walking out or of dismissing, where, in a nutshell, the employment relationship is sundered.

Suppose, for instance, an employer has dismissed with inadequate notice (distinguish Cheshire and Fifoot's example of dismissal where the employee is in breach), has the employee so dismissed got an option to go or to stay or is his employment automatically terminated? Can he, in accordance with general contract theory, refuse to accept the repudiatory breach and turn up for work and, although not given work, claim his remuneration on the ground that he is ready

146. [1971] 1 WLR 361; [1971] 2 All E.R. 216.
147. At 227 (All E.R.).
148. *Laws v. London Chronicle Ltd.* [1959] 2 All E.R. 285, 287 *per* Evershed L.J.
149. 8th edition, 566.

and willing to do the work?[150] (There is no question as to enforcement of the contract in relation to the provision of work as an employee cannot claim specific performance of an employment contract.)[151] Until recently, the predominant view of the common law courts was that a special rule operated in the context of employment to the effect that repudiation in the form of wrongful dismissal unilaterally terminated the contract of employment without the need for its acceptance by the injured party.[152] It gradually became clear that, in the same way, wrongful repudiation by an employee automatically brought the employment contract to an end. In 1971, however, the tide began to turn. In *Decro-Wall Int. S.A.*,[153] above, Lord Justice Salmon expressed some misgivings as to whether a wrongful dismissal brings a contract of service to an end in law, 'although no doubt in practice it does'. Lord Justice Sachs[154] expressed a similar view. Both Lords Justice recognised, *obiter,* that a dismissed servant's remedy must lie only in damages and that he could not sue in debt for remuneration under the contract in respect of any period after his employment had actually ceased. The doubts expressed in this case became positive affirmations in *Thomas Marshall (Exports) Ltd. v. Guinle*[155] when Vice Chancellor Megarry held that a contract of personal service was no exception to the general rule that repudiation did not automatically discharge the contract. And in *Gunton v. Richmond upon Thames L.B.C.*[156] this approach of the common law was reconfirmed by the Court of Appeal. The majority of the Court (Buckley and Brightman L.JJ., Shaw L.J. diss.) held that the elective theory of termination applied to all forms of wrongful repudiation of the contract of employment, wrongful dismissal being no exception. The influence of this case is potentially great.

Lord Justice Buckley in *Gunton* recognised that there had been much judicial difference of opinion on the question whether wrongful dismissal of a servant puts an immediate end to the contract of service or whether such repudiation must be accepted in order to terminate the contract. He questioned why the doctrine should operate differently in the case of contracts of personal service from

150. Cf. *G.K.N. (Cwmbran) Ltd. v. Lloyd* [1972] ITR 160, 166 (NIRC); *Sanders v. Ernest A. Neale Ltd.* [1974] ITR 395; 400-'1 (NIRC).
151. See p. 87, chapter four *post.*
152. *Vine v. NDLB* [1956] 1 QB 658, 674; [1957] AC 488, 500; *Francis v. Kuala Lumpur Councillors* [1962] 1 WLR 1411, 1417; *Denmark Productions Ltd. v. Boscobel Productions Ltd.* [1969] 1 QB 186; *Sanders, supra.*
153. Fn. 146 *ante* at 369. See, too, *Hill v. C.A. Parsons Ltd.* [1972] 1 Ch. 305, generally regarded as an exceptional decision ([1975] ICR 351 *per* Roskill L.J.).
154. At 375.
155. [1978] IRLR 174.
156. [1980] ICR 755; see notes (1981) CLJ 33; (1981) ILJ 50.

the way in which it operates in respect of other contracts. In principle he saw no reason why there should be any difference. He rejected the argument commonly advanced in support of the automatic theory, namely, that the courts will not decree specific performance of a contract of personal service, on the basis that there are innumerable kinds of contract which the court would not order to be specifically enforced to which the doctrine would undoubtedly apply.[157] In the absence of special circumstances, however, he observed that a wrongfully dismissed employee has no option but to accept the employer's repudiation of contract. Consequently, in the absence of special circumstances, Buckley L.J. was of the view that the court in a case of wrongful dismissal should easily infer that the innocent party has accepted the guilty party's repudiation. In any event, if a dismissed employee sues for damages for wrongful dismissal, he must by so doing accept the employer's repudiation of the contract.[158] The majority in *Gunton* argued that either party may have a legitimate interest in keeping certain aspects of the contractual relationship alive. For example, an employer may wish to enforce a restrictive covenant (cf. *Guinle's* case, above) or an arbitration clause. The employee, as in *Gunton*, may wish to rely upon a disciplinary procedure, or he may wish to prolong the duration of his contract for the purposes of qualifying as to continuity of employment under unfair dismissals legislation. Upon closer examination, however, only where an employer tries to speed up the effective date of termination, thereby precluding statutory terms, is it of the essence that an employee should be free to 'accept' repudiation. It is unnecessary otherwise to pray in aid 'incidental or collateral terms' (*per* Buckley L.J.) as a justification for wanting to keep the contract on foot. In ordinary contract cases, arbitration and limitation of damages clauses continue to exist after the main contract has been terminated and there is no reason why restrictive covenants or disciplinary procedures should not likewise be kept alive.

This last proposition may be asserted with particular confidence in the wake of the House of Lord's decision in *Photo Productions Ltd. v. Securicor Ltd.*[159] The case concerned fundamental breach of a commercial security contract but the broad statements of principle enunciated therein are of general application in the law of contract.

---

157. In substance, this was the rationale of Shaw L.J.'s disagreement with the reasoning of the majority in *Gunton*.

158. Of course, if the contract persists after a wrongful repudiation, the wage-work bargain will no longer be a part of it, so the employee will not be able to claim an agreed sum of wages, but only damages for breach of contract.

159. [1980] 2 WLR 283; [1980] 1 All E.R. 556; See L. Melville: 'The Nature of Fundamental Breach' (1980) 130 NLJ 307; [1980] CLJ 252; (1980) MLR 567; (1980) LQR 324.

For puspoes of employment law, they appear to go one step further than *Gunton* in relation to the meaning of contractual termination (although the difference may be no more than semantic). Certain it is, however, that great caution must be exercised from now on in relation to the meaning of 'termination'. A contract can never be said to be 'terminated' in the strict meaning of the word. Rather, when one speaks of termination:

> '. . . what is meant is no more than that the innocent party or, in some cases, both parties are excused from further performance.'

Lord Diplock developed these thoughts further in *Photo Productions Ltd.* and, according to Lord Wilberforce and the other Law Lords, they 'state correctly the modern law of contract in the relevant respects'.[160] His speech, therefore, is the most instructive. According to Lord Diplock:

> 'every failure to perform a primary obligation is a breach of contract, but the unfulfilled obligations of each party remain unchanged [here he was referring to what is known as a breach of warranty] except in two cases and these are:
>
> (a) fundamental breach: this is where the event resulting from the failure by one party to perform a primary obligation has the effect of depriving the other party of substantially the whole benefit which it was the intention of the parties that he should obtain, in which case the party not in default may elect to put an end to all primary obligations of both parties remaining unperformed;
>
> (b) breach of condition: this is where the contracting parties have agreed, whether by express terms or by implication of law, that any failure by one party to perform a particular primary obligation . . . irrespective of the gravity of the event that has in fact resulted from the breach, shall entitle the other party to elect to put an end to all primary obligations of both parties remaining unperformed.'

Where the innocent party does elect to put an end to all the unperformed obligations of both parties the following principles apply:

> '(i) there is substituted by implication of law for the primary obligations of the party in default which remain unperformed, a

160. At 563 (All E.R.).

secondary obligation to pay monetary compensation to the
other party for the loss which he will sustain in the future in
consequence of such future non-performance [this his Lordship
called 'anticipatory secondary obligation'; in relation to statutory unfair dismissal the anticipatory secondary obligation is
supplied by Act of the Oireachtas and comprises the various
remedies provided thereunder] and

(ii) the unperformed primary obligations of the other party are
discharged.'

Confusion must be avoided in regard to the source of secondary
obligations. It is a mistake, said Lord Diplock, to use words such as
contractual 'rescission' or 'determination'. The contract is just as
much a source of secondary, as it is of primary obligations, even
though the effects of breach may arise by implication of law.[161]
Applying modern contract principles, then, a contract of employment can never be said to be 'terminated' as such. This operates as a
further gloss upon the elective theory of 'termination' in the event of
breach.

The clarification of general contract principles in *Photo Productions Ltd.* was much needed and worthwhile but it should not be
assumed that the common law boot can be applied to every foot
without discrimination. This is evident from *Gunton*. To apply the
general language of acceptance unreflectively to the contract of
employment as the Court of Appeal did in that case is to fail to appreciate the latter's relational, as distinct from its transactional, aspect
and to obscure the structure of the implied mutual undertakings
contained therein. The matter will not be further explored at this stage
but it will surface once more in chapter five where various
interpretative difficulties under the Unfair Dismissals Act, 1977, are
attributed to the influence and the ambiguity of the common law. In
the concluding chapter of this work the contract model will be looked
at afresh, to see whether it is capable of being so tailored as to safeguard employment interests.

---

161. At 566 (*loc. cit.*).

CHAPTER FOUR

Remedies for Wrongful Dismissal

A. Ordinary Employees

A breach of contract by one party confers upon the other, as of right, a power to sue for damages.[1] Where an employer wrongfully dismisses an employee and thereby discharges the contract by his breach, the remedy of damages is by far the most usual remedy given by the common law, or by the rules of equity, for the protection of an employee's job security.[2] A claim for damages for wrongful dismissal must be brought within six years.[3] In practice, it is the only remedy for ordinary employees because specific performance, injunctions or declarations of invalidity of dismissal will not normally be allowed. Equally important in practice is the high cost of bringing civil proceedings. For this reason, a wrongful dismissal will often go unremedied at common law.

(1) *Equitable remedies*

It is the contractual nature of the employment relationship which produces the result that damages are a wrongfully dismissed employee's only real option. To award equitable remedies, it is argued, would be a contradiction in terms as dismissal legally terminates both the contract and the relationship of employment. (This may be refuted, however, see chapter three, page 86). It is also maintained that equitable remedies are not available because of the general rule that the courts will not decree specific performance of contracts involving the performance of a personal service.[4] The court's refusal of equitable remedies to compel performance of a contract of employment applies both in relation to a refusal of orders

---

1. *Fray v. Voules* (1859) 1 E. & E. 839; *Marzetti v. Williams* (1830) 1 B. & Ad. 415. Some contracts must be viewed separately as they may incorporate usage or custom, e.g., seamen's contracts: cf. *Byrne v. Limerick Steamship Co. Ltd.* |1946| I.R. 138; (1946) 80 I.L.T.R. 142 (seaman's maritime lien upon the ship enforceable against it for recovery of wages).
2. For a good exposition of English law see M. R. Freedland, *The Contract of Employment*, 244-272; also *McGregor on Damages* paras. 883-904. P. Lehain: 'Calculating the quantum of Damages for Wrongful Dismissal' (1979) 129 NLJ 887. On Irish law, see P. Connolly: 'Damages in Tort and in Breach of Contract' (1975) Lecture no. 87, Society of Young Solicitors.
3. Section 11(1) Statute of Limitations, 1957. This limitation does not apply to specific performance or equitable remedies.
4. *Whitwood Chemical Co. v. Hardman* [1891] 2 Ch. 416, 426 (CA).

of reinstatement directed against an employer and to a refusal to work directed against an employee. Historically, objections to such orders were not operative before the 19th century.[5] The rationale behind the refusal of the courts of equity to order specific performance of an obligation to perform personal services lies in the principle that equity will not make an order the performance of which it cannot effectively supervise or where performance would require constant supervision.[6] To force one person to work for another, it is said, would be to turn contracts of service into contracts of slavery.[7] The status of a former employee may also be relevant. In *Shiels v. Clery & Co. (1941) Ltd.*,[8] for example, the High Court was 'not prepared to thrust upon the company a servant [managing director] whom they did not wish to employ'.

Refusal of equitable remedies has been justified on a further ground, namely, lack of mutuality. An order of reinstatement cannot be obtained against an employer because, it is contended, specific performance will not lie to compel the rendering of personal services.[9] But the argument as to mutuality should be approached with caution in relation to the contract of employment. The merits of granting specific performance against an employee may well be very different from those of granting reinstatement to an employee. To treat the two arguments as if they stood or fell together imposes what Freedland has described as a formal equality between the parties which is far removed from the realities of their relationship.[10]

In *C. H. Giles & Co. Ltd. v. Morris*,[11] Megarry J. referred to the 'strong reluctance' of the courts to grant equitable remedies. In his view, such remedies were not refused as a rule and

> 'some day, perhaps, the courts will look again at the so-called rule that contracts for personal services or involving the continuous performance of services will not be specifically

---

5. See *Ball v. Coggs* (1710) 1 Bro. Parl. Cas. 140; and dicta of Sir John Leach V.C. thereon in *Adderly v. Dixon* (1824) 1 Simons & Stuart 607, 611; also *East India Co. v. Vincent* (1740) 2 Atkyns 83.

6. *Ryan v. Mutual Tontine Association* [1893] 1 Ch. 116.

7. Cf. *De Francesco v. Barnum* (1890) 45 Ch. D. 430, 438 *per* Fry L.J. But 'Fry and his fellow judges were clearly thinking in terms of a farmer or the master of a small workshop and their servants. In modern conditions it is hardly turning contracts of service into contracts of slavery to order the reinstatement of an engineer in a factory employing 5,000 people': G. de N. Clark: 'Remedies for Unjust Dismissal' PEP Broadsheet 518, June, 1970, 8.

8. High Court unreported, 13 October 1979.

9. *Page One Records Ltd. v. Britton* [1968] 1 WLR 157. See statutory endorsement of this in Britain: TULRA 1974, s. 16.

10. M. R. Freedland *op. cit.*, fn. 2 *ante*, 276.

11. [1972] 1 All E.R. 960; [1972] 1 WLR 307 (Ch. D.).

enforced. Such a rule is plainly not absolute and without exception, nor do I think that it can be based on any narrow consideration such as difficulties of constant superintendence of the court.'[12]

Proof that the so-called rule concerning refusal of specific performance is not absolute may be found in *Hill v. C. A. Parsons Ltd.*,[13] a case which has been described as 'highly exceptional'.[14] In *Hill*, a majority in the Court of Appeal granted an interlocutory injunction restraining an employer from dismissing an employee. Mutual confidence still existed between the parties and damages would not have been an adequate remedy particularly in view of the fact that the Industrial Relations Act, 1971, which gave employees the right not to be unfairly dismissed in the circumstances, was shortly to come into force.[15] The majority of the Court was required to, and did, deny the absolute standing of the rule of equity against injunctions of this kind. Thus Lord Denning M.R.:

'It may be said that by granting an injunction in such a case, the court is indirectly enforcing specifically a contract for personal services. So be it.'[16]

But the case has intruded only very slightly upon the established attitude of the courts towards compulsory reinstatement.

Sometimes (albeit in non-dismissal situations) the courts are willing to grant injunctions as against employees, restraining the breach of a contractual undertaking not to work for a rival employer. But, true to more established principles, they will not do so if the effect would be to drive the defendant 'either to starvation or to specific performance of the positive covenants'.[17] Likewise the courts will not grant an injunction where duties of a personal and fiduciary nature are con-

---

12. At 969 (All E.R.).

13. [1972], Ch. 305 (CA), (1972) 1 ILJ 37; (1972) 35 MLR 310; [1972] 30 CLJ 37 (notes).,

14. Soon afterwards, in *Chappell v. Times Newspapers Ltd.* [1975] ICR 145, *Hill's* case was so treated. It was also described as 'unusual, if not unique' by Sir John Donaldson in *Sanders v. Ernest A. Neale Ltd.* [1974] ICR 565, 571.

15. The Act did not give an unfairly dismissed employee any legal right to reinstatement. It simply provided for a tribunal to recommend re-engagement, or otherwise, compensation.

16. At 315A.

17. *Warner Bros. Pictures Inc. v. Nelson* [1937] 1 KB 209, 216 *per* Branson J. The defendant, Bette Davis, had contracted not to act in a film for any other company without the permission of the plaintiffs. An injunction was granted restraining her from doing so since she would not thereby be driven 'although she may be tempted' to perform her contract with the plaintiffs.

cerned and where at least one of the parties has lost confidence in the other.[18]

There are grounds for arguing that the equitable remedy of a declaration[19] should not be viewed in the same light as that of specific performance or injunctions, that it should be spared some of the court's 'strong reluctance'. A declaration that dismissal was null and void will not be granted in the case of an ordinary contract of employment.[20] But a declaration will lie to declare a breach of contract[21] and there would be no objection, it seems, to a declaration that dismissal was wrongful.[22] For practical reasons, this course of action is not adopted by ordinary employees, although it might be useful to seek a declaration as to breach where other rights might be affected,[23] or

---

18. *Page One Records Ltd. v. Britton* [1968] 1 WLR 157.

19. *Pace* Lord Morris of Borth-y-Gest who described the law in *Francis v. Municipal Councillors of Kuala Lumpur* [1962] 1 WLR 1411 (PC), 1417

> 'When there has been a purported termination of a contract of service, a declaration to the effect that the contract still subsists will rarely be made. This is a consequence of the general principle that the courts will not grant specific performance of contracts of service. Special circumstances will be required before such a declaration is made and its making will normally be in the discretion of the court.'

See, too, *Hill v. Parsons Ltd.* [1972] 1 Ch. 305 (CA) *per* Lord Denning and Sachs L.J. at 314 and 319.

20. *Vine v. NDLB* [1957] AC 488, 500 *per* Viscount Kilmuir L.C.

21. Zamir: *The Declaratory Judgment* 129-'37. See now *Gunton v. Richmond Upon Thames LBC* [1980] ICR 755; [1980] IRLR 321 in relation to breach of a procedural term in the contract of employment, discussed at chapter three, page 63 *ante*. A declaration as to a dismissed person's rights under a compromise agreement following personal injuries as a result of an accident which happened in the course of work was granted in *Kingston v. Irish Dunlop Co. Ltd.* [1969] IR 233. On declaratory relief, see *Rules of the Superior Courts,* Order 19, Rule 29 which derives from the Rules of 1877. This form of relief has been common to England and Ireland since the passing of the Judicature Acts. For a good general discussion of the background to the Rule and some judicial reactions to it see *Guaranty Trust Co. of New York v. Hannay & Co.* [1915] 2 KB 536, 568.

22. Barry J., in *Barber v. Manchester Regional Hospitals Board* [1958] 1 WLR 181, 194-'5, made it clear that a declaration would not be granted to the effect that the plaintiff's employment with the Board had never been validly determined. If, however, the plaintiff had sought a declaration that his employment had never been lawfully or rightly determined, such a declaration, if necessary, might have been made. These fine distinctions undoubtedly flow from the unavailability of specific performance.

23. As in *Taylor v. National Union of Seamen* [1967] 1 QBD 767 where the plaintiff's position as a member of his trade union and his prospects of a future career in the union were 'very seriously' affected by his wrongful dismissal. He was an official of the union concerned and had been dismissed for alleged insubordination. Ungoed-Thomas J (Ch. D.) held he 'should have the protection of a declaration'.

where an employer is guilty of repudiatory conduct which the employee is not willing to accept as terminating the contract.[24] To sue for damages in the latter circumstances would be tantamount to 'acceptance'; to seek an appropriate declaration would not. The essential point to stress is that to declare a purported dismissal wrongful would not lead to anything like 'a contract of slavery'. And since an employer can pay wages in lieu of notice a declaration would not require the employee to continue working with the employer in question (see *Stevenson v. United Road Transport Union*).[25]

The reservations outlined above in regard to equitable remedies have manifested themselves in unfair dismissals legislation. The primary remedies of reinstatement and re-engagement, if awarded in cases of unfair dismissal, cannot be enforced against an employer and in any event are awarded only in the very smallest proportion of cases. Once again, the importance of a constitutional jurisdiction comes to the fore. The possibility of obtaining 'whatever redress is appropriate in the circumstances',[26] e.g., a declaration that the purported dismissal of an ordinary employee is *ultra vires* the Constitution, hence invalid and of no effect, is all the more significant in the light of the common law's uncertainties.

(2) *Damages*

(i) *General principles on which damages are awarded for wrongful dismissal*

The rules governing compensation for termination of employment are fragmented and uncoordinated and it would be misleading to call them a system. The general principle underlying the assessment of damages in contract is that of *restitutio in integrum*. The courts have applied this principle restrictively both as to the heads of damages which may be considered and as to the assessment of damages under those heads. The underlying aim of the principle of *restitutio in integrum* is that of restoring the plaintiff to the position he would have

---

24. See chapter three, page 81, above. A declaration has not been sought in these circumstances to date. To do so might be important in order to establish that the innocent party has not deliberately aggravated his loss by 'sitting in the sun'.

25. [1977] ICR 893, 907 *per* Buckley L.J. See Elias, Wallington & Napier: *Labour Law Cases and Materials* 512. It should be added that there are some doubts as to whether an employer is entitled always to pay wages in lieu of notice. There are judicial authorities to the effect that such payment might well be contrary to the actual terms of a given contract; if this were so, a purported termination would be wrongful. This view is described and endorsed by M. R. Freedland: *The Contract of Employment*, 181.

26. *Glover v. BLN Ltd.* [1973] IR 388, *per* Walsh J. at 427.

been in had he not sustained the wrong.[27] The plaintiff is entitled to compensation for damage or loss suffered. Where damages for breach of contract are concerned it is not always easy to determine whether items of actual damage are sufficiently proximate or whether, as consequences of the breach, they are too remote to be the subject of damages. In this respect, as was noted in chapter one, the Irish courts[28] have accepted the principle of *Hadley v. Baxendale*,[29] which requires a plaintiff to prove either that the damage arose naturally from the breach or that it arose from special circumstances contemplated by the parties.

A basic ambiguity of *restitutio in integrum* in the context of contract is as between the two meanings of: (1) putting the plaintiff in the position he would have been in had he never made the contract, i.e., restoring the *status quo ante*; or (2) putting him in the position he would have been in if the contract had been duly performed. According to Fuller and Perdue,[30] it is possible to protect three kinds of interest:

(i) *the restitution interest* — the interest in compelling the defendant to disgorge value received when the defendant's promise was unfulfilled, i.e., the prevention of unjust enrichment;

(ii) *the reliance interest* — the interest in obtaining compensation from the defendant in respect of benefit lost, or of detriment incurred, in reliance upon his promise; and

(iii) *the expectation interest* — the interest in obtaining compensation from the defendant in respect of the benefit lost, or detriment incurred, as the result of non-fulfilment of the promises made by him.

The interpretation of *restitutio in integrum* adopted in the context of contract is that of protecting the expectation interest, and perhaps to a slight extent the reliance interest. Protection of the restitution

27. See A. I. Ogus: *The Law of Damages* 17-21; 282-'8; H. Street: *Principles of the Law of Damages* 3; M. R. Freedland, *op. cit.*, fn. 25 *ante* 245.

28. See *Irvine v. Midland Gt. W. Rly. (Ir.) Co.* (1879) 6 L.R. Ir. 55; *Parker v. Cathcart* (1866) 17 I.C.L.R. 778; *Boyd v. Fitt* (1863) 14 I.C.L.R. 43. In *Duffy v. Sutton* [1955] I.R. 248, Lavery and Kingsmill Moore JJ. in the Supreme Court assumed that the principle of *Hadley v. Baxendale* (fn. 29 *post*) governed the question of remoteness of damage.

29. (1854) 9 Exch. 341. See Sir Robin Cooke: 'Remoteness of Damage and Judicial Discretion' [1978] C.L.J. 288; C. Manchester: 'Remoteness of Damage — Contract and Tort reconciled?' (1978) 128 N.L.J. 113; R. G. Lawson: 'Damages — Some Recent Developments' parts I and II (1978) 128 N.L.J. 600, 627.

30. 'The Reliance Interest in Contract Damages' (1936) 46 Y.L.J. 52, 373, cited by Freedland, *op. cit.*, fn. 25 *ante*, 246.

interest is almost entirely relegated by common law to the sphere of quasi-contract.[31]

Where an employee is wrongfully dismissed he is entitled, subject to the rules on mitigation, to damages equivalent to the wages he would have earned under the contract from the date of dismissal to the end of the contract. The general principle applied by the courts to fixed term contracts recognises an employee's right to damages in respect of loss of employment for the remainder of the fixed term, subject only to the rules concerning mitigation of loss.[32] Thus, in *Glover v. B.L.N. Ltd.*,[33] the plaintiff was employed on a fixed term contract for five years. He was awarded damages *inter alia* for loss of salary over twenty months, the remainder period of his contract. For the more usual contract of indefinite length, Lord Denning M.R. described the law as to the measure of damages in *Hill v. Parsons Ltd.*[34]

> '[a servant] is left to his own remedy against the master for breach of the contract to continue the relationship for the contractual period. He gets damages for the time he would have served if he had been given proper notice, less, of course, anything he has, or ought to have earned in alternative employment. He does not get damages for the loss of expected benefits to which he had no contractual right.'

Limitations of damages in respect of loss of earnings to an employee's expectation interest, to the period of notice required for proper termination of the contract, is based upon a general principle that damages are to be assessed on the assumption that the defendant would have performed the contract in the manner least disadvantageous to himself. This was originally stated in England as a rule that

> 'where there are several ways in which the contract may be performed, that mode is adopted which is the least profitable to the plaintiff, and the least burthensome to the defendant.'[35]

It later appeared in the form that 'a defendant is not liable in damages

---

31. See, e.g., *O'Connell v. Listowel U.D.C.* (1957) *Ir. Jur. R.* 43.

32. In UK see *Davis v. Marshall* (1861) 4 L.T. 216: *Smith v. Thompson* (1849) 8 C.B. 44; *Re Golomb & William Porter & Co. Ltd.'s Arbitration* (1931) 144 L.T. 583.

33. [1973] I.R. 388.

34. Fn. 13 *ante*, at 314.

35. *Cockburn v. Alexander* (1848) 6 C.B. 791, *per* Maule J. 814 (charter-party).

for not doing that which he is not bound to do'.[36] The principle of performance in the manner least disadvantageous to the defendant has now been recognised as applying to an employer's right to give notice.[37]

(ii) *Specific cases*
(a) *Breach of substantive limitations*

The principle described above limits the courts in computing damages where wrongful dismissal takes the form of termination with no or with incorrect notice of the contract of employment, or where summary dismissal is held to be unlawful. If dismissal were in breach of contract in the sense of being on impermissible substantive grounds (and not, of course, a lawful summary dismissal) it would not always be sufficient, in this writer's view, to assess damages on the same basis. It may be true that a defendant is not liable in damages for not doing that which he is not bound to do but if, on the contrary, he has in fact bound himself not to do something, he should be liable to compensate the plaintiff if he acts in disregard of this.

Since by agreeing to substantive limitations an employer may be found to have limited his prerogative to dismiss, it would be illogical to award an amount of damages to compensate the plaintiff for the time he would have served under the contract if he had been given proper notice. The very giving of notice would impliedly be restricted by the contract. If, e.g., a person is employed for life, subject to restrictions on the employer's power to dismiss for misconduct, there would seem to be no reason in principle why such an employee, if wrongfully dismissed, should not be compensated in respect of the full loss consequent upon breach. This would be subject to the law on mitigation of damages but the significant difference would be that the employee's expectation interest in the contract would extend beyond the period of reasonable notice to the remainder of the contract term.

(b) *Breach of procedural limitations*

Again, where an employee is dismissed in breach of an express or implied term in the contract as to procedure, the measure of damages

---

36. *Abrahams v. Herbert Reiach Ltd.* [1922] 1 K.B. 477 *per* Scrutton L.J. at 482 (contract with author for publication of series of articles).

37. *British Guiana Credit Corporation v. Da Silva* [1965] 1 WLR 248 at 259 H-260 B *per* Lord Donovan. Short-term fluctuation of earnings in ascertaining the week's wages upon which the damages are to be based were dealt with in *Devonald v. Rosser & Sons* [1906] 2 K.B. 728: damages were assessed on the basis of 'the average wages earned by the plaintiffs for some time preceding the stoppage'. This problem arises especially in connection with manual employees where their notice period is likely to consist of weeks rather than months or years.

may be different. In *Taylor v. NUS*[38] damages were awarded for
wrongful dismissal in breach of a contractual duty to hear but the law
reports are unhelpful on the question of computation. The approach
of the Court of Appeal in *Gunton v. London Borough of Richmond*[39]
is unequivocal, however. There the plaintiff was held to be entitled to
a contractual right not to be dismissed on disciplinary grounds before
the contractual disciplinary procedure had been carried out in due
order but with reasonable expedition. Consequently, the period by
reference to which the amount of damages should be assessed was
held to be a reasonable period from the date of dismissal for properly
carrying out those procedures, plus the period of notice to which the
employee was entitled. The employer's common law right to dismiss
with due notice did not override the contract's express provisions.
The reasoning in *Gunton* is attractive, superficially, but it may be
criticised for failing to take into account the nature or chief purpose
of a disciplinary or dismissal procedure, namely, to ensure that,
before a dismissal decision is taken, management provides an
employee with the opportunity to defend himself. The process of
establishing the facts should be distinguished from that of deciding
whether dismissal is justified. The facts may indicate a repudiation of
such gravity on the employee's part as to have justified his instant dismissal at the time of breach. Or they may indicate breach of a lesser
nature in which case an employer wishing to terminate the employment relationship must give proper notice. Again they may suggest a
breach such as would justify instant dismissal once the procedures
are exhausted. Or they may establish that an employee could not
have been dismissed at all. *Gunton* is premissed on the assumption
that, once the procedures have been gone through, an employer can
dismiss lawfully. This is surely unsound. Moreover, the principle of
performance in the manner least disadvantageous to the employer is
simply inapplicable in these circumstances.

(c) *Damages and the elective theory of repudiatory breach*

In chapter three, the approach of the civil courts in Britain
concerning repudiatory breach and termination of the contract of
employment was discussed. In *Gunton,* it may be recalled, the Court
of Appeal held that wrongful dismissal does not terminate the
contract of employment until the employee has accepted the
employer's repudiation of the contract. This theory poses difficulties
for the law of damages. Prior to acceptance, for example, could an
employee claim in debt rather than in damages? The advantages of a
claim in debt would be that the rules on mitigation would not apply.

38. [1967] 1 W.L.R. 532.
39. [1980] ICR 755; [1980] IRLR 321.

But to sustain such a claim, it would be necessary to establish that an employee's willingness to do the work, not his actual performance of it, sufficed to ground his entitlement to wages.

Suppose an employee is entitled to three months' notice and his employer dismisses him summarily or on a month's notice and the facts are such as to justify the view that the employee did not accept the employer's repudiation of the contract until the end of ten weeks from the employer's exclusion from his employment. Does the contract continue to subsist during the ten weeks? Alternatively, may one assume the employer is guilty of a breach of contract continuing *de die in diem* for refusing to offer the employee employment from the date of exclusion down to the date of acceptance, and that he is thereafter liable for damages on the basis of a wrongful repudiation of the contract? If the latter, could the employee properly claim damages under the second head in relation to a period of three months from the date of acceptance as well as damages (or, indeed, debt) under the first head in relation to the ten week period? The Court of Appeal answered these interrogatories in *Gunton*. It declared that the employee's cause of action in such circumstances would arise at the time he was wrongfully excluded from his employment and his subsequent acceptance of the repudiation would not create a new cause of action, although it might affect the remedy available for it. In Lord Justice Buckley's words:

> 'the question must, I think, be for how long the servant could have insisted at the date of the commencement of his cause of action upon being continued by the master in his employment.'[40]

From the context, it is clear that this length of time constitutes the employee's notice period. This particular application of the principle of performance least disadvantageous to the defendant removes what might have been a major problem with the elective theory. Lord Justice Buckley's remarks were *obiter,* however, and arguably, incorrect. It will be assumed, for present purposes, that the elective theory is correctly applicable to employment contracts (as to doubts concerning this, see chapter three above). First, as a matter of principle, there is no reason to justify an employer's non-action in the face of an employee's refusal to accept breach. If the former is legally entitled to end the contract of employment by giving proper notice and does not do so, either at all or for an inexcusably long time, why should the victim have to bear the brunt of this? Secondly, if one's baseline principle in law is that the expectations created by the

40. [1980] I.R.L.R. 321, at 329.

contract are protected, it would be at variance with this to award compensation only for the notice period where a plaintiff by his conduct made it abundantly clear that he wished to carry on in employment. What would be the nature of the employee's claim in respect of the period beginning with the employer's breach up to his, the employee's, acceptance of it? Could an employee claim in debt rather than in damages? This question strikes at the core of the contract bargain. Are wages paid in return for work or for willingness to do the work agreed? Caselaw on entitlement to pay during absence on grounds of illness supports the notion of pay for willingness to work[41] but such cases differ significantly from the example under discussion in that both parties are there willing to continue the relationship of employment. In sick pay cases, the employer is not in breach. Where an employer is in breach, it would be difficult to uphold the argument that the innocent party, in virtue solely of his willingness to work, could insist on payment for 'performance'. That would be to confuse the correlative nature of the various obligations in the employment contract. At its simplest, performance in the contract of employment is not an independent phenomenon capable of execution without co-operation from the employer. In *White and Carter (Councils) Ltd. v. McGregor*[42] the House of Lords held that if a defendant repudiates a contract the plaintiff need not take steps to mitigate until he has decided to treat the repudiation as having by anticipation put an end to the contract. The plaintiffs were always ready to perform the contract. But the case was peculiar in that the plaintiff was able to perform his part without any co-operation from the defendant and it is generally admitted that, if he had been unable to perform for lack of such co-operation, he could not have sued in debt and must have tried to mitigate the damages.[43] Because of the importance of dependent and conditional promises, and of trust and co-operation in the employment relationship, it is suggested that an employee's claim up to the time of acceptance of the breach by him should lie in damages rather than in debt. That the employee would therefore be under a duty to mitigate his loss need not cause concern. In many cases it will be unreasonable to expect a plaintiff-employee to mitigate by 'accepting' breach in one fashion or another. It is scarcely unreasonable for a plaintiff to want to remain on in his job. In contract, no less than in tort, the wrongdoer must take his victim *talem qualem*. Just as it is nonsense to talk about a suit for wrongful dismissal at any stage prior to termination of the contract of employment, so it should be regarded as objectionable to apply the same

41. See a discussion of the authorities in *Osman v. Saville Sportswear Ltd.* [1960] 1 WLR 1055 (QBD).
42. [1962] AC 413.
43. F. H. Lawson: *Remedies of English Law*, 69.

measure of damages to any breach taking place during that time. In theory, as well as in fairness, if the elective theory is to be logically consistent, there should be no obstacle in the way of recovering (a) damages for breach of contract up to the time of acceptance of the breach (subject, where appropriate, to the rules on mitigation); and (b) damages thereafter for wrongful dismissal.

(iii) *Specific application of principles relating to damages for wrongful dismissal*

The first major difficulty in this respect concerns compensation for loss of reputation and injury to feelings.[44] Until very recently, as Kennedy C.J. observed in *Kinlan v. Ulster Bank Ltd.*[45]

> 'It [was] very clearly settled, both in this country and in England, and affirmed in many cases, that in actions for breach of contract, damages may not be given for such matters as disappointment of mind, humiliation, vexation or the like.'

Hurt feelings have no place in traditional commercial relationships and judicial reluctance to award damages for mental distress, or to take into account the way in which the defaulting party acted in breaching the contract flows from the assumption 'that businessmen have thick skins and care only about compensation for losses to the pocketbook'.[46]

The Chief Justice in *Kinlan's* case cited a number of authorities in support of his statement,[47] among them the notorious *Addis v. Gramophone Co. Ltd.*,[48] which left as its legacy a restrictive approach to the measure of damages for wrongful dismissal. In *Addis,* the plaintiff was dismissed in a harsh and humiliating manner. It was held that the manner of his dismissal could not affect any damages to which he was entitled. Until recently the decision was looked upon as illustrating that in actions for wrongful dismissal a plaintiff was unlikely to recover exemplary damages, aggravated

44. See Mr. Justice Declan Costello: 'Measuring Damages in Breach of Contract cases — some recent Irish decisions' (1978) Lecture no. 112, Society of Young Solicitors; H. E. Markson: 'Commercial Contracts: Damages for Distress?' (1979) 129 N.L.J. 359.

45. [1928] I.R. 171, 184. See, in similar vein, *Parker v. Cathcart* (1866) 17 ICLR 778 (Common Pleas).

46. K. Swinton: 'Contract Law and the Employment Relationship: the Proper Forum for Reform' in *Studies in Contract Law,* 364; also same: 'Foreseeability and Where Should the Award of Contract Damages Cease?' *op. cit.,* 61.

47. *Breen v. Cooper* I.R. 3 C.L. 621; *Hamlin v. Gt. Northern Rly.* 1 H. & N. 408.

48. [1909] A.C. 488, *per* Lord Atkinson at 495, 496.

damages, damages for non-economic loss consisting of injury to feelings, or damages in respect of loss of reputation caused by the manner of dismissal.[49] Four of the five Law Lords rejected the plaintiff's claim representing injury to his feelings and the increased difficulty he experienced in obtaining other employment as a result of the defamatory nature of his dismissal from employment.[50]

In Britain damages for loss of reputation have always been recoverable in one exceptional situation — where loss of publicity would be sustained by the plaintiff. This arises where enhancement of a plaintiff's reputation by publicity was particularly contemplated by the contract, so that it might be regarded as a head of damage contemplated by the parties themselves when entering into the contract. The proposition was first established with regard to actors in *Marbé v. Geo. Edwardes*[51] and confirmed by the House of Lords in *Clayton v. Oliver.*[52] In the latter, Lord Buckmaster said he thought 'loss of reputation' was not the exact expression and 'loss of publicity' should be used.[53] This head of damage was extended from actors to authors, or at least to the author of a screen play entitled to a screen credit, in *Tolnay v. Criterion Films.*[54] Goddard J. pointed out that:

> 'all persons who have to make a living by attracting the public to their works, be they . . . painters or . . . literary men . . . or . . . pianists and musicians, must live by getting known to the public.'[55]

49. See *British Guiana Credit Corporation v. Da Silva*, fn. 37 *ante*, wherein the Privy Council refused to allow damages for wrongful dismissal under the head of 'humiliation, embarrassment, and loss of reputation'. See too *Withers v. General Theatre Corporation* [1933] 2 K.B. 536 (C.A.).

50. One aspect of the decision has often been criticised (e.g., *Freedland, op. cit.*, fn. 25 *ante*, 248) i.e., the difficulty of deciding whether the House of Lords went to the further lengths of holding that damages could not be recovered for loss of prospects of other employment resulting from the *fact* of the dismissal as opposed to the damaging *manner* of dismissal. One of the five Law Lords. Lord Loreburn. committed himself to such a proposition (at 491). If that further rule were to result from the case, an employee could not recover damages attributable to the fact that dismissal prevents him from obtaining a qualification or a fund of experience which he would have gained from the employment had he not been dismissed. and which would have increased his ability to obtain, or his earnings in, subsequent employ ment. A belief that the majority of the House of Lords endorsed that view appears from the Court of Appeal decision in *Dunk v. George Waller & Son Ltd.* |1970| 2 Q.B. 163. But see Freedland *op. cit.*, 248.

51. [1928] 1 K.B. 269 (C.A.).

52. |1930| A.C. 209, followed in *McLaren v. Chalet Club* (1951) 1 C.L.C. 2508.

53. At 220.

54. |1936| 3 All E.R. 1625.

55. At 1626-'7. Goddard thought that the loss of publicity to an actor whose worth the public can only establish by seeing him perform, is more serious than in the case of an author: at 1626.

Not all claims for loss of publicity have succeeded. Thus, a chief sub-editor,[56] a surveyor to a local authority[57] and a company director[58] have failed to establish loss of publicity as a result of dismissal.

The law concerning damages for disappointment recently underwent some very important developments. It is now well established that in appropriate cases the victim of a breach of contract can claim for mental distress as a result of the breach. In *Heywood v. Wellers*[59] Lord Justice James described the law:

> 'if it is within the contemplation of the contracting parties that a foreseeable result of a breach of the contract will be to cause vexation, frustration or distress, then if a breach occurs which does bring about that result, damages are recoverable.'[60]

Cases on damages for disappointment cover two separate lines of development. A high proportion involve spoiled holidays or something akin thereto,[61] where the disappointment suffered on breach is the reverse side of the contract (see McMahon J. in *Johnson v. Long-leat Properties (Dublin) Ltd.*[62] a case concerning breach of a building contract). The second category of cases constitutes the most significant development in this area of contract damages.[63] Here, pleasure and distress are not so intimately connected with the contract. Cases have concerned, e.g., wrongful demotion: *Cox v. Phillips Industries*.[64] *Cox*, which came before Lawson J. in the EAT, concerned an industrial engineer who had been relegated to a position of lesser responsibility. His salary remained the same but his relegation, which was in breach of a term in his contract whereby the employing company promised him a position of higher responsibility, was held to have exposed him to a good deal of depression, vexation and frustration and to have led to ill health. The question was whether he could be

---

56. *Collier v. Sunday Referee Publishing Co.* [1940] 2 K.B. 647.
57. *Moss v. Chesham U.D.C.* (1945) 172 L.T. 301.
58. *Re Gollomb* (1931) 144 L.T. 583 (C.A.).
59. [1976] 1 All E.R. 300.
60. At 308.
61. The relevant authorities are: *Diesan v. Samsan* [1971] S.L.T. 49; *Jarvis v. Swan's Tours Ltd.* [1973] 1 All E.R. 71; *Jackson v. Horizon Holidays Ltd.* [1975] 3 All E.R. 92; *Cox v. Phillips Industries Ltd.* [1976] 3 All E.R. 161.
62. High Court unreported, 19 May 1976: McMahon J.; see, too, *Quinn & Another v. Quality Homes and Others,* High Court unreported, 21 November 1977; Finlay P.
63. Canadian cases also deal with this head of damages. See *Tippett v. International Typographical Union Local 226* (1977) 71 DLR (3rd) 146; *Newell v. Canadian Pacific Airlines* (1977) 14 O.R. 752.
64. [1976] 3 All E.R. 161.

awarded damages in respect of such matters for breach of contract?
In the judgment of Lawson J:

> '. . . this is a case where it was in the contemplation of the
> parties in all the circumstances that, if that promise of a
> position of better responsibility without reasonable notice was
> breached, then the effect of that breach would be to expose the
> plaintiff to the degree of vexation, frustration and distress which
> he in fact underwent.'

The judge saw no reason why, if a situation arises which within the
contemplation of the parties would have given rise to vexation,
distress and general disappointment and frustration, the person who
is injured by a contractual breach should not be compensated in
damages for that breach. In *Cox* the emphasis was skillfully replaced
to rest upon breach of the contract of employment. Since he had
already received the appropriate compensation (wages in lieu of
notice) to which he was entitled under his contract, Cox would have
recovered nothing at all had he brought an action for damages for
wrongful dismissal. It may be that *Cox* will give added impetus to the
courts to imply a term into the individual's contract of employment
not to be deprived of job satisfaction.[65] In *Garvey v. Ireland and
Others*[66] the Irish High Court seemed to prefer the decision in *Addis*
to that in *Cox*.[67]

(iv) *Other forms of pecuniary loss and deductions: pensions,
     perquisites and liability to income tax*

The law concerning damages for wrongful dismissal is neither well
developed nor consistent in the matter of protecting an employee
against pecuniary loss other than loss of basic earnings. Mere factual
expectations in excess of legal rights are not, it would seem, recoverable. Pension rights are perhaps the most important fringe benefits to
be considered in calculating damages for wrongful dismissal.[68] The
general principle applicable to assessing damages for loss of pension
rights is the same as that which is applied to compensation generally
for wrongful dismissal: namely, an employee ought to be put in as

---

65. Elias, Napier & Wallington, *op. cit.*, fn. 25 *ante*, 519, fn. 1.
66. High Court unreported, 19 December 1979.
67. The authority of the judgment in this respect may, however, be doubted. See
page 113 *post*.
68. They form a recognised head of damages in calculating damages for wrongful
dismissal: see in UK *Bold v. Brough, Nicholson & Hall Ltd.* [1964] 1
W.L.R. 201; cf. *Judd v. Hammersmith Hospital Board of Governors* [1960] 1
W.L.R. 328.

good a position as he would have been if the employer had performed the contract, assuming that the employer had performed the contract in the manner least disadvantageous to himself.[69] A claim for damages for loss of pension rights resulting from dismissal essentially takes the form of a claim in respect of the loss of the increase in the value of pension rights which would have been enjoyed had it not been for the dismissal. If an employee had remained in employment, his pension would have become more valuable. He is compensated for the fact that this increase in value has not occurred. If, however, the continuation of pension contributions, or the ultimate payment of benefit, is a matter within the discretion of the employer and not a legal obligation upon him, then the rule of least disadvantageous performance may be applied, and no damages are payable under this head.[70]

If there is any question of deprivation of a vested right in a company's pension scheme the courts adopt a more rigid approach. This was illustrated in the case of *Glover v. B.L.N. Ltd.*[71] where the general rules governing the employing company's pension scheme were to the effect that no damages could be recovered for loss of benefit thereunder. A rule headed 'Employer's right to discharge employees' read:

> 'Membership of the scheme shall not in any way restrict the right of the employer to discharge any of his employees and the benefits provided under the scheme shall not be made the grounds for increasing a claim for damages in any action brought by a member against his employer.'

Clause 3 of the declaration of trust executed by the employer's trust company was also relevant. It provided that the assurances would be held by the trustee (i.e., the trust company) upon certain trusts and:

> 'in the event of the employment being terminated by the employer before normal pension date for any reason other than fraud or misconduct, [the assurances would be held on trust] . . . for the member.'

Judge Kenny held that, as Glover had not been lawfully discharged

---

69. *Op. cit.*, fn. 25 *ante*, 253.
70. *Beach v. Reed Corrugated Cases Ltd.* [1956] 1 W.L.R. 807. But the rule of least disadvantageous performance does not apply to the employer's right (if any) to discontinue his entire pensions scheme in relation to his employees at large — Phillimore J. in *Bold's* case, fn. 68 *ante*, at 211-'2; Diplock L.J. in *Lavarack v. Woods of Colchester Ltd.* [1967] 1 Q.B. 278 at 295 F-297B.
71. [1973] IR 436.

for fraud or misconduct, he had a vested right in the policy of assurance when his contract was terminated. A rule which is intended to deprive anyone of a vested right must be very clearly worded. In his view, the above rule meant that an employee who had been discharged could not include future benefits under the scheme as part of his damages if his dismissal was not lawful. It did not take away Glover's vested rights in the policy.

Apart from loss of pension rights, a wrongfully dismissed employee is entitled to damages representing loss of earnings in kind[72] but bonus payments,[73] overtime, incentive payments or commission[74] may be recovered only if the employee can show the employer was contractually bound to allow him to earn them. Because the courts have built on the traditional theory of the commercial nature of the employment contract, *ex gratia* payments and discretionary future financial benefits cannot be secured, no matter how much they may enhance the incentive to work.

New statutory benefits are likely in future to complicate the issue. It is arguable that there should be recognition in damages of the loss of statutory seniority rights, e.g., for the loss of accrued service for purposes of entitlement to a minimum period of notice under the Minimum Notice and Terms of Employment Act, 1973, or to remedies for unfair dismissal under the Act of 1977, or for purposes of entitlement to redundancy pay under the Redundancy Payments Acts, 1967-'79. Although the point is not quite the same, in England, redundancy payments are not deducted from damages for wrongful dismissal: *Basnett v. J. & A. Jackson Ltd.*[75] In *Basnett's* case the

72. See, on board and lodgings: *Mulcahy v. O'Sullivan and Walsh* [1944] IR 336; in relation to domestic servants see the anomaly that 'board wages' are not recoverable: *Gordon v. Potter* (1859) 1 F. & F. 644, qualified by *Lindsay v. Queens Hotel Ltd.* [1919] 1 KB 212; free luncheon vouchers are unlikely to be recoverable: *McGrath v. de Soissons* (1962) 112 L.J. 60; expenses for remainder of fixed term contract are not recoverable: *Glover v. B.L.N. Ltd.* [1973] IR 388, 435. The last case makes it clear that a claim may be made for loss of a company car where this was available under a person's contract of employment.

73. Bonus payments must be distinguished from separate 'consensual emoluments': *Cox v. E.S.B.* [1944] IR 81, 89. 'Danger money' was awarded in *Byrne v. Limerick S.S. Co.* [1946] IR 138. Loss of future discretionary bonuses is not recoverable: *Lavarack v. Woods of Colchester Ltd.* [1967] 1 QB 278 (CA). Compare Lord Denning's dissenting judgment with the view of Lush J. in *Manubens v. Leon* [1919] 1 KB 208, 211. See Freedland, *op. cit.*, fn. 25 *ante*, 259.

74. See Freedland *op. cit.*, fn. 25 *ante*, 260, who is of the view that the courts will be likely to hold that there is an obligation to enable the total remuneration to reach a reasonable level, following *Bauman v. Nulton Press Ltd.* [1952] 2 All E.R. 1121. See, on the question of commission agents, *Ward v. Spivack Ltd.* [1957] IR 40.

75. [1976] ICR 63; Crichton J. See, *contra*, the earlier case of *Stocks v. Magna Merchants Ltd.* [1973] ICR 530, which the NIRC declined to follow in *Yorkshire Engineering and Welding Co. Ltd. v. Burnham* [1974] ICR 77. See a note on *Basnett's* case in (1976) 5 ILJ 180.

court accepted that a redundancy payment is analogous to a pension; it is payable regardless of wrongful dismissal and may be equated with a private insurance scheme paid for by the employer's work.[76]

(v) *Liability to Income Tax*

A wrongfully dismissed employee, it seems, lacks the foresight to engage in tax planning in order to reduce his liability to income tax. The law governing calculation of the effect of tax liability on damages for loss of earnings or earning capacity is unsatisfactory and controversial. Liability to income tax is not something which concerns only the plaintiff and the Revenue Commissioners, for the courts have decided that in computing damages for wrongful dismissal regard must be had to the fact that, but for the dismissal, a plaintiff would have had to pay tax in respect of the income which he would have received. As the law stands, it is cheaper for an employer to break a contract of employment with an employee than to perform it. The question of deduction for tax purposes came to a head in *British Transport Commission v. Gourley*.[77] There, the House of Lords[78] held that when a plaintiff's damages arising out of personal injuries include a sum for loss of future earnings and that sum is not chargeable to income tax or sur-tax, a deduction for the tax which the plaintiff would have had to pay if he had received the earnings in the future must be made. When damages had to be computed in the Irish case of *Glover v. B.L.N. Ltd.*[79] Kenny J. followed the House of Lords. Before that time, deduction of notional tax liability from damages had not been the practice of the Irish courts, although Judge

76. *Parry v. Cleaver* [1970] A.C. 1.
77. [1956] AC 185. See a devastating analysis and demolition of *Gourley* in G. Bale: 'British Transport Commission v. Gourley Reconsidered' (1966) 44 Can. B.R. 66; it deals with all the cases and literature. See also, H. Luntz: *Assessment of Damages for Personal Injury and Death* 159; Prof. H. Street: *Principles of the Law of Damages* 88; O. P. Wylie and J. E. McGlyne: 'Taxation, Damages and Compensation for Unfair Dismissal' (1978) NLJ 550; A. Samuels: 'Gourley Revisited and Rejected' (1967) 30 MLR 83 *re* rejection of *Gourley* by Supreme Court of Canada in *Ontario v. Jennings* (1966); G. Dworkin: 'Damages and Tax, a Comparative Survey' [1967] *British Tax Review* 315; Harvey McGregor: 'Compensation versus Punishment in Damages Awards' (1965) 28 MLR 629; J.S. Hall: 'Taxation of Compensation for Loss of Income' (1959) 73 LQR 212; A. J. Jolowicz: 'Damages and Income Tax' [1959] CLJ 86; P. M. Roach: 'Damages for loss of earnings in personal injury claims' (1959) 33 ALJ 11; J. Powell: 'Taxation of Payments received on Termination of Employment' (1981) ILJ 239.
78. By a majority of 6:1.
79. [1973] IR 388.

Kenny had raised the matter in *Carvill v. Irish Industrial Bank Ltd.*[80] In *Glover*, the High Court was prepared to have regard to 'realities rather than technicalities'[81] and, following the reasoning of the House of Lords, it took cognisance of the importance of income tax and sur tax in the 'economic lives of so many of our citizens'. Kenny J. rejected counsel's contention that *Gourley* applied only to loss of remuneration in accident cases and not, as in the case before him, to loss of remuneration arising out of wrongful dismissal. The principle was the same in both instances:

'the damages are compensation for being deprived of the opportunity to earn.'

There could be no logical basis for the application of a different rule in each case.[82] In *Glover*, the House of Lords decision only affected taxation of such amount of the damages as was not in excess of (now) £6,000; the sum above this figure was liable to tax in any event under sections 8 and 9 of the Finance Act, 1964 (cf. sections 114 and 115 of the Income Tax Act, 1967, as amended by s. 10, Finance Act, 1980).

Glover's case may be criticised on a number of grounds. First, it enables an offender to profit at the expense of an injured party while at the same time, it must be remembered, the Revenue do not get the amount by which the damages are reduced. Further, a judicial estimation of the amount of tax is open to the possibility of being inaccurate and consequently of working injustice to the victim.[83] It is arguable that such calculations are inappropriate to a court of law; a plaintiff might be promoted, for instance, or marry a spouse with an

---

80. [1968] I.R. 325, 338: 'I do not think it necessary to express any opinion on whether there should be a deduction for the income tax which the plaintiff would have had to pay on the sum of £2,500 or on the question whether this sum, if awarded to the plaintiff without any deduction for income tax, would have been taxable in his hands'. See, too, Kenny J.'s judgment in *In re Trusts of Will of Simon Sheil; Browne v. Mulligan and Others* (Supreme Court unrep., 23 Nov. 1977): no information put before the court re plaintiff's income tax, hence court had no way of assessing appropriate deduction.

81. *Parry v. Cleaver* [1970] AC 1, 13 *per* Lord Reid explaining *Gourley*.

82. At 440. The restriction of the rule to damages awarded in accident cases had already been rejected in Britain in *Beach v. Reed Corrugated Cases* [1956] 1 WLR 807; *In re Haughton Main Collieries Co.* [1956] 1 WLR 1219; *Parsons v. BNM Laboratories Ltd.* [1964] 1 QB 95; and *Bold v. Brough, Nicholson & Hall Ltd.* [1964] 1 W.L.R. 201.

83. See Kenny J.'s example at 441: X earning £4,000 p.a. involved in an accident in 1965 who gets damages assessed in February, 1967. The estimate of sur-tax would have been made grossly inaccurate by s. 10 of the Finance Act, 1967, and the extension of that relief by the Finance Act, 1968.

income, or move to a country where taxation is lower.[84] Further, damages should represent compensation for loss of earning capacity, not loss of earnings: they should restore the *status quo ante* in so far as possible. Nor is the logic of the decision impeccable. Judson J. pointed out in the Canadian case of *R v. Jennings*:[85]

> 'Income tax is not an element of cost in earning income. It is a disposition of a portion of the earned income required by law.'

From the defendant's point of view it is irrelevant what the plaintiff would have done with his earnings if he had not been injured — tax is a charge on income after it has been received. Lawful tax planning might have enabled a plaintiff to have reduced his liability to tax. It is not surprising that the English Law Reform Committee, following on *Gourley*, concluded a report on the question of taxation of damages[86] as follows:

> '. . . it may turn out that the difficulties to which the law gives rise in practice are greater than some of us at present are disposed to believe and we are therefore agreed in thinking that it may well become desirable to review the practical implications of the decision in *Gourley's* case after a further lapse of time.'

If there is a plain duty to tax damages, and the argument is not altogether convincing that there is, the mode of so doing in circumstances of dismissal requires more subtlety and ingenuity.[87]

---

84. See *Stewart v. Glentaggart Ltd.* [1963] SLT 119; for difficulties see *Simon on Income Tax* Vol. C (1970), C4. 413-'17.

85. (1966) 57 DLR (2d) 644.

86. Seventh Report, Cmnd. 501, last par. (1958).

87. One solution might be to make the award of damages itself liable to income tax. Where the damages represent several years' loss of income it would be necessary to introduce income averaging or 'top slicing' provisions to ensure that these damages were not subjected to unduly high rates of tax by virtue of being taxed wholly in one tax year. 'Top slicing' provisions are no strangers to the tax code. The Government would then receive the tax it would have received had the person being compensated continued to receive taxable income. The employer could be required to withhold a portion of the award and account for it to the Revenue (it could be subject to the PAYE system). The balance would be paid to the employee and, provided the correct amount of tax had been withheld and paid, the employer's liability would be discharged. The employee would be liable to tax on the gross award but would be credited with payment of the tax withheld by his employer. An alternative suggestion is made in relation to compensation for unfair dismissal, see chap. 7, page 192 *post*, although a uniform system would obviously be more desirable.

(vi) *Social Welfare Benefits*

The law on deductability of benefits such as social welfare benefits is uncertain. It is perhaps too much to expect a perfectly interlocking structure when different benefits have different objectives. But in principle it is clear that an employer should not be permitted to break his contract with impunity by enabling him to deduct an assortment of benefits from the damages he would otherwise have to pay. It is equally clear that where a plaintiff by thrift or foresight has contributed the whole or part of the premiums in respect of contingency insurance, a deduction should not be made. In Ireland a deduction was made from damages in respect of compensation under the old Workmens Compensation Acts, 1934-1955 (see now State Occupational Industrial Injury benefit under the Social Welfare (Consolidation) Act, 1981): *Flynn v. Great Northern Railway Co. (Ir.) Ltd.*[88] And in Britain the Court of Appeal has held that a sum in respect of unemployment benefit received should be deducted from an award of damages: *Parsons v. B.N.M. Laboratories Ltd.*[89]

(vii) *The mitigation of loss*

An employee who has suffered damage following breach of contract is not entitled to compensation in respect of any loss he could reasonably have avoided after the occurrence of the breach. So, for example, in *Herman v. Owners of S.S. Vicia*,[90] seamen who had been wrongfuly dismissed were not awarded damages for a period in which they were unemployed and did not seek alternative employment. *McGregor on Damages* lists the rules of mitigation.[91] Two are relevant in an action for damages for wrongful dismissal. They are:

(a) the rule as to avoidable loss — no recovery for loss which the plaintiff ought to have avoided; and
(b) the rule as to avoided loss — no recovery for loss which the plaintiff has avoided,[92] unless the matter is collateral.

The first of these presents the greater problem. To assess whether a plaintiff ought to have avoided loss it may have to be determined whether he should have accepted new work which is geographically

88. (1955) 89 ILTR 46.
89. [1964] 1 QB 95.
90. [1942] I.R. 305; cf. *Irvine v. Midland Gt. W. Rly. (Ir.) Co.* (1879) 6 LR Ir. 55. The best known early statement of the principle governing the measure of damages for wrongful dismissal is in *Beckham v. Drake* (1849) 2 HLC 579, 606-'7 *per* Erle J. For the historical development of the rule see R. G. Lawson: 'Mitigation of Damages: Recent Developments' (1978) Vol. 128 NLJ 1185.
91. 13th ed. 1972, para. 205.
92. *See Cotter v. Ahern*(High Court unreported, 25 February 1977).

or occupationally different from his old position. Secondly, it may have to be determined whether and if so, how far, a plaintiff was entitled to insist upon congenial personal relations in new employment.

The victim of a breach of contract need do no more by way of mitigation than is reasonable in all the circumstances. An employee is not obliged to strain himself for the benefit of his employer. Lord Macmillan's words in *Banco de Portugal v. Waterlow & Sons*[93] have been cited approvingly on a number of occasions.[94] In his view:

> ·'the measures which he [the victim] may be driven to adopt in order to extricate himself ought not to be weighed in nice scales at the instance of the party. whose breach of contract has occasioned the difficulty . . . he will not be held disentitled to recover the cost merely because the party in breach can suggest that other measures less burdensome to him [might] have been taken.'

Applying the reasonableness test, it has been held that an employee need not mitigate by accepting another offer of employment from his present employer where dismissal has taken place in such a manner as to prejudice good personal relations between the parties.[95] Damages are likely to be nominal, however, where an employee's dismissal comes about technically as a result of a change in the composition of an employing partnership and he refuses an offer of continued employment by the reconstituted partnership.[96] Again, applying the reasonableness test, refusal of an offer of re-engagement at a lower salary has been held reasonable for the purposes of the rule as to mitigation of loss.[97] An employee is entitled to refuse an offer of alternative employment by his existing employer where it involves a demotion.[98] Finally, loss of employment will not be treated as avoid-

---

93. [1932] A.C. 452, 506.

94. Recent examples are *Rumsey v. Owen White and Catlin* (1978) 245 EG. 225; *Daily Office Cleaning Contractors Ltd. v. Shefford* [1977] RTR 361.

95. *Payzu Ltd. v. Saunders* [1919] 2 K.B. 581, 588-'9 per Bankes L.J.; *Yetton v. Eastwoods Froy Ltd.* [1967] 1 WLR 104; *Shindler v. Northern Raincoat Co. Ltd.* [1960] 1 WLR 1038 (Diplock J.). *Semble*, an employee can properly doubt the genuineness of an offer made by the employer at a time when the relations between them have been handed over to a solicitor, above all when the offer requires the employee to abandon such common law rights as he has already acquired for wrongful dismissal: *Shindler's* case.

96. *Brace v. Calder* [1895] 2 Q.B. 253.

97. *Jackson v. Hayes, Candy & Co. Ltd.* [1938] 4 All E.R. 587.

98. *Yetton's* case, footnote 95 *ante*.

able where acceptance of employment would bring an employee into serious conflict with his trade union.[99]

B. Office-holders and Public Employees

The most effective and in Ireland the most frequently sought remedies for wrongfully dismissed workers in special categories of employment are a declaration that dismissal is null and void or an order of *certiorari* quashing a purported decision to dismiss. More infrequently an injunction may be sought to restrain dismissal.[100] Office-holders and persons whose dismissal is governed by statute or regulation constitute the main exceptions to the general rule that equitable remedies will not be granted in the face of wrongful dismissal.[101]

(1) *Declaratory relief*

In former times the action for a declaration had not attained its present popularity. It was almost unknown before 1865 and its scope has been immensely widened in the last 100 years or so.[102] A declaration that a dismissal was in breach of contract may be made but that is unlikely to assist a wrongfully dismissed worker in any practical way. It has been observed that in theory such a declaration is available to an ordinary employee. The advantage of seeking a declaration for an office-holder or public employee lies in the precise nature and content of the declaration he may seek. In fact the content of a declaration is likely to be critical. As in *Vine v. National Dock Labour Board*,[103] or *The State (Gleeson) v. Min. for Defence*,[104] a declaration may be made that a purported act of dismissal was *ultra vires*, null and void. Or, as in *Francis v. Municipal Councillors of Kuala Lumpur*,[105] the court may be asked to declare that the

99. *Morris v. C. H. Bailey Ltd.* [1969] 2 Lloyd's Rep. 215 — recognised it was not necessary to mitigate loss where acceptance of employment would have brought employee into breach of contract of membership with trade union or have rendered him liable to expulsion therefrom, in a closed shop trade.

100. As in *Shiels v. Clery & Co. (1941) Ltd.* (High Court unreported, 13 October 1979).

101. Contrast the insecure position of probationary office-holders: *Delaney v. Garvey* (High Court unreported, 14 March 1978); *Hynes v. Garvey* [1978] I.R. 174; *The State (McGarrity) v. The Deputy Commissioner of the Garda Síochána* (High Court unreported, 10 August 1977).

102. In former times when the holder of an office was removed and he claimed that this was not justified he applied for the issue of an information in the nature of a *quo warranto* directed to the new holder of the office to show how he held the office from which the prior holder had been removed.

103. [1957] AC 488.

104. [1976] IR 280.

105. [1962] 1 WLR 1411.

appellant still continued in the employment of the respondents or, as in *National Engineering and Electrical Trade Union & Ors v. McConnell*,[106] the court may declare that an officer of a trade union has never ceased to hold that position. In the latter two situations, it follows that the contract has not ended by other events taking place between the purported dismissal and the date of the declaration. This is by no means the case where a purported dismissal is declared *ultra vires* and void. In such circumstances, an employee may, e.g., have applied for and commenced work elsewhere before the date of the declaration. In most cases, of course, as Henchy J. observed in *Garvey v. An Taoiseach and the Government*,[107] it is open to an employer — in spite of any declaration — to recommence dismissal or disciplinary procedures in accordance with natural justice or fairness. Judges, it seems, can rarely resist dropping a broad hint to this effect.[108]

(2) *Damages as an alternative remedy*

The theory of the law is that equity steps in to provide a remedy where damages would be inadequate to compensate the plaintiff. The adequacy of damages as an alternative remedy to the declaratory action has not come up for discussion in Ireland but guidelines may be found in British cases. In the first place, there must be a contractual element before it is appropriate to compare the two remedies. In *Vine's* case, Lord Justice Jenkins rejected the defendant's plea that damages would be inadequate. Vine had been employed in the docks as a dock worker for 30 years or more.

> 'It was his life's work; it was a trade which he had pursued from boyhood. Why should he be removed from that employment if he wishes to continue in it? Why should it not be a consideration in deciding whether damages is an adequate remedy or not, that a man prefers one way of life to another? I can see no reason for holding that damages here are necessarily an adequate remedy.'

In *Vine* dismissal for the plaintiff meant loss of his status as a registered dockworker, and that would put an end to any possibility of working in the docks.

106. High Court unreported, 20 June 1977.
107. [1981] I.R. 75.
108. E.gg., Henchy and Griffin JJ. in *Gleeson's* case fn. 104 *ante* at 297 and 298; Jenkins L.J. in *Vine v. NDLB* [1956] 1 QB 658 (CA) at 678; Deputy Judge Dillon at first instance in *Stevenson v. United Road Transport Union* [1976] 3 All E.R. 29, 45. By the time the last case came on appeal the union had dismissed the plaintiff a second time.

If, however, a dismissed employee would be likely to acquire similar work elsewhere, it is doubtful whether a declaration would be given. For example, in *Francis* case, *supra,* a clerk dismissed by the Municipal Council whose status was accepted to be statutory failed to obtain a declaration that he was still employed by the Council. He could easily obtain other work as a clerk.

Where an employment is regulated by statute, it may be possible for an employee, provided his employment is public or he succeeds in establishing a special status, to challenge his dismissal by way of the prerogative orders.[109] In this respect, as in general, recruit officers are not secure in their tenure.[110]

(3) *Damages as an additional remedy*

A wrongfully dismissed plaintiff may seek a declaration that his purported dismissal was wrongful or was ineffective, null and void and at this stage seek damages as an additional remedy. Damages may or may not be inconsistent with the declaration. If the latter is to the effect that an employee is still validly in employment, an inquiry as to damages would not be appropriate[111] but arrears of salary could be claimed as an ordinary contract debt. If, on the other hand, the declaration related to a purported dismissal in time past, averring to a breach of contract, this would not preclude an award of damages.

In *Cox v. E.S.B.,* the plaintiff, an employee of the E.S.B., was removed from office by the Board as and from August, 1933, without the Board's having obtained the requisite prior consent of the Minister for Local Government and Public Health. In 1941, the plaintiff sued the Board, claiming a declaration that the order made by it was *ultra vires,* void and of no legal effect. His employment was governed by the Local Authorities (Officers and Employees) Act, 1926, which required the prior consent of the Minister for a person's removal from office. Gavan Duffy J. made an order declaring the order made by the Board purporting to dismiss the plaintiff *ultra vires,* void and of no legal effect. He also directed an inquiry as to damages. On appeal, the Supreme Court[112] affirmed the declaration in favour of the plaintiff. The Court was of opinion, however, that the

---

109. It has been held that *certiorari* will not lie to enforce the disciplinary procedure applicable to a Post Office employee where this was held to be a matter solely regulated by his contract of employment: *R. v. P.O., ex parte Byrne* |1975| ICR 221. Examples of Irish cases in which certiorari was sought are *St. (Gleeson) v. Minister for Defence,* fn. 104 *ante; St. (McGarrity) v. Deputy Commissioner of the Garda Síochána,* fn. 101 *ante; St. (Sheehan) v. McMahon & Others* (Supreme Court unreported, 25 October, 1977).

110. See fn. 101 *ante.*

111. In this respect, *NEETU v. McConnell,* fn. 106 *ante,* is arguably incorrect.

112. [1943] I.R. 94, 109; 231, 233.

inquiry as to damages was inconsistent with that declaration and varied the order of Gavan Duffy J. by discharging so much thereof as directed an inquiry. The plaintiff thereupon brought an action against the Board claiming, first, a declaration that he was then and had been since 1933 in the employment of the Board as a whole-time, permanent, and pensionable officer under a statutory contract of employment; secondly, a declaration that he was entitled to a certain sum in respect of arrears of salary and cost of living bonus calculated in accordance with the cost of living index figure from September, 1933, to the date of issue of the summons; thirdly, an inquiry, if necessary, as to the sum due to him for arrears of salary and cost of living bonus for the said period. Gavan Duffy J. held that Cox was lawfully entitled to the arrears of his salary with normal increments from August, 1933, to February, 1942. The Minister for Local Government had in fact dismissed the plaintiff from office on the latter date. Further, the plaintiff was held entitled in respect of the same period to the cost of living bonus, subject to its stabilisation in May, 1941, but it was held that he would have to give credit to the Board for any earnings during working hours over the same period. The defendants contended that Cox's action was defeated by his alleged acquiescence or laches. But since Cox had been ready and willing to perform his duties for the Board during the period in question, Gavan Duffy J. rejected this contention.[113] By awarding arrears of salary and a cost of living bonus the court was putting the plaintiff in the position he would have been in had the contract not been terminated illegally and the plaintiff allowed to continue in his work. Judge Kenny was later to declare in *Glover v. B.L.N. Ltd.*[114] that:

> 'An award of damages by a court is intended to compensate the plaintiff for the loss which he has suffered: in some cases the damages may be punitive but compensation or restoration (so far as money can do it) to the position before [termination] . . . is the main element.'

---

113. The judge also held that the Board's defence of a six years limitation to the plaintiff's claim was unsustainable as the greater part of the claim was founded upon a statutory liability and hence the plaintiff had 20 years within which to sue, applying *Cork & Bandon Rly. Co. v. Goode* 13 C.B. 826. In that case the statute deemed the defendant to be a shareholder in the events that had happened to him and as a shareholder rendered him liable to pay calls made by the directors; here the relevant statute (Electricity Supply Act, 1927, s. 29(9)) transformed the plaintiff into a servant of the Board on the making of the vesting order and rendered the Board liable to pay him remuneration on a scale indicated by the statute.

114. [1973] IR 433, 441.

Quantum of Damages

Where a contract of employment exists or may be inferred, compensation or restoration is likely to involve more for office holders and special category employees than for ordinary employees. Because of the additional factor of office or status, benefit lost or detriment incurred as a result of non-fulfilment of the defendant's promises is likely to encompass more. In *Cotter v. Ahern and Others*,[115] for example, the principle of performance least disadvantageous to the defendant was departed from as it would have been unrealistic and not in accordance with the facts to suggest that it was within the real contemplation of the parties that a post should last merely for the duration of the notice period. The plaintiff succeeded in establishing a breach of contract on the part of a school manager when, on account of trade union pressure, he was not appointed principal of a national school. The High Court was influenced, not only by the plaintiff's status as principal, but also by the unlikelihood that he would leave in the middle of the school year.

The High Court decision on the question of redress in *Garvey v. Ireland and Others*[116] is somewhat curious. Among other things, the original pleadings before the High Court questioned the power of the Government of Ireland, under the Police Forces Amalgamation Act, 1925, to terminate the office of the Commissioner of the Garda Síochána at any time: whether without prior notice; or without giving reasons; or without giving the holder of the office an opportunity of making representations in relation thereto. McWilliam J. ruled that the Government had no such power and the defendants appealed to the Supreme Court against his finding. Their appeal was rejected by a majority (4:1) of the Court. The case was sent back to Mr. Justice McWilliam to make such order as he thought fit in the circumstances. The High Court summarised the finding of the Supreme Court thus:

> 'that the circumstances of [Mr. Garvey's] purported removal from office . . . were such that his appointment was not validly terminated.'

Given that this was the Court's decision it is surprising that the arguments in the High Court centred on whether the plaintiff was entitled to 'damages' for his wrongful removal from office and, if

115. High Court unreported, 25 February 1977 (Finlay P.).
116. [1981] I.R. 75; the question of 'damages' was determined by the High Court (McWilliam J.) on 19 December 1979. The facts are outlined at page 75, chapter three, above.

so, the measure of those damages.[117] The purported removal from office took place in January, 1978 (see page 75, chapter three, above). Garvey resigned his position in May, 1979. A sum representing the amount of his salary from January, 1978, was paid to the former Commissioner on resignation but, as payment was in arrears, McWilliam J. made an award of special damages representing the interest to which Garvey was entitled from the date of his purported removal from office to that of his actual resignation:

> '. . . the plaintiff did suffer loss by not receiving his salary at the proper times because either he had to borrow money by investment or otherwise so as to make a profit.'

So far, the judgment is unobjectionable.[118] But McWilliam J. went on to discuss general and exemplary damages both of which were claimed by the plaintiff. General damages were claimed for loss of job satisfaction, loss of opportunity to prepare for his retirement, invasion of privacy due to the public interest in his removal from office, injury to his health and general distress aggravated by the effect the events had upon his family. Both *Cox v. Phillips Industries Ltd.*[119] and *Addis v. Gramophone Co. Ltd.*[120] were cited in court. McWilliam J. espoused the decision in the latter, above all its emphasis that, where a claim is made for breach of contract, whether of a contract of employment or otherwise, circumstances of malice, fraud, defamation or violence which might sustain an action of tort cannot be taken into consideration.

> 'Accordingly, unless some injury was occasioned by the plaintiff as a result of the wrongful removal from office of the

117. See Kenny J. in the Supreme Court on the trial judge's decision: 'These findings meant that the plaintiff had been wrongfully removed from the office which he held *and was, at least, entitled to damages*' (emphasis added).

118. With one reservation, however. The judgment implies that the plaintiff who delays longest, provided he remains within the Statute of Limitations, 1957, and is not guilty of acquiescence or laches, will receive the greatest award. A new approach is suggested by *Taylor v. National Union of Seamen* [1967] 1 W.L.R. 532 where the possibility is suggested of a declaration which preserves all those prospective rights of the employee which flow from a continuance in employment, without giving him the right to wages between purported dismissal and trial, because the latter might lead to considerable over-compensation of the employee. Freedland suggests that occasions might well arise in which it might be a useful remedy to declare a dismissal invalid for the purpose only of pension rights depending upon the continuity of employment and not for the purpose of continuing remuneration: *op. cit.,* fn. 25 *ante,* 292.

119. [1976] 1 WLR 638.

120. [1909] AC 488.

plaintiff which could reasonably have been foreseen by the defendants I am of opinion that he is not entitled to any general damages under this heading.'

But Garvey was the holder of a statutory office whose attempted removal was held to have been devoid of legal validity. Insofar as the High Court based its decision on principles relating to wrongful breach of contract one can remark only that it was misconceived and wrong. The Court's discussion of exemplary damages is equally unsatisfactory. It is unclear whether these damages were considered as a claim in contract or in tort. The general tenor of the Court's judgment is contractual, yet the authority cited in respect of exemplary damages involved tortious liability: *Rookes v. Barnard*.[121] In *Rookes'* case, Lord Devlin stated:

'that there are certain categories of cases in which an award of exemplary damages can serve a useful purpose in vindicating the strength of the law and thus affording a practical justification for admitting into the civil law a principle which logically ought to belong to the criminal. The first category is oppressive, arbitrary or unconstitutional action by the servants of government.'

This statement was not elaborated on in *Rookes* as the case itself did not deal with actions by servants of government. It was, however, very fully discussed in *Broome v. Cassel & Co.*[122] and McWilliam J. was satisfied from the judgments in that case that he should award exemplary damages 'related to the injury which the plaintiff has suffered by reason of the arbitrary and oppressive conduct of the Government'. Having regard to the view that similar injury would to a large extent have been sustained by the plaintiff had he been lawfully removed from office, the judge awarded £500 on that part of the claim. It is submitted that, since *Addis'* case held that exemplary damages cannot be admitted in contract, this aspect of the award should be seen as recovered in tort.

121. [1964] 2 WLR 269, 328.
122. [1972] 2 WLR 645.

CHAPTER FIVE

Statutory Unfair Dismissal

A. The Need for Legislation Concerning Dismissal: Background Influences

Before 1977, the need for legislation in Ireland to deal with dismissal for unjust cause was great. The common law action for wrongful dismissal was cumbersome, inadequate and very often expensive. It existed for an élite of workers. Dismissal was also a serious cause of industrial unrest. Of the disputes recorded in the Labour Court reports for the years 1972-1975 inclusive, 187 were classified as disputes relating to engagement or dismissal, in which 26,299 people were involved, accounting for over a quarter of a million man days lost in industry. In 1975, one third of all man days lost were due to these reasons.

International influences were also at work. During the years leading up to the introduction of the Unfair Dismissals Act, individual dismissal was the subject of an International Labour Organisation Recommendation, a Proposal for Legislation in the European Economic Communities and statutes in individual countries in Western Europe and elsewhere.[1] A number of International Labour Conventions and Recommendations dealt with matters relating to dismissal prior to ILO Recommendation no. 119 on the Termination of Employment (Geneva 1963).[2] But comprehensive treatment of

---

1. See a comprehensive treatment of 'Protection against Unfair Dismissal: A Comparative View' by J. Stieber (Michigan State University): paper presented to International Industrial Relations Association (Paris) 1979.
2. Certain of these instruments provided protection against dismissal in particular circumstances (i.e., during maternity leave: Maternity Protection Convention 1919 (no. 3) Art. 4; Maternity Protection Convention (Revised) 1952 (no. 103) Art. 6; Maternity Protection Recommendation 1952 (no. 95) para. 5, or for certain reasons (such as union membership or participation in union activities): Right to Organise and Collective Bargaining Convention 1949 (no. 98) Art. 1; seeking or holding office or acting as workers' representatives: Workers' Representatives Convention 1971 (no. 135) Art. 1 and Workers' Representatives Recommendation 1971 (no. 143) Part III; and grounds constituting racial, religious or other discrimination: Discrimination (Employment and Occupation) Convention 1958 (no. 111) Arts. 1-2; Discrimination (Employment and Occupation) Recommendation 1958 (no. 111) para. 2. Others provided for special measures to be taken in certain cases in the event of dismissal (as in the case of redundancy of migrants during their term of employment: Migration for Employment Recommendation (Revised) 1949 (no. 86) Arts. 22, 24, 26 of the Annex to the Recommendation) or for certain rights upon dismissal (i.e., the right to receive holiday pay for the part of holiday entitle-

termination of employment was not formally envisaged until the adoption in 1950 by the International Labour Conference of a resolution which noted the absence of international standards on the matter and called for the preparation of a report on the law and practice of different countries in respect of termination of employment.[3] The subsequent adoption of the recommendation on Termination of Employment in 1963 marked the culmination, internationally, of a growing recognition that the individual worker required protection against arbitrary and unwarranted termination of his employment and against the economic and social hardship resulting from loss of employment.

ILO Recommendation no. 119 lays down general standards relating to termination of employment at the initiative of the employer.[4] It provides that termination of employment by an employer should not take place unless there is a valid reason for such termination connected with the capacity or conduct of the worker or based on the operational requirements of the undertaking, establishment or service. The reasons to be considered valid for this purpose are left to be defined nationally. At the same time it is provided that certain enumerated reasons should not constitute valid reasons for termination of employment, namely, union membership or participation in union activities; seeking office as, acting or having acted as a

---

ment not taken at the time of termination of employment): e.g., Holidays with Pay Convention (Revised) 1970 (no. 132) Art. 11. The protection provided by certain of these standards was incorporated in para. 3 of ILO Recommendation no. 119 which is considered in the text. A list of the relevant instruments and decisions is given in *ILO: Termination of Employment (dismissal and lay-off)* Report VII (1) International Labour Conference, 46th sess., 1962, Appendix.

3. *ILO: Record of Proceedings* Int. Lab. Conf., 33rd Sess., (1950) 579; the Office undertook a series of studies in the field, certain of which formed the basis of discussion at the technical meetings.

4. These are supplemented by a number of further standards applicable to cases of termination of employment involving reduction of the work force. A Working Party of the ILO was set up in the late 1970s by the Governing Body to carry out a systematic review of all the existing instruments and classify them in a number of categories. The first category comprises instruments whose ratification and application should be promoted on a priority basis; the second, those whose revision would be appropriate; and the third, all other existing instruments. Some instruments were included in both categories 1 and 2. Among them was ILO Recommendation no. 119. The Recommendation is therefore to have priority status and, also, to be revised. See N. Valticos: 'The future prospects for international labour standards' (1979) 118 *Int. Lab. Rev.,* 679. Recommendation no. 119 was discussed at the 67th session of the ILO, Geneva 1981. See *Report VIII (2)* on *Termination of Employment at the Initiative of the Employer.* A more conclusive debate is expected in 1982. The *Report* is not referred to in detail in the text as it would be premature at this stage. However, it is clear that before the Irish Unfair Dismissals Act is amended, very serious consideration will have to be given to the *Report* as it was agreed, at least in 1981, to implement most of it by way of Convention, not, as in 1963, by Recommendation.

worker's representative; the filing of a complaint or participating in proceedings against an employer involving an alleged violation of laws or regulations; race, colour, sex, marital status, religion, political opinion, national extraction or social origin.[5] In 1963, the Irish Government indicated that they accepted the provisions in the Recommendation, subject to minor reservations. The Irish Congress of Trade Unions made it known that they were in favour of appropriate legislation. In 1973, in accordance with Article 19 of the Constitution of the ILO, the Governing Body of the ILO requested the governments of all member States to supply reports indicating the position of their law and practice in regard to the matters dealt with by the Recommendation.[6] Although the essential principle of the Recommendation had by then been adopted in many countries, Ireland's report could point only to three areas of statutory activity: namely, redundancy, industrial disputes and minimum notice and terms of employment.[7] Speaking generally, the Committee remarked that:

> '... the existence of notice periods or severance allowances, although necessary aspects of the more comprehensive protection aimed at by the Recommendation, [do not] meet [the] fundamental requirement [i.e., of general guarantees against unjustified termination].'[8]

The message was clear. Further indirect pressure on Ireland to review her dismissal laws arose on another international front. In connection with the decision taken on the then proposed EEC Directive on the approximation of the legislation of Member States concerning mass dismissals in December, 1974,[9] the Council of the European Communities requested the Commission to submit a comprehensive report on legislation on behalf of workers in the event of individual

---

5. '... [It] is this provision for protection against unjustified termination of a worker's employment that represents both the core of the instrument and its major element of impact': *Report* fn. 11 *post*, — para 159.

6. *Report III: Termination of Employment* Int. Lab. Conf., 59th Sess., 1974. It was the first occasion on which reports on the Recommendation were requested under Art. 19 of the Constitution of the ILO and thus was the first opportunity the Committee had to examine reports of governments on their law and practice relating to termination of employment.

7. Respectively, — Redundancy Payments Act, 1967, amended 1971 and 1973; Industrial Relations Act, 1946, amended 1969; Minimum Notice and Terms of Employment Act, 1973. The two first mentioned Acts have since been further amended.

8. Para. 164.

9. As a result, see in Ireland the Protection of Employment Act, 1977.

dismissals.[10] Part I of the report, which was submitted in 1976.[11] gives a comprehensive summary of the legal position in the Member States of the Community. Once more Ireland could mention only redundancy and minimum notice legislation; at times she was forced to reveal that 'No special provisions' existed (as in relation to the grounds for 'Normal Dismissal'). Ireland submitted that:

> 'Disagreements are normally dealt with by means of negotia tions between management and workers. To help the negotia tions the Government provides mediation offices and industrial tribunals which management and workers can use.'

'By means of this procedure', it was maintained, 'voluntary continued employment can be achieved'. At the time, Ireland's 'mediation offices' (*sic*) for individual termination were primarily the Rights Commissioners, established under the Industrial Relations Act, 1969. Her 'industrial tribunals' were the Labour Court[12] and the Redundancy Appeals Tribunal.[13]

The Anti-Discrimination (Unfair Dismissals) Bill, as it was first styled, was introduced into Dáil Éireann in 1976 by the Minister for Labour in the Coalition Government.[14] Omitting any reference to international influences, the Minister stated that:

> 'the general impulse for this legislation related to the number of disputes which had been caused in recent years as a result of disagreement on the disciplinary methods used in particular cases. Disputes had arisen because an employee felt aggrieved, and his sense of grievance, in the existing lacuna in our legisla tion, meant he sought the assistance and support of fellow workers in his disagreement with the employer. We had many strikes. We reckon that one-fifth of man days lost in the year before last arose from disputes relating to dismissals . . .'[15]

As passed by both Houses of the Oireachtas in April, 1977, the Un fair Dismissals Act does not conform in every respect to the require

10. R3632/74 (SOC) 280. The European Parliament was also in favour of the Commission drawing up such proposals, see its Resolution of 12 March 1973; OJC 19 of 12.4.1973; see similarly OJC 95 of 28.4.1975.
11. V/812/75 — E; see 'EC Commission Proposals on Individual Dismissals': *European Industrial Relations Review* (no. 30) June 1976.
12. Established by the Industrial Relations Act 1946.
13. Established by the Redundancy Payments Act 1967.
14. *Dáil Debates*, 30 June 1976.
15. *Ibid.*, Vol. 294, col. 503 (23 Nov. 1976); see, too, Vol. 293, col. 1076 (4 November 1976).

ments of ILO Convention no. 119.[16] The Convention therefore comprises a vital set of standards against which to judge how far the Act ensures fair treatment and valid procedures.

B. The Unfair Dismissals Act[16a]

(1) *Basic principles*

The Act provides for the bringing of claims for redress for unfair dismissal before a Rights Commissioner or the Employment Appeals Tribunal within six months of the date of dismissal. The advantages of a statutory claim reside chiefly in time, costs, informality and in the fact that the draftsmen were committed to the necessity of devising a criterion of lawfulness of dismissal which would be at once more exacting and yet more flexible than the implied terms offered by the law of the contract of employment. They achieved this by the combination of requiring an employer to show good cause for dismissal and of an overriding test of the reasonableness of an employer's decision to dismiss.[17]

The Act is cast in a pluralist framework. Companies cannot be run solely in the interests of management; workers' rights must be consulted as well. Section 6(1) floods the entire Act. It deems the dismissal of an employee to be an unfair dismissal for the purposes of the Act

'unless, having regard to all the circumstances, there were substantial grounds justifying the dismissal.'

The specific conception of fairness espoused by the Act distinguishes it clearly from the common law action for wrongful dismissal. The formal justice of the common law is rejected, i.e., the narrow and often socially inadequate dictates of contract law which make the uniform application of general rules the keystone of justice, and which establish principles whose validity is supposedly independent of choices among conflicting values. Procedural and substantive

16. For example, para. 7(2) stipulates that during the notice period the worker should, as far as practicable, be entitled to a reasonable amount of time-off without loss in pay for this purpose. Ireland has not made any provision in respect of time-off. Nor is the employer required by legislation or otherwise, in accordance with para. 8 of the Recommendation, to provide an employee upon termination of his employment with a certificate indicating the dates of entry into and termination of the employment and specifying the type or types of work on which he was employed (nothing unfavourable to the worker should be inserted in such a certificate: para. 8(2)). Further discrepancies are noted throughout the text.

16a. The full text of the Unfair Dismissals Act, 1977, is given in Appendix I.

17. See P. Davies and M. R. Freedland: *Labour Law Texts and Materials* 349; R.M. Unger: *Law in Modern Society* 194-5; see too, R. Dworkin: *Taking Rights Seriously* 134-5.

rules of justice are preferred. Where breaches of implied or other contractual terms are concerned, the Act imports notions of fairness in order to arrive at an overall assessment of the lawfulness of dismissal. The balance between procedural and substantive justice is in itself crucial — both within the Act and in its application.

The Act in section 13 renders void any provision in an agreement, whether a contract of employment or not, and whether made before or after the commencement of the Act, to the extent that it purports to exclude or limit the application of, or is inconsistent with, any provision in the Act. This may be crucial where an agreed settlement has been negotiated between an employer and employee. If the agreement is concluded before, rather than after, dismissal in such a way as to exclude a statutory claim, it will be void under section 13.[18]

(2) *Enforcing authorities under the Act*

A major advance brought about by the Unfair Dismissals Act was the provision of an adjudicatory service which was speedy and free. This service comprises the Rights Commissioners and the Employment Appeals Tribunal. Unfortunately, however, the emphasis both in the Act and in the operation of these authorities is upon finality rather than consistency of decision-making. This manifests itself in a number of ways.

In the first place there is very little scope for public comment upon decisions of the Commissioners or of the EAT. Proceedings before a Commissioner are held 'otherwise than in public'[19] and their recommendations are not available to members of the public. To analyse their role in relation to unfair dismissal is therefore impossible and little information may be gleaned from such of their recommendations as are appealed to the EAT. When it comes to determinations of the Tribunal the position is only marginally better. These are in loose form, unindexed, and there is no annual binding service. Points of law are discussed only exceptionally and then scantily. Important facts are frequently omitted and the reasons for a determination are scarcely ever made explicit. Much depends on the actual composition of the Tribunal in any particular case. The one and only attempt to make potential users of the Act or the general public more aware about the work of the EAT is found in a slim pamphlet entitled *Reports of Important Decisions by the Employment Appeals Tribunal under the Unfair Dismissals Act 1977: Years 1977 to 1978*.[20] The booklet appeared in 1981. It contains an

18. *Eate v. Semprit (Ireland) Ltd.* UD 46/1977. See, further, chapter 7, page 202 below, fn. 110.
19. Unfair Dismissals Act, s. 8 (6).
20. Prl. 8765, Government Publications Office.

abbreviated account of 27 cases. It is apparently the Tribunal's intention to produce a follow-up for succeeding years' 'Important Decisions'.

The base-line of the Unfair Dismissals Act is furnished by quite clear legal rules, but this is not apparent in EAT practice. There is a danger that Tribunal determinations are beginning to belie the expectations of potential claimants. A 'wilderness of single instances' is imminent, if not already with us. The remaining chapters in this book attempt a rationalisation of the principles and practice of the EAT. Subject to the impediments listed above, an effort is made to detect patterns and trends. Such statements of principle as have emerged from Tribunal determinations are recorded and presented within what purports to be a framework of legal if not of logical consistency. It must not be assumed that these statements appear regularly in Tribunal decisions. Where gaps appear in the framework, decisions of the British EAT or civil courts will be cited. These must be viewed with the caution owed to decisions of another jurisdiction operating similar, not identical,legislation. A certain amount of speculation as to how the Act ought to be construed or interpreted is unavoidable. Again and again, a return will be made to the statute. Its importance cannot be over-emphasised.

A second way in which finality is seen to operate at the expense of consistency concerns the Act's appellate system. Tribunal autonomy is promoted. The Act provides that

> 'A party concerned may appeal to the Circuit Court from any determination of the Tribunal in relation to a claim for redress under this Act.'[21]

Where, at the expiration of the time for bringing such an appeal,[22] no appeal has in fact been brought, the Minister for Labour may step in if an employer fails to carry out a determination of the Tribunal.[23] The Minister may institute and carry on proceedings in the Circuit Court in his name on behalf of the employee against the employer 'for redress under this Act'.[24] This will amount to an appeal by the

---

21. Section 10 (4).
22. Page 133 below.
23. Section 10 (1).
24. The advantage of the Minister's taking the matter before the Circuit Court resides in the fact that, as a result, neither employer nor employee will be liable to pay costs, s. 10 (3). The Department of Justice's Scheme of Legal Aid and Advice does, however, apply to advice and representation in respect of appellate proceedings before the Circuit Court. The Scheme is means-tested. To qualify for the services available, a person's annual disposable income may not exceed £3,500 (this ceiling is subject to periodic review). The Scheme excludes proceedings before administrative tribunals such as the EAT, and test cases.

employer because the Act states that where the Court 'finds that an employee is entitled to redress', it shall order the employer concerned to make to the employee concerned 'the appropriate redress'.[25]

Appeals to the Circuit Court may be on questions of law or fact. The Act is not specific either way. In theory, the Circuit Court could play a most important role in preventing Tribunal determinations from being wildly at variance with one another. The British EAT fulfils this role in respect of industrial tribunals[26] (in many ways the Irish EAT is equivalent to the latter). The Circuit Court could also prescribe guidelines for the Act's operation; this would be a most valuable exercise in the absence of a Code of Practice in Ireland. Once more, however, there is darkness instead of light. The Circuit Court Rules[27] do not require an appellant to notify the EAT of the appeal. Hence the number and outcome of appeals to the Circuit Court is unknown. Moreover, in most cases the Circuit Court does not issue a written judgment and parties are forced to rely upon their own transcript of the case, presuming they have had foresight enough to take one. Once again, but more culpably in the case of an ordinary court, points of law are not analysed in any depth. In its *Report* for 1978, the EAT noted, in somewhat ruffled tones, that it 'became aware of' 14 appeals to the Circuit Court and that 5 of these had been upheld. The number of appeals doubled in 1979 and 1980. Some of these did not uphold the Tribunal's determinations but, beyond recording that fact, no further explanation is given or can be found.

Generally speaking, in civil cases, an appeal lies to the High Court from decisions in cases originating in the Circuit Court. Appeals from EAT determinations do not fit clearly into this category. The Act does not refer to the High Court's jurisdiction. In spite of this there have been two appeals to that Court from a Circuit Court decision.[28]

25. If, *ex hypothesi,* an employee wishes to enforce a determination of reinstatement or re-engagement, could the Circuit Court endorse an order to that effect? Because of the common law's reluctance to enforce employment contracts, chapter four, page 87 above, it is suggested that an employee's redress could lie only in damages. Contrast the EPCA, s. 71: if an employer's non-compliance extends to a failure to reinstate or re-engage on any terms, an industrial tribunal may award compensation in the form of an additional award over and above the other elements of compensation.

26. See, e.g., a total of 181 recorded cases of the EAT in relation to fairness alone under the EPCA: P. Elias 'The Concept of Fairness in Unfair Dismissal' (1981) ILJ 201. Elias analyses the recent trend of the Court of Appeal to favour limited intervention by the EAT and to display a high degree of respect for the conclusions of the industrial tribunals.

27. No. 1 of 1979, S.I. no. 10 of 1979.

28. *Ryder & Byrne v. Commissioners of Irish Lights* (unreported 16 April, 1980, chapter six, page 148, fn. 16, below); *McCabe v. Lisney and Son* (unreported 16 March, 1981, chapter seven, pages 197-'8, fn. 82, below). In *McCabe,* counsel for the respondents contended that the Act provided no right of appeal to the High Court but Ellis J. held the wording of the Act was too indefinite and uncertain to

A brief comment is necessary about the enforcing authorities them selves. Rights Commissioners adopt an informal, inquisitorial approach and enjoy a wide discretion concerning procedures.[29] They were established and appointed by the Minister for Labour under the Industrial Relations Act, 1969, to deal with trade disputes arising out of individual grievances.[30] At present there are three Commissioners. There is a right of appeal from their recommendations to the more formal, more legalistic Employment Appeals Tribunal, where the procedure tends to be adversarial. Likewise, where a Commissioner's recommendation is not carried out by an employer, an employee may bring the claim before the EAT.

The forerunner to the present Employment Appeals Tribunal was set up under the Redundancy Payments Act, 1967. Before the Unfair Dismissals Act, the Redundancy Appeals Tribunal, as it was then known, dealt with cases under redundancy and minimum notice legislation. It was renamed the Employment Appeals Tribunal under s. 18 of the Unfair Dismissals Act. Much of the Redundancy (Redundancy Appeals Tribunal) Regulations of 1968 and '69 are applicable to the EAT. (See Appendix IV). In addition, regulations have been made under s. 17 of the Unfair Dismissals Act concerning claims and appeals[31] and the calculation of weekly remuneration.[32]

The Tribunal consists of a Chairman who is a practising barrister or solicitor of not less than 7 years standing; and, since the Redundancy Payments (Amendment) Act, 1979, was passed, not more than 5 Vice-chairmen and not less than 12 or more than 30

---

deprive the applicant of his right of appeal to the High Court to which he would otherwise be entitled in the absence of a sufficiently clear or express provision or intention in the Act to that effect.

29. Contrast the conciliation machinery of ACAS under the EPCA, ss. 133-134.

30. Section 13 of the Act of 1969. See an (unsigned) article by the author: 'The System of Rights Commissioners in Ireland' (1974) 108 ILTSJ 252; see also 'Ireland — Dismissals law two years on': *European Industrial Relations Review* April 1979, No. 63, 20. When the Commissioner is approached by an aggrieved employee he notifies the employer and informs him that he wishes to investigate the matter. The latter is expected to attend the hearing. If the claim is settled before or during the hearing, or if it is withdrawn, the Commissioner does not need to make a recommendation. The Rights Commissioner may provide for legal representation and 'except as so provided, no person shall be entitled to appear by counsel or solicitor before [them]'. The Commissioner may not hear a claim if any party concerned notifies him in writing that he objects to the claim being heard, page 125 below. Once the Commissioner is notified in writing of objections concerning his hearing a particular case, the file concerning the claim must be closed. The words of the Act may be strictly construed, however, so that if an objecting party does not notify the Commissioner in writing but merely ignores his notification the Commissioner may proceed to hold a hearing in his absence.

31. S.I. no. 286 of 1977, see Appendix II.

32. S.I. no. 287 of 1977, see Appendix III.

ordinary members who are representative, in equal numbers, of workers and employers.[33] All members of the EAT are appointed by the Minister for Labour. There are at present 3 vice-chairmen and 24 ordinary members. Half of the ordinary members are nominated by the Irish Congress of Trade Unions and half by a body or bodies representative of employers. A person may represent himself before the EAT or be represented by, e.g., a lawyer or a trade union official. The annual reports of the EAT refer to the increasing complexity of appeals occasioned by the growing legal representation of parties under the Act of 1977.[34] There is no legal aid for claimants either before the Rights Commissioners or the EAT.[35]

In two instances the Act stipulates that the Rights Commissioners may not hear a claim for redress.[36] They are where:

(a) the Tribunal has made a determination in relation to the claim, or

(b) any party concerned notifies the Commissioner in writing that he objects to the claim being heard by a Rights Commissioner.

In the same way, the Tribunal may not hear a claim for redress under the Act (except by way of appeal from, or where an employer has failed to carry out,[37] a recommendation of a Rights Commissioner)

33. Redundancy Payments Act, 1967, s. 31(2) as amended by Redundancy Payments Act, 1979, Schedule.

34. See, e.g., *Annual Report* for 1977 (Government Publications Office, Prl. 7110) and chapter nine *post*.A witness before the Tribunal is entitled to the same immunities and privileges as if he were a witness before the High Court. (UDA, 1977, s. 8(9) incorporating IRA, 1946, s. 21(2)). The Tribunal may take evidence on oath and impose penalties for wilful and corrupt perjury, false evidence and swearing. (UDA 1977, s. 8(9) incorporating RPA, 1967, s. 39(17)). It may require persons to attend when specified in a notice to that effect or to produce documents in their possession, custody or control which relate to any matter. If a person receives a notice about attendance or the production of documents and refuses or wilfully neglects to observe its terms, he is guilty of an offence and liable on summary conviction to a fine not exceeding £150. (RPA, 1979 (Schedule)). The Tribunal has no power to punish for contempt; it is unable to restore the *status quo ante* of the parties pending a hearing of the claim. A system of precedent is very slowly growing up in relation to determinations of the Tribunal, although past decisions are persuasive rather than conclusive authority.

35. The fact that the Scheme of Legal Aid and Advice (fn. 24 *ante)* does not apply to administrative tribunals now merits critical re-examination. Apparently there has been some opposition to the idea from the trade union movement.

36. Section 8(3) and (5). The latter is directly adopted from the Industrial Relations Act, 1969 (cf. *Dáil Debates*, cols. 128-9, 25 January, 1977).

37. Section 8(4).

    (a) if a Rights Commissioner has made a recommendation in
        relation to the claim, or
    (b) unless one of the parties concerned notifies a Com-
        missioner in writing that he objects to the claim being heard
        by a Rights Commissioner.

If, therefore, an employee wishes to present his claim straightaway
before the Tribunal, or if an employer wishes to present his defence
only in that forum, the party concerned must notify the Commissioner in the terms set out above. This cumbersome procedure has
been criticised by the EAT.[38] Where an employer expresses his
preference for the more formal approach of the Tribunal by objecting to a claim being heard by a Commissioner, an aggrieved
employee has no option but to present his claim before the EAT.

By far the most rapid development of unfair dismissal law is taking
place before the EAT.[39] From the first half-year of its existence in
1977 to the last full year for which a report is available, 1980, the
grand total of cases decided by the EAT under the Unfair Dismissals
Act was 16, 151, 331 and 754 respectively. At the same time there
was a drop in the number of applicants who chose to come before the
Rights Commissioners. It is impossible to say why this should have
occurred but it is not fanciful to suggest that the total lack of any
reliable yardstick by which to predict the outcome of a claim before
the Commissioners may be one of the factors involved.[40]

In general the EAT does not award costs against a party to an
appeal or claim. Where, however, one of the parties has acted
frivolously or vexatiously, the Tribunal may make an order that he
shall pay to another party a specified amount in respect of travelling
expenses and other costs or expenses reasonably incurred by that
other party in connection with the hearing.[41]

Unlike its British counterpart, the act regulates alternative
remedies. Where, under s. 8 of the Act, an employee gives notice to a
Rights Commissioner or to the EAT, he is not entitled to recover
damages at common law for wrongful dismissal.[42] Equally, where an

---

    38. *O'Donovan v. Gillen* UD 101/1978. The Tribunal described it as '. . . a bit
futile to be required by statute to put in writing a statement to the effect that the
writer does not wish to have his case dealt with by a Rights Commissioner'.

    39. See further on trends in EAT practice, chapter 9 below.

    40. See analogously in relation to the conciliation machinery of ACAS, R.
Munday 'Tribunal Lore: Legalism and the Industrial Tribunals' (1981) ILJ 146,
152.

    41. S.I. no. 286 of 1977, Appendix II.

    42. Section 15(2). The constitutionality of this sub-section may be doubted. A
personal right of fundamental importance is that of access to the courts, or the right
to litigate a claim. See *The State (Quinn) v. Ryan and Others* [1965] I.R. 70; 100
ILTR 105; *Macauley v. Minister for Posts and Telegraphs* [1966] I.R. 345. On

employee has initiated proceedings at common law, he cannot seek redress under the Act.

The Act attempts to channel disputes concerning unfair dismissal away from the Industrial Relations Act, 1969. Section 8(10) enacts

> 'A dispute in relation to a dismissal that is an unfair dismissal for the purposes of this Act shall not be referred to a rights commissioner under section 13(2) of the Industrial Relations Act, 1969.'

The wording of the sub-section is ambiguous. Only by inserting the words 'deemed to be' before 'an unfair dismissal for the purposes of this Act' would its sense be unequivocal. If a claimant recommenced proceedings before a Rights Commissioner under the Act of 1969 on the basis either that his dismissal had been found to be fair by the EAT or that there is no such thing as a dismissal which 'is' unfair 'for the purposes' of the Unfair Dismissals Act, arguably the Commissioner should decline to hear the case, applying the administrative law principles of 'issue estoppel'. To agree to hear a claim relating to the same issue under each Act successively (the one providing for appeal to the EAT, the other to the Labour Court) would be to frustrate the aims of the Oireachtas in relation to unfair dismissals law. Section 15 of the Act of 1977 attempts to regulate alternative proceedings at common law. *A fortiori* section 8(10) must be seen as attempting to regulate alternative proceedings under statute. Its purport is clear: not only is a claimant intended to be debarred from recommencing proceedings under the Act of 1969 when he has proceeded under the Act of 1977 but also, if his case is one which appropriately comes under the latter, he may not choose the Act of 1969 as his preferred route. For as long as the sub-section remains unamended, however, a claimant may want two bites of the statutory cherry and on one occasion to date this has not been refused.[43]

these see J. M. Kelly *The Irish Constitution,* 365. Note the way in which the right to litigate claims was viewed as a personal right by the Supreme Court in *O'Brien v. Keogh* [1972] I.R. 144, and as a personal and a property right later on in *O'Brien v. Manufacturing Engineering Co. Ltd.* [1973] I.R. 334 although doubt was cast, *obiter,* on the two last-mentioned decisions in the Supreme Court by O'Higgins C.J. in *Moynihan v. Greensmyth* [1977] I.R. 55, 69. There seems to be no reason why an employee who commences proceedings under the Unfair Dismissals Act might not initiate an action at common law later on. It is significant that in *Mid-Western Health Board v. Ponnampalam* (Circuit Court unreported, 26 March 1980) Judge Gleeson did not regard it as '... a matter for this Court to decide whether it is constitutional for the legislature to enact as it did in Section 15(2) of the Unfair Dismissals Act that because he embarked on the present procedure [under the Act] the claimant is not entitled to damages at common law.'

43. *Kennedy v. Dataproducts (Dublin) Ltd.* UD 12/1981 (at the time of writing, on appeal to the Labour Court under The Industrial Relations Act, 1969).

(3) The Winds of Change?

A detection of patterns and trends and an analysis of the Unfair Dismissals Act itself are timely since the Act is currently under review in the Department of Labour. At the same time, ILO Recommendation no. 119 is under review at an international level. Improvements to the Act will be suggested or hinted at in the following pages against a background of what attempts to be a comprehensive chart or map of the Act. The two most important defects in the Act, as will be seen, concern the definition of 'dismissal',[44] and the nature of the presumption of unfairness.[45]

The conceptual basis for the Act is, and must be, the contract of employment. The Act employs and in some cases, it defines, terms already familiar at common law such as 'termination', 'dismissal', 'contract of employment' and 'fixed term contract'. The view cannot be sustained, it is suggested, that the Unfair Dismissals Act turned over a leaf so new as to jettison the vast body of common law relating to the contract of employment. In the first place, this is nowhere stated in the Act and, as a matter of statutory construction, a change or a beginning so fundamental could not be presumed *ex silentio*. Secondly, there is the likelihood that such a view — involving an intuitive construction of the Act — would lead to chaos. However artificial and defective it may be, however obsolete, the contract of employment provides a mechanism for regulating the individual employment relationship. It affords a measure or standard by which critically to assess decisions relating to unfair dismissal. It enables one to speculate as to where the law is going, and where it ought to go.

Not every worker is covered by the Unfair Dismissals Act. There are technical qualifications to be satisfied. An employee must come within the appropriate definitions and he must present his claim in time. He also bears the burden of proving he has been dismissed within the Act and he must establish the date of his dismissal. The remaining part of this chapter will examine the portals through which an aggrieved employee must pass in order to qualify for the Act's protection.

C. Preliminary Requirements in the Act

(1) Qualifications and exclusions

The right not to be unfairly dismissed applies to every employee except in so far as its application is qualified or excluded by or under

44. Page 134 below.
45. See chapter eight, page 206 below.

the Act. In this respect, the Act falls below the standards of ILO Re
commendation no. 119.[46] To be a qualified employee, an individual
must

    (i) be an 'employee' as defined by section 1 of the Act;[47] and
    (ii) have the requisite continuous service[48] of not less than one

46. Para. 18 of ILO Recommendation no. 119 provides that the Recommendation should apply to all branches of economic activity and to all categories of
workers, except four, which may be excluded, namely, (a) workers engaged for a
specified period of time or for a specified task in cases in which, owing to the nature
of the work to be effected, the employment relationship cannot be of an indeterminate
duration; (b) workers serving a period of probation determined in advance and of a
reasonable duration; (c) workers engaged on a casual basis for a short period; and (d)
public servants engaged in the administration of the State to the extent only that
constitutional principles preclude the application to them of one or more provisions
in the Recommendation. The list of excepted categories in the Irish Act is far wider
than that encompassed by the Recommendation or in the proposed new Convention,
see *Report* fn. 4 *ante,* para 6. The permitted exclusions at (a) and (b) above are given
separate treatment in the Unfair Dismissals Act. The ILO *Report* (fn. 11 *ante)* referred to problems which arise in the implementation of Recommendation no. 119
where, *inter alia,* significant groups of persons covered by the Recommendation are
excluded from the protection afforded nationally 'e.g. . . . where legislation is limited in
scope, excludes certain groups of persons or imposes qualifying periods other than the
probationary periods authorised by the Recommendation' (para. 165). This would
seem to be of direct application to the Irish Act.

47. 'Employee' means 'an individual who has entered into or works under (or,
where the employment has ceased, worked under) a contract of employment and, in
relation to redress for a dismissal under this Act, includes, in the case of the death of
the employee concerned at any time following the dismissal, his personal representative.' See chapter 3, page 46 *ante;* and cases such as *Kirwan v. Dart Industries Ltd.*
UD 1/1980; *O'Cearnaigh v. ITGWU* UD 383/1979.

48. Continuous service is calculated by reference to the rules in the amended
First Schedule, Minimum Notice and Terms of Employment Act, 1973: section 2(4)
(as amended by s. 20 of the Unfair Dismissals Act 1977). See *Phipps v. Laffin* UD
18/1979 (*re* First Schedule of Minimum Notice and Terms of Employment Act,
1973, para. 7, concerning transfer of a trade or business: continuity unbroken where
employee dismissed and immediately re-employed by new employer); *McGrath v. C.
A. Jenkins & Sons Ltd.* UD 227/1978 (informal transfer of a business as a going
concern without de facto break in service will not break continuity of service); *Caulfield v. Campbell Catering Ltd.* UD 341/1979 (previous employer had no 'direct
relationship' with respondent company: therefore no transfer of trade or business);
Murray v. Antolec Ltd. UD 51/1980 (previous service with associated companies in
England could not be counted in addition to claimant's service in Ireland — *semble,*
the wording of the definition of transfer excludes transfers between associated
companies, contrast the Redundancy Payments Act, 1967, s. 16). Other cases of
note are *Maher v. B & I Line* UD 271/1978 (holiday entitlement cannot be added to
period of service in order to qualify a claimant under the Act of 1977); *Oakes v.
Lynch* UD 214/1978 (employee broke service for purposes of Act of 1977 by
terminating employment of own accord); *Fitzgerald v. Williams Transport Group
Ltd.* UD 151/1978, UD 165/1978 (EAT had to make a positive finding as to the
date of commencement and as to the date of dismissal for purposes of ascertaining
one year's continuity of service).

Under the Schedule, employment hours cannot average less than twenty-one

year with the employer where dismissal is related to pregnancy,[49] maternity,[50] or is connected with trade union membership or activities.

There is no provision excluding a foreigner nor is the dismissal by a foreign employer of a foreigner working in Ireland excluded. The term 'employee' is so defined as to remove any doubt that, in the case of the death of an employee at any time following dismissal, the term applies to his personal representative. The definition of employer is not so explicit but by interpretation it has been taken to follow common law principles,[51] i.e., contract claims enforceable against a person in his lifetime are enforceable against his personal representative after his death.

Even if an employee is qualified in terms of his period of continuous service he may be excluded if he falls into any one of the categories set out in s. 2(1):

employees who have reached the normal retiring age in their firm or who, due to age, would be excluded from the operation of the Redundancy Payments Act, 1967 to 1979;[52]

persons employed by a close relative in a private house or on a farm where both reside;[53]

---

hours per week (the corresponding figure for Social Welfare legislation is eighteen hours) see *Flanagan v. Magnier* UD 365/1979; *Murphy v. Sweeney* UD 216/1978; *Reid v. Sharkey* UD 132/1978; but see *Bartlett v. Kerry County Council* UD 178/1979 (claimant employed as part-time fireman with no specific hours of work; employment comparable to that of district midwife in *Limerick Health Authority v. Ryan* [1969] IR 194 hence covered by the Act even if he might work less than 21 hours a week). Temporary employees, unless they fall within section 2(2) of the Unfair Dismissals Act, are covered: *Kearney v. Midland Health Board* UD 247/1979; *Quigley v. Western Health Board* UD 114/1978; *Ryder & Byrne v. Commissionerss of Irish Lights* UD 31/1977; UD 82/1977; High Court unreported, 16 April, 1980.

49. Section 6(2) (f) UDA 1977.

50. Maternity Protection of Employees Act, 1981, s. 25.

51. *Hutton v. Major George Philippi* UD 291/1980.

52. Pensionable age for purposes of redundancy is now sixty-six (Social Welfare Act, 1977, s. 13(2)): *O'Neill v. Breffni Proteins Ltd.* UD 78/1981; *Stenson v. Fluid Dynamics* UD 251/1978. Contrast ILO *Report* fn. 11 *ante*, para. 35, '... where termination is left to the initiative of the employer the fact that the worker has reached a certain age or has become entitled to an old age pension should not in itself constitute a justified ground for termination'. In the proposed new Convention, fn. 4 *ante*, age is likely to be an invalid reason for termination.

53. *Dáil Debates*, Vol. 294, cols. 489-92 (23 November 1976). An Opposition amendment to exclude small employments of less than 5 persons was not agreed to: *ibid.*, cols. 492-8. Note the development in EAT practice in Britain to distinguish small employers in relation to standards of procedural fairness: e.g., *The Royal Naval School v. Hughes* [1979] IRLR 383. And see now, Employment Act, 1980, s. 6.

members of the Defence Forces and of the Garda Síochána;

AnCO trainees and apprentices;

Persons employed by or under the State[54] other than persons designated for the time being under s. 17 of the Industrial Relations Act, 1969;[55]

officers of local authorities, health boards, vocational education committees and committees of agriculture.[56]

54. In *Hayes & Caffrey v. B & I Line* UD 192/1979 respondents claimed that, as their company was wholly owned by the Minister for Finance, their employees, including the claimants, were persons 'employed by or under the State'. By a 'person employed by or under the State' the Tribunal understood the Unfair Dismissals Act to designate a person in employment as a civil servant. Having regard to the decision of the High Court in *O'Loughlin v. Minister for Social Welfare* [1958] IR 1, the Tribunal construed the phrase 'a person employed by the state' as referring to a person who is a civil servant of the State and 'a person who is employed under the State' as a 'civil servant of the Government' as those expressions were described in the case cited. The Tribunal observed that 'If the legislature intended to exclude employees of semi-state bodies or companies with a share capital the entire of the shares in which were held for the time being by or on behalf of the Minister for Finance or otherwise by or on behalf of the State, the Tribunal considers that the Act would have said so.' The provisions of the Act do not apply to unestablished staff in the non-industrial civil service. See Dáil Questions nos. 351 and 352, 13 December 1979, col. 1898. The principal staff categories involved are as follows: Postmen; Telephonists; Installers; Technicians; Labourers; Cleaners; Messengers. The numbers of staff in the non-industrial civil service excluded from the scope of the Unfair Dismissals Act is 52,000: *Trade Union Information* Summer 1980, 21.

55. The categories of unestablished State employees designated under the Industrial Relations Act, 1969, the date of designation, the categories of unestablished State employees appearing to be outside the scope of section 2 of the Unfair Dismissals Act and the categories of established State employees listed in the Schedule to the Civil Service Commissioners Act, 1956, as (i) designated under the Act of 1969 and (ii) not designated, were dealt with by the Minister for the Public Service in answer to Dáil Questions no. 387 and 388 on 20 November 1976 (Col. 1952). On 8 October, 1969, State industrial employees and civilian employees serving with the Defence Forces were so designated. The number of employees in the designated categories is 8,200: *Trade Union Information* Summer, 1980, 21. See *Watson v. Department of Posts & Telegraphs* UD 220/1979 (porter in Department not included in list of designated persons).

56. Note that non-officers are covered: *Dáil Debates* Vol. 294, cols. 479-82 (23.11.1976). This particular exception has generated most opposition and has often been the subject of criticism. See *Sullivan v. Western Health Board* UD 131/1979 (clinical psychologist); *Ponnampalam v. Mid Western Health Board* UD 300/1979 (consultant surgeon) appointed in temporary capacity to carry out clinical surgery duties, allegedly appointed to replace someone else: EAT held he did not fill officer post to which this other surgeon had been appointed — accordingly, as Mid Western Health Board had not obtained required statutory authority for him to fill this post, he was not an officer of a Health Board within s. 2(1) (j) UDA 1977. The Tribunal ordered that the claimant be reinstated and their decision was appealed to the Circuit Court. Judge Gleeson (former chairman of the EAT) allowed the appeal (26 March 1980), basing his reasons on s. 2(1) (j). Counsel for the claimant argued that a

Much discussion during the parliamentary debates on the draft Unfair Dismissals Bill concerned excluded and special categories of applicants.[57] Approximately one-fifth of the working population in Ireland comes within these groups. Some are already covered by particular statutory provisions, e.g., members of the Defence Forces and of the Garda Síochána; others have their own internal procedures, e.g., civil servants. But not all employees in the excluded categories have other rights to appeal in the event of dismissal.[58]

In so far as fixed term contracts or contracts for a specified purpose are concerned, a dismissal consisting only of the expiry of the term (without renewal) or the completion of the specified purpose is not covered by the Act if (i) the contract is in writing, (ii) it was signed by both parties and (iii) it contains a statement that the Act shall not apply to the dismissal: section 2(2). It is interesting to contrast the EPCA under which a fixed term contract cannot be excluded unless it is for a term of one year or more.[59] Likewise, under that Act, a contract for a fixed purpose is not covered.[60]

Workers serving a period of probation are dealt with in section 3.[61] The Act does not apply to the dismissal of an employee during a period at the commencement of employment when he is on probation or undergoing training if the contract is in writing and the duration of probation or training is one year or less and is specified in the contract. The Act also excludes dismissal during training for qualification or registration as a nurse, pharmacist, health inspector, medical laboratory technician, occupational therapist, physiotherapist, speech therapist, radiographer or social worker. Persons engaged under a statutory apprenticeship[62] in an industrial activity designated by AnCO, the Industrial Training Authority, are

---

temporary officer was not an 'officer' in the sense intended by s. 2(1) (j) but the judge was satisfied that by custom and practice senior medical employees of public or Health authorities had been called officers); see, too, *O'Callaghan v. Cork Corporation* UD 309/1978 (baths officer employed by Cork Corporation: held officer of Corporation and as such excluded from UDA); *Quigley v. Western Health Board* UD 114/1978 (State Registered Psychiatric Nurse — full discussion on what constitutes an officer of a Health Board: applicant held not to be an officer of a local authority).

57. E.g., *Dáil Debates* Vol. 294, cols. 499-522 (23 November 1976).
58. *Ponnampalam v. Mid Western Health Board* UD 300/1979.
59. Section 42 (1), as amended by the Employment Act, 1980, s. 8.
60. *Ryan v. Shipboard Maintenance Ltd.* [1980] ICR 88.
61. See *Dáil Debates*, Vol. 295, cols. 174-83 (8.12.1976); also Vol. 297, cols. 593-600 (2.3.1977). Also *Stevenson v. Dalton Secondary & Preparatory Schools* UD 10/1978; *Fleming v. Athlone Manufacturing Co. Ltd.* UD 140/1978; *Marsh v. UCD* UD 27/1977; *Doyle v. Nitrigin Eireann Teo.* UD 148/1978.
62. E.g., *O'Callaghan v. Denis Mahony Ltd.* UD 117/1979; *Quinn v. Ken David Ltd.* UD 264/1979.

covered except during (i) the six months after commencement of the apprenticeship and (ii) the period of one month following completion of the apprenticeship.[63]

The restrictions just mentioned concerning probationary workers and apprentices, and the requirement of one year's continuous service do not apply to workers claiming under the Maternity Protection of Employees Act, 1981.[64] A further exclusion is provided under s. 24 of the Act of 1981. The Unfair Dismissals Act does not apply to dismissal where an employer at the commencement of employment informs an employee in writing that his employment will terminate on the return to work of another employee who is absent from work on maternity leave or additional maternity leave or time off as defined by the Act of 1981 and the dismissal of the first-mentioned employee occurs for the purpose of facilitating the return to work of that other employee.

(2) *Time-Limit for presentation of claims and appeals*

It is essential for a dismissed employee to present his claim in time.[65] To initiate a claim for redress a person must give notice in writing to a Rights Commissioner or to the Tribunal subject to the particulars specified in the Unfair Dismissals (Claims and Appeals) Regulations, 1977,[66] (see Appendix II). This notice must be given within 6 months of the date of the relevant dismissal and the Act says that a copy of the notice 'shall be given to the employer concerned within the same period': section 8(2). 'Shall' in the latter sense has been interpreted as directory or regulatory only, so that failure to notify an employer within the six month period is not fatal to an employee's claim.[67]

63. *Dáil Debates*, Vol. 295, cols. 183-88 (8.12.1976); *ibid.*, Vol. 296, cols. 50-58 (25.1.1977); *ibid.*, Vol. 297, cols. 601-2 (2.3.1977); section 4, UDA 1977.

64. Section 25.

65. A useful account of the practical considerations involved in proceeding under the Unfair Dismissals Act is given by N. Wayne: *Labour Law in Ireland* chapter 5. Fortunately, no adverse consequences arose as a result of the postal dispute in 1979, although the fact that such consequences were likely apparently did not suggest to the Minister for Labour that the Act merited amendment: see Dáil Question No. 26, 6 December 1979, Col. 1135. In general if representations are made to the EAT for an early hearing, e.g., because of industrial action, they will be acceded to, if well founded.

66. (Government Publications Office, Dublin, Prl. 6581) S.I. No. 286 of 1977. An employee will have to bypass the Rights Commissioner stage if he wants to claim simultaneously under the Minimum Notice and Terms of Employment Act, 1973, and/or the Redundancy Payments Acts, 1967-79.

67. *Hayes & Caffrey v. B & I Line* UD 192 and 193/1979, followed in *Higgins v. Donnelly Mirrors Ltd.* UD 104/1979. Contrast EPCA, s. 67(2): in Britain the time limit of three months may be extended for 'such further period as the tribunal considers reasonable in a case where it is satisfied that it was not reasonably practicable for the complaint to be presented before the end of the period of three months'.

The time limit for bringing an appeal to the EAT from a recommendation of the Rights Commissioner is six weeks. This limit is absolute.[68] Appeal must be by notice in writing containing such particulars as are specified in the Unfair Dismissals (Claims and Appeals) Regulations, 1977 (see Appendix II). Where one party appeals, this will not enable the other party to bring a cross-appeal at the same hearing without fulfilling the requirement of bringing a notice of appeal within the six week period.[69] On appeal, the parties and the evidence are heard *de novo*.[70]

Proceedings before the Circuit Court for redress under the Act[71] must be initiated within six weeks from the date on which the EAT's determination has been communicated to the parties.

(3) *Fact of dismissal*

Before the enforcing authorities will examine the fairness or unfairness of dismissal, they must be satisfied by an employee that he has been 'dismissed' in accordance with the Unfair Dismissals Act, 1977. 'Dismissal' is defined in section 1 to mean:

'(a) the termination by his employer of the employee's contract of employment with the employer, whether prior notice of the termination was or was not given to the employee,

(b) the termination by the employee of his contract of employment with his employer, whether notice of the termination was or was not given to the employer, in circumstances in which, because of the conduct of the employer, the employee was or would have been entitled, or it was or would have been reasonable for the employee, to terminate the contract of employment without giving prior notice of the termination to the employer, or

(c) the expiration of a contract of employment for a fixed term without its being renewed under the same contract or, in the case of a contract for a specified purpose (being a purpose of such a kind that the duration of the contract was limited but was, at the time of its making, incapable of precise ascertainment), the cesser of the purpose.'

---

68. *Byrne v. Clayton Inns Ltd.* UD 21/1978; *Cherubini v. J. Downes & Son Ltd.* UD 22/1978 (where the EAT expressed dissatisfaction with the rigidity of s. 9(2)).
69. *Greely v. Handcraft Lampshades* UD 96/1978; UD 130/1978.
70. *Fullam v. Curragh Knitwear Ltd.* UD 76/1978. The EAT cannot order the implementation of a Recommendation. If there is no appeal, the EAT may not in any circumstances hear the claim *de novo:* Section 8(5) (a), Unfair Dismissals Act.
71. Section 10(1) and (4).

These three events constitute an exhaustive list. None, unfortunately, is free from interpretative difficulties.

To take fixed term contracts (c) first. When a contract for a fixed term expires, it has not been 'terminated' by either employer or employee. At common law there will be no remedy. For this reason it was important to include fixed term contracts within the Act, thereby removing what might otherwise have been a useful device for employers to avoid responsibility.[72] At the same time, however, the Act recognises that genuine fixed term contracts, e.g., for temporary, once-off jobs, are an important part of the range of employment relationships: hence, section 2(2).[73] But a 'fixed term contract' is not defined in the Act, and British experience shows that it may be interpreted with varying degrees of narrowness or breadth. If the the same degree is adopted both in relation to s. 1 and to s. 2(2), a dilemma arises. A wide meaning broadens the range of situations where the employee may validly contract out of his statutory rights. On the other hand, a narrow meaning removes many forms of dismissal from the Act's protection and a major loophole is opened. The latter became apparent from *British Broadcasting Corporation v. Ioannou*,[74] although the loophole was subsequently removed by the Court of Appeal decision in *Dixon v. British Broadcasting Corporation*.[75] The Court made it clear that a fixed term contract is not limited to a contract for a term which cannot be unfixed by notice within its terms.[76]

Likewise, the definition of dismissal in (a) and (b) above, the conceptual core of the legislation, is far from clear in its meaning. In chapter three, various difficulties surrounding the concept of termination at common law were discussed. An attempt was made to describe the effect of breach of the employment contract on the concept of termination. The latter raised a question vital to the statutory as well as to the common law jurisdiction, namely, whether repudiatory conduct automatically terminates the contract or whether, on the other hand, termination depends upon some further act or election by the injured party. It will be recalled that in the British case of *Gunton v. Richmond upon Thames L.B.C.*[77] the Court of Appeal by a majority decision rejected the automatic theory. *Prima facie,* this decision is significant for unfair dismissal because

72. See *Fitzgerald v. St. Patrick's College* UD 244/1978.
73. Page 132 above.
74. [1975] ICR 267.
75. [1979] QB 546; [1979] ICR 281; [1979] 2 All E.R. 112; [1979] 2 WLR 647; [1979] IRLR 114.
76. For difficulties surviving *Dixon* see Elias, Napier & Wallington: *Labour Law — Cases and Materials* 559.
77. [1980] ICR 755.

the Unfair Dismissals Act rests on an edifice of common law contract principles. An elective theory presents little difficulty in relation to repudiatory conduct short of dismissal. But where breach takes the form of an 'out and out dismissal' or of an employee's leaving the job, i.e., where the employment relationship is struck at, an act of election seems far removed from reality. As will be seen, there is a difference of approach between the ordinary courts in Britain and the EAT on the precise effects of repudiatory breach.

In Ireland, the meaning of 'dismissal' has not yet troubled the EAT. The position is one of uncertainty. A vital question stems from the discussion is chapter three, namely, what does it mean to talk about 'termination of the contract of employment'? The phrase appears in both (a) and (b) of section 1 of the Unfair Dismissals Act.

In 1978, Elias' attempt to unravel the concept of dismissal in British legislation constituted a major advance,[78] although by now his work is dated. Borrowing his terminology, the discussion which follows concentrates on dismissal as in (a) of section 1, which will be called Limb 1 dismissal, and dismissal as in (b) which will be called Limb 2 dismissal. The definition of constructive (Limb 2) dismissal differs as between Ireland and Britain, Ireland having provided not only for dismissal in circumstances of contractual entitlement but also for dismissal where an employee terminates the contract of employment in circumstances where it was or would have been reasonable for him to do so without giving prior notice of termination to his employer. Only that aspect of section 1 (b) to which it is appropriate to apply traditional contractual methods of argument will be considered here.[79] Parts (i) and (ii) to follow deal with the legal definition of 'dismissal'; while part (iii) concerns itself with evidential or factual aspects.

(i) *Termination, repudiatory breach and unfair dismissal*

In the context of unfair dismissal, whether an elective or automatic theory is adopted could be of considerable effect. If repudiatory action automatically terminates the contract, then dismissal will fall under Limb 1 and constitute a termination of the contract by the employer. If the automatic theory is applied to all forms of breach, however, repudiatory conduct by an employee will likewise bring the contract to an end. The employee will be taken to have 'dismissed' himself; he will not be able to come within section one of the Act. Moreover, it is difficult to see how Limb 2 dismissals could have any meaning: an employer by his repudiatory conduct would already have

---

78. P. Elias: 'Unravelling the Concept of Dismissal' (1978) ILJ 16 and 100.
79. Constructive dismissal is further dealt with below, chapter six, page 169.

terminated the contract. The category of constructive dismissal would appear to be rendered redundant.

An elective theory equally presents difficulties. It suggests that the contract of employment is terminated by an employee when he actually accepts his employer's wrongful act. If acceptance constitutes termination, and an act of election is open only to the innocent party, this presupposes that wrongful dismissal falls within Limb 2. Likewise, it presupposes that Limb 1 dismissals relate solely to situations where the employer was not in default. Mr. Justice Phillips once described statutory unfair dismissal as an artificial creature not easily to be understood by the layman — it is 'dismissal contrary to the statute'.[80] But he scarcely envisaged a distortion of the sort just outlined.

A further possible consequence flowing from the elective theory concerns the date of dismissal. In theory, and not forgetting about mitigation of loss,[81] an employee dismissed before he has attained the requisite period of one year's continuous employment could extend his employment by refusing to accept termination for the length of notice due in an effort to make up the shortfall.[82]

In Britain, the EPCA (s. 55(2)) defines Limb 1 and Limb 2 dismissals in a way which for purposes of the present discussion may be taken to have been later mirrored in the Irish Act. The EAT in Britain, in *Brown v. Southall & Knight*,[83] reaffirmed a preference for a distinction between repudiation which does not strike at the root of the employment relationship and which requires acceptance, and out and out dismissal or 'sending away' of an employee, involving precisely such a consequence for the relationship between the parties. A straightforward dismissal was regarded as falling squarely within the definition of employer-initiated termination in s. 55(2)(a), such dismissal (or so it appears from the statutory wording) being effective, whether or not a dismissal in breach, immediately to terminate the contract.[84]

In *Brown*, a letter of summary dismissal in breach of contract was delivered to the appellant's home while he was away on holiday. It was argued unsuccessfully that this repudiation was ineffective unless and until accepted, i.e., until it was time to return to work, or alternatively, until the moment the employers were required to do something to enable him to do his work, e.g., admitting him to the premises at the end of the holiday period. In reply the EAT held that

80. *W. Devis & Sons Ltd. v. Atkins* [1976] ITR 15, 22 (QBD).
81. Chapter seven, page 199.
82. This construction may be barred, however, by the actual wording of 'the date of dismissal', see further below, page 143.
83. [1980] IRLR 130.
84. *Per* Slynn J. at 133.

'termination' of the contract does not necessarily depend on whether there has been repudiation. Further, there is no absolute rule either way that there is always automatic termination after a fundamental breach or that there is always an option which the employee must accept before the employer can dismiss. The EAT distinguished between out and out dismissals and those cases where some other repudiation is alleged. The sending away may or may not be a breach of contract but the employee may not refuse to go. The employer can unilaterally determine the contract and no acceptance of that determination is required to effect it; nor does the employee have the right to say 'no' until the moment comes when the employer must do something, such as giving work or admitting to the premises. Acceptance may be required in other cases, e.g., where the employee is in breach of contract by failing to carry out work with the requisite skill. The employer must accept that repudiation before the contract comes to an end but, if he does, it is he who terminates, not the employee. There may also be cases where the employee leaves the employer no option by refusing to continue the relationship and this, according to the EAT, could amount to automatic unilateral termination by the employee thus depriving him of statutory remedies.

Very much the same approach has been applied to self-dismissal. In Britain, a so-called doctrine of "employee repudiation" threatened for a time to drive a coach and four through unfair dismissals legislation. There were decisions to the effect that an employee in fundamental breach of his contract of employment dismissed himself, thereby relieving the employer of all managerial responsibility.[85] Self-dismissals did not come within the Act but a timely deathblow to this theory was delivered by the EAT in *Rasool & Others v. Hepworth Pipe Co. Ltd*.[86] In a manner foreshadowing *Brown*, Waterhouse J. analysed 'two groups of fundamental breach'

(i) those which being or entailing a deliberate curtailment of the contract effectively terminate it without more and
(ii) those which merely entitle the other party at his option to treat it as discharged by 'accepting' the repudiation.

In *Rasool*, the employee's fundamental breach (unauthorised attendance at mass meetings during working hours at the employer's factory) fell into the latter category. The commonsense reality was that the employer did have an option which he exercised to terminate

---

85. See *Gannon v. Firth* [1976] IRLR 415; *Thompson v. Eaton (GB) Ltd.* [1978] IRLR 483; *Marsden v. Fairey Stainless Ltd.* [1979] IRLR 103, 105; *Smith v. Arana Bakeries Ltd.* [1979] IRLR 423; *Kallinos v. London Electric Wire* [1980] IRLR 11.
86. [1980] IRLR 80.

the contract.[87] The EAT expressly disapproved of *Gannon v. Firth*,[88] the progenitor of constructive resignation cases, and implied that other cases which followed it were wrongly decided. The first type of breach referred to above[89] relates to those breaches where 'effectively' an aggrieved party cannot elect to ignore the breach and carry on under the contract:[90] the relationship of mutual trust and confidence has broken down or is completely severed. *Nihil posse creari de nilo.* Thus, some breaches will, while others will not, end the contract depending on their seriousness — contrast wrongful dismissal and wrongful repudiation.

In *London Transport Executive v. Clarke*[91] a majority in the Court of Appeal (Templeman and Dunn L.JJ., Lord Denning M.R. diss.) held that an employee's contract of employment was not terminated by his own conduct in absenting himself from work for seven weeks without leave; rather it was terminated by the employer's acceptance of his conduct as a repudiation of the contract. Thus far the ratio in *Rasool* is consistent with the Court's decision. But again a divergence of approach becomes manifest between the EAT and the ordinary courts. The Court of Appeal went on to reiterate the general principle that contracts of employment are not exceptions to the general rule that a repudiated contract is not terminated unless and until repudiation is accepted by the innocent party. Any such exception would be contrary to principle, unsupported by authority binding on the Court of Appeal, and undesirable in practice.[92] Lord Justice Templeman saw the main difficulties as centering around the decision as to whether breach was of a special kind or not.[93]

87. See the implications in relation to striking employees, *Harvey's Industrial Relations and Employment Law* (ed. Elias) 1981, p. 11/66.

88. Fn. 85 *ante.*

89. Waterhouse J. cited an industrial tribunal decision, *Sealey & Others v. Avon Aluminium Co. Ltd.* [1978] IRLR 285. To the extent that the *obiter dicta* conform to the analysis of the Master of the Rolls in *Harbutts Plasticine Ltd. v. Wayne Tank & Pump Co. Ltd.* [1970] 1 QB 447, 464, *Rasool* must be regarded as incorrect. See *Photo Productions Ltd. v. Securicor Ltd.* [1980] 2 WLR 283 which overruled the effect of *Harbutt's* case.

90. E.g., *Hare v. Murphy* [1974] 3 All ER 940; [1974] IRLR 343 (employee sentenced to twelve months imprisonment).

91. [1981] IRLR 166.

92. At 171.

93. Whereas, he opined, the acceptance theory was far less complicated. If a worker walks out of his job and does not thereafter claim to be entitled to resume work, then he repudiates his contract and the employer accepts that repudiation by taking no action to affirm the contract. No question of unfair dismissal can arise unless the worker claims that he was constructively dismissed. If a worker walks out of his job or commits any other breach of contract, repudiatory or otherwise, but at any time claims that he is entitled to resume or to continue his work, then his contract of employment is determined only if the employer expressly or impliedly assents and accepts repudiation on the part of the worker. Such acceptance constitutes termina-

Which approach is to be preferred? Each presents its own peculiar difficulties, either of interpretation or of consequence, but there is no doubt that the automatic theory adheres more closely to the reality of the employment relationship. There is an implied suggestion, based on the internal language of the Irish Act (specifically the definition of 'date of dismissal', see page 143 below), that the automatic theory was intended by the Oireachtas. But doubts inevitably remain. More than anything else a legislated solution is called for which will enable the Act to be interpreted free from the doctrinal ambiguities and pitfalls of the common law notion of 'termination'.

(ii) *The 'fact' of constructive dismissal: criteria involved in its establishment*

In the preceding discussion, constructive dismissal was explored only to the extent that the circumstances 'entitle' an employee to terminate the contract of employment on account of the employer's breach of contract. An employee may also terminate his contract where it is reasonable for him to do so. This option, as already noted, is not open to an employee under s. 55 (2) (c) of the EPCA. Paradoxically both a contract and a reasonableness test emerged from British case-law before the important Court of Appeal decision in *Western Excavating (ECC) Ltd. v. Sharp*[94] (it had not been delivered at the time of the Irish Act's introduction). The Court considered the criterion which ought to be applied to ascertain whether an employee was 'entitled' to put an end to the contract without notice. The contract test was summarised thus by Lord Denning M.R.:

'If the employer is guilty of conduct which is a significant breach going to the root of the contract of employment, or which shows that the employer no longer intends to be bound by one or more of the essential terms of the contract, then the employee is entitled to treat himself as discharged from any further performance.'[95]

tion; it may take the form of writing or of refusing to allow the worker resume or continue his work.

94. [1978] ICR 221; [1978] IRLR 332; followed by the Irish EAT in relation to unilateral alteration of a term of employment in *O'Brien & Others v. Murphy Plastics (Dublin) Ltd.* UD 142-4/1980.

95. At 226 (ICR). See *Pedersen v. London Borough of Camden* [1981] IRLR 173 (CA); [1979] IRLR 377 (EAT); and *Woods v. WM Car Services (Peterborough) Ltd.* [1981] IRLR 347. The EAT in the latter case seem to derive from *Pedersen* the principle that employment law constitutes an exception to the general rule in contract law whereby the existence of fundamental breach is a question of law. Instead the EAT see it as a mixed question of fact and law. Further clarification is necessary.

The alternative reasonableness test asks whether the employer:

> 'conducts himself or his affairs so unreasonably that the employee cannot fairly be expected to put up with it any longer, [if so] the employee is justified in leaving.'[96]

The Court of Appeal rejected this test in favour of the contract test which it felt was the more stringent of the two. The reasonableness test had led to findings of constructive dismissal on the most whimsical grounds.[97] In Britain, therefore, only cases where an employer's conduct amounts to a breach of contract can now be looked upon as authoritative.

The difference between the two tests is significant. The contract test seeks to make a vertical division of type between one kind of conduct and another, as distinct from a mere horizontal division of degree. 'Unreasonableness is primarily a test of degree: conduct in any area of life can be as reasonable as the individual cares to make it. In that sense it may be an apt test for distinguishing one substantive area of conduct from another. On the other hand the contract test is a composite test which embodies criteria both of type and degree, neither of which has much to do with reasonableness. The test of type is simply whether or not the conduct complained of is regulated by the terms (express or implied) of the contract of employment. If not, no matter how unreasonably, capriciously or oppressively an employer acts in respect of it, the conduct cannot amount to a repudiation of the contract by the employer. Elias expresses a preference for the reasonableness test because:

> 'To adopt a reasonableness test directly rather than, as is tending to happen at present, indirectly through the contract,[98] would seem to be a more secure foundation for regulating constructive dismissals and also more in keeping with the

---

96. At 226 (ICR).
97. It has led to some of the most bizarre and eccentric decisions in the whole of employment law. Anderman has some reservations about confirmation that the test of constructive dismissal is contractual in Britain but, he says, the interpretation of the relevant statutory definition in the EPCA (then TULRA, para. 5(2) (c)) to provide a solely contractual test, is justified by the language of that provision: *The Law of Unfair Dismissal* 241. The Court of Appeal in *Sharp's* case, fn. 94 *ante,* also argued that the language of para. 5(2) (c) of TULRA was more consistent with the contractual test, and it is to be inferred, according to Elias ('Unravelling the Concept of Dismissal' (1978) ILJ 100 at 101) that when the statute talks of the employee being entitled to terminate, it means 'legally entitled' to terminate in response to the employer's repudiatory conduct.
98. See further, chapter six, page 171, below.

general framework of unfair dismissal laws which are designed to subject managerial prerogative to a reasonableness standard.'[99]

To date, both tests have been applied by the Irish EAT although it is often a matter of inference which test is followed in the circumstances. The contract test is more stringent than the test of reasonableness. It is curious that both should have been provided in the form of alternatives.

(iii) *Doubt as to facts surrounding dismissal*

Because of the presumption of unfairness in relation to dismissal it might be thought the benefit of any doubt surrounding the fact of dismissal would accrue to an employee. In determinations of the Irish EAT, the trend is markedly in the other direction.[100] The employer likewise benefits where there is a conflict of evidence as to dismissal and the EAT is unable to make up its mind which side to believe.[101]

Not infrequently, employers attempt to avoid the consequences of dismissal, e.g., by providing in the works rules that on a particular breach employees will be 'assumed' to have left their employment or to have dismissed themselves. Breach of such a rule does not automatically exclude a claim under the Act.[102] An employer may, for example, instruct an employee to perform the contract and tell him that if he fails to do so he will be deemed to have resigned. Where the employee actually resigns, everything will depend on whether the instruction issued by the employer was one which he could lawfully issue under the contract of employment. If it was, and the employee chooses to ignore it, there will be no dismissal in law. If an employer was acting *dehors* the contract, his conduct may constitute a breach which is sufficient to justify the employee leaving and claiming he has been constructively dismissed. The so-called doctrine of employee repudiation was mentioned earlier, page 138. It is only exceptionally, it is suggested, that employee repudiation should be held to amount to a termination of the contract by the employee.

99. *Art. cit.*, fn. 97 *ante*, 111. See, too, J. B. Capstick: 'Constructive Dismissal' (1979) 129 NLJ 499.

100. Particularly if the employer's account is supported by a memorandum which he prepared on the day of the alleged dismissal: *Glass v. Lissadell Towels Ltd.* UD 320/1979. See, on conflict of evidence, *O'Connor and O'Connor v. Guiry* UD 65/1978; *Freeman v. O'Flaherty* UD 9/1978.

101. *Hyland v. Balmoral Dublin Ltd.* UD 63/1978.

102. *Corrigan v. Rowntree Mackintosh (Ireland) Ltd.* UD 39/1978. Suppose the rule-book indicated that an employee would be 'deemed to have terminated his employment' upon breach: such a clause would most probably be held to contravene section 13 of the Unfair Dismissals Act, 1977 (being a provision in an agreement purporting to exclude or limit the application of the Act).

(4) *Date of Dismissal*

The final hurdle for an employee at the preliminary stage of a claim under the Act is to ascertain the date of dismissal. This date establishes the end of an employee's length of continuous service and hence the qualifying period of service for a complaint and the period for the calculation of an award of compensation. The date is also important to establish the time when an employee is entitled to a written statement of reasons, his age at the time of dismissal, the particular version of the statutory enactment that is applicable and whether an employee's claim has been presented within the six month time limit.

Under s. 1 of the Unfair Dismissals Act, the 'date of dismissal' is defined as the date on which an employee's notice of termination[103] expires or would have expired where the notice is or would have been in accordance with the contract of employment or of the Minimum Notice and Terms of Employment Act, 1973, whichever is the greater. For fixed term or specified purpose contracts the date of dismissal is the date of the expiry or cesser.

If wages in lieu of notice are paid the case is treated as a 'no notice' one. The EAT explained in *O'Reilly v. Pullman Kellog Ltd.*:[104]

'A notice period . . . is a warning to an employee that at a given date his employment will end. The absence of a warning period . . . means that no notice of termination [is] given.'

The giving of notice *per se* does not constitute dismissal within the meaning of the Act as such notice, by agreement between the parties, may be withdrawn prior to its expiration.

Implicit in the Act's definition of the 'date of dismissal' is the notion that dismissal operates automatically to terminate the contract.[105] In s. 1 (b), when dealing with situations where no notice is given to an employee, the Act defines the date of dismissal as the date on which notice (as set out thereafter) would have expired

'If it had been given on the date of such termination.'

103. It is essential to distinguish **mere warnings** from a notice to terminate. Once an employer has given notice to **terminate**, he cannot revoke the notice unless the employee consents: *Murphy v. Binchy & Sons Ltd.* UD 243/1978. The same is true, *mutatis mutandis,* where an employee gives notice. Where a disciplinary procedure provides a right of appeal against dismissal and treats an employee as suspended without pay until an appeal is heard, and if the appeal is rejected, the effective date of dismissal is likely to be the date upon which dismissal initially took effect, not when the appeal was rejected: see *Savage v. J. Sainsbury Ltd.* [1980] IRLR 109.

104. UD 340/1979.

105. See discussion, page 135 above.

Although it is an unsatisfactory way to resolve the interpretative difficulties surrounding 'termination' it would be difficult, arguably, to accommodate a theory within these statutory words enabling an employee purportedly dismissed without notice to 'sit in the sun'. Termination is taken to have occurred when the employee was sent away. Elias has argued[106] that the automatic theory should apply to the date of dismissal as defined in the EPCA (s. 55)(4)) as acceptance of that theory is implicit in s. 55(5). Under this subsection, if an employer is required to give notice to the employee and he gives inadequate or no notice, the effective date of termination will be considered for certain statutory purposes to be the date as calculated according to s. 55(4) plus the statutory minimum period of notice. This assumes that dismissal without notice, or with inadequate notice, involves a termination by the employer. Elias' theory, that termination in the British statute derives its meaning from the internal grammar of the Act, thus avoiding confrontation with the common law, was recently confirmed by the EAT in *Robert Cort & Son Ltd. v. Charman*.[107] In the context of s. 55(4), it was held that dismissal takes effect on the day the employee is told he is dismissed. The reasoning was based *inter alia* on the drafting of the Act.

---

106. *Harvey*, para. 249.
107. [1981] IRLR 437.

CHAPTER SIX

Reasonableness and the Employer's Role Under the Unfair Dismissals Act

A. The Employer's Reason for Dismissal

The concept of fairness is located within a framework which accepts that the employer has the right to dismiss where this is necessary to protect his business interests. To that extent it adopts an employer perspective.[1] At the same time the law requires that employers should not remorselessly pursue their own interests. The worker's interests must be considered as well. The function of fairness is to reconcile these interests. It does so in different ways depending on the kind of dismissal involved. There are two stages. First of all, an employer's reason for dismissal must be identified. Secondly, whether the reason was one which is deemed fair or unfair, or whether there were other substantial grounds for dismissal, an employer must be able to justify his decision to dismiss.[2] The test of reasonableness is applied to determine the fairness or unfairness of his action.

In the first part of this chapter, the employer's reason for dismissal is discussed. The reasonableness of his decision is then analysed. Fairness in the context of constructive dismissal is considered separately because of the existence in Ireland of two tests for constructive dismissal, namely, the contract and the reasonableness tests.[3] If the reasonableness test is followed initially, a danger arises that the overall question of the employer's reasonableness may be considered prematurely and merged with the test itself.

(1) Identifying the employer's reason

The first step in assessing fairness is to isolate the employer's

1. See the introduction to C. Drake and B. Bercusson's *The Employment Acts 1974-1980*, 36-38.
2. These two stages have been referred to as 'casual' and 'capacious' respectively: S. R. Carby-Hall: *Studies in Labour Law* 240, 243. Both the casual and the capacious approaches are intrinsic in every case. The casual approach cannot stand alone. A combination of both approaches lends itself to an adaptability in relation to all relevant matters. They are plesiomorphic in character. On the Irish Act see, by the author: 'Justifying his decision to dismiss: the Employer's Role under the Unfair Dismissals Act 1977' (1980) IBAR 58. On the British: P. Elias: 'The Concept of Fairness in Unfair Dismissal' (1981) ILJ 201. Note the statutory requirement concerning the onus of proof has been amended in Britain: Employment Act, 1980, s. 5.
3. Section 1, Unfair Dismissals Act. See chapter five, page 140, *ante*.

reason for dismissal — or his principal reason if he has more than one. In *Abernethy v. Mott Hay & Anderson*,[4] Lord Cairns described:

> '|a| reason for the dismissal of an employee |as| a set of facts known to the employer, or it may be of beliefs held by him, which cause him to dismiss the employee.'

It is not necessary for the reason to be correctly labelled at the time. In the same case, Lord Denning M.R. declared that:

> 'the reason shown for dismissal must be the principal reason which operated on the employer's mind.'[5]

It is the reason which in fact operated on the employer's mind which is important. To assist an employee the Act lays down that, if requested, an employer must provide a dismissed employee, within fourteen days of the request, with a written statement of particulars of the grounds of dismissal: s. 14(4).[6] At the same time, however, in determining whether a dismissal was fair or unfair,

> 'there may be taken into account any other grounds which are substantial grounds and which would have justified the dismissal.[7]

An employee has no grievance or right to redress under the Act if an employer unreasonably refuses to provide a written statement or if the written statement is inaccurate or untrue.[8] But failure to comply

4. |1974| IRLR 213, [1974] ICR 323.
5. *Ibid.*, at 329 (ICR).
6. E.g., *Du Bois v. Meic Teo Hydromarine International* UD 222/78.
7. This accords in principle with British law. In *Abernethy's* case, footnote 4 *ante*, an employer honestly, but wrongly, believed that the facts of the case constituted redundancy. The tribunal concluded, after looking at the facts, that the employer's reason related to the capabilities of the employee to do the work he was employed to do. Lord Denning M.R. commented in the Court of Appeal 'I do not think that the reason has got to be correctly labelled at the time of dismissal. It may be that the employer is wrong in law in labelling it as dismissal for redundancy. In that case the wrong label can be set aside'. See *Hilton v. Carrigaline Pottery Co. Ltd.* UD 153/1979 (employer gave vague reasons in response to s. 14 request; nevertheless EAT allowed him to present his case in full at the hearing).
8. Contrast s. 53(4) EPCA. In that jurisdiction, an employee may present a complaint to an industrial tribunal if an employer unreasonably refuses to furnish a written statement or if the written particulars are inaccurate or untrue. A delay by the employer in providing the information may amount to a refusal: e.g., *Keen v. Dymo Ltd.* [1977] IRLR 118; *Joines v. B. and S. (Burknale) Ltd.* [1977] IRLR 83. To meet the statutory test of adequacy 'the document must be of a kind that the employee, or anyone to whom he may wish to show it, can know from reading the

with s. 14(4) may assist the Tribunal in assessing the fairness of an employer's behaviour and in determining the appropriate redress to award an aggrieved employee.

(i) *Dismissals deemed not to be unfair*

The burden of proof lies with an employer to establish his reason or reasons for dismissal. To avoid a preliminary finding of unfairness he must establish not only what his reason was, but also that the reason fits within one of the general categories likely to be regarded as 'fair' under s. 6(4) of the Act of 1977 namely, that it concerns:

(a) the capability, competence or qualifications of the employee for performing work of the kind he was employed to do,[9]
(b) the conduct of the employee,
(c) the redundancy of the employee, or
(d) that the employer was prohibited by statute[10] from continuing to employ the individual in his job.

If dismissal did not result wholly or mainly from one or more of these matters there must have been other substantial grounds which justified the dismissal (s. 6(6)). To meet the burden of proof at this stage, an employer must show that his reason was one that can justify the dismissal, not one that necessarily does justify it. If he fails to show that his reason for dismissal was potentially valid, the dismissal will be unfair at this preliminary stage.[11]

---

document itself why an employee was dismissed': *Horsley Smith & Sherry Ltd. v. Dutton* [1977] IRLR 172 (EAT). A statement of the main factual grounds must be given, not merely a reference to one or more of the statutory heads in the legislation. An award may be made to an employee in respect of an inadequate written statement equal to the amount of two weeks pay subject to no maximum limit. This is additional to any compensation the employee may receive for unfair dismissal.

9. The EPCA (s. 57(2) (a)) refers to 'capability and qualifications' as a ground for dismissal in this respect. Unlike the Irish Act, these terms are defined in the EPCA: 'capability' is assessed by reference to skill, aptitude, health or any other physical or mental quality: 'qualifications' means any degree, diploma or other academic, technical or professional qualification relevant to the position which the employee held (s. 57(4) (a) and (b)). Contrast *Malone v. Lewicki Microelectronics Ltd.* UD 249/1979 and *Woods v. Olympic Aluminium Co. Ltd.* [1975] IRLR 356.

10. See *Ponnampalam v. Mid-Western Health Board* (Circuit Court unreported, 26 March 1980); *Stephens v. Mid-Western Health Board* UD 67/1979. In Britain, driving qualifications have been the main cause of dismissal in this respect. The Health and Safety at Work Act, 1974, is another source of dismissal contrary to statute. See A. Samuels: 'Safety and Dismissal: Dismissal and Safety' (1980) 130 NLJ 395.

11. In Britain, reasons fall into three categories, broadly speaking. There are automatically fair, potentially fair and automatically unfair reasons. Unless the reason is automatically fair or automatically unfair, the employer must show that 'in

(a) *Capability, competence or qualifications*

From an employer's point of view, and from the Tribunal's, cases involving alleged efficiency or inefficiency at work are among the most difficult under the Act.[12] The line between dismissal for incompetence and for misconduct is very difficult to draw.[13] Incapability may be affected by ill-health which is not, of course, an employee's fault. Persistent short absences over a long period, or substantial single periods of absence for sickness, disability or mental illness – or their effects on the job – may be grounds for dismissal under s. 6(4) (a).[14] Even where the courts declare that the contract of employment is frustrated by a long illness, a conclusion they are always reluctant to make, the EAT (illogically, from a strictly legal point of view) will consider the reasonableness of an employer's decision to dismiss.[15] Perhaps the most difficult problems in relation to competence and qualifications arise where an employee's original qualification is no longer good or sufficient owing to new machines or techniques or to a desire on the employer's part to improve work standards.[16] Problems may also arise where employees cannot acquire the technical expertise expected of them or a particular piece of paper to accompany their practical ability; or where paper qualifications are not accompanied by real and developing ability; or where someone with good qualifications is 'outgrown' by his job. The reasonableness of the employer's approach in all these situations will be the determining element as to the fairness of dismissal.

---

the circumstances (having regard to equity and the substantial merits of the case) he acted reasonably in treating [the reason] as a sufficient reason for dismissing the employee': EPCA, s. 57(3) as amended, EA, s. 6. See Hepple & O'Higgins: *Employment Law* Chapter 17.

12. As the EAT acknowledged in *Harrison v. Alan Gay Ltd.* UD 58/1978. Cf. *Cook v. Thomas Linnell & Sons Ltd.* [1977] ICR 770.

13. See the British EAT in *Sutton & Gates (Luton) Ltd. v. Boxall* [1978] IRLR 486 – where a person does not come up to standard through carelessness, negligence or idleness, this is better dealt with as misconduct.

14. *Bennett v. Byrne & Sons Ltd.* UD 173/1980; *Reardon v. St. Vincent's Hospital* UD 74/1979; *Bevan v. Daydream Ltd.* UD 31/1978.

15. *Nolan v. Brooks Thomas Ltd.* UD 179/1979, adopting the test set forth in *Marshall v. Harland & Wolff Ltd.* [1972] 7 ITR 150. See further *Tarnesby v. Kensington and Chelsea and Westminster Area Health Authority (Teaching)* [1981] IRLR 369; *Hart v. A. R. Marshall & Sons* [1978] 2 All ER 413; *Egg Stores (Stanford Hill) Ltd. v. Leibovici* (1976) ITR 289, [1976] IRLR 376. On the application of frustration in statutory unfair dismissal and redundancy claims see the interesting criticisms of H. G. Collins in (1977) ILJ 185; also C. Manchester: 'Frustration or Dismissal' (1978) 128 NLJ 674. And see fn. 118 *post*.

16. See *Ryder & Byrne v. The Commissioner of Irish Lights* UD 81 and 82 of 1977, the first case under the UDA to be appealed to the High Court (unreported judgment, 16 April 1980).

(b) *Conduct*

'Misconduct' for the purposes of the Unfair Dismissals Act need not mean anything which would amount to misconduct in the ordinary sense.[17] The employee may have been dismissed for gross misconduct,[18] for a single breach of discipline or for misconduct consisting of a series of acts and following a series of warnings. An employer's honest belief will be of influence. It is generally possible to justify dismissal for a first offence of gross misconduct.[19] Many house agreements provide that an employee can be sacked instantly for 'gross misconduct', although this will not be conclusive for purposes of the Unfair Dismissals Act. What constitutes gross misconduct is not purely a question of fact, it is a mixed question of fact and law. It is far less likely to ground an appeal from a decision of the EAT, however, than the broader issue of reasonableness. Gross misconduct generally presupposes intentional and deliberate misconduct.[20] The common law can provide useful categorisations of statutory misconduct, e.g., theft,[21] assault, deliberate refusal to obey a legitimate order, gross negligence. Where these, together with the requirement of intention, are regarded as gross misconduct by an employer, the common law can assist the Tribunal in determining the

---

17. *Waters v. Kentredder (Ire.) Ltd.* UD 3/1977. During the Report Stage of the Bill in Dáil Eireann, the Opposition spokesman (later Minister for Labour) attempted unsuccessfully to have the relevant subsection modified to read: 'the conduct of the employee which results in damage to the business or is detrimental to the business of the employer or to the performance of the employee in the execution of his duties': *Dáil Debates* 2 March 1977, Vol. 297, Cols. 657-9. The Deputy was reassured by the Minister that 'We are talking in an industrial relations context and the conduct of the employee has a relatively narrow application in that context': *ibid.*, col. 658. See discussions on Committee Stage also: *Ibid.*, Vol. 296 (25 January 1977) Cols. 86-98.

18. In contradistinction to the Irish Act, the question of summary dismissal in cases of serious misconduct is dealt with separately in para. 11 of ILO Recommendation no. 119. In view of the very nature of this reason for termination of employment the Recommendation provides on the one hand that the worker concerned may be deprived of certain rights (period of notice, or compensation in lieu thereof, separation benefits) and on the other that certain additional safeguards and procedures should be observed. For instance, dismissal should only take place where the employer cannot be expected in good faith to take any other course; there is an implied waiver by the employer of the right to dismiss and by the worker of the right to appeal if such action has not been taken within a reasonable time; further the worker has a right before dismissal becomes finally effective to state his case promptly and to be appropriately assisted.

19. *Doyle v. J. J. Carron & Co. Ltd.* UD 236/1978.

20. *Doyle supra;* also *Devlin v. Player & Wills (Ire.) Ltd.* UD 90/1978.

21. It may also be consulted as a standard in the absence of disciplinary rules on the grounds that cetain acts or serious misconduct are known and understood to be such by employees: see *Fullam v. Curragh Knitwear Ltd.* UD 76/1978.

reasonableness of an employer's attitude.[22] The basic core of recognised categories of gross misconduct derives from the duties of employers which the common law applies in the contract of employment.

(c) *Redundancy*

The dismissal of an employee is deemed not to be unfair if it results wholly or mainly from redundancy (s. 6(4)(c)) but redundancy situations can be complex because s. 6(3) of the Act[23] creates a presumption of unfairness where there has been an unfair selection for redundancy. A dismissed employee may therefore be entitled to an award of unfairness on top of his redundancy pay.[24] Under subsection 3, dismissal is deemed unfair:

> if an employee was dismissed due to redundancy but the circumstances constituting the redundancy[25] applied equally to one or more other employees[26] in similar employment[27] with the

22. For instance, the duty of care, the duty of honesty, the duty of obedience to lawful orders, the duty of faithful service. If an employee breaches any of these wilfully this may be viewed as a breach of an essential contractual condition.

23. See EPCA 1978, s. 59. Termination of employment for economic, technological, structural or similar reasons features prominently in the *Report* of the ILO, chapter five, fn. 4, *ante,* and will form a crucial part of the proposed new Convention.

24. An employee may complain of unfair dismissal for redundancy where he has already received and accepted a lump sum redundancy payment: this does not preclude the EAT from hearing the claim for unfair dismissal on its merits: *Oglesby v. McKone Estates Ltd.* UD 61/1979. Presumably the same would apply where the employee claimed concurrently for a redundancy payment. The amount of compensation awarded by the Tribunal is likely to be further reduced by any redundancy payment already received by an employee: this is clear from *obiter dicta* in *Friel v. John Sisk & Son Ltd.* UD 71/1978. Under s. 13(9) of the EPCA, 1978, the amount of any redundancy payment awarded or paid expressly reduces the amount of the 'Basic Award'. Where such redundancy payment is more than the Basic Award any excess is taken into account so as to reduce the 'Compensatory Award'.

25. Under redundancy legislation 'place of employment' in, e.g., the building industry has been interpreted as referring to more than one particular site. The EAT has read a mobility term into almost all building contracts. The converse of this appears to apply under the UDA. The EAT has left open the question as to how s. 6(3) should be applied in the building industry. It is unclear whether 'the circumstances constituting the redundancy' may be taken to apply equally to an employee on one site that is closing and to similar employees on other sites: *Gould v. O'Shea's Ltd.* UD 323/1978.

26. Where a claimant is the only employee in a particular grade or employment he loses any entitlement to claim under s. 6(3): *Flynn v. Brendan L. Brophy Ltd.* UD 329/1979; *Conlon v. PMPA Farm Machines Ltd.* UD 173/1978; *Whelan v. Hartley & Synden (Tube Investment) Ltd.* UD 49/1978. The claimant's comparators must be 'employees' in similar employment: *Deegan v. Chums Ltd.* UD 103/1979.

27. The precise meaning of similar employment is unclear but the type of work

same employer who have not been dismissed, and either—

(a) the selection of that employee for dismissal resulted wholly or mainly from one or more of the matters specified in sub section (2) of this section or another matter that would not be a ground justifying dismissal, or

(b) he was selected for dismissal in contravention of a pro cedure relating to redundancy and there were no special reasons justifying a departure from that procedure.

Paragraph (b) is dealt with in chapter eight in the context of collec tive aspects of dismissal. Redundancy has the same meaning for unfair dismissal purposes as for the Redundancy Payments Acts, 1967-1979.[28] Broadly, this refers to moving or closing down a busi ness, or having a diminishing need for employees to do the particular work they have been employed to do. The burden of proving dismissal for a redundancy reason in unfair dismissal claims is the opposite to that under redundancy payments legislation. In the latter, redundancy is presumed unless the employer proves otherwise.[29] In

---

done and the skill or specialised knowledge required to do it would be crucial factors in any assessment of similarity: *Moloney v. J. & L. F. Goodbody Ltd.* UD 6/1978; *Kennedy v. Same* UD 8/1978. The EAT looks at the actual work being done and its interchangeability with other work. It does not rely on job titles or job grading schemes: cf. *Gargrave v. Hotel and Catering Industrial Training Board* [1974] IRLR 85; *Simpson v. Roneo Ltd.* [1972] IRLR 5.

28. Section 7(2) of the Redundancy Payments Act, 1967, as amended by section 4 of the Redundancy Payments Act, 1971, provides that a person who is dismissed shall be deemed to have been dismissed by reason of redundancy if his dismissal results wholly or mainly from one of the following:

'(a) the fact that the employer has ceased or intends to cease to carry on the busi ness for the purposes of which the employee was employed by him, or has ceased or intends to cease, to carry on that business in the place where the employee was so employed, or

(b) the fact that the requirements of that business for employees to carry out work of a particular kind in the place where he was so employed have ceased or diminished or are expected to cease or diminish, or

(c) the fact that his employer has decided to carry on the business with fewer or no employees, whether by requiring the work for which the employee had been employed (or had been doing before his dismissal) to be done by other employees or otherwise, or

(d) the fact that his employer has decided that the work for which the employee had been employed (or had been doing before his dismissal) should henceforward be done in a different manner for which the employee is not sufficiently qualified or trained, or

(e) the fact that his employer has decided that the work for which the employee had been employed (or had been doing before his dismissal) should henceforward be done by a person who is also capable of doing other work for which the employee is not sufficiently qualified or trained.'

29. Section 10, Redundancy Payments Act, 1971.

resisting a redundancy payments claim an employer will be denying the fact of redundancy. In defending an unfair dismissal claim, an employer may wish to do the opposite, i.e., to establish the fact of redundancy.

To satisfy the EAT that an employee was dismissed for redundancy under section 6(3) there must be a redundancy situation[30] and redundancy must be the main reason for dismissal. If the employer cannot prove both, and cannot prove one of the other potentially fair reasons, dismissal will be unfair. Redundancy has become a common justification for dismissal. For this reason strict proof is required.[31] A company which has processed many redundancies in the past will be assumed to be well versed in proper redundancy procedures. If an employee is not notified early on of the reason for his dismissal or if this is recorded long after the appropriate time in the minutes of the company, dismissal will be unfair.[32] There is a difference between dismissal for redundancy and dismissal merely to cut costs.[33] But if, in making economy cuts, a company re-examines the need for a particular employee, this may suggest a redundancy situation. One way of facilitating proof of redundancy is to show that dismissal has resulted from company re-

---

30. E.gg., *O'Neill v. Murphy* UD 122/1980; *Carroll v. Condons Cash & Carry Ltd.* UD 160/1979; *O'Byrne v. Orchard Insurance Ltd.* UD 172/1979; *O'Dowd v. Collis Lee Ire. Ltd.* UD 170/1979; *Kennedy v. Cappineur Joinery Ltd.* UD 38/1977. Statements made by a Minister in Dáil Éireann regarding security of employment in a particular workplace and his promises that redundancy would not take place constitute, in the EAT's opinion, 'unilateral statements' that cannot be taken to amount to a guarantee by an employer that, if an employee's job comes to an end, he will be assured of suitable alternative employment and if he does not secure such employment that he will be entitled to redress for unfair dismissal: *Riordan v. Dairy Disposal Co. Ltd.* UD 55/1979. (The EAT suggested in passing that the employee might have some redress at common law.) Examples of cases finding no redundancy are: *Costello v. Kellys Carpetdrome* UD 78/1980; *Gallivan v. Irish Commercial Society Ltd.* UD 319/1979; *Garrett v. The Botany Weaving Mill Ltd.* UD 355/1979; *Byrne v. P. J. Hegarty & Sons Ltd.* UD 126/1978.

31. See the criticisms by Kilner Brown J. in *O'Hare and Another v. Rotaprint Ltd.* [1980] ICR 44 — because Department of Employment partly refunds employer where he has paid redundancy payments, public has right to insist that entitlement to redundancy payment be properly and strictly challenged. Original intention of redundancy legislation has been 'clouded by a slipshod acceptance of a bottomless purse'. Unless proof of redundancy is strict, there is a real danger that the security of employment which employers are now urged to give will remain constrained by their own perception of market forces: see H. Forrest: 'Political Values in Individual Employment Law' (1980) 43 MLR 361, 375; and R. Hyman and I. Brough: *Social Values and Industrial Relations* 9.

32. *McCabe v. Lisney & Son* UD 5/1977.

33. *Woods v. Apollo Shopfitting Ltd.* UD 202/1979. Cf. *Delanair Ltd. v. Mead* [1976] ICR 552.

organisations (even if not yet in operation) designed to improve performance and efficiency.[34]

(d) *Other substantial grounds*

The category of other substantial grounds is a general residual category of reasons for dismissal, not restricted to those otherwise listed in sub. s. 4 of section 6 of the Unfair Dismissals Act.[35] The preliminary stage of showing a potentially valid reason is made more difficult by the requirement that an employer's reason be 'substantial'. For example, disruption or bad example[36] among fellow employees is harmful to production and the company's business interests but if it reaches a substantial level, it is a potentially fair ground for dismissing those seen as responsible either through their conduct or attitudes. Where an employee in a position of responsibility gives bad example, even though he has no intention to defraud, his dismissal is likely to be adjudged fair.[37]

In Britain, unlike Ireland,[38] nearly all cases of other substantial reasons concern employees who have refused to accept changes in their contract terms following some kind of reorganisation.[39] Often the contractual position is unclear and requires investigation. The Tribunal may find the proposed change already catered for in the contract or other collective agreement because some prior productivity bargaining has produced a 'mobility' or 'flexibility' clause which is incorporated into an employee's individual contract.[40] The question

---

34. E.gg., *White v. Scotts Foods Ltd.* UD 29/1979; *O'Connor v. Galeo Ltd.* UD 208/1979; *Sheehan v. Cork Fruit Co. Ltd.* UD 187/1978; *Sinclair v. Armstrong Autoparts (Ire.) Ltd.* UD 225/1978.

35. Where an employer does not attend a hearing under the Unfair Dismissals Act but attempts by way of written submission to adduce substantial grounds justifying the dismissal, it will be most unlikely that his submissions will satisfy the requirements of the statute: *Keneally v. Ballinahina Dairies* UD 254/1978; cf., too, absences of first-hand evidence in *Tormey v. Display Development Ltd.* UD 2/1977. See J. Bowers and A. Clarke: 'Unfair Dismissal and Managerial Prerogative: A Study of "Other Substantial Reason" ' (1981) ILJ 34.

36. Persistent flaunting of company rules constitutes a clear form of bad example: *Ryan v. Solus Teoranta* UD 106/1977; compare *McCoy v. AET Ltd.* UD 60/1979.

37. *Wachuku v. Redmond* UD 102/1979; *O'Rourke v. E. M. Halpin & Co. Ltd.* UD 45/1977.

38. A rare example is *Waters v. Kentredder (Ire.) Ltd.* UD 3/1977 (employee insisting on demarcation following death of fellow employee when work for sake of convenience and economy redistributed among remaining employees: held substantial ground justifying dismissal). See, too, a case involving similar principles: *Walsh v. J. D. Carr & Co.* UD 91/78.

39. See *Banerjee v. City & East London Area Health Authority* [1979] IRLR 147.

40. The courts, however, may review such clauses, pages 173-4 below.

then becomes one of employee disobedience, refusing to obey instruc
tions to transfer jobs or to work at a different site, rather than stand
ing on existing contractual rights. Dismissal is based on a 'conduct'
reason.[41] Employers who insist on making changes not provided for
in the contract may be held to have constructively dismissed their
employees if the latter leave (see page 170 below). In such circumstances, an employer may still claim that dismissal is fair for some
other 'substantial grounds' under s. 6(1). So a constructive dismissal
may not necessarily be unfair.

(ii) *Dismissals deemed to be unfair*

Certain reasons for dismissal are deemed unfair under sections 5
and 6 of the Unfair Dismissals Act. Section 5 concerns dismissal for
participation in strike or other industrial action. This is separately
considered in chapter eight. Subsections 2 and 3 of section 6 deem
the following grounds unfair, namely;

    (a) trade union membership or activities,
    (b) religious or political opinions,
    (c) involvement by an employee in civil or criminal proceedings
        against or involving an employer,
    (d) race or colour,
    (e) pregnancy,
    (f) maternity,
    (g) unfair selection for redundancy.

These reasons do not constitute automatically unfair grounds for dis
missal, because subsections (2) and (3) of section 6 begin

      'Without prejudice to the generality of subsection (1) of this
      section'

and subsection (1), it will be recalled, deems every dismissal unfair for
purposes of the Act unless, having regard to all the circumstances,
there are substantial grounds justifying the dismissal. Reasonable
ness enters the Act at every point. The grounds set out at (b), (c) and
(d) above (all of which have constitutional implications) have yet to be
considered by the EAT. Chapter eight deals with (a) and (g), i.e., with
those grounds which relate to collective aspects of dismissal, where
there is a conflict of interests rather than of rights. Dismissals deemed
unfair on grounds of pregnancy or of maternity are dealt with here.

---

41. E.g. *Wicks v. Smethurst Ltd.* (1973) COIT 251/83; *Hamm v. Edwards*
[1972] IRLR 102; contrast *Cullen v. Keal Ltd.* UD 324/1979.

In order to rebut the presumption of unfairness in relation to dismissal because of pregnancy or matters connected therewith,[42] an employer must establish an employee's inability to do the work, either adequately as required by her contract[43] or without effecting a contravention of statute or of some statutory instrument.[44] In addition, he must show that at the time of dismissal there was no other work suitable for the employee and available for her to do or, alternatively, that:

> 'the employee refused an offer by her employer of alternative employment on terms and conditions corresponding to those of the employment to which the dismissal related, being an offer made so as to enable her to be retained in the employment of her employer notwithstanding pregnancy.'

If the employer can establish that the real reason for dismissal was not pregnancy, so much the better. In general it is difficult to do this[45] but if an employee, e.g., failed to reveal at interview that she was pregnant,[46] her dismissal thereafter is unlikely to result 'wholly or mainly' from pregnancy but from failure to disclose.[47] The Unfair Dismissals Act is not specific in relation to what constitutes alternative employment. When the Act refers to other 'suitable' employment, presumably this must be suitable taking into account the employee's pregnancy, state of health, and her particular skill, ex-

---

42. Such as absence connected with a miscarriage: e.g. *George v. Beecham Group* [1977] IRLR 43.

43. *Corcoran v. Weatherglaze Ltd.* UD 20/1981. An employer may fairly dismiss a pregnant employee if she is incapable of doing adequately the work she was employed to do at the time of dismissal. However the onus is on the employer to show he acted reasonably in deciding that the inability of a pregnant employee was sufficient to justify dismissal, cf. *Brear v. W. Wright Hudson Ltd.* [1977] IRLR 287.

44. See *Callaghan v. CIE* UD 278/1981. Currently there are no laws forbidding the employment of pregnant women as distinct from other women. A distinction between pregnant and other women is made in the Factories (Ionising Radiations) Regulations S.I. Nos. 17 and 249 of 1972: these specify that pregnant women may not be subjected to levels of radiation as high as those for women who are not pregnant.

45. An employee with a very bad attendance record, whose absences on account of pregnancy came as a 'last straw', but who nevertheless was dismissed because of pregnancy, would come within the statutory protection, see *George's* case, fn. 42 *ante*. Allowances are made for slight inefficiencies during pregnancy so a defence of misconduct is difficult to sustain: *Gleeson v. Sheehan* UD 14/1979.

46. *Mullins v. Standard Shoe Co. Ltd.* UD 134/1979.

47. In *Mullins* case, the Tribunal were satisfied that the employee did not know she was pregnant until after she began working for the respondents. The Tribunal appeared to condone (or be prepared to condone) employers who take on female staff on the basis of not expecting pregnancy.

perience and qualifications. The Act appears to place an employer under an (implied) obligation to see if a vacancy exists for other suitable employment. The sub-paragraph cited above refers to 'alternative employment' the terms and conditions of which must 'correspond' to those of the employment to which the dismissal related. Alternative employment could not be said to correspond to an employee's former job if it was less favourable in any substantial way as to capacity, workplace, or other terms and conditions. This interpretation is supported by the Maternity Protection of Employees Act, 1981, which, *inter alia,* lays down the right to return to work after maternity leave.[48] A refusal to give the employee her job back is deemed to be a dismissal, and this in turn is deemed unfair. However, the presumption of unfairness may be rebutted.[49] An employee has the right to be reinstated in her job and 'job' is flexibly defined; it refers to:

> 'the nature of the work which she is employed to do in accordance with her contract of employment and the capacity and place in which she is so employed.'

But since reinstatement may not always be practicable, an employee may alternatively be re-engaged. The Act prevents an employer from over-diluting an employee's entitlement to return to work.[50] The work required to be done under the new contract must be suitable in relation to the employee concerned and appropriate for her to do in the circumstances; in addition, its terms and conditions relating to the place where the work is to be done, the capacity in which the employee concerned is to be employed and any other terms or conditions of employment must be 'not substantially less favourable' than those of the original contract of employment.

(2) *Evidence of the employer's reason*

In general the reason an employer shows for dismissal must have been in existence at the time an employee was given notice or was summarily dismissed. This may be inferred from the wording of the Act. Section 6(6) requires the employer to show that the dismissal:

> 'resulted wholly or mainly from one or more of the matters specified in subsection 4 of this section or that there were other substantial grounds justifying the dismissal.'

It may be implied that any matters which occur or are discovered

48. See Part III of the Act of 1981.
49. Section 26(4).
50. Section 21.

subsequent to dismissal normally have no relevance in ascertaining the reason for dismissal.[51] Since they were not known to an employer at the time they could not have provided a motivation for dismissal. It is firmly the law in Britain that the Tribunal must judge matters as they stand at the date of dismissal upon information known or available to the employer at that time.[52] There is no reason why in Ireland there should be a departure from the common law[53] where matters coming to light following dismissal may be taken into account when assessing the appropriate redress to be awarded an unfairly dismissed employee. The Irish Tribunal has permitted an employer to take prior incidents (good or bad) into account, even where they differed in type from the reason which precipitated the dismissal.[54] And the EAT has recognised an employer's right to introduce evidence, acquired after the date of dismissal, to reinforce or corroborate an act of misconduct of a similar nature which formed part of the basis of the decision to dismiss.[55]

An employer is not entitled to put forward his subjective view without any supporting evidence that it was his real view.[56] For instance, the opinions and views of management in monitoring the performance of an employee may constitute positive evidence of incompetence, the more so when monitoring is in conjunction with trade union representatives,[57] or it may be proved that an employee was not performing his work in accordance with a standard in itself reasonable. Statistical evidence is helpful;[58] equally, complaints as to performance by outsiders will be taken into account but there must be clear evidence of these.[59] The EAT may itself visit the employer's premises to examine matters such as work pattern, flow of stocks and

---

51. See C. Carr: 'Unfair Dismissal — Exclusion of Subsequent Evidence' (1977) 127 N.L.J. 128.

52. See *W. Devis & Sons Ltd. v. Atkins* [1977] 3 All E.R. 40, [1977] IRLR 314 (HL); *Bates Farms & Dairy Ltd. v. Scott* [1976] IRLR 214; *Earl v. Slater Wheeler (Airlyne) Ltd.* [1973] 1 All E.R. 145, [1973] IRLR 115.

53. See chapter three, page 61, *ante*.

54. UD 29/1977. According to the Tribunal, 'if [the claimant] could say that he previously had a very good record it would be surely unjust to ignore it. Therefore, we think that it would be unfair to the employers not to take notice of the previous incidents in this case.' See, too, *Arklow Pottery Ltd. v. O'Reilly* UD 241/1979.

55. *Loughran v. Bellwood Ltd.* UD 206/1978.

56. Compare *Trust Houses Forte Leisure Ltd. v. Aquilar* [1976] IRLR 251 in which an employee was dismissed for defrauding customers. The EAT held it was not necessary for the employer to prove actual guilt if he could show that his view of the employee's guilt was the real reason for the dismissal.

57. *Gallagher v. Linson Ltd.* UD 87/1979.

58. *Harrison*, footnote 12 *ante*.

59. *Callanan v. Messrs. Thomas, John and Edward McWilliams* UD 299/1978; on the other hand it may be a case of *res ipsa loquitur*; *Kirwan v. Northside Motors Ltd.* UD 12/1979.

stock control methods.[60] In regard to misconduct, while the Tribunal's function is not to determine the guilt or innocence of a claimant,[61] at the same time it is not sufficient for an employer to dismiss an employee merely because he, the employer, believes him guilty of some offence, e.g., serious misconduct in the form of fraud. On the evidence, the Tribunal must be satisfied that the employer has reasonably arrived at that conclusion.[62]

An employer may fail to come forward with any supporting evidence apart from a bare assertion of belief. In such a case, the Tribunal will be entitled to conclude that this stated reason for dismissal was not the real reason. The evidence itself may cast doubts upon the genuineness of an employer's asserted beliefs and suggest another reason.[63] Where an employer's own description of events suggests a reason contrary to his stated one, the possibility of convincing the Tribunal that the latter is the real reason is greatly reduced.[64] It is generally possible for the EAT to determine the principal reason where an employer presents a battery of reasons.[65] Of itself, industrial pressure does not constitute a ground for dismissal although it may be relevant in assessing the overall reasonableness of an employer's decision.[66]

B. Reasonableness of the Employer's Decision to Dismiss

'Perfect' procedural justice has been defined as the ideal of a procedure guaranteed to lead to an outcome where justice is identified by

---

60. *Bux v. Toohey & Co. Ltd.* UD 137/1978.
61. *Hennessy v. Read & Write Shop Ltd.* UD 192/1978; endorsed by *Dunne v. Harrington* UD 166/1979.
62. See, in this context, *Devlin v. Player & Wills (Ireland) Ltd.* UD 90/1978 (employee accused of theft by management; Tribunal looked, *inter alia*, to definition of theft in Larceny Act, 1916, when rejecting the accusation.)
63. See, e.g., *O'Hare v. The Curtain Centre Ltd.* UD 149/1978; *McLeish v. Ten Pin Bowling Co. of Ireland* UD 94/1978; *Mulcahy v. Seaborn Ltd.* UD 157/1978. See, in UK, *Chris v. John Lichfield* [1975] IRLR 28; *Yates v. British Leyland* [1974] IRLR 367; *Castledine v. Rothwell Engineering Ltd.* [1973] IRLR 99; *Price v. Gourley Bros. Ltd.* [1973] IRLR 11; *Raynor v. Remploy Ltd.* [1973] IRLR 3.
64. *Zambra v. F. G. Duffy* UD 154/1978. See *Castledine's* case, fn. 63 *supra*.
65. UD 310/1978; see, too, *Smith v. de Jong* UD 207/1978; *Clarke v. CIE* UD 104/1978, contrast *O'Brien v. Int. Harvester Co. of Great Britain* [1974] IRLR 374.
66. *McSweeney v. OK Garages Ltd.* UD 107/1978 distinguished in *O'Leary v. Tracy Shoes (Douglas) Ltd.* UD 350/1979; cf. EPCA 1978, s. 63 and see, e.g., *Ford Motors Co. Ltd. v. Hudson* [1978] IRLR 66 (EAT); *Hazells Offset Ltd. v. Luckett* [1977] IRLR 430 (EAT). Pressure exerted by outsiders, e.g., suppliers, may be relevant; *Jackson v. D. J. McCarthy & Co. Ltd.* UD 297/1978.

some independent criterion.[67] The balance between substantive and procedural justice becomes most crucial in relation to the reasonableness of an employer's decision to dismiss. The EAT eschews an interventionist role; it is reluctant to scrutinise the substance of an employer's decision to dismiss. But its determinations have made a considerable impact on the procedures adopted by management concerning dismissals. More and more, procedural justice is being taken for granted by all concerned and the EAT's function is to decide how exacting its tenets shall be. An employer will be regarded as having fairly dismissed an employee only if he both gave the employee the full benefits of fair procedure and accorded him his just deserts or established a functional necessity for his dismissal. In *Hennessy v. Read & Write Shop Ltd.*,[68] the Tribunal described 'the test of reasonableness'. It is applied to:

'(1) the nature and extent of the enquiry carried out by the employer prior to the decision to dismiss the claimant, and
(2) the employer's conclusion following such enquiry that the claimant should be dismissed.'

The Tribunal will scrutinise an employer's conduct very closely where he is faced with a problem requiring investigation. In *Dunne v. Harrington*[69] it declared that an employer may investigate either:

(a) personally in a fair and reasonable manner, i.e., as fully as is reasonably possible, confronting the "suspected" employee with "evidence", checking on and giving fair value to the employee's explanation or comments and allowing the employee to be represented at all such meetings/confrontations if the employee requests it or a union/management agreement requires it and to produce "counter evidence"[70]

or he may

(b) rely on the reports of others. If he does so without confronting the accused employee with the contents of same, without hearing, investigating and giving value to his replies, giving him reasonable opportunity to produce rebutting

---

67. See Rawls: *A Theory of Justice* 85. Note the development in Britain which distinguishes standards of procedural fairness for small employers, e.g., *The Royal Naval School v. Hughes* [1979] IRLR 383. This, in principle, is unsound.

68. UD 192/1978, followed in *O'Leary* footnote 66 *supra*, and *Goggin v. AnCO* UD 344/1979.

69. UD 166/1979.

70. The EAT referred to *Hennessy* fn. 68 *supra*, to *Murray v. Meath Co. Council* UD 43/1978, and to *British Home Stores Ltd. v. Burchell* [1978] ITR 560.

"evidence", and to be represented if the employee feels this
to be desirable, then such employer breaches a fundamental
rule of natural justice, *viz.*, that the other party (i.e., the
employee in these circumstances) should be heard. In short,
an employer acting on the reports of third parties and not
acquainting the employee with same does so at his peril if it
results in the dismissal of that employee.'[71]

Where an employer is confronted with information amassed by a fair
and reasonable investigation he should apply himself to it in a fair and
reasonable way 'as a prudent and concerned employer' and reach his
conclusion as to the appropriate disciplinary measure which should
relate reasonably to the offence.[72] By talking in terms of 'a prudent
and concerned employer' the EAT appears to be setting an objective
standard of fairness. This is infinitely preferable to the attitude which
the EAT in Britain has displayed upon occasion. It has been reluctant to assert that certain management styles are unacceptable and
instead has hidden behind the commonly held opinions of some
employers.[73]

The nature of an employer's enquiry and the reasonableness of his
conclusion in the light of all the circumstances will be distinguished
for purposes of the present analysis.

(1) *The nature of the employer's enquiry*

When deciding to dismiss an employee, an employer will normally
be expected to observe the rules of natural justice.[74] He must observe

71. The EAT pointed out that they were basing their comments on an internal
enquiry of an industrial or business nature. Reference was made to *White v. Fry-
Cadbury (Irl.) Ltd.* UD 44/1979.

72. *Dunne* fn. 69, *supra*. The EAT expressly refrained from commenting on the
importance of complying with disciplinary procedures in union/management agreements as no such agreement applied in the case. However, the general view of the EAT
was described as 'in accordance with that expressed in *Blackman v. Post Office* [1974]
IRLR 46' wherein the NIRC took the view that dismissal in accordance with a
management/union agreement was a substantial reason for dismissal under the legislation then applicable, namely the Industrial Relations Act, 1971, s. 24(1)(b). This was
so even where the agreement was not legally binding. It was wholly unreasonable and
wrong to break such agreements.

73. E.g. *Saunders v. Scottish National Camps* [1980] IRLR 174. 'It is a
dangerous development, for if this kind of argument becomes widely accepted it will
result in being defined by the attitude of the most prejudiced body of employers
rather than by the tribunal's perception of how an enlightened employer might
behave': thus P. Elias: 'The Concept of Fairness in Unfair Dismissal' (1981) ILJ 201,
213.

74. A system of 'precedent' is developing in relation to the rules of natural justice
before the EAT: e.gg., *Warner-Lambert Ltd. v. Tormey and Hegarty* UD 255/1978;
Hynes v. Frederick Inns Ltd. UD 172/1978.

'industrial due process'. An employee has a fundamental right to defend himself when accused of an act which, if not adequately explained to the satisfaction of his employer, would or might place his job in jeopardy.[75] He is also entitled to be confronted with any evidence that may exist; and an employer is under a duty to satisfy himself, by inquiring as fully as possible, that when he reaches his decision he is in possession of all the facts, including the views of the employee concerned. But an employer's duty to operate fair procedures is not absolute. Procedural defects will not make a dismissal automatically unfair.[76] At the same time, findings of unfair dismissal have been made entirely on the grounds that an employer failed to live up to the rules of natural justice. The legitimacy of the processes adopted by an employer may be subordinated to the substantive merits of a particular case. An employer may be able to justify a procedural omission if he meets the onus of proving that, despite the omission, he acted reasonably in the circumstances in deciding to dismiss an employee. The correctness of this proposition was tested in *Meath County Council v. Creighton*[77] 'by an extreme example of a purely hypothetical case'[78]

> '. . . two employees are proved to go to the end of a remote field and one comes back seriously and bodily injured and complains to his employer that he was brutally assaulted by his fellow employee and the employer dismisses his fellow employee on the spot without waiting for any explanation.'

If, having been convicted of causing grievous bodily harm to his workmate, the dismissed employee claims under the Act of 1977

> 'does that employee, who has been proved beyond all doubt to be guilty of misconduct, have a right to claim compensation for an unfair dismissal merely because his employer failed to give him a hearing in accordance with natural justice? We think not.'

The onus of proof on an employer seeking to justify, having dispensed with or disregarded fair procedures, will of course be considerable. Achieving a balance between procedural and substantive justice is

---

75. *Hynes* case, *supra*. The EAT referred to an earlier determination of its own, *Hennessy v. Read & Write Shop Ltd*. UD 192/1978, also to Judge Kenny's judgment in the High Court in *Glover v. BLN Ltd*. [1973] I.R. 388.

76. *Byrne v. Allied Transport Ltd*. UD 11/1979.

77. UD 11/1977.

78. The example is similar to the facts in *Carr v. Alexander Russell Ltd*. [1976] IRLR 220.

exceedingly difficult. The functional importance of manifest justice in industrial relations cannot be underestimated: good industrial relations depend upon management not only acting fairly but being seen to do so.[79] Fair industrial practices are important, above all, in relation to:

    (i) Warnings of dismissal, and
    (ii) Adequate hearings.

(i) *Warnings*

With the exception of cases of gross misconduct, serious ill-health, or other circumstances entitling an employer to dismiss without notice, an employer is normally expected to give a final formal warning before dismissing an employee[80] although, as a matter of law, the omission of a warning will not render a dismissal unfair. Where a warning, if duly given, is likely to influence the result, its omission may make a dismissal unfair. In *O'Reilly v. Dodder Management,*[81]

79. As Sir John Donaldson rightly indicated in *Earl v. Slater & Wheeler (Airlyne) Ltd.* [1972] IRLR 115 (NIRC). For an interesting analysis of the way in which standards of fairness have changed in emphasis in Britain see P. Elias, *art. cit.,* fn. 73 *ante.* The test now laid down by the EAT in *British Labour Pump v. Byrne* [1979] IRLR 94, is whether on the balance of probabilities the employer would have taken the same course even if he had held an enquiry. The Court of Appeal has equally been placing less emphasis on procedure. Note, however, the importance accorded to procedure both prior to and at the time of termination in the ILO *Report,* chapter five, fn. 4 *ante,* paras. 11-13.

80. See, *O'Connor v. Marley Extrusions (Irl.) Ltd.* UD 135/1979. A typical example of an agreed procedure for dismissal might be—

    (a) a verbal warning to be given to the employee by his supervisor,
    (b) a formal warning in writing to be given and, where appropriate, a copy to his shop steward,
    (c) a final warning in writing to be given and, where appropriate, a copy to his shop steward,
    (d) suspension,
    (e) dismissal in the absence of a settlement.

81. UD 311/1978. See the approach in *Mansfield & Hosiery Mills Ltd. v. Bromley* [1977] IRLR 301, where the industrial tribunal noted that if the applicant had been given an opportunity to improve his performance 'it was questionable whether he could have succeeded' and indeed it was 'on the whole unlikely because the employee had been appointed to a post that was rather beyond him'. The EAT on appeal upheld the tribunal and declared that the fact that, 'it can be said in some very plain circumstances [that an opportunity to improve is otiose] does not mean . . . that it is a case where the industrial tribunal was bound to have said it'. This decision was given strong support by the House of Lords in *Devis'* case, fn. 52 *ante.* In *Mansfield,* the EAT modified its view in the earlier less satisfactory case of *Lowndes v. Specialist Heavy Engineering Ltd.* [1976] IRLR 246, [1977] ICR 1. But see the analysis in the article by P. Elias, fn. 73 *ante.*

the Tribunal stated most emphatically that an employer cannot dismiss without, where appropriate, giving an employee warnings. Where capability and competence are concerned, the standard of job performance that is required must be made clear to an employee and he should be told clearly that failure to reach that standard will result in dismissal:

> 'a warning should place the appellant under clear notice of his general[82] or particular areas of deficiency, so as to enable him to rectify same, or if aggrieved, to make representations to his employer, either personally or through his trade union re presentative.'[83]

In particular a final warning should specify that an infringement will lead to the sanction of dismissal.[84] A reasonable employer must ascertain the possibilities of correcting an employee's behaviour before dismissing him.[85] This may be less important in dismissal for ill-health, or for redundancy, where consultation is likely to provide the necessary information for employees; similarly, in dismissal for incapability. In cases of misconduct, an employer is required not only to make reasonable efforts to communicate to an employee that his actions are placing his job in danger, but he is also required to ensure that an employee is given a reasonable opportunity of rectifying his actions to meet the required standards of behaviour.[86] Fighting or

---

82. In some instances, it seems, notification of a general area of deficiency will not be enough. In *Gaffney v. Press Knives Ltd.* UD 304/1978, the Tribunal expressed a wish to put on record that where vague complaints such as 'non-cooperation' are made or found against an employee, specific instances of non-cooperation should be given to the employee, so that he will understand clearly the employer's complaints and also ways should be indicated to him, in which an improvement might reasonably be expected.

83. *Kerr v. Tower Hotel Group Ltd.* UD 11/1977; see, too, *Richardson v. H. Williams & Co. Ltd.* UD 17/1979; *Newman v. T. H. White Motors Ltd.* |1972| IRLR 49; *Phipps v. Laffin* UD 18/1979.

84. *Kerr, supra. Allen v. Wellman International Ltd.* UD 152/1979; *Connolly v. Midland Tarmacadam Ltd.* UD 19/1979; *O'Reilly v. Dodder Management* UD 311/1978; *Walsh v. Smiths (Portlaoise) Ltd.* UD 164/1978; *Corcoran v. Kelly & Barry & Associates* UD 174/1978. Where there is a sudden and uncharacteristic deterioration in an employee's work performance, the employer should make reasonable efforts to find out the causes of this: *McGibbon v. Mark Royce Ltd.* UD 90/1978; also, *Belford v. Doyle* UD 286/1978.

85. See *Fullam v. Curragh Knitwear Ltd.* UD 76/1978; *Bartley v. Royal Dublin Golf Club* UD 151/1978; *Byrne v. North Strand Furniture Ltd.* UD 12/1980.

86. *Healy v. Cormeen Construction Ltd.* UD 98/1978. See, too, *Byrne v. Bradden Design Centre Ltd.* UD 176/1978; *Redmond v. Royal Marine Hotel* UD 196/1978 (where the employer had in any event confused the claimant with another employee); *O'Reilly v. Furlong & Sons Ltd.* UD 75/1978.

violence is well established as a category of misconduct for which a single offence may justify dismissal. The general principle expounded by the Tribunal is that 'fighting *per se* is not a dismissable offence certainly in the first instance'[87] but a reasonable employer is expected to indicate in his disciplinary rules that fighting or violence is liable to be punished by instant dismissal, although failure to provide such a rule or to warn will not always make a dismissal unfair. In effect the rule itself may act as a substitute warning.

Where an employer has tacitly accepted or condoned a particular practice and decides to take a firm disciplinary line, he must give adequate warning to employees that he is taking a new approach. If he has previously tended to interpret a disciplinary rule rather lightly, a sudden decision to dismiss employees for breaking the rule without adequate warning of the change in approach may be unfair. In *Harris v. P. V. Doyle Hotels*[88] the claimant was dismissed for drinking on the premises. The Tribunal observed that management had not sufficiently made known to employees of the hotel that drinking on the premises would result in instant dismissal and:

> '[a] rule which is not expected to be enforced may be so diluted that its breach *per se* might not justify dismissal. There was a duty on management to make clear beyond doubt to employees any 'house rules' such as the drinking rule in this hotel, the breach of which would result in automatic dismissal.'[89]

Where management has condoned a certain amount of laxity on the part of employees they are under a clear duty not to act prematurely and to dismiss without adequate warning that they expect a higher standard.[90]

(ii) *Adequate hearings*

The provision of a fair hearing for employees is a very important element of fair procedure. Ideally, an employer should have a

---

87. *Warner-Lambert (Ire.) Ltd. v. Tormey and Hegarty* UD 255/1978. In the general context of this form of misconduct see *Kelly v. Steward & Son Ltd.* UD 320/1978; *Sheils and Bonner v. Engineering Ltd.* UD 67/1977, UD 18/1978; *Ryan v. Tender Meats Ltd.* UD 42/1978; *Meath County Council v. Creighton* UD 11/1977.

88. UD 150/1978. See *Bendall v. Pain & Betteridge* [1973] IRLR 44.

89. The fairness of the rules themselves and the question of whether they are binding on an employee would always be reviewable by the Rights Commissioners and the EAT.

90. *O'Neill v. Furlong & Sons Ltd.* UD 75/1978. Also, *Hertz Rent A Car Ltd. v. Hughes* UD 10/1980. Contrast *Redland Purple Ltd. v. O'Halloran* UD 51/1978; *Sloan & Co. Ltd. v. Dunne* UD 69/1978 (a bad precedent) and *W. J. Dwan Ltd. v. Tynan* UD 120/1980. Cf. too, *Hadjioannou v. Coral Casinos Ltd.* [1981] IRLR 352.

disciplinary procedure providing the right for an individual to be informed of complaints against him and to be given an opportunity of stating his case before any decisions are reached.[91] Under the Code of Practice in Britain:

'. . . before a decision is made or penalty imposed the individual should be interviewed and given the opportunity to state his or her case and should be advised of any right under the procedure, including the right to be accompanied.'[92]

Natural justice demands that alleged misdemeanours of an employee be brought to his notice and that he be given an opportunity to defend himself.[93] It is uncertain whether one has the right to an oral hearing: depending on the circumstances, written representations may be regarded as satisfying the test of fairness.[94] It is a fundamental requirement of fairness that an accused employee be given a full and reasonable opportunity to examine all relevant witnesses and to be represented if he so wishes.[95] A denial of trade union representation will amount to a breach of natural justice. In *Devlin v. Player & Wills Ltd.*[96] the Tribunal was satisfied that the denial of trade union representation to the claimant on a matter which the respondent company regarded as serious and on which it intended to take the most serious action of dismissal amounted to 'unfair industrial practice'.

Where criminal conduct is involved on an employee's part, some form of representation will be crucial. In *Kelly v. CIE*[97] the appellant was suspended pending an investigation into an alleged theft of goods from a Catering Service Car. His dismissal was later confirmed after an internal investigation by the company. While the investigation was

---

91. Where employers have no definite or formal procedure for dismissal they are in a weak position: *Ennis v. Donabate Golf Club Ltd.* UD 118/1978. Further, see the unsatisfactory attitude of the EAT in *Condron v. Rowntree Mackintosh Ltd.* UD 195/1979.

92. Para. 11 Code of Practice (UK).

93. *Moran v. Bailey Gibson Ltd.* UD 69/1977. See, similarly, *Garrett v. CIE* UD 177/1980, approving *Khanum v. Mid-Glamorgan Area Health Authority* [1978] IRLR 215; *McCarthy v. Irish Shipping Ltd.* UD 100/1978.

94. In this context see *Ayanlowo v. IRC* [1975] IRLR 253.

95. *Kelly v. CIE* UD 28/1978.

96. UD 90/1978; also, *Murray v. Meath County Council* UD 43/1978. Contrast *Dacres v. Walls Meat Co. Ltd.* [1976] IRLR 20, [1976] ICR 44 (QBD) (held trade union representation could have made no difference in the circumstances and therefore its precision did not render the dismissal unfair). See too *Rank Xerox (UK) Ltd. v. Goodchild* [1979] IRLR 185. (EAT held, in matters where serious criminal conduct is alleged, it is essential if it can be arranged that there should be representation in accordance with agreed disciplinary procedure.)

97. UD 28/1978.

pending, the Garda Síochána were contacted and the appellant was charged with larceny. The charge was later dismissed. The Tribunal noted that:

> 'it is a fundamental right of a person accused of a criminal offence to act on the advice of his legal adviser.'

and went on to state its belief that

> 'the involvement of the Gardai in a criminal investigation should properly have resulted in the suspension of the company's internal investigations insofar as they required the appellant/accused person to comment on the allegations, the subject of the criminal charge, unless the accused person consents with the knowledge and agreement of his legal representative, where such a representative has been instructed.'

In cases involving misconduct the correct procedure will generally be to suspend an employee pending full and proper enquiry into his conduct.[98] But where an employer unreasonably delays before dismissing an employee in order to suit his own convenience, his *laches* will render the dismissal unfair.[99] By suiting the convenience of the business, an employer is overlooking the fact that an employee's character is in question and fairness requires 'that the employee be at once challenged and be immediately given an opportunity and an adequate means to meet the challenge'. Again, it may suit an employer's convenience to operate disciplinary procedures which are described as 'final and inappellable'. But no matter how acceptable these procedures, any decisions based thereon may be reviewed by the enforcing authorities under the Act.[100]

(2) *Reasonableness of the employer's conclusion in the light of all the circumstances*

As a last step, an employer has to satisfy the EAT that his decision to dismiss was reasonable 'having regard to all the circumstances'. He is allowed some discretion. In *Vokes Ltd. v. Beer*[101] the Court of Appeal suggested that the net must be cast fairly wide:

---

98. *Ledwidge v. Peter Mark Ltd.* UD 70/1978. Where the misconduct consists of a criminal offence, however, and charges have been laid against an employee, a hearing may be inappropriate.

99. *Zambra v. Duffy* UD 154/1978.

100. *Marsh v. UCD* UD 27/1977.

101. [1973] IRLR 363, [1974] ICR 1.

'The circumstances embrace all relevant matters that should weigh with a good employer when deciding at a given moment in time whether he should dismiss an employee.'

As it happens, the enforcing authorities have considerable latitude in determining as a question of fact whether or not the employer's decision to dismiss was reasonable in all the circumstances. In this respect, they act as 'industrial juries'.[102] Any important consideration that mitigates the fault of the employee or which calls into question the wisdom of dismissal must be considered.

In relation to incompetence, for example, an employer's own duties may have a bearing on whether an employee has met his responsibilities. Management is under a general duty not only to define the work but also to provide adequate supervision.[103] Where physical or mental illness is concerned, the EAT will ask whether a proper investigation of the claimant has been carried out, although essentially, it should be added, the decision to dismiss is an employment, not a medical matter. The question will turn on a balance of the employee's and company's interests respectively. An employee's long record of good service in the past may be taken into account by the EAT. Likewise, age and relative inexperience will not be overlooked. An employer's decision to dismiss is not likely to be upheld where he took on an employee knowing he was not better than other applicants for the position.[104] If an employee's appointment is probationary, the test of reasonableness is adjusted to take into account a duty on the employee's part to establish himself, as well as the employer's duty to give him a reasonable opportunity to do this. The trauma of a family death may be relevant although in such circumstances it may be more reasonable for an employer to re-assign an employee to some other section within the company rather than to dismiss him.[105]

The EAT may hold it unfair to dismiss for disobedience to a legitimate instruction if it was unreasonable for an employer to issue the order in the first place and to insist on obedience to the point of

---

102. As a general rule the ordinary courts should approach with caution decisions on questions of fact arrived at by the EAT or by the Rights Commissioners. That is not to say, however, that their decisions ought not to be overturned.

103. It may be that an employee's incapability is more apparent than real and that proper training by the employer would have produced more efficient work performance: *Bux v. Toohey & Co. Ltd.* UD 137/1978.

104. *McGrath v. Short* UD 315/1978.

105. *Bastow v. Anderson & Co.* UD 314/1978; contrast *Farrell v. Rotunda Hospital* UD 35/1978.

dismissal.[106] The boundary line is thin between this sort of situation and one where an employee is deemed to have 'terminated' his employment himself by wilful disobedience.[107] Further, an employee's refusal to obey may be looked upon as unreasonable if he ought to have foreseen that his action could produce adverse consequences, for instance, a worsening of the company's financial position.[108] In relation to misconduct in the form of fighting or violence, all relevant factors will be taken into account such as the extent of the violence, any element of self defence or other mitigating circumstances.[109] The degree of provocation will also be assessed and if an assault was totally unprovoked this justifies summary dismissal.[110] The standard of proof required to establish provocation is very high.[111] Where two workers engage in a constant battle of provocative observations, whatever words they use are unlikely to warrant a physical assault by one on the other.[112] An employee's task is to convince the Tribunal that his employer's assessment of the surrounding circumstances was not that of a reasonable employer. A general plea for leniency will not suffice.[113]

The reasonableness test in relation to theft or dishonesty applies more to a showing of deliberate dishonesty than to any amounts of money that may be involved. It may be related to the degree of trust which is expected from an employee in the circumstances. The higher standard that is required of a harbour master was taken into account

106. *Fergus O'Farrell Ltd. v. Nugent* UD 120/1978; UD 123/1978; also *Durnin v. Building & Engineering Co. Ltd.* UD 159/1978; *McGowan v. Kelleher Public Works Ltd.* UD 9/1980; *Nolan v. Steel and Engineering Supplies Ltd.* UD 34/1981. Contrast *Canavan v. K. A. Burke (Carriers) Supplies Ltd.* UD 15/1977; see, further, in relation to disobedience: *Cannon v. John Bolton Motors Ltd.* UD 58/1979; *Fitzgerald v. Williams Transport Ltd.* UD 151/1978; UD 165/1978; *Stamp v. A. N. Stamp Ltd.* UD 11/1978; *Galway Crystal Ltd. v. McMorrow* UD 1/1977. A case of particular interest is *Walsh v. F. N. Woolworth & Co. Ltd.* UD 296/1978 which may be criticised for a failure by the EAT to apply the test of reasonableness to a mobility clause in the employee manager's contract of employment.

107. *Floody v. Charles Dougherty & Co. Ltd.* UD 46/1980.

108. *Fullam* fn. 85 *ante.*

109. See *Warner-Lambert's* case, fn. 87 *ante:* an important aspect was that the appropriate disciplinary procedures operating in the firm were not complied with in any real way.

110. *Cox v. Industrial Contract Engineers Ltd.* UD 133/1978; also *Challoner v. Irish Meat Producers Ltd.* UD 56/1977. Assault may be reasonable in the face of severe provocation: *Mullen v. Linenhall (1972) Ltd.* UD 94/1980.

111. *Ledwidge v. Peter Mark Ltd.* UD 70/1978; see too, *Ferodo Ltd. v. Clusker* UD 139/1979.

112. *O'Shea v. P. J. Cullen & Sons* UD 17/1977.

113. *Hogan, Farrell and Dolan v. Cantrell & Cochrane Ltd.* UD 41-3/1979.

in *Hevey v. Dublin Port & Docks Board*[114] where the applicant was dismissed for taking six tins of fruit. Where pilfering and embezzlement are concerned, it may be relevant that the Gardai were not called in with a view to investigating the circumstances;[115] although if a detailed procedure already exists in the company for dealing with such acts, non-involvement of the Gardai may assume far less relevance. An employee may commit a criminal act outside employment. Where this affects the business in some way,[116] or if an employee holds a position of trust[117] or his own reputation is affected, an employer may be able to establish that it was not unfair to dismiss. Otherwise, the commission of a crime outside employment may be held an unsufficient ground for dismissal particularly where it is a first offence. Where, however, a jail sentence is imposed for a criminal offence, an employer will not normally be expected to keep an employee's job open. The contract of employment is arguably frustrated.[118]

All of the matters so far mentioned relate to mitigating circumstances affecting an employee. It is equally clear — although it may be difficult for an employer to succeed in justifying dismissal on this basis — that any important circumstance which relates to the business interests of the employer may be taken into account.[119]

C. Constructive Dismissal: the Reason Therefor

In relation to constructive dismissal, the emphasis or process of investigating claims is quite different from ordinary dismissals. The first stage focuses on the employer's behaviour. So closely related that it would be difficult to call it a second stage is the employee's response to that behaviour. Either of two interrogatories will be raised at this juncture: was the employee entitled in a contractual sense to

114. UD 161/1978; see, too, *White v. Cadbury (Ire.) Ltd.* UD 44/1979; *Devlin v. Player & Wills (Ire.) Ltd.* UD 90/1978; *Williams Transport Group Ltd. v. McCafferty* UD 152/1978; *Sloan & Co. v. Dunne* UD 69/1978.
115. *Maguire v. Dunnes Stores (Drogheda) Ltd.* UD 19/1978.
116. An argument raised but not sustained in *Morrissey v. Morton* UD 115/1980.
117. Cf. *Clarke v. CIE* UD 104/1978.
118. Cf. *Hare v. Murphy Bros.* [1974] ICR 603 (CA): 12 month prison sentence imposed by a court frustrated the contract of employment (*per* Lord Denning) or terminated it by making it impossible for the employee to perform his part of the contract (*per* Stephenson and Lawton L.JJ.). See *Norris v. Southampton City Council* (*The Times* 3 February 1982) where the EAT held that where an employee, by his own conduct, made the performance of his contract of employment impossible, as, e.g., if he committed an offence resulting in imprisonment, the contract was not frustrated but rather the employer could treat it as repudiated and dismiss the employee.
119. *Lavery v. Irish Silver Ltd.* UD 68/1977.

resign or otherwise to terminate his contract of employment, or, was it reasonable for him so to do? The employee's burden of establishing dismissal in either sense may be onerous. The bulk of a hearing concerning constructive dismissal is likely to concern the employee's proof of dismissal. An examination of one or more of the reasons deemed fair or unfair under the Act may or may not be relevant. In any event it will be necessary as a final step to enquire whether dismissal was reasonable in the light of all the circumstances. Here the onus is on the employer. Rarely if ever have cases in Ireland reached that stage with any clarity. Indeed, as earlier mentioned, the initial test of reasonableness may obscure the test of reasonableness overall. If an employee seeks to argue that his constructive dismissal satisfies the test of reasonableness, in practice this may be tantamount to requiring him to prove that his dismissal was unfair.[120] Although it is generally very difficult to state whether the Irish EAT applies one test rather than the other in relation to constructive dismissal, where it has applied the reasonableness test, it has not always avoided the danger of merging the two notions of reasonableness.[121]

But the treatment of reasonableness in each of the two contexts in which it may arise is not the only neuralgic issue in assessing the employer's role in the matter of constructive dismissal. Other problems may appear at the first stage, if the contract rather than the reasonableness test is invoked. Where an employee relies on the contract test, it will be of cardinal importance to ascertain the precise scope of the contract. Express terms present little difficulty.[122] Thus constructive dismissal may arise where an employer unjustifiably reduces an employee's remuneration,[123] or insists upon a change in

120. A different but equally disquieting perspective was outlined by Phillips J. in *Scott v. Aveling Barford Ltd.* [1977] IRLR 419.
'If the Tribunal has answered question 1 — whether the employee has been dismissed — in the employee's favour on the ground that the employer acted so unreasonably as to entitle the employee to leave — then it is hardly likely that the same Tribunal would hold that the same employer, acting in the same way, had been "fair" in pushing the employee out of his (that is, the employee's) job.'
121. See, e.g., *Reddington v. Duffy's Bakery* UD 153/1978.
122. Although it should be noted that from time to time the EAT's interpretation of express contract terms has allowed perhaps too wide a scope for managerial prerogative. See, e.g., *Riddell v. Mid-West Metals Ltd.* UD 687/1980.
123. As happened in *Owens v. Ramsbottom* UD 103/1980 although the point was not taken up. An employee must actually resign in order to be able to claim constructive dismissal. This point could assume considerable importance in relation to claims based on breach of implied terms. See *Hunt v. British Railways Board* [1979] IRLR 379. In *Western Excavating (ECC) Ltd. v. Sharp* [1978] QB 761, [1978] ICR 221, Lord Denning M.R. said that an employee must decide to leave soon after the conduct of which he complains. But if an employee were to stay on for a few weeks after, say, demotion, it should still be possible for him to claim under the

the nature of the employee's contractual performance or obligations such as the kind of work he is required to perform, the hours of work he is required to do,[124] and the place at which he is required to do the work.[125] Difficulties may arise, however, where constructive dismissal is alleged in the face of breach of an implied term. An employee may encounter problems in identifying such terms, although the process has been facilitated by a change in judicial attitude to the status of the employment relationship.[126] Examples of terms[127] which have been implied in Irish cases include the maintenance of trust and confidence by an employer,[128] the provision of managerial support and

---

legislation provided he has never agreed to the demotion but in fact protested about it: *Marriot v. Oxford and District Co-Op. Soc. (No. 2)* [1970] 1 QB 186, [1969] 3 All ER 1126 (CA). Some evidence will be required that the employee objected to the employer's treatment: *Luckhurst v. Kent Litho Co. Ltd.* (1976) EAT 302/76; *Sheet Metal Components Ltd. v. Plumridge* [1974] IRLR 86, [1974] ICR 373. In Ireland where the compensation awarded to an unfairly dismissed employee does not include a basic award the amount likely to be awarded to an employee who stays on in order to find another job is likely to be so small as to make a claim not worth bringing, except perhaps to establish a finding of unfair dismissal.

124. *Keenan v. Raheny and District Credit Union Ltd.* UD 111/1980.

125. In Britain, the case of *R.S. Components Ltd. v. Irwin* [1973] IRLR 239; [1973] ICR 535 was responsible for a new mood on the part of industrial tribunals where employees are dismissed for refusal to accept changes not contractually permitted. The NIRC accepted the possibility there that dismissal for refusal to accept a unilateral variation in a contractual condition which restricted an employee from acting in competition could count as 'some other substantial reason'. Since *Irwin*, an employer's business interests have been accepted as a substantial ground justifying dismissal in several cases, concerning, e.g., Change of hours: *Smithson v. Sydney Chambers & Co. Ltd.* [1976] IRLR 13; *Wilson v. Leslie Blass Ltd.* [1975] IRLR ITR 75; *Robinson v. Flitwick Frames Ltd.* [1975] IRLR 261; *Knighton v. Rhodes* [1974] IRLR 71; *Moreton v. Selby Protective Clothing Co. Ltd.* [1974] IRLR 269; Flexibility changes: *Smith & Tickell v. Cornwall CC* COIT 803/182, *Finnerty v. Devro Ltd.* [1974] IRLR 175; New Payments System: *Sycamore v. Myer & Co. Ltd.* [1976] IRLR 84. In general, see H. Forrest: 'Political Values in Individual Employment Law' (1980) 43 MLR 361.

Equally, the contract of employment may define the conditions of employment concerning working hours and type or place of work in such a way that insistence upon some change in these would not amount to a constructive dismissal. If a woman is contractually described as a 'waitress', for instance, she cannot complain if she is asked to work in the canteen rather than the directors' dining room. *Grace v. Northgate Group Ltd.* [1972] IRLR 53. See, too, *Managers (Holborn) Ltd. v. Hohne* [1977] IRLR 230.

126. It is primarily the development of unfair dismissal law which has provided the impetus for the courts in Britain to examine carefully the obligations which an employer owes to an employee: P. Elias: 'Unravelling the Concept of Dismissal' (1978) ILJ 100 at 107. See, too, B. Napier: 'Judicial Attitudes towards the Employment Relationship — Some Recent Developments' (1977) 6 ILJ 1, 6.

127. These terms have never formed the basis of comment by the EAT: their existence is generally assumed.

128. *Byrne v. R. H. M. Foods (Ire.) Ltd.* UD 69/1979; see similarly, *Courtaulds Northern Textiles Ltd. v. Andrew* [1977] IRLR 84; *Donovan v. Invicta Airways* [1969] 2 Lloyds Rep. 413.

security for an employee,[129] the payment by an employer of the statutory wage for workers in the industry,[130] non-competition on the part of an employee[131] and the right to be treated with respect by an employer and not to have to endure physical violence and humiliation.[132] Mere doubts and misunderstandings concerning, e.g., an employee's holiday position or other terms and conditions of employment would not justify resignation.[133]

In *BAC Ltd. v. Austin*,[134] the British EAT observed that it must ordinarily be an implied term of the contract 'that employers do not behave in any way which is intolerable or in a way which employees cannot be expected to put up with any longer' and that that would include any serious departure from 'good industrial practice'.[135] This appeal to good industrial relations practice invokes a very wide-ranging criterion which could apply to a protean variety of individual circumstances. In fact, British cases on constructive dismissal for breach of an implied term cover a very wide variety of circumstances.[136] There are many forms of distasteful and unreasonable

---

129. *McGrath v. C.A. Jenkins & Sons Ltd.* UD 227/1978; see, similarly, *Wigan Borough Council v. Davies* [1979] IRLR 127.
130. *McGrory v. Campbell* UD 49/1979.
131. *O'Neil v. Flynns Garage* UD 122/1981.
132. *O'Leary v. Cranehire Ltd.* UD 167/1979; *Higgins v. Donnelly Mirrors Ltd.* UD 104/1979 (although no violence was involved). The right to be treated with respect would not be violated if, e.g., an employee were passed over for promotion: *Corcoran v. Central Remedial Clinic* UD 7/1978.
133. *O'Grady v. Cornelscourt Shopping Centre Ltd.* UD 210/1979.
134. [1978] IRLR 332.
135. Albeit this pronouncement was *obiter* and subject to the express reservation that industrial tribunals must apply the judgment in *Western Excavating Ltd. v. Sharp*.
136. They include instances of persistent and unwanted amorous advances: *Western Excavating Ltd. v. Sharp* fn 123 *ante, obiter:* prematurely calling in the police to investigate an employee: *Fybe & McGrouther Ltd. v. Byrne* [1977] IRLR 29; refusal to pay commission: *Logabox v. Titherley* [1977] IRLR 97; reduction in pay: *Industrial Rubber Products v. Gillon* [1977] IRLR 389; *Gilles v. R. Daniels & Co. Ltd.* [1980] IRLR 457; malice in excluding employee from promotion: *Turner v. London Transport Executive* [1977] IRLR 441; employee's refusal to move to a new place of work: *George Wimpey & Co. Ltd. v. Cooper* [1977] IRLR 205; *Little v. Charterhouse Magna Assurance Co. Ltd.* [1980] IRLR 19; employee's refusal to undertake temporary duties pending discussions with trade union: *Scott v. Aveling Barford*, fn. 120 *ante; Milthorn Toleman Ltd. v. Ford* [1978] IRLR 306; requirement to drive overloaded vehicle: *Wilkins v. Cantrell & Cochrane Ltd.* [1978] IRLR 483; failure to take action on a safety complaint: *BAC v. Austin*, fn. 134 *ante; Keys v. Shoefayre Ltd.* [1978] IRLR 476; allegations of inefficiency and incompetence of employee: *Wetherall (Bond St. WI) v. Lynn* [1977] IRLR 333; change in emphasis in job duties: *London Borough of Camden v. Pedersen* [1979] IRLR 377; deductions from pay of cash deficiencies caused by dishonesty: *Bristol Garage (Brighton) Ltd. v. Lowen* [1979] IRLR 86; false accusations that employee is guilty of theft: *Robinson v. Crompton Parkinson Ltd.* [1979] IRLR 61; arbitrary and discriminatory refusal to

behaviour on the part of employers which, although not amounting to breach of an express term in the contract of employment, may find a remedy in the doctrine of the implied term. The British EAT recognised early on that contractual repudiation could include abusive, intolerable and unreasonable treatment by an employer:

> 'What is conduct on the part of the employer showing intention not to be bound by the contract will depend on the circumstances of each case, and upon the terms of the contract, express or to be implied, in each case; these terms will reflect the changes in the relationship between employer and employee as social standards change.'[137]

Not all findings by industrial tribunals in Britain may be justified. It is difficult to agree, for example, that the use of abusive language by an employer evinces an intention not to be bound by the contract.[138] If the contract test is applied with too broad a brush,[139] its supposed basis in contract law becomes little more than a formality.

An employer may seek to justify an alleged constructive dismissal

offer employee a pay rise: *F. C. Gardner Ltd. v. Beresford* [1978] IRLR 63; refusal to allow time off in an emergency: *Warner v. Barbers Stores* [1978] IRLR 109; foul language by employer: *Palmanor Ltd. v. Cedron* [1978] IRLR 303; employee underemployed: *V. A. Hemmings v. International Computers Ltd.* [1976] IRLR 37; conduct of workmates: *McCabe v. Chicpack Ltd.* [1976] IRLR 38; change of job content, demotion: *J. B. Robson v. Cambrian Electric Products Ltd.* [1976] IRLR 109; *Ford v. Milthorn Ltd.* [1980] IRLR 30; demotion as a disciplinary sanction (no repudiation): *Theedom v. British Railways Board* [1976] IRLR 137; no suitable work for employee: *F. T. Breach v. Epsylon Industries Ltd.* [1976] IRLR 180; unreasonable overtime: *Gilbert v. Goldstone* [1976] IRLR 257; lay off without pay: *Burroughs Machines Ltd. v. Timmoney* [1976] IRLR 343; suspension: *D. & J. McKenzie Ltd. v. Smith* [1976] IRLR 345 (Court of Session); lack of management support: *Associated Tyre Specialists (Eastern) Ltd. v. Waterhouse* [1976] IRLR 386; rudeness to secretary: *Isle of Wight Tourist Board v. Coombes* [1976] IRLR 413.

137. *Wetherall's* case fn. 136 *ante*. If an employee is abused by other employees this would not amount to constructive dismissal unless the employer condoned the behaviour or failed to take reasonable steps to prevent it: *McCabe v. Chicpack Ltd.* [1976] IRLR 38.

138. See earlier cases in which it was suggested it may be 'the tone in which the words are delivered which is as important as the words themselves and we find that they were intended to be, and in fact were, abusive and insulting to the employee ['bloody fat sod — stupid stuck up bitch']: *Mac Neilage v. Arthur Roye (Turf Accountants) Ltd.* [1976] IRLR 88 (IT). See, further, *Wares v. Caithness Leather Products* [1974] IRLR 162. It seems that case-law in Britain has distinguished between male and female employees: words like 'fuck off' may not amount to dismissal: *Witham v. Hills Shopfitters Ltd.* (1976) IT 17091/76/B; *Davy v. J. A. Sollins (Builders) Ltd.* [1974] IRLR 324. (Contrast Irish case, *Carroll v. Peter Lyons Ltd.* UD 229/1979). But abusive behaviour of other sorts may amount to constructive dismissal: *Bariamis v. John Stephen of London Ltd.* [1975] IRLR 237; *Fanshaw v. Robinsons & Sons Ltd.* [1975] IRLR 165.

139. See page 174 below.

by pointing to an express or implied[140] 'flexibility' or 'mobility' clause in the employee's contract of service. For instance he may have included a clause to the following effect:

> 'Should the interests of the company demand it, you may be required to serve at various offices of the company's head-quarters in Dublin, and the particular nature of your job may be changed.'[141]

Similarly a clause could be inserted:

> 'If you are employed [e.g., on site] you may be required to work overtime on being given reasonable notice.'[142]

In the latter case, an employer's insistence that his employee work overtime following due notice could not be regarded as being in breach of contract. Managerial prerogative in drawing up flexibility clauses is not unbridled, however. If an employer is given wide discretion by contract to alter the conditions of employment of employees, it is likely that the courts or the Tribunal would imply a term limiting the scope of that discretion. For instance, if a clause enabled an employer to transfer an employee to another job with a higher or lower rate of pay, whether day work, night work or shift work, it is unlikely that this would be interpreted so as to allow an employer to behave unreasonably, for example, to transfer a carpenter to a plumber's job or to transfer a process worker in a Dublin factory to a factory in Co. Kerry.[143]

---

140. Tribunals and courts in Britain have shown a strong dislike of implying such terms without fairly substantial evidence of their existence: e.g., *Overseas School of English v. Hartley* (1977) EAT 86/77.

141. A similar clause defeated an employee's claim for constructive dismissal in *Bex v. Securicor Transport Ltd.* [1972] IRLR 68 (business manager transferred to position of customer liaison officer).

142. *Dowsett Engineering Construction Ltd. v. Fowler* (1977) EAT 425/76. Where an employer alleges that an employee's original contract has been widened by agreement of the employee, he must clearly establish that the employee consented to the change.

143. Cf. *Briggs v. Imperial Chemical Industries* (1968) 3 ITR 276. It is impossible to say where the line limiting managerial prerogative would be drawn. One could argue that the employer is under a duty not to exercise his prerogative powers in a way which undermines the trust and confidence in the employment relationship, so that if he habitually insists on a particular employee changing jobs under a flexibility agreement, or transferring under a mobility clause, or being required to work overtime, or being refused overtime, this may in certain circumstances constitute a repudiation of the contract: according to Elias, fn. 126 *ante,* 100 at 106, *Gardner Ltd. v. Beresford* [1978] IRLR 63 is but a short step from this proposition.

CHAPTER SEVEN

Remedies for Unfair Dismissal

Introduction: Proprietas in Employment

On a number of occasions[1] the EAT has declared that:

'The Unfair Dismissals Act, 1977, establishes for an employee a propriety right to his employment, which, if taken away without there being substantial grounds justifying his dismissal, entitles him to redress for unfair dismissal.'[2]

In *Wynes v. Southrepps Hall Broiler Farm Ltd.*[3] Sir Diarmuid Conroy explained the concept of job ownership in redundancy legislation:

'Just as a property owner has a right in his property and when he is deprived he is entitled to compensation, so a long-term employee is considered to have a right analogous to a right of property in his job, he has a right to security, and his rights gain in value with the years . . .'

---

1. See generally F. Meyers: *Ownership in Jobs;* S. Brittan: *The Economic Consequences of Democracy* chapter 20; also 'Property Rights in Jobs' *Financial Times,* 2 April 1980; R. Holmes: 'The Ownership of Work: A Psychological Approach' (1967) 5 BJIR 19; for an analogy with social welfare rights see Wade & Phillips: *Constitutional and Administrative Law* 95; more generally, see G. de N. Clark: 'Remedies for Unfair Dismissal: A European Comparison' (1971) 20 ICLQ 397, 401. See also, same: *Remedies for Unfair Dismissal* (PEP Broadsheet 1970); V. Shrubsall: 'Some Rulings by the EAT on Unfair Dismissal' (1977) Vol. 127 NLJ 606. And, by the author: 'Section 7: Primary Remedies for Unfair Dismissal' (1977) 111 ILTSJ 245.

2. *McBride v. Midland Electrical Co. Ltd.* UD 37/1979; similarly, *O'Connor v. Heat Recovery Ltd.* UD 105/1980; *Bartley v. Royal Dublin Golf Club* UD 151/1978. See, by the author, 'Workers' Rights' in *Trade Unions and Change in Irish Society* (ed. D. Nevin) 82.

3. (1968) ITR 407, 407-8. See, too, G. de N. Clark: 'The compensation under discussion must be related to the value of the employee's accrued, quasi-proprietary rights in his job . . .' *Remedies for Unfair Dismissal* (PEP Broadsheet 518, 1970) 49. The late Professor Kahn-Freund was of the opinion that the property analogy could be taken too far. He saw it as a rule of social ethics that he who sacrifices an asset should receive a fair amount of compensation: *Labour Law: Old Traditions and New Developments* 38. Although he admitted 'there is something in the analogy' as 'for the large majority of people their job is their principal asset. They have invested their skill and their strength in the job'. See, further, D. Jackson: *Unfair Dismissal* 41.

The purpose, he said, is to compensate a worker for loss of job, irrespective of whether that loss leads to unemployment. It is to compensate him for loss of security, possible loss of earnings and fringe benefits, and the uncertainty and anxiety of change of job. These may all be present even if a man gets a fresh job immediately.

The claim that a worker has something akin to a property right in his job is not an enforceable claim-right. Nor can a job be bought, sold, or left to one's dependants. The property analogy belongs more to the sphere of morality or of social ethics. Legal manifestation of the rule 'that he who sacrifices an asset should receive a fair amount of compensation'[4] is confined mostly to the question of remedies. The property analogy explains why an unfairly dismissed worker's chief remedy is reinstatement, not re-engagement or compensation. Reinstatement recognises that, where a job has been wrongly expropriated, the person divested of his 'property' is entitled to recover what he has lost or had taken from him. Herein lies the difference between having a right to a job and simply having a job. Again, (as in Ireland or Britain) compensation is provided as an alternative to the primary remedies of reinstatement and re-engagement, it is not strictly a consequential award. Unlike its common law equivalent, compensation purports to be for loss of the job *per se*. In Part A of this chapter the property analogy is measured against the extent to which an employee who is unfairly dismissed can insist upon returning to his job. It will be seen that, in Ireland, the statutory attempt to create a legal right to remain in one's job has not succeeded. In Part B the part played by compensation in the evolution of *proprietas* in employment will be contrasted.

A. **Primary Remedies under the Act**

(1) *The Constitution*

From an individual worker's point of view, as the preceding chapters make apparent, the Constitution may be highly beneficial. It is ironic, therefore, that when it came to formulating the primary remedies for unfair dismissal the Constitution was presented as a stumbling block. It was alleged that reinstatement and re-engagement were inconsistent with an employer's right to freedom of association under Art. 40, s. 6, sub-s. 1 (iii).[5] Since freedom of

4. Kahn-Freund,*op. cit.*, fn. 3 *ante*, 38.
5. See a useful discussion on 'The Constitution and the Right to Reinstatement after Wrongful Dismissal' by M. Robinson and J. Temple Lang in the *Gazette of the Incorporated Law Society of Ireland*, My-Ju 1977, 78. A right to reinstatement is afforded by the constitutions and national legislation of other European countries without the suspicion that by so doing an employer's constitutional rights are being infringed. The right to reinstatement has been recognised in international documents

association carries with it a right not to associate it was argued that statutory provision for compulsory reinstatement or re-engagement would be *ultra vires*. The proponents of this view were not deterred by the fact that the freedom of association generally presupposes a common interest, not a contractual relationship — most frequently, it protects an employee's right to join, or to form, unions or associations. Protection is afforded against a particular employer and/or other workers and/or the State who may not interfere with the exercise of the freedom. But even if it is permissible to talk about an employer's rights under Art. 40, s. 6, sub-s. 1 (iii) in the context of primary remedies, such right of association as the employer may have is more accurately a freedom. It cannot hold sway against the rights, *strictu sensu,* of other persons. To argue that an employer is constitutionally entitled, on account of a freedom, to take advantage of his own wrong, is indefensible, the more so as the wrong in question is likely to involve a violation of the constitutional rights of former employees. The presumed 'right' or freedom of a former employer not to associate with his wrongfully dismissed employee is hardly more worthy of protection than the latter's right to continue to earn a livelihood. Besides, an employer's right in this respect, if it exists, may be subjected to regulatory legislation. In its final clause, Article 40, s. 6, sub-s. 1 (iii) says that:

'Laws . . . may be enacted for the regulation and control in the public interest of the exercise of the foregoing right.'

There is no doubt, in principle, that legislation regulating the right of association (such as the Unfair Dismissals Act) is constitutional.[6]In the end, primary remedies were included in the Act, the Constitution notwithstanding. Political considerations, it seems, won the day. On the Second Stage reading of the Bill in Seanad Éireann the Minister for Labour asserted that:

'It would be tragic to think that legislation that Deputies and Senators in both Houses agree is desirable should be held back or rendered less strong because of legal advice that the Constitution could be cited against these provisions. It would be nonsense to think that legislation did not offer the option to the aggrieved party of reinstatement . . . [We] have accepted the

such as the European Social Charter and ILO Recommendation No. 119 on the Termination of Employment (Geneva 1963). The question would present no difficulty if the right to reinstatement were given directly or indirectly under European Community Law.

6. See *NUR v. Sullivan* [1947] IR 77, 88 for discussion of 'regulation' in Art. 40. s. 6, sub-s. 1 (iii). And see Walsh J.'s balancing exercise in *Meskell v. CIE* [1973] IR 135.

possibility of certain elements of the Constitution being cited against the legislation before us. On the other hand, there is conflict in relation to this advice.'[7]

(2) *Reinstatement and Re-engagement defined*

Section 7 of the Act sets out the primary remedies. An employee unfairly dismissed under the Act is entitled to redress consisting of whichever of the following primary remedies the Rights Commissioner, the EAT, or the Circuit Court, as the case may be, considers appropriate having regard to all the circumstances:

'(a) reinstatement by the employer of the employee in the position which he held immediately before his dismissal on the terms and conditions on which he was employed immediately before his dismissal together with a term that the reinstatement shall be deemed to have commenced on the day of the dismissal, or
(b) re-engagement by the employer of the employee either in the position which he held immediately before his dismissal or in a different position which would be reasonably suitable for him on such terms and conditions as are reasonable having regard to all the circumstances.'[8]

---

7. *Seanad Debates* Vol. 86, Cols. 540-41 (March 1977).
8. Primary Remedies have slowly evolved in Britain. There, under the Industrial Relations Act, 1971 (Sched. 6, para. 5), only re-employment could be recommended for an unfairly dismissed employee. The recommendation was used in as little as 4% of the cases arising under the Act. The provisions in the Industrial Relations Act gave way to those in the Trade Union and Labour Relations Act, 1974 (sched. 1, para. 17), which gave tribunals power if they thought it practicable, and in accordance with equity, to recommend either reinstatement or reengagement and to lay down terms on which an employee was to be taken back. The Employment Protection Act, 1975, and the consolidating Act of 1978, have effected significant changes. The original recommendation by a tribunal is turned into two kinds of order, (s. 69), of which an order for reinstatement is the most important. Re-engagement must approximate to it wherever possible.
In the past, tribunals did not seem willing to apply the remedies of reinstatement and re-engagement. (See Report of Standing Committee F on the Employment Protection Bill, 21st sitting, July 3, 1975, cols. 1098-1100.) Now, under s. 68 of the EPCA, the tribunal's attention is forcibly directed to the equity of the case before it. It must publicly recite the law for its own benefit as well as that of the complainant. Following this public recitation, the employee complainant has the opportunity again of affirming his wish to be reinstated or re-engaged or otherwise. If he wishes to be reinstated or re-engaged the tribunal still has discretion to refuse to grant the remedy but its discretion is bounded by criteria set out in the Act: s. 69 (5) and (6). As a result, the onus of raising the possibility of reinstatement or re-engagement lies clearly on the tribunal and there cannot be any doubt as to whether a tribunal needs to consider a primary remedy where a claimant does not seek an order for such a

Reinstatement[9] requires an employer to treat an employee in all respects as if he had not been dismissed. An unfairly dismissed employee is entitled to any arrears of salary from the date of dismissal to the date of implementation of the order less any Social Welfare benefits received by him.[10] The Tribunal has spelled it out on a number of occasions[11] that the term 'salary' includes any benefits, including any salary increases which a claimant might reasonably be

---

remedy, a doubt which exists as far as the Irish Act is concerned. In general, see *Northman v. London Borough of Barnet* (no. 2) [1980] IRLR 65.

Under s. 71 EPCA, in a case where an employer has reinstated or re-engaged an employee in response to an order but compliance is only partial in any respect, a tribunal must make an award of compensation which it considers to be fit having regard to the loss sustained by the employee as a consequence of the employer's failure fully to comply with the terms of the order. Where the employer's non-compliance extends to a failure to reinstate or re-engage on any terms, the tribunal may award compensation in the form of an additional award over and above the other elements of compensation. The additional award normally consists of an award on a scale from a minimum of 13 to a maximum of 26 weeks pay. The amount of compensation under this head may not exceed £6,760 (SI 1980/2019). A tribunal has discretion not to make an additional award of compensation if the employer satisfies it that it was not 'practicable' to comply with the order: EPCA, s. 71(2) (b). See *Williams v. Lloyds Retailers Ltd.* [1973] IRLR 262 (refusal by employer); *Hackwood v. Seal (Marine) Ltd.* [1973] IRLR 17; *Hallam v. Baguley & Co. Ltd.* (355/73); *Curtis v. Paterson (Darlington) Ltd.* [1973] ICR 496 (refusals by employee); *Burdekin v. Dolan Corrugated Containers Ltd.* (5376/72), *Dobson v. K.P. Morritt Dolan Corrugated Containers Ltd.* (5376/72), *Dobson v. K.P. Morritt Ltd.* [1972] IRLR 101. In relation to Britain, it is interesting to note that the Donovan Commission, apparently seduced by what the courts had always done, in the end preferred compensation despite describing reinstatement as the ideal remedy: Cmnd. 3623 (1968) para. 551. Professor Kahn-Freund described this 'unfortunate conclusion' as the result of 'the power of a legal shibboleth': 'Uses and Misuses of Comparative Law' (1974) 37 MLR 1, 24. Draft Orders — The Unfair Dismissal (Increase of Compensation Limit) Order 1981, and The Employment Protection (Variation of Limits) Order 1981 — have been laid before Parliament proposing increases in the maximum basic, additional and compensatory awards to £4050, £7020 and £7000 respectively.

When the Irish Unfair Dismissals Bill first appeared, it provided for one primary remedy only, namely, re-engagement. During the Second Stage reading of the Bill the Minister for Labour's attention was drawn to the legal difference between reinstatement an re-engagement: *Dáil Debates*, 25 Jan. 1977, Col. 67. The solitary inclusion in the bill of the latter was questioned; an amendment was moved to delete the word 're-engagement' and to substitute 'reinstatement' instead (*Ibid.*, col. 115). Ultimately both remedies appeared in the Bill: *ibid.*, 2 March 1977, Col. 661.

9. See *Plan for Reinstatement* (Industrial Welfare Society, LSE 1945); K. Williams: 'Job Security and Unfair Dismissal' (1975) 38 MLR 292.

10. The principle of deducting social welfare benefits allows an employer to benefit at the expense of the State and may be criticised on that account. The issue is central to the computation of compensation awards and is discussed more fully at page 191 below.

11. E.gg., *Clarke v. Hogan* UD 135/1978; *Kelly v. CIE* UD 28/1978; (implied by) *McMahon v. Cootehill Livestock Sales Ltd.* UD 102/1980.

expected to have had but for the dismissal. Furthermore, a claimant will have restored to him all rights and privileges (including seniority and pension rights, if applicable) which he might reasonably be expected to have but for the dismissal. Re-engagement, on the other hand, may be in a different job[12] provided it is comparable to the old one or is otherwise suitable.[13] This remedy provides the EAT with considerable latitude. The stated terms of re-engagement, if sufficiently wide, could in effect amount to reinstatement.[14] A person may be re-engaged only by his former employer (in Britain he may be re-engaged by his employer, a successor of his, or by an associated employer, see chapter eight, page 212, fn. 42 below). Where re-engagement is a likely remedy, it would appear desirable, *inter alia,* for the employer to provide information about relevant vacancies in his own or any associated organisation either before or at the hearing.[15]

It is a widespread belief that all rights dependant upon continuity are lost when re-engagement rather than reinstatement is effected. But continuous service for purposes of the Minimum Notice and Terms of Employment Act, 1973, and of the Unfair Dismissals Act, is preserved where the dismissal of the employee is 'followed by the immediate "re-employment" of the employee.'[16] It is possible to

12. Note the unusual case of *Coates v. Ryan* UD 51/1979 (applicant not seeking any redress, merely a 'finding that he had been dismissed'. Correctly, the EAT did not proceed to a Determination but the employer conceded the fact of dismissal rather than argue the matter).

13. As first drafted and debated in Dáil Éireann, if a position were offered to an employee, it had to be one that was 'reasonably suitable *to* him' (emphasis added). The revised paragraph substituted 'for' for 'to'. Further, in the earlier definition, one of the terms and conditions expressly required was 'a term that the re-engagement shall be deemed to have commenced on the day of the dismissal or on any subsequent day'.

14. This was accepted in Britain in the debate on the Industrial Relations Bill when Lord Drumalbyn said: 'it may be appropriate . . . to recommend that an employee be given his old job back on such terms as if the dismissal had never taken place': 801 H.L. Deb. 197. The remarks to the contrary in *Morris v. Gestetner Ltd.* [1973] 1 WLR 1378, 1382, *per* Sir John Donaldson, are not merely *obiter*, it is suggested, but wrong in principle — though they may explain why it was thought desirable to include in TULRA 1974 a specific power to recommend reinstatement as well as re-engagement (Para. 17(2) Sch. 1). The difference between reinstatement and re-engagement is one of degree only and not of kind. To award reinstatement *simpliciter* or re-engagement on terms amounting to reinstatement leads to no injustice. Where monetary compensation is given it will normally include sums to represent loss of seniority rights which have pecuniary value. To do less for a person who is re-employed would be gratuitously restrictive.

15. In a Code of Practice to accompany the Act at a future date, such a provision might usefully be included. A statutory penalty might also be envisaged for an employer who fails to adduce reasonable evidence as to the availability of the job from which the complainant was dismissed or of comparable or suitable employment.

16. Minimum Notice and Terms of Employment 1973, First Sched. Rule 6; Unfair Dismissals Act, 1977, s. 2(4).

salvage seniority rights under an earlier contract by incorporating them into any new contract negotiated (a process which is sometimes an important feature of strike settlements).[17]

(3) *No right to primary remedies*

A fundamental point about the legislation in both jurisdictions is that there is no right to insist on keeping one's job — the award of one or other of the primary remedies must be appropriate in the light of all the circumstances. In determining the appropriateness of re-instatement or re-engagement the EAT will take a number of factors into account. First, an employee's wishes are important — though not overriding.[18] At times his wishes may be tempered by those of his trade union.[19] They may be overruled by the EAT as where an employee's reluctance to request reinstatement was put down to his tender years.[20] Normally if one party — and certainly if both — are opposed to reinstatement or re-engagement, the Tribunal will respect this. Employer opposition may be treated somewhat sceptically, however. The EAT has awarded reinstatement, such opposition notwithstanding, when it was aware that work performance would necessarily be suspended pending recovery of a claimant's health.[21]

The EAT may also consider the practicality of compliance. There is no statutory equivalent in Ireland of s. 70(7) of the EPCA which lays down the general rule that tribunals shall not take into account the fact that a dismissed employee has been permanently replaced when they are considering whether it is practicable for an employer to comply with a re-instatement order or an order for re-engagement.[22]

17. See *Mason v. The Post Office* [1973] IRLR 51.
18. See *Marsh v. University College Dublin* UD 27/1977; *McBridge v. Midland Electrical Co. Ltd.* UD 48/1979; *Gahan v. Lalor* UD 326/1079.
19. *McSweeney v. Sunbeam Ltd.* UD 62/1978.
20. *Healy v. Joseph Brennan Bakeries Ltd.* UD 622/1980.
21. *Foley v. Mahon R. McPhillips Ltd.* UD 267/1979.
22. The exception is where the employer shows that it was not practicable (see *Meridian Ltd. v. Gomersall* [1977] ICR 597; *Oliso-Emosingoit v. Inner London Magistrates Courts Services* EAT 139/77) to arrange for the dismissed employee's work to be done without engaging a permanent replacement *or* that the replacement was engaged after the lapse of a 'reasonable period without having heard from the dismissed employee that he wished to be reinstated or re-engaged' *and* that when the employer engaged the replacement it was 'no longer reasonable' for him to arrange for the dismissed employee's work to be done except by a permanent replacement. This is the one issue upon which an industrial tribunal's discretion is specifically curtailed by the Act. Prior to the EPA amendment to TULRA, industrial tribunals had a wide discretion to decide when the appointment of a replacement made a recommendation of reinstatement impracticable. The cost of dismissing an innocent employee, i.e., the replacement employee, was a consideration that resulted in few recommmmendations of reinstatement being made in such circumstances: see *Farthing v. Midland Household Stores Ltd.* [1974] IRLR 354.

In practice, however, the Irish EAT administers the law in similar fashion, although where it was impracticable to let the replacement go, e.g., for industrial relations reasons[23] or where the replacement's standard of work was higher and therefore better for the enterprise,[24] the Tribunal chose to award compensation to an unfairly dismissed employee rather than to order reinstatement or re-engagement.[25] Again, industrial relations practice may determine the exact nature of the remedy.[26] Where an employer's establishment is of a special nature, e.g., one which caters for handicapped children, it is unlikely that reinstatement or re-engagement will be deemed appropriate.[27] A university teaching post might be regarded as one where service was of a special or personal nature. But although good staff relations are desirable in a university department, in the opinion of the EAT they are not necessary:

> 'The good of the department should not prevent a proper examination of the fairness of the dismissal, no matter how inconvenient the result.'[28]

In ordinary circumstances, there will be no basis for an order of reinstatement where a job has disappeared owing to redundancy or where the workplace has closed down. The circumstances in *Ferenka Ltd. v. Lewis*[29] were unusual. The company ceased to operate between the date of the Rights Commissioner's Recommendation and the hearing of the appeal before the Tribunal. The EAT held that the applicant was entitled to reinstatement from the date of dismissal to the date the factory closed. He was to be treated as an employee in continuous employment for all purposes up to that time.[30]

There may be a question of contributory conduct. Although the

---

23. *McSweeney v. Sunbeam Ltd.* UD 62/1978.

24. *Lavery v. Irish Silver Ltd.* UD 68/1977.

25. The longer the delay between dismissal and hearing, the more likely it is that a replacement will have been hired, the less likely it is that a person will be offered reinstatement or reengagement. With this in mind, employees should take the opportunity to lodge a complaint of unfair dismissal as soon as notice of that dismissal is received.

26. *Doyle v. Nitrigin Éireann Teo.* UD 148/1978.

27. *Rossiter v. Sisters of La Sagesse* UD 92/1978.

28. *Marsh v. UCD* UD 27/1977.

29. UD 26/1977.

30. The company was held entitled to offset the employee's weekly social welfare benefit against any monetary compensation payable as a result of the EAT's determination. The period of three weeks' lay-off before the date of closure of the company was disregarded when calculating the monetary compensation payable as Lewis, if still employed, would not have been paid social welfare benefit during that time. It seems a defence of redundancy on the employer's part (s. 7(4) (c) of the Unfair Dismissals Act) was not raised.

Unfair Dismissals Act deals with contributory action in the specific context of compensation awards (s. 7(2)) it is clear from the Act that this factor may be reflected in the terms of an order for re-engagement. Section s. 7.1(b) enables the Tribunal, when ordering re-engagement, to set such terms and conditions 'as are reasonable having regard to all the circumstances'. In relation to reinstatement, the Tribunal may take into account the employee's degree of 'fault' only when considering whether or not to order reinstatement; it has no discretion otherwise to do so: s. 7(1)(a). As a general rule, however, misconduct is likely to defeat an employee's claim for unfair dismissal altogether.

In all cases, regard will be had to the industrial relations realities of the situation. It is improbable that either of the primary remedies will be awarded where shop floor feeling would be against it or if strikes or industrial action would follow.[31] The size of the business will have an important influence on industrial relations aspects. Where the enterprise is small, and industrial friction is likely to follow reinstatement or re-engagement, the Tribunal will probably conclude that compensation is the more appropriate remedy.[32] On the other hand, if an applicant worked for a large company in a relatively impersonal employer/employee relationship, particularly if his was a minor position, either of the primary remedies may be appropriate.[33]

Where an employee is reinstated or re-engaged by an employer in pursuance of a determination or order under the Unfair Dismissals Act, he is obliged to repay any moneys received by him from his employer under the Redundancy Payments Acts, 1967 to 1979: s. 19 of the Unfair Dismissals Act. The moneys may be recovered as a simple contract debt in a court of competent jurisdiction. Likewise any moneys due and owing to an employee under those Acts in relation to dismissal cease to be due or owing.[34]

The fact that either of the primary remedies will be awarded only

31. Cf. *Bateman v. British Leyland UK Ltd.* [1974] IRLR 101; [1974] ICR 403; 16 KIR 284; 9 ITR 266.
32. See *Bateman,* above. This is likely to be the case with dismissals in a closed shop situation: *Sarvent v. Central Electricity Board* [1976] IRLR 66. But even in such circumstances an order for reinstatement may be made where a tribunal finds that 'there is not likely to be any difficulty in the parties agreeing the terms of that reinstatement': *Goodbody v. British Railways Board* [1977] IRLR 84.
33. See *Clarke v. CIE* UD 104/1978; contrast *Todd v. N.E. Electricity Board* [1975] IRLR 130.
34. Section 19 was inserted, when the situation in regard to reinstatement and re-engagement was strengthened in the Bill. Section 16 of the Unfair Dismissals Act, 1977, provides that unfair selection for redundancy will constitute unfair dismissal under the Act. It is conceivable that an employee who has already been paid redundancy money could later be awarded reinstatement or re-engagement on an unfair dismissal claim based on unfair selection for redundancy. The section reasonably requires redundancy payments to be refunded in such circumstances.

where it is practicable represents a serious qualification to the view that unfair dismissals legislation protects a worker's *proprietas* in employment, thus achieving a supposed new balance in the employment relationship. The vast majority of claimants before the EAT who are declared to have been unfairly dismissed do not receive their jobs back. This is amply documented in the *Annual Reports* of the EAT for 1978, 1979 and 1980 respectively (the first three full years of the Act's operation). In 1978 out of a total of 65 successful claims the EAT made 10 awards of reinstatement and four of re-engagement. In 1979, out of a total of 130 successful claims, reinstatement was ordered in 12 cases and re-engagement in one. In 1980 the picture altered slightly. Out of 115 successful claims, reinstatement was ordered in 21 cases and re-engagement in one. These figures are only partly accounted for by the fact that many of the respondents before the Tribunal are small employers.[35]

B. Compensation

(1) *Broad approach of the EAT*

From the start, the EAT has preferred a broad approach in awarding compensation. An employer is required to compensate an employee fully if he cannot prove the reason for dismissal and it cannot be shown that he acted reasonably in treating it as 'a substantial ground' for dismissing a particular employee. There is no doubt that the deterrent effect of this upon employers gives an

---

35. In Britain statistics reveal the startling fact that only a tiny proportion of all complainants are reinstated or re-engaged, and it has declined since these were made the primary remedies in 1976. In 1973, 4.2 per cent of those whose cases were settled before a hearing were given back their jobs. This has fallen each year and was only 1.8 per cent in 1979. Of those who went to a hearing 2.3 per cent were recommended to be given back their jobs in 1973. In 1977 only 1.4 per cent were reinstated or re-engaged and in 1979 this declined to 0.8 per cent. See *D.E. Gazette* for the relevant years. See the interesting suggestion made by B. Hepple that a procedure of automatic continuation of the contract pending decision by the EAT would help to overcome the psychological resistance of employees against returning to an employment after the unpleasant rupture of a dismissal which they consider to be unfair: 'A Right to Work?' (1981) ILJ 65, 78. A recent study in Britain suggests that it is unsatisfactory to explain the infrequency of re-employment in terms of the remedy being unwanted or not viable because the evidence suggests this is often not the case and because such an explanation ignores the fact that the tribunals and ACAS in Britain are less than enthusiastic about promoting re-employment: L. Dickens and others: 'Re-employment of Unfairly Dismissed Workers: The Lost Remedy' (1981) ILJ 160. See too a valuable DES Research Paper (no. 23 of 1981) on 'The aftermath of tribunal reinstatement and re-engagement'; P. Lewis: 'An analysis of why legislation has failed to provide employment protection for unfairly dismissed employees' (1981) BJIR 316.

employee greater job security.[36] The average award of compensation in Ireland is £1,732[37] — unlike Britain where the figure is less than half that sum.[38] In practice the EAT faces considerable difficulties when calculating the amount of compensation under s. 7(1)(c) of the Unfair Dismissals Act. In contrast to the EPCA, 1978, which speci-

36. The ILO Committee of Experts in their *Report* (Report III: *Termination of Employment* Int. Lab. Conf. 59th Sess., 1974, para 169) observed that compensation 'is most effective as a remedy when it can act as a deterrent against unjustified termination' and added the following reservation:

'In some cases, where the amount of compensation is limited to the amount of loss that the worker can show that he has suffered, a question may arise as to whether such compensation would be sufficient to afford the protection required.'

But a deterrent effect must not be over-emphasised, see the *Donovan Report*, fn. 8 *ante*, para. 524.

37. See *Annual Reports* of the EAT and see Appendix VI.

38. The median level of compensation in 1979 was £400, about five weeks at the average wage. See *D.E. Gazette* for 1979. This may be compared to the theoretical maximum figure in 1979 of £14,800. In Britain, the Employment Protection (Consolidation) Act, 1978, (s. 72) says that where no order for reinstatement or re-engagement has been made, or where such an order has been made but not effected, the tribunal may make a basic award (calculated in accordance with s. 73) *and* a compensatory award (calculated in accordance with s. 74). The granting of a basic award supports the philosophy of a property interest in employment. Formerly, as part of the basic award, every employee who was found to have been unfairly dismissed was always awarded an irreducible minimum of two weeks pay or the equivalent of his entitlement to a redundancy payment, whichever was the greater. This has been repealed by the Employment Act, 1980 (s. 9). The basic award is calculated like a redundancy payment, on the basis of the dismissed employee's age, continuous service and weeks' pay. See, *re* maximum amount, SI 1980/2019 and fn. 8 *ante*. Deductions from the basic award may arise from the employee's contributory action: s. 73(7), or prior redundancy payments: s. 73(9). See *Thomas & Betts Manufacturing Co. Ltd. v. Harding* [1978] IRLR 213.

The compensatory award is 'such amount as the tribunal considers just and equitable in all the circumstances having regard to the loss sustained by the complainant in consequence of the dismissal in so far as that loss is attributable to action taken by the employer': s. 74. The maximum compensation that may be awarded is £6,250 (SI 1723, 1979 but see fn. 8 *ante)*. When compensation for unfair dismissal was at an embryonic stage in Britain it was unclear whether the relevant legislation (s. 116 of the Industrial Relations Act, 1971) intended damages to be consequential or to compensate fully on the basis of what was just and equitable in all the circumstances. (At the time, tribunals could make only a compensatory award: the basic award did not appear until 1975.) In 1968, the Donovan Commission seemed to have been directed towards a broader, property interest concept. It stated that the tribunal '. . . should normally be concerned to compensate the employee for the damage he has suffered in the loss of his employment and legitimate expectations for the future in that employment, in injured feelings and reputation and in the prejudicing of further employment opportunities.': fn. 8, *ante*, para. 553. Before *Norton Tool Co. Ltd. v. Tewson* [1973] 1 All E.R. 183; [1973] 1 WLR 44; 117 Sol. Jo. 33; [1972] IRLR 86; [1972] ICR 501; 13 KIR 328; 8 ITR 23; Digest Cont. Vol. D

fies a formula to be used in calculating the basic award, regulations under s. 17 of the Unfair Dismissals Act deal only with the calcula tion of weekly remuneration. The Tribunal is therefore faced with imponderables: it is required to put immediate cash values on items such as pension rights, future loss of wages and the likelihood of re-employment.

(2) *Compensation described*

The remedy of compensation is described in s. 7(1) (c) as:

> payment by the employer to the employee of such compensa tion (not exceeding in amount 104 weeks remuneration in respect of the employment from which he was dismissed calculated in accordance with regulations under section 17 of this Act) in respect of any financial loss incurred by him and attributable to the dismissal as is just and equitable having regard to all the circumstances.[39]

'Financial loss' includes:
  (i)   any actual loss and
  (ii) any estimated prospective loss of income attributable to the dismissal and
  (iii) the value of any loss or diminution, attributable to the dis-

---

977; see note by B. Reynolds in (1973) M.L.R. 424: industrial tribunals in Britain had varied opinions as to how they should compute compensation awards. This and subsequent cases support the view that the legislation should be interpreted in its widest sense and that any compensation awarded should be based upon a principle nearing the concept of a 'property right in employment'. *Tewson's* case clearly influenced s. 7 of the Irish Act concerning the assessment of compensation. Compensation was there considered under four headings:- immediate loss of wages; manner of dismissal (was there, as a result, any risk of financial loss at a later stage?); security of future employment; loss of future protection for unfair dismissal and redundancy. The principles enunciated in *Tewson* were not intended to be exhaustive. They have been added to since, in e.g., *Scottish Co-Op. Ltd. v. Lloyd* [1973] ICR 137.

39. The Regulations referred to are S.I. no. 287 of 1977 (see Appendix III). If redress has been awarded by the Labour Court . . . in respect of a dismissal under ss. 9 or 10 of the Anti-Discrimination (Pay) Act, 1974, or under s. 3(4) of the Employment Equality Act, 1977, no redress may be given by the EAT under s. 7 of the Unfair Dismissals Act, 1977. The converse also applies. This is provided in s. 27 of the Employment Equality Act, 1977. 'Dismissal' in the two Acts just mentioned refers to circumstances where a person has been penalised by being dismissed for having in good faith brought or taken part in proceedings under the relevant legisla-tion. The Labour Court may not award compensation which exceeds 104 weeks' remuneration. The Court is not bound by the same considerations or criteria as those which the EAT must observe under section 7 of the Unfair Dismissals Act.

missal, of the rights of the employee under the Redundancy Payments Acts, 1967 to 197[9], or the value of any loss or diminution in relation to superannuation.

The object of compensation is to make reparation fully for the loss suffered by a dismissed employee. It is for the applicant to prove his loss but it is not necessary for him to bring precise and detailed proof of every item of loss. The EAT makes allowance for the fact that proceedings are informal and that claims are often presented by lay persons.

Sub-section 2 says that for the purposes of determining compensation regard shall be had to:

(a) the extent (if any) to which the financial loss referred to in that subsection was attributable to an act, omission or conduct by or on behalf of the employer,
(b) the extent (if any) to which the said financial loss was attributable to an action, omission or conduct by or on behalf of the employee,
(c) the measures (if any) adopted by the employee or, as the case may be, his failure to adopt measures, to mitigate the loss aforesaid, and
(d) the extent (if any) of the compliance or failure to comply by the employer or employee with any procedure of the kind referred to in s. 14(3) of this Act[40] or with the provisions of any code of practice relating to procedures regarding dismissal approved of by the Minister.[41]

The employee is entitled to compensation only if there has been a finding of unfair dismissal. This may seem all too obvious but the Rights Commissioners on occasion have recommended *ex gratia*

40. This refers to a procedure that has been agreed upon by or on behalf of the employer concerned and by the employee concerned or a trade union, or an excepted body under the Trade Union Act, 1941 to 1971, representing him or has been established by the custom and practice of the employment concerned. Section 7(2) (d) was intended, *inter alia*, to promote the use of procedures in relation to disciplinary and dismissal grievances.

41. When the Unfair Dismissals Bill was being debated in Dáil Éireann, the following insertion was proposed by Deputy Gene Fitzgerald: '(e) The effect of the payment of compensation on the financial and employment viability of the employer'. The object was to avoid very severe burdens being cast on small companies or businesses: *Dáil Debates* Vol. 296, Col. 121 (25 January 1977). The proposal was defeated. Outside of this discussion the remedy of compensation was not commented on in Parliament. See the British Employment Act, 1980 (s. 6), which requires the size and administrative resources of the employer's undertaking to be considered in determining the fairness of dismissal.

severance payments[42] while not holding a dismissal unfair. Where these Recommendations have been appealed to the EAT, they have always been overruled.[43]

Section 7(1)(c) of the Unfair Dismissals Act places a limitation on the amount of compensation a claimant can receive. It cannot exceed 104 weeks' gross pay in respect of the employment from which he was dismissed. Remuneration is calculated in accordance with Statutory Instrument No. 287 of 1977 (see Appendix III). The regulations cover certain categories of employee: those on hourly time rates or fixed wages or salary, employees on piece work, commission or bonuses. They also deal with 'normal working hours', work-related payments and shift work.

In brief, the EAT computes an employee's net loss from dismissal to the date of the hearing, taking into account his basic pay, average bonuses and average overtime pay. If an employee has sustained no loss by reason of the dismissal as, e.g., by obtaining immediate employment without injuring his pension or other rights, he will not be entitled to compensation under the Unfair Dismissals Act. Social Welfare benefits are deducted. An employee's prospective loss of income also has to be estimated: this involves computing any reduction he is likely to suffer in future net earnings and fringe benefits. Loss of protection in respect of statutory rights under Unfair Dismissals, Redundancy and Minimum Notice Acts will also be computed and an assessment made as to any expenses, perquisites or pension rights lost by an employee as a result of his dismissal. These items are now considered in more detail.

(i) *Actual loss*

The most important aspect of actual loss concerns notice. The EAT will want to discover whether an ex-employee has received adequate notice or wages in lieu thereof. If he has been summarily dismissed, and there are no relevant contractual provisions, the EAT will have recourse to the Minimum Notice and Terms of Employment Act, 1973, to determine an ex-employee's entitlement to notice.[44] The former employee may also make a claim in express terms under the Minimum Notice and Terms of Employment Act

42. E.gg., *A la Francaise Ltd. v. Monaghan* UD 13/1977; *Wheatley v. Ulster Bank Ltd.* UD 18/1977; *Warren v. Cross Channel Carriers Ltd.* UD 44/1977; *Chevalier v. Herve Mahy, Ty Ar Mor Restaurant* UD 60/1977; *Sheils v. Bonner Engineering Ltd.* UD 67/1977.

43. *Warren's* case and *Chevalier's* case, above.

44. *O'Farrell Ltd. v. Nugent* UD 120/1978; UD 123/1978; see, also, *Evode Industries Ltd. v. Hearst and Others* UD 396-8/1979.

when he is claiming unfair dismissal.[45] The amount awarded in such circumstances is based on the employee's 'take home' (i.e. net) wages. Where a dismissed employee refuses suitable employment elsewhere immediately after his dismissal on the grounds that he will be paid for his due notice period anyway, this may be regarded as a breach of the employee's duty to mitigate. According to recent British authority[46] the fact that a dismissed employee has earned money during the 'due notice' period may be taken into account so as to reduce his compensation award under the heading of immediate loss of wages. Where a figure is being computed for immediate loss of wages, and the claimant is ill for the relevant period, his loss of earnings may be assessed as nil if, under his contract of employment, an employee is not entitled to wages during sick leave. In such circumstances assessment of compensation will be based on availability for work.[47]

Expenses and perquisites may also be taken into account.[48] Legal

---

45. *Healy v. Cormeen Construction Ltd.* M. 263; UD 98/1978; see too *Murtagh v. O'Connor & Breen Ltd.* UD 186/1978; *O'Hare v. The Curtain Centre Ltd.* UD 149/1978. From *Healy*, it is clear that any bonuses and average overtime pay to which the employee is entitled is taken into account. (See Regulations 4, 5 and 6 of S.I. No. 287 of 1977, Appendix III); also *Ledwidge v. Peter Mark Ltd.* UD 70/1978 (average weekly bonus); *Greely v. Baker* UD 96/1978, UD 130/1978 (commission of about £10 per week); but see *Eate v. Semprit (Ireland) Ltd.* UD 46/1977 (claim for overtime in the circumstances not legally sustainable). Accrued holiday entitlements will also be awarded: *Byrne v. Bradden Design Centre Ltd.* UD 136/1978.

46. *Tradewinds Airways Ltd. v. Fletcher* [1981] IRLR 272. Earlier authorities to the contrary may now be regarded as incorrectly decided, e.gg., *Stepek Ltd. v. Hough* [1973] 8 ITR 516 (NIRC); *Vaughan v. Weighpack Ltd.* [1974] ICR 261; *Hilti (Great Britain) Ltd. v. Windridge* [1974] ICR 352; *Everwear Candlewick Ltd. v. Isaac* [1974] ICR 525; *Blackwell v. G.E.C. Elliott Process Automation Ltd.* (1976) 11 ITR 103. These last mentioned authorities were criticised and described as wrongly decided before *Fletcher* 'containing as they must the paradoxical statement that a positive gain to the employee can amount to a "loss"': J. E. McGlyne: *Unfair Dismissal Cases* 298.

47. *Murray v. Reilly* M.137; UD 3/1978; and similarly *McSweeney v. Sunbeam Ltd.* UD 62/1978. Contrast *Murray* with *Kerr v. Marley Extrusions (Ireland) Ltd.* UD 78/1978 where the employee's loss to date in respect of wages was assessed at nil as he had been in continuous receipt of disability benefit from the date of dismissal to the date of hearing. See, also, *O'Shea v. P. J. Cullen & Sons* UD 17/1977 — where the claimant whose jaw had been broken in an argument with a fellow employee was incapacitated for work for the first five weeks of his unemployment. No compensation was given in respect of that period. In the decisions above, the EAT did not scrutinise the employee's contractual entitlement to pay during sick leave, rather it assumed an absence of such entitlement. This approach may be faulted.

48. Examples of the sort of expenses the Tribunal might take into account are private use of a company car, but not the use of a colour television. *Murray v. C.T.V. Services Ltd.* UD 109/1978; free meals, *Kerr v. Tower Hotel Group Ltd.* UD 12/1977; expenses incurred in looking for another job; compensation for loss of

costs will not be granted by the EAT although a party may be ordered to pay costs for having acted frivolously or vexatiously.[49] May legal costs be claimed as 'expenses' on the basis that costs and expenses are not the same? The British case of *Hill v. AUEF*[50] gave an affirmative answer to this question. In what was a highly complex case, the Tribunal held that the applicant had acted reasonably in employing a solicitor and counsel. The expense of paying his lawyers was regarded as an expense reasonably incurred in consequence of the matters to which the complaint related.

There is no reason why 'actual loss' should not be interpreted to cover loss relating to the manner of dismissal where it involves injury to pride or feelings. This head of damage is developing at common law in Britain.[51] A strict approach may be forecast, however, from *Vaughan v. Weighpack*,[52] wherein Sir Hugh Griffiths stated the view that it is only if there is cogent evidence that the manner of the dismissal caused financial loss, as, for example, by making it more difficult to find future employment:

> 'that the manner of dismissal becomes relevant to the assessment of compensation . . . The court believes that it will only be on the very rarest occasions that it will be found that the evidence justifies an award under this head.'

income from shares bought by an ex-employee under a scheme for employers providing that on dismissal such shares had to be sold back at par; removal expenses: *Doheny v. Allplast Ltd.* UD 120/1979; the cost of printing a *curriculum vitae.* It is unlikely that gratuities will be recovered.

49. Reg. 19(3) of Redundancy (Redundancy Appeals Tribunal) Regulations 1968, S.I. No. 24 of 1968; see Appendix IV. In Britain the position is similar. In *Raynor v. Remploy Ltd.* [1973] IRLR 3, the London Tribunal explained that: '. . . [Rule 10(d) of the Industrial Tribunals (Labour Relations) Regulations 1947] provides that a tribunal shall not normally award costs unless a party to the proceedings has in its opinion acted frivolously or vexatiously. In the face of that clear direction, we think it inappropriate to award costs in the guise of an allowance under [s. 74] of the Act . . .' See, now, Industrial Tribunals (Rules of Procedure) Regulations, 1980 (S.I. 1980 No. 884) Sch. 1. R.11.

50. June 1973: Industrial Tribunal Case No. 1509/73 (unreported), though see *Robert Normansell (Birmingham) Ltd. v. Barfield* (1973) 8 ITR 171.

51. See chapter four above, page 98. The Labour Court takes personal injury to a claimant into account when awarding compensation under the Employment Equality Act, 1977: *Coughlan v. Contract Cleaners Ltd.* DEE 1/1978; EE 3/1978.

52. [1974] ICR 261. See, too, *Brittains Arborfield Ltd. v. Van Uden* [1977] ICR 211. In *Tewson's* case, fn. 38 *ante,* Sir John Donaldson indicated that if the manner and circumstances of dismissal could give rise to any risk of financial loss at a later stage by, for example, making the dismissed employee 'less acceptable to potential employers or exceptionally liable to selection for dismissal, account should be taken of such circumstance and assessment of compensation increased accordingly'. But note Sir John Donaldson in the same case: 'Loss does not include injury to pride or feelings'. See A. Hiller: 'Compensation for Stress in Unfair Dismissal' (1978) Vol. 128 NLJ 1212.

(ii) *Deductions*

The most important deductions from actual loss are Social Welfare benefits. These are subtracted from compensatory sums for loss of earnings other than those which relate to an award of wages in lieu of notice.[53] It may happen that a dismissed employee is receiving a higher sum in Social Welfare benefits than his take home pay prior to dismissal − if so, his loss, paradoxically, will be nil.[54] If an employee contributes to his loss he will not be compensated. For example, where a dismissed employee did not sign on at her local employment exchange and was not in receipt of Social Welfare benefits during unemployment, the maximum personal rate of unemployment benefit which she could have received was deducted from her compensation.[55] But where an employee received no Social Welfare payments because of difficulties in obtaining his P45 form from his employer, no deductions were made.[56]

On a strict construction of s. 7 of the Act, it is difficult to justify deduction of Social Welfare benefits. Deduction effectively permits an employer who has acted unfairly to benefit from the State's contribution by way of Social Welfare payments. The fact that he is not permitted to benefit where an employee has been dismissed from part-time employment[57] begs the question as to why the advantage should be afforded in one case and not in the other. Since 1978, dissatisfaction with the deduction of Social Welfare benefits has been expressed in unfair dismissal cases by individual members of the EAT.[58] In Britain, the Employment Protection (Recoupment of Unemployment Benefit and Supplementary Benefit) Regulations, 1977, attempts to remedy the injustice caused by this particular deduction.[59]

53. *Ennis v. Donabate Golf Club Ltd.* UD 118/1978. See, too, *Martin v. Weldon Ltd.* UD 30/1978; *McLoughlin v. Cappincur Joinery Ltd.* UD 36/1977; UD/1977; *Branigan v. Collins (Godolfin Gallery)* UD 28/1977; *Kerr v. Tower Hotel Group Ltd.* UD 12/1977.

54. *Farrell v. Rotunda Hospital* UD 35/1978.

55. *Trans Irish Lines Ltd. v. Delaney* UD 6/1977.

56. *Doheny v. Allplast Ltd.* UD 120/1979.

57. See *Clifford v. Galvins Hardware Ltd.* UD 1/1978.

58. E.gg., Mr. Cornelius Donovan in *Murray v. C.T.V. Services Ltd.* UD 109/1978; *O'Donovan v. Gillen* UD 101/1978; *McCarthy v. Irish Shipping Ltd.* UD 100/1978; *Buckley v. Disabled Artists Ltd.* UD 3/1978; *McSweeney v. Sunbeam Ltd.* UD 62/1978; Mr. P. Murphy in *Halpin v. Aemec Engineering Ltd.* UD 333/1979; also legal submission to EAT in *Gaffney v. Hughes* UD 269/1978; Mr. Mulhall in *Fay v. The Order of Hospitalers of St. John of God* UD 92/1980.

59. S.I. 1977, No. 674, operative from May, 1977. Before these Regulations, industrial tribunals regularly made allowances in respect of unemployment benefit, and so on, received by the dismissed employee. (See e.g., *Field v. Leslie & Goodwin Ltd.* [1972] IRLR 12 and *Ward v. British Domestic Appliances* [1972] IRLR 8.) The recoupment regulations are complex. A good summary is found in Hepple & O'Higgins: *Employment Law* 717.

(iii) *Liability to income tax*

It might be expected that, as at common law, a sum would be deducted representing a claimant's notional tax liability.[60] The Income Tax Act, 1967, renders liable to tax any payment (not otherwise chargeable to income tax) which is made:

> 'whether in pursuance of any legal obligation or not, either directly or indirectly in consideration or in consequence of, or otherwise in connection with, the termination of the holding of the office or employment . . .'

The key words are 'whether in pursuance of any legal obligation or not'. If an employee is awarded a compensatory payment under the Unfair Dismissals Act, the sum is covered by the Act of 1967 to the extent that it exceeds £6,000.[61] At the present time the EAT does not take this factor into account. Instead, in all cases, it calculates compensation on the net figure of an employee's wages. Where the sum awarded is below £6,000 this method of computation presents no difficulties: a rough and ready approximation of an employee's actual loss is in line with the nature of the legislation. But where an award of compensation exceeds £6,000, the EAT would do well to remember that in theory an employee is liable to income tax under the Act of 1967. (In 1978 there was one award of £19,200 — later reduced to £15,000 and in 1979, 10 awards exceeded £6,000). Because net figures are used in the calculation of compensatory awards there is no reason why such awards should not be expressly exempted from income tax.[62] Until such time, the EAT might perhaps apply different computational bases depending on whether an award falls above or below £6,000.

(iv) *Prospective loss*

Having assessed an employee's actual loss on account of dis-

60. See S.D. Keigher: 'Unfair Dismissals Awards and Taxation' (1979) 113 ILT 301, is the only reference to the topic in Irish literature to date. Also, Wylie and McGlyne: 'Taxation, Damages and Compensation for Unfair Dismissal' (1978) 128 N.L.J. 550.

61. Income Tax Act, 1967, s. 115, as amended by Finance Act, 1980, s. 10.

62. Statutory redundancy payments are completely tax free. Where an additional payment over the statutory minimum is negotiated, and it exceeds £6,000, it is subject to income tax: N. Wayne: *Labour Law in Ireland,* 46. A similar approach might be adopted in relation to unfair dismissal. See the suggestion made in chapter 4, page 106, fn. 87, concerning taxation of damages for wrongful dismissal. Although, as there stated, a uniform approach would be preferable for both common law and statutory purposes, the most immediate need arises in the latter context where because of the prevailing practice of the EAT to use net figures in the calculation of compensation, and because of the importance of informality, the amendment proposed in the text might afford an easier solution.

missal, the EAT is required under s. 7 to award a sum for prospec tive loss of income. If a dismissed employee has found other employ ment, the EAT will calculate the actual difference between his present and former wage. But if he is still out of work it will have the more difficult task of assessing the claimant's chances of obtaining employment in the future.[63] This requires knowledge and information as to the particular employment situation. In *Bux v. Toohey & Co. Ltd.*,[64] the EAT awarded a sum which took into account the likelihood of the claimant's not being able to commence new employment at his previous level of wages. Normally, inflation and increases due, e.g., to National Wage Agreements, will be taken into account.[65] The less skilled the nature of the job, the less likely it will be that an ex employee will find it difficult to find new employment.[66] If an ex employee succeeds in getting a new job and is secure in that job, and if his qualifications and job opportunities are very good, the Tribunal will make no award in respect of future loss of earnings.[67] But if an unfairly dismissed employee would probably have lost his old job in any event by reason of redundancy, this will be reflected in his entitle ment to compensation.[68] Receipt of disability benefit disentitles an employee to compensation in respect of future or prospective loss.[69]

---

63. In *Dunne v. Duignan* UD 261/1979 the EAT had to assess future loss of earnings for a claimant who was pregnant. On the evidence it was found she would have returned to work after the birth had she not been dismissed. Accordingly she was entitled to compensation for the loss of future income (although the EAT did not think claimant would have returned immediately after the six weeks post-natal Maternity Benefit ended). See, too, *Ennis v. Donabate Golf Club Ltd.* UD 118/1978; *O'Callaghan v. Quinnsworth* UD 68/1978 (EAT called upon to assess compensation against background of former employee's ill-health).

64. UD 137/1978; see, similarly, *McCarthy v. Irish Shipping Ltd.* UD 100/1978.

65. National Wage increases were taken into account in *Mullins v. Standard Shoe Co. Ltd.* UD 134/1979.

66. *Buckley v. Disabled Artists Ltd.* UD 3/1978. See, too, *Ahern v. Ahern Fabrics Ltd.* UD 74/1977; *O'Shea v. P. J. Cullen & Sons* UD 17/1977.

67. *Healy v. Cormeen Construction Ltd.* UD 98/1978. It very often happens that an unfairly dismissed employee receives no reference from his employer. This is likely to be a handicap in the search for new work. See *Hunt v. Gordon & Thompson Ltd.* UD 34/1977. In *Loughran v. Bearcroft Caterers*, UD 61/1978, the Tribunal recognised the handicap of no reference but 'hoped that this Order will to some extent take the place of a reference in satisfying would-be employers that she is a good and conscientious canteen manageress and cook'. See, too, *Greeley v. Baker* UD 96/1978, UD 130/1978 and contrast *Kerr v. Tower Hotel Group Ltd.* UD 12/1977.

68. *Branigan v. Collins (Godolfin Gallery)* UD 28/1977, also *Trans Irish Lines Ltd. v. Delaney* UD 6/1977. Contrast the British case of *Young's of Gosport Ltd. v. Kendell* [1977] ICR 907 in which the EAT considered there was a chance that Kendell would have been made redundant and the future loss aspect would have been reduced from 12 to 9 months.

69. *Corcoran v. Kelly & Barry & Associates* UD 174/1978.

The task of assessing future loss may be very difficult for the EAT. If an employee is in poor health, for example, compensation will be higher as he is less likely to get fresh employment. At the same time, if he is so ill as to be liable to be fairly dismissed in the near future, that factor too must be taken into account.

When, in its definition of 'financial loss', the Act refers to the value of any loss or diminution, attributable to the dismissal, of an employee's statutory rights, it mentions only the Redundancy Payments Acts. There is no reference to loss of protection in respect of unfair dismissal or minimum notice legislation. Notwithstanding this, the EAT considers loss of protection under each of these as well. With regard to compensation for unfair dismissal rights, the amount awarded is generally nominal.[70] Loss of protection concerning rights in any new employment under the Minimum Notice and Terms of Employment Act, 1973, during the qualifying period under the Act (13 weeks continuous service), is also likely to be nominal. No allowance is made where a claimant has re-established his rights under the Act in new employment.[71] Loss of protection under the Redundancy Payments Act, 1967-79, is more complex. The Tribunal may have to take into account that an unfairly dismissed employee will receive no redundancy payments if he is dismissed on account of redundancy within the first two years of employment. It may have to examine whether a redundancy situation is likely to arise in the new employment and, if so, whether an employee will be more likely to be made redundant in his new employment on the normal practice of 'last in first out'. The amount of compensation will be affected by evidence of the likelihood that, had the ex-employee not been dismissed when he was, he might thereafter have been dismissed by reason of redundancy.[72] Each case differs in its treatment of this item.[73]

---

70. This may be defended, (see McGlyne: *Unfair Dismissal* 305), since the very fact that a dismissed employee is before the Tribunal and is receiving compensation manifests that he is exercising his 'protection' in this regard. His future losses will be catered for. The figure awarded most often in this context is £10: e.gg., *Murtagh v. O'Connor & Breen Ltd.* UD 186/1978; *Healy v. Cormeen Construction Ltd.* UD 98/1978; *Rossiter v. Sisters of La Sagesse* UD 92/1978; but see *O'Rourke v. Ryans Meat Market Ltd.* UD 112/1978 in which £6 was awarded under this heading.
71. See *Healy's* case, *supra*.
72. If he has reached the age of over 41, his loss is certain to be greater (Sch. 3, Redundancy Payments Act, 1967, s. 1). The issues were considered in *Tewson's* case (fn 38 *ante*) − in detail being slightly different because of differences in the British legislation. The NIRC thought it just and equitable to award compensation upon approximately one half of Tewson's accrued protection in respect of redundancy as he was aged 50 and had been continuously employed for 11 years. This principle was followed in *Scottish Co-Op. Ltd.*, fn. 38 *ante*.
73. Contrast *Murtagh v. O'Connor & Breen Ltd.* UD 186/1978; *Healy v. Cormeen Construction Ltd.* UD 98/1978; *Rossiter v. Sisters of La Sagesse* UD 92/1978; *Fergus O'Farrell Ltd. v. Nugent* UD 120/1978; UD 123/1978;

(v) *Superannuation*

Assessment of the 'value of any loss or diminution in relation to superannuation' represents a further task for the EAT under s. 7. The assessment of loss of pension rights is exceptionally difficult.[74] It straddles time present and time future. It is essential for the Tribunal to adopt a 'forward looking' approach. The return of an employee's own contributions to a pension scheme (less tax plus interest) is not sufficient *per se* to compensate for lost pension rights because an employee is entitled to these as a matter of course. It is not sufficient to put an applicant in the same position as if he had not been dismissed. What the applicant loses is 'the value of the employer's contributions from the date of his dismissal. . . . He is also entitled to the value of the employer's contributions from the date of the dismissal until such time as he finds further employment.'[75]

McSweeney v. Sunbeam Ltd. UD 62/1978; *Madigan v. Yvonne Models Ltd.* UD 295/1978; *Geraghty v. Abouds Pages Ltd.* UD 46/1978; UD 50/1978; *O'Rourke v. Ryans Meat Market Ltd.* UD 112/1978; *Byrne v. P. J. Hegarty & Sons Ltd.* UD 126/1978; *Ahern v. Ahern Fabrics Ltd.* UD 74/1977.

74. In the British case of *Copson v. Eversure Accessories Ltd.* [1974] ICR 636, Sir John Donaldson summarised the principles involved in assessing loss of pension rights under various headings, *inter alia,* burden of proof, types of loss, loss of pension position, loss of future pension opportunity. He stressed that it was impossible
> . . . 'to cover every eventuality and permutation and that there is no single right way of assessing the loss in respect of pension'.

At the cost of considerable simplification, the essentials of the problem of compensation for loss of pension rights have been set out by D. Jackson: *Unfair Dismissal* 32. See, too, his article: 'Compensation for loss of Pension Rights in Cases of Unfair Dismissal' in (1975) ILJ, 24, and see D.G. Ballantine: 'Assessment of Pensions Loss on Unfair Dismissal' (1980) 130 NLJ 516.

75. In *Eate v. Semprit (Ireland) Ltd.* UD 46/1977, the applicant agreed to accept £4,000 on severance of his employment in full settlement of all outstanding claims he might have had. Later he initiated proceedings under the Unfair Dismissals Act 1977. The EAT found the claimant's dismissal unfair. A breakdown of his lump sum compensation included a figure for 'Return of Superannuation contributions' — assessed at £247.77. It is interesting to contrast the British case of *Scottish Co-Op. Wholesale Society Ltd. v. Lloyd* [1973] ICR 137. Lloyd during his employment contributed to a pension scheme run by his employers. The employers contributed on an equal basis. When Lloyd was unfairly dismissed he received £805 in respect of his contributions, plus interest, but minus income tax. If he had continued in employment until 1985 Lloyd would have paid a further £817 in contributions and would have qualified for a pension of £700 per annum. His 'invalidity pension right' at the time of his dismissal was about £400 per annum. In his new employment there was no superannuation scheme. The employee's loss in this respect was assessed by the tribunal at £2,000 and, after deducting the sum received, i.e., £805, the tribunal awarded him £1,195. The employers appealed that the gross money returned, i.e., £895, should have been deducted but the Industrial Court held that the money received after tax was the appropriate deduction. Lord Thomson made it plain that, in assessing the loss of superannuation rights, there was no one right way of assessing the loss to the exclusion of all other methods of

Most claimants before the EAT are likely to know very little about the details of their pension schemes, if any. The absence of appropriate professional advice enhances their difficulties. The Tribunal has produced a useful form to assist claimants in computing loss of pension rights. The procedure usually followed by the EAT is to obtain details of pension schemes from claimants and to send these to an independent actuary for assessment of estimated loss in regard to superannuation.[76] The same course is adopted where a claimant produces his own actuarial report and this is disputed by his employer.[77]

The figure awarded for loss of pension rights is increasingly becoming the greatest single item in the assessment of compensation for unfair dismissal. Pension rights have also become a very important bargaining factor where claims are settled before a hearing. Even if a dismissed employee obtains new employment immediately following dismissal, and has been repaid his contributions, less tax, to the pension fund — and above all, if he has armed himself with an actuarial assessment — he will be able to negotiate a sum in settlement of prospective loss of pension rights. Many cases are settled or resolved following agreement on the question of pension rights.

Transferable pensions present no problems.[78] Where a pension scheme in new employment has a lower rate of benefit compared to that in the old, a sum will be given as compensation for loss of expected benefit in that regard. This is likely to take the form of a loss of benefit period. For example, the EAT might consider the difference between the benefits offered by the two schemes and discount the difference by the possibility that an employee might not live to enjoy them. If an employee is unfairly dismissed from a job with a non-contributory scheme and moves to a job with a contributory scheme the additional cost of the new scheme would be a further basis for compensation.[79]

---

approach. Actuarial evidence, he said, might be properly regarded as not only not conclusive but also quite unnecessary. The 'broad commonsense approach' should be adopted. He emphasised that the former employee was entitled to the return of his contributions to the superannuation fund and also to compensation for future loss of benefits.

> 'Another approach, and one favoured by us, is to think of the employer's future contribution to the superannuation fund as an addition to the employee's salary. The result is virtually the same.'

76. *O'Neill and O'Connor v. PMPA Ins. Co. Ltd.* UD 124 and 130/1980; *Fox v. Ashling Hotel Ltd.* UD 108/1978.

77. *Maguire v. Ofrex Group (Ireland) Ltd.* UD 90/1980.

78. *McCarthy v. Irish Shipping Ltd.* UD 100/1978.

79. The amount will be based upon the annual costs of contribution times a multiplier applicable to the individual: see, e.gg., *Powrmatic Ltd. v. Bull* [1977] IRLR 145; [1977] ICR 469, in which a multiplier of fifteen years was allowed.

(vi) *Contributory action by complainant or by employer: s. 7(2) (a) and (b)*[80]

An employer bears the burden of satisfying the Tribunal that an employee contributed to his own loss.[81] The EAT has interpreted s. 7(2) (a) and (b) as requiring action that is 'blameworthy' in some way.[82] The percentage of an employee's contributory action is often high where the EAT finds dismissal unfair solely or chiefly because of a denial of natural justice.[83] In such cases procedural justice is regarded by the EAT as of paramount importance. At the same time, substantive justice is subtly achieved by adjusting a claimant's compensatory award. It is sometimes difficult for the EAT to agree on the percentage to be deducted on account of contributory action. In *McCabe v. Lisney & Son*[84] this was variously assessed at 25%, 50% and 75% by the three members of the Tribunal. In the end, 50% was held to represent a fair percentage. *McCabe's* case brought to light an ambiguity in s. 7 of the Unfair Dismissals Act. The net question related to the proper stage at which the reduction allowed

80. It is submitted that the conduct, competence, and so on, of the employee must be known to the employer at the time of the dismissal in order to rank as contributory action: s. 7(2) (b). If the employer is unaware of, e.g., certain misconduct of the employee until after he has decided to dismiss him, it is obvious that that conduct, although it occurred prior to the decision to dismiss, could not have contributed to the dismissal. However, the Tribunal might well have regard to subsequently discovered facts when assessing compensation under s. 7(1) (c). Any deduction made thereunder would not be made under the contributory action provisions but under the general provision in s. 7(1) (c) and, particularly, taking into account the words 'such compensation . . . as is just and equitable having regard to all the circumstances' (see House of Lords in *W. Devis & Sons Ltd. v. Atkins* [1977] 3 All ER 40; [1977] IRLR 314, particularly Viscount Dilhorne. See, too, common law position in *Carvill v. Irish Industrial Bank* [1968] IR 316, 345-6, and chapter three, page 60 above).

81. *Per* Sir John Donaldson in *A.G. Bracey Ltd. v. Iles* [1973] IRLR 210 — the same principle holds in Ireland. Section 7(2) (a) enables the EAT, when determining the amount of compensation to be awarded, to have regard to the extent, if any, to which the financial loss referred to in s. 7(1) (c) was attributable to an act, omission, or conduct by or on behalf of the employer. There is no equivalent provision in Britain. See s. 74(6) EPCA, 1978. A rare example of the EAT's alluding to employer's contributory action is *Hennessy v. McCann Nurseries Ltd.* UD 7/1979 (a minority view). Clearly, if the determination of the EAT is one of unfair dismissal, any contribution on the employer's part will go towards that finding and have no significance on its own. It is difficult to see the point of s. 7(2) (a).

82. In *McCabe v. Lisney & Son* (High Court unreported, 16 March 1981) counsel for the claimant appellant submitted that s. 7(2) (b) should be construed so as to relate only to conduct affecting the amount of the employee's financial loss after dismissal and not to conduct relating to his employment before then. The argument was, not surprisingly, rejected. See fn. 80 above.

83. E.g., *Barr v. Marley Extrusions (Ire.) Ltd.* UD 78/1978; also, *Kerr v. Hotel Group Ltd.* UD 12/1977.

84. UD 5/1977.

under s. 7(2) (b) should be made: should it be in respect of a dismissed employee's overall loss or in respect of the maximum amount of compensation he is allowed under s. 7(1) (c), namely, 104 weeks' remuneration? Section 7(1) (c) refers to compensation in respect of 'any financial loss', and the repetition of this phrase and its definition in s. 7(2) and (3) respectively, suggest that the figure to be reduced is the overall one. On the wording of the Act a majority of the Tribunal applied the reducing factor to the claimant's overall loss, not to the lesser figure of 104 weeks' remuneration (the difference being between £40,000 and £19,200). The claimant was therefore awarded the full figure of two years' remuneration by way of compensation. *McCabe's* case was appealed to the Circuit Court by the employers where the amount of compensation was reduced to £6,234.[85] The Court completely side-stepped the EAT's interpretative dilemma by making no reference at all to overall loss. But the EAT's earlier interpretation was restored on appeal to the High Court.[86] It is clear that deductions are to be made from the full financial loss if it exceeds the maximum permitted sum, and any resulting excess over this must then be reduced, waived or abandoned to this maximum level.

Whether large deductions are just and equitable has been questioned. In Britain the opinion was expressed, prior to *Devis v. Atkins*,[87] that a contributory factor of more than 80% was verging on the inconsistent. In *Devis'* case, Viscount Dilhorne, who delivered the major speech, observed that:

'The Act requires the tribunal to consider whether a dismissal was "to any extent" caused by action of the employee. It does not preclude the tribunal from coming to the conclusion that the dismissal was wholly caused by his conduct and, in the light of that conclusion, thinking it just and equitable to reduce the compensation it otherwise would have awarded to a nominal or nil amount.'

Viscount Dilhorne referred to Phillips J. who thought there was an inconsistency in finding a dismissal unfair and then not awarding compensation.[88] He disagreed:

85. Circuit Court 1/79.
86. High Court unreported, 16 March 1981.
87. [1977] AC 941; [1977] 3 All ER 40. See S. D. Anderman: *Unfair Dismissal* 213, 231.
88. He referred to *Kemp v. Shipton Automation Ltd.* [1976] IRLR 305; [1976] ICR 514; 11 ITR 232, where the opinion was expressed that to award less than 20 per cent (i.e., a contribution of more than 80 per cent) was likely to be seen as verging on the inconsistent and that the Employment Appeals Tribunal would feel free to vary the tribunal's award if satisfied that it is based on a wrong principle, e.g., is inconsistent with the finding of unfair dismissal.

'... a man may bring about his dismissal wholly by his own misconduct and yet ... that dismissal may be unfair through failure to warn him that his employment was in jeopardy. In such a case, and there may be others, there is no inconsistency [in holding that] the just and equitable award might be of nil compensation.'[89]

The Irish EAT has tacitly approved Viscount Dilhorne's *dicta* on a number of occasions.[90]

In line with the Act's policy of promoting procedural fairness, and of encouraging collective bargaining in this respect, section 7(2) (d) enables the Tribunal to take into account the extent, if any, of compliance or failure to comply by an employer or employee with any procedure of the kind referred to in s. 14(3) of the Act or with the provisions of any code of practice relating to procedures regarding dismissal approved of by the Minister for Labour. As yet no code of practice has been approved by the Minister.[91] Procedures in s. 14(3) relate to procedures agreed upon by or on behalf of the employer concerned and by the employee concerned or a trade union,[92] or an excepted body under the Trade Union Acts, 1941-71,[93] representing him or procedures that have been established by custom and practice in the employment concerned.

(vii) *The duty to mitigate: s. 7(2) (c)*

The common law rule of mitigation of damages applies to compensation for unfair dismissal.[94] Questions of mitigation are questions of fact. The burden of proof lies on the party seeking to allege that another has failed to mitigate loss.[95] Sir John Donaldson explained the duty in *A.G. Bracey Ltd. v. Iles:*[96]

89. Numerous examples of contributory action may be found in Britain: *Jamieson v. Aberdeen County Co.* [1975] IRLR 348: *Wells v. E. & A. West Ltd.* [1975] IRLR 269; *Deegan v. Norman & Sons Ltd.* [1976] IRLR 139; *Bowie v. British Leyland (UK) Ltd.* [1976] IRLR 48; *Chrystie v. Rolls Royce (1971) Ltd.* [1976] IRLR 336 (EAT); *Thornton v. Champion Association Weavers Ltd.* [1977] IRLR 385; *Wells v. Derwent Plastics Ltd.* [1978] ICR 424.
90. See, *White v. Cadbury (Ireland) Ltd.* UD 44/1979; *Condon v. Rowntree Mackintosh Ltd.* UD 195/1979; *Murray v. Meath Co. Council* UD 43/1978. See, too, Dáil Question No. 403, 31 October 1979, Col. 1007.
91. See chapter 8, page 203, fn. 2, below.
92. *Kerr v. Tower Hotel Group Ltd.* UD 12/1977; *O'Connor v. Marley Extensions (Irl.) Ltd.* UD 135/1979.
93. These are staff associations; civil service unions; teachers unions; Joint Labour Committees; any other organisations which the Minister for Labour declares excepted.
94. *Fay v. The Order of Hospitalers of St. John of God* UD 92/1980.
95. *Bessenden Properties Ltd. v. Corness* [1974] IRLR 338 (CA).
96. [1973] IRLR 210.

'The law is that it is the duty of a dismissed employee to act reasonably in order to mitigate his loss. It may not be reasonable to take the first job that comes along. It may be much more reasonable, in the interests of the employee and of the employer who has to pay compensation, that he should wait a little time. He must, of course, use the time well and seek a better paid job which will reduce his overall loss and the amount of compensation which the previous employer ultimately has to pay . . .'

These principles are illustrated in decisions of the EAT. A dismissed employee is generally expected to register with an employment agency such as the National Manpower Service. Otherwise, his compensation may be reduced.[97] If he attends a training course during unemployment and receives a training allowance, it seems his compensation will be reduced thereby.[98] Where an employee attends a fulltime course following his dismissal and this effectively withdraws him from the labour market he is likely to receive no compensation at all for loss during that period.[99] Paradoxically, if he attends a relatively short course with the aspiration of finding work again as soon as possible, he is likely to be compensated for loss during this period. If an unfairly dismissed employee cashes a life assurance policy as part of his efforts to alleviate loss, the Tribunal may allow him the difference between the amount actually paid to the Assurance Company and the surrender value he receives.[100] An employee's efforts to mitigate loss can be severely handicapped without a reference[101] and an employer who persists in refusing to give a reference may have to 'pay' for his intransigence before the Tribunal.[102]

Refusing other employment merely because it involves lower wages can be a breach of the duty to mitigate.[103] Conversely, accept-

97. *Kearney v. Standard (1938) Ltd.* UD 138/1978; *Tormey v. Display Development Ltd.* UD 2/1977.

98. *Martin v. Weldon Ltd.* UD 30/1978 where the claimant attended an AnCO training course during unemployment and received a training allowance. He was awarded the difference between his earnings and the allowance by the EAT. The decision as to dismissal was reversed on appeal to the Circuit Court (23 November 1978). See, too, *Ledwidge v. Peter Mark Ltd.* UD 70/1978.

99. See *Pagano v. HGS* [1976] IRLR 9 — where Pagano took up fulltime study 3 months after dismissal. His loss was assessed at his net wage loss prior to going to college.

100. Footnote 98 above.

101. See ILO Recommendation No. 119, chapter 5, page 120, fn. 16, in relation to certificates of character.

102. Footnote 98 above.

103. As in British case of *Connolly v. Robinson* (1946/72). Refusal of an offer of re-employment with the same employer was held to be a failure to mitigate loss and hence a disentitlement to compensation in *Murphy v. Valley Investment Ltd.* UD 112/1980.

ing other employment which is very much lower paid can be a breach of the duty. The test is one of reasonableness.[104] If an employee is close to retiring age he should be ready favourably to consider work he would not normally have considered, in order to mitigate his loss.[105] An employee's reluctance in regard to seeking alternative employment may be regarded as reasonable in certain circumstances if, e.g., he wishes first of all to clear his name.[106] Where it is reasonable for an employer to become self-employed straightaway or within a short time after dismissal, any fall in income is likely to be taken into account.[107] The duty to mitigate ceases when an order of reinstatement or re-engagement is made by the Tribunal. It does not revive unless and until an employee is informed that the employer is unwilling to take him back.[108]

The duty to mitigate succeeds the heading of contributory action in section 7(2) of the Unfair Dismissals Act. In a case where deductions were made in respect of each such heading the statutory order was reversed.[109] The Tribunal considered this more equitable: 30% of the compensatory award was deducted for failure to mitigate and 75% deducted from the remainder for contributory conduct.

(viii) *Ex-gratia or severance payments*

What are the implications for a statutory claim of unfair dismissal of *ex-gratia* or severance payments? Theoretically, these may be

104. See *dicta* of Sir John Donaldson in *Archbold Freightage v. Wilson* [1974] IRLR 10; and in Ireland *McCabe v. Lisney & Son* UD 5/1977; *Eate v. Semprit (Ireland) Ltd.* UD 46/1977. In *Riordans Travel Ltd. v. Acres Co. Ltd.* (High Court unreported, 17 January 1979) McWilliam J. referred to the following words from *Mayne on Damages* which were approved by Davies L.J. in *Moore v. Der Ltd.* [1971] 1 WLR 1476, at 1479:-
> 'Although the plaintiff must act with the defendant's as well as his own interests in mind, he is only required to act reasonably, and the standard of reasonableness is not too high in view of the fact that the defendant is an admitted wrongdoer.'

105. As in *Lloyd v. Standard Pulverised Fuel Co. Ltd.* [1976] IRLR 115.

106. *Zambra v. Duffy* UD 154/1978.

107. *Dowling v. W.B. Peat & Co. Ltd.* UD 93/1978. Contrast, however, *Hassett v. Leonard T.V. Consultants (Limerick) Ltd.* UD 76/1977 — where claimant set up on his own and no account whatsoever was taken of expected fluctuations in future earnings. In fact the Tribunal remarked that the employers were 'lucky that his [employee's] compensation must turn out to be small'. Distinguish *Fletcher v. Photo Precision Ltd.* [1973] IRLR 169.

108. 'Where re-engagement is recommended on different terms, the employee can do no more than wait for the offer' *per* Sir Hugh Griffiths in *Curtis v. Paterson (Darlington) Ltd.* [1973] ICR 496 at 502. See *Dobson & Heather v. K. P. Morritt Ltd.* [1972] IRLR 99; *Williams v. Lloyds Retailers Ltd.* [1973] IRLR 262; *How v. Tesco Stores Ltd.* [1974] IRLR 194; *Kendrick v. Aerduct Productions* [1974] IRLR 322; *Crampton v. Dacorum Motors Ltd.* [1975] IRLR 169.

109. *Lissadel Towels Ltd. v. O'Halloran* UD 203/1978.

complex but, in practical terms, they are straightforward. After (rather than before)[110] dismissal proceedings have commenced, if a settlement is reached to the agreement of both parties in which all claims under the Unfair Dismissals Act (and, where appropriate, other Acts) are struck out on the payment of a lump sum compensation, the Tribunal will register this agreement. The effect will discharge all statutory claims.[111] If such an agreement is concluded after proceedings commence before the Rights Commissioner, no appeal will be entertained by the EAT.[112] An employee's best course of action in the event of non-compliance with a lump sum agreement by his employer is to initiate proceedings once more under the Act – provided he comes within the statutory time limit.[113] Alternatively, provided he comes within the six year period laid down by the Statute of Limitations, 1957 (s. 11), he may commence civil proceedings in a court of appropriate jurisdiction for recovery of a contract debt. A settlement agreed before dismissal proceedings is likely to be void as contravening s. 13 of the Unfair Dismissals Act. Where an employer refuses to implement such an agreement, an employee could not seek to enforce it before the ordinary courts nor, being a 'sword-holder', could he rely on the doctrine of promissory estoppel.[114] His sole form of redress would be via a statutory claim, provided he met the Act's requirements.

110. See the approach adopted by the EAT in circumstances where an agreed settlement was negotiated before rather than after dismissal: *Eate v. Semprit (Ireland) Ltd.* UD 46/1977. The Tribunal cited s. 13 of the Act which states that 'a provision in an agreement shall be void in so far as it purports to exclude or limit the application of, or is inconsistent with, any provision of this Act'. The Chairman considered the section in the light of the British case of *Maddison v. Council of Engineering Institutions* [1976] IRLR 389; [1977] ICR 30; [1976] ITR 272, and held that Eate's agreement purported to exclude or limit the application of the Act. It was therefore void under s. 13 and did not preclude a claim for compensation under the Unfair Dismissals Act, 1977. But the claimant was not held entitled to any more compensation; in all the circumstances he had been adequately compensated.

111. *Cuneen v. Prendeville (Waterville Lake Hotel)* UD 19/1980.

112. *Doyle v. Pierce (Wexford) Ltd.* UD 50/1979; *Timmins v. Munster Simms Hardware Ltd.* M 384/1980.

113. See *Millar v. P. Faulkner & Sons Ltd.* UD 200/1978. See, too, *Savage v. Ruaine* UD 59/1978 – claim struck out upon employer's undertaking to pay claimant £45; *Lyons v. O'Meara Camping (Ireland) Ltd.* UD 188/1978 – in which an undisclosed settlement was reached; *Reid v. H.B. Prosser Ltd.* UD 185/1978 – same; *Cassidy v. Connolly* UD 75/1977 – claim settled for payment by employer to claimant of £750 and the issue by employer of character reference.

114. Cf. *Coombe v. Coombe* [1951] 2 KB 215; [1951] 1 All ER 767 *per* Denning L. J. at 769 (All ER).

CHAPTER EIGHT

Collective Aspects of Unfair Dismissal

A. The Individualisation of Collective Issues in the Act

'Where labour is weak — and its strength or weakness depends largely on factors outside the control of the law — Acts of Parliament, however well intentioned and well designed, can do something, but cannot do much to modify the power relation between labour and management.'[1]

This is a fundamental point. A highly significant feature of the Unfair Dismissals Act is its individualisation of dismissal which may also be a collective issue.[2] The concern of the legislators was that dismissal should be taken out of the arena of industrial conflict, thus separating discipline and dismissal from the wider issue of collective control. Dismissal is treated in relative isolation from the bargaining context. The authorities are resorted to after dismissal has taken place, not when it is apprehended or threatened. Those who seek not selective but universal job protection through the extension of collective organisation and collective action find this unsatisfactory but their arguments, it is suggested, are irreconcilable with substantive justice.

The Act is most often used by workers within the so-called 'secondary' sector of the labour market, where 'labour is weak' and pay and job security relatively low.[3] The evidence is far from conclusive that the Act has provided an individual remedy which is used where there may be a collective alternative. It is true, for

---

1. Professor Otto Kahn-Freund: *Labour and the Law,* 8.
2. Because collective issues have been made justiciable by the UDA it is regrettable that the code of practice referred to in s. 7 (2) (d) of the Act has not been drawn up. It would have a most important contribution to make, bearing in mind the many difficulties which face the EAT when it has to have regard to both collective and individual interests. A code would suggest the appropriate matters to consider in dispute resolution and throw some light on the concept of reasonableness where collective and individual interests clash. It is essential that industrial action should not be governed by the same criteria as, e.g., misconduct. The appropriate rules governing management discretion in disciplining the workforce in the ordinary course of production are not suitable for deciding what economic sanctions should be permitted to both sides during industrial conflict.

On the general question of individualisation of collective issues see M. Mellish and N. Collis-Squires: 'Legal and Social Norms in Discipline and Dismissal' (1976) 5 ILJ 164; S. Anderman: *The Law of Unfair Dismissal,* 3-4.

3. B. Hepple: 'A Right to Work?' (1981) IJL 65, 68 from which source the terminology in the text has been extracted.

instance, that the number of official disputes relating to engagement or dismissal of workers (including redundancy) fell from 48 in 1977 to 25 in 1978 and dropped to 23 in the following year.[4] But against this apparent decrease in the number of industrial disputes must be placed the figures relating to unofficial disputes. For 1978 and 1979, the percentage of unofficial disputes to the local number of industrial disputes was 68%. In 1980, it was 81%. Among the reasons for unofficial disputes during 1977-'80, disputes as to dismissal represent about as high a proportion of unofficial disputes now as in 1977.[5] This suggests that 'dispute dismissals' have not in fact been brought within the Act. Collective issues have remained collective issues[6] and bargaining control remains unaffected. If anything, the Act has strengthened collective bargaining by providing a base upon which trade unions may build.

To argue that collective aspects of the Unfair Dismissals Act are unimportant or without impact because few cases have been dealt with internally, is to miss the point that the law and lawyers are concerned with moments of crisis and therefore with the very few cases that cannot be dealt with internally. For this reason the cases that have been initiated under the Act cannot be ignored. In addition, there is what may be a large silent statistic relating to the number of collective disputes which have been resolved, or resolved more speedily, because of the Act and an awareness of its potential effects.

4. According to figures released by the Central Statistics Office, Dublin. See *Irish Statistical Bulletin* (1980) Vol. LV, No. 3, 215.

5. In general, the pattern is that unofficial disputes involve either fewer workers and/or are of relatively short duration. The reasons or causes of unofficial industrial disputes have been estimated (unofficially) as follows, for 1977-1979.

	1977	1978	1979
Pay and Conditions	64	49	47
Dismissal/suspension	36	25	19
Manning/productivity/bonus	23	28	12
Promotion	4	2	7
Demarcation	4	2	5
Redundancy/lay-off	12	4	5
Recognition	5	3	2
TOTAL	148	113	97

6. Where industrial disputes concern dismissal they may end up before the Labour Court (established under the Industrial Relations Act, 1946). In its *Annual Report* for 1979 the Court gave a breakdown of disputes by cause. Dismissal accounted for 7 disputes before the Court out of a total in excess of 500.

B. The Trade Disputes Act and Dismissal

Workers who engage in industrial action are protected against civil suit for 'simple' civil conspiracy,[7] picketing, including breaches of employment contracts or interference with business. This immunity is provided under the Trade Disputes Act, 1906, as amended,[8] but only if workers are acting:

'in contemplation or furtherance of a trade dispute'

and provided also that their action is not inconsistent with the Constitution.[9]

The definition of 'trade dispute' in s. 5 covers disputes relating to dismissal and also disputes which might give rise to a claim of constructive dismissal under the Unfair Dismissals Act. A 'trade dispute' means

'any dispute between employers and workmen, or between workmen and workmen, which is connected with the employment or non-employment or the terms of the employment, or with the conditions of labour, of any person.'

and the expression 'workmen' refers to:

'all persons employed in trade or industry, whether or not in the employment of the employer with whom a trade dispute arises.'

Section 5 (the 'golden formula') has been restrictively interpreted in Ireland.[10] It has been held, however, that a trade dispute within the

---

7. See, by the author: 'The Tort of Conspiracy in Irish Labour Law' (1973) *The Irish Jurist* Vol. VIII, 225.

8. The Trade Union Act, 1941, s. 11, restricts the protection of ss. 2, 3 and 4 of the Act of 1906 to apply only in relation to authorised trade unions who for the time being are holders of negotiation licences as defined in the Act, and members and officials of such unions, but not otherwise. The section covers members and officials of an authorised trade union whether acting officially or unofficially: *Gouldings Chemicals Ltd. v. Bolger* [1977] IR 211. Doubt was cast on the constitutionality of s. 11 in *Gouldings* case but it was not necessary for the Court to explore the matter further.

9. *Educational Co. of Ireland Ltd. v. Fitzpatrick* [1961] IR 345.

10. This has particularly been so in relation to the parties to a trade dispute: e.gg. *B. & I. Steam Packet Co. Ltd. v. Branigan* [1958] IR 128; *Brendan Dunne Ltd. v. Fitzpatrick* [1958] IR 29; *Smith v. Beirne* (1955) 89 ILTR 24. The courts have

Act arises where an employer relies solely upon his common law right of dismissal and is not prepared to state or to discuss his reasons therefor.[11]

C. Express limitations on Managerial Prerogative in the Act

In the Act of 1977, collective aspects of unfair dismissal law are found among the express limitations on an employer's power to dismiss. In subsections (2) and (3) of section 6, trade union membership and activities, and unfair selection for redundancy are deemed, respectively, to constitute unfair reasons for dismissal. Section 5 concerns unfair dismissal for participation in strike or other industrial action. The aim of these provisions, apart from providing a refuge for workers where there is an irreconcilable conflict of interests, is to strengthen collective bargaining by encouraging trade union membership and activities and by forcing employers to take due regard of collective agreements where they exist, e.g., in relation to redundancy. During the Dáil debate on the draft Bill, the Minister for Labour said that:

> '. . . anybody who looks over the history of unfair dismissals will realise that membership of a trade union has been one of the commonest reasons for it.'[12]

---

been less restrictive concerning the issues involved in a trade dispute: e.g., *Becton Dickinson Ltd. v. Lee* [1973] IR 1; *Esplanade Pharmacy Ltd. v. Larkin* [1957] IR 285. However the recent Supreme Court decision in *Talbot (Ireland) Ltd. v. Merrigan and Others* (unreported, 1 May 1981) may reduce considerably the scope of the Act. See fn. 43 *post*. In general, concerning earlier cases, see, M. Abrahamson: 'Trade Disputes Act — Strict Interpretation in Ireland' (1961) 24 MLR 596.

11. *Quigley v. Beirne and others* [1955] IR 62. Two employees were given notice of termination. The employer declined to provide the reasons for dismissal and picketing began at the premises the day after notice expired. The Supreme Court accepted that the dispute did not concern the legal rights of the men (at 76). There is no right at common law to know the reason for one's dismissal once correct notice has been given. Lavery J. described the Trade Disputes Act as designed to permit, within carefully defined lines, certain actions to secure recognition of extra-legal claims of a particular nature and to bring pressure to bear on employers to observe certain principles and standards which the law does not impose. Trade disputes may involve matters of legal right but ordinarily they are concerned with other matters. Lavery J. held that the trial judge was wrong in so far as he had based his conclusion that there was no trade dispute on the fact that no legal right had been infringed. Analogous cases concerning wrongful dismissal and the Trade Disputes Act, 1906, are *Riordan v. Butler* [1940] I.R. 347; *Doran v. Lennon and O'Kelly* [1945] I.R. 315; *Corry v. NUVGATA and Others* [1950] I.R. 315; *Silver Tassie Co. Ltd. v. Cleary and Others* and *Same v. Beirne and Others* (1958) 91 I.L.T.R. 27; *Maher v. Beirne and Others* (1959) 93 I.L.T.R. 101.

12. *Dáil Debates* Vol. 298, col. 840 (11 March 1977).

It is appropriate to begin by examining this ground. Before doing so, however, the point may be reiterated that none of the grounds discussed in this chapter constitute automatically unfair reasons for dismissal. Section 6(1) is no less relevant here than in relation to other grounds in the Act. That is to say, it is always open to an employer to adduce evidence that he had substantial grounds justifying the dismissal. If he succeeds in convincing the Tribunal, dismissal will be adjudged not to be unfair. There is a common misunderstanding about the nature of the Act's presumptions in the matter of unfairness. Particularly where collective issues are involved, such as trade union membership or activities or dismissal for participation in strike action, it is believed that the Act provides complete protection. The fact is that it does not. Whether it should provide more than statutory descriptions of what are likely to be regarded as unfair dismissals is a separate issue and one which should loom large in any debate concerning amendments to the Act.

(1) *Trade union activities*

Under the Unfair Dismissals Act, 1977, s. 6(2) (a), dismissal is deemed unfair if it results wholly or mainly from:

> 'the employee's membership,[13] or proposal that he or another person become a member of, or his engaging in activities[14] on behalf of, a trade union or excepted body under the Trade Union Acts, 1941 and 1971, where the times at which he

---

13. Note the Irish Act does not cover non-membership of a trade union (cf. s. 58(1) (c) EPCA).

14. Presumably this refers to activities of the trade union whether at national, branch or sectional level. From British cases, it may not be enough for the activities to be 'matters which people associate with trade union activities' but which are basically individual grievances treated as such by the individual concerned: *Gardner v. Peeks Retail Ltd.* [1975] IRLR 244. The activity should be connected with the more institutional aspects of trade union organisation activity, such as taking part in trade union meetings *(Miller v. Rafique* [1975] IRLR 70); attempts to recruit a fellow employee *(Brennan & Ging v. Ellward (Lancs.) Ltd.* [1976] IRLR 378); consulting a shop steward or fulltime trade union representative, or attempting to form a workplace union group *(Lyon v. St. James Press Ltd.* [1976] IRLR 215; [1976] ICR 413). See, too, *Crouch v. P.O.* [1973] 3 All ER 225, 244 (CA). The British EAT has pointed to the need to distinguish the activities of a trade union from the activities of an individual trade unionist. Only the union's activities fall within the statutory protection against dismissal or lesser penalty: *Chant v. Acquaboats* [1978] ICR 643 (EAT). However, this distinction cannot be followed too rigidly. Pre-employment union involvement is not protected: *City of Birmingham v. Beyer* [1977] IRLR 211; *McKendry v. Avery Hardoll* [1977] IRLR (369/77 EAT).

engages in such activities are outside his hours of work[15] or are times during his hours of work in which he is permitted pursuant to the contract of employment [16] between him and his employer so to engage.'[17]

Section 6(7) of the Act is also relevant. It incorporates an amendment initiated in Seanad Éireann during the debate on the Unfair Dismissals Bill.[18] The sub-section gives universal access to the Act to employees who feel they have been dismissed due to trade union membership or activities, i.e., employees are not excluded because they have less than one year's service,[19] are beyond retiring age, or are dismissed during probation, training or apprenticeship. As a *quid pro quo* the provision removes the presumption of unfairness on the part of an employer and purports to put employer and employee on an equal basis. The burden of proving an unfair union dismissal rests with an employee, and unless a company's motives are glaringly obvious,[20] the onus will be very difficult to discharge.[21]

Section 6(2) (a) of the Act of 1977 covers dismissal for union membership only (unlike the British Act)[22] although presumably dismissal for non-membership — if it could not be accommodated within the subsection — could be dealt with as an 'other substantial

---

15. This presumably refers to the time when an employee is contractually required to be at work and therefore would not include lunch hours, dining breaks or just before or after starting or quitting work: *Post Office v. UPOW* [1974] 1 All ER 229; [1974] IRLR 22.

16. It is interesting that permission must be pursuant to the contract of employment (see, e.g., *Miller v. Rafique* [1975] IRLR 70). Permission presumably may be implied. Therefore, activities such as raising members' grievances with management during working hours should cause no problems even if no express permission has been given: permission is implied from the willingness of management to work with the union: *Marley Tile Co. v. Shaw* [1978] IRLR 238. Presumably management's permission can be implied in cases where an employer raises an unusual and unexpected problem which goes to the root of the union's standing at the workplace (e.g., management's refusal to accredit a properly elected shop steward).

17. The British provisions contained in s. 58 of the EPCA are more complex, dealing with, for example, the dismissal of shop stewards and protection of the closed shop (the section has been amended by the Employment Act, 1980, s. 7).

18. See *Dáil Debates* Vol. 298, col. 837 (31 March 1977); see, similarly, s. 64(3) EPCA.

19. E.g., *McCormac v. P.H. Ross Ltd.* UD 206/1979.

20. On the burden of proof, see *Smith v. Hayle Town Council* [1978] ICR 996 and see, too, *McMorn v. Exquisite Knitwear* [1975] COIT 346/226.

21. See, e.g., *A La Francaise Ltd. v. Monaghan* UD 13/1977; *Grassick v. T.P. O'Connor & Sons Ltd.* UD 114/1979 (the claimant appeared in person; a dismissed employee is unlikely, without the benefit of advice or representation, to appreciate the way in which the burden of proof operates in trade union dismissals).

22. See fn. 13 *ante*.

ground' under section 6(1) of the Act.[23] The right to join a trade union is guaranteed and protected under Article 40, s. 6, sub-s. 1(iii) of the Constitution and the right not to join also enjoys constitutional protection.[24] Because these rights are constitutionally protected, an employee dismissed for union membership (or non-membership) could rely not only on the Unfair Dismissals Act but also, by way of separate proceedings, on the Constitution.[25] Because of its constitutional ramifications, dismissal for trade union membership is the only ground within the Act of 1977 which is likely to render a dismissal automatically unfair. While recognising that no right under the Constitution is absolute, it would almost certainly be contrary to Article 40, s. 6, sub-s. 1(iii) to construe the Act in such a way as to permit an employer to adduce substantial grounds justifying dismissal within section 6(1). To penalise an employee for exercising a right which under the Constitution he is entitled to do would be likely to be unlawful, no matter what the circumstances.

(2) *Unfair selection for redundancy*[26]

Unfair selection for redundancy is likely to amount to unfair dismissal. If an employee is dismissed due to redundancy and he is unable to show that his selection for redundancy resulted wholly or mainly from an inadmissible reason in section 6(2), (see chapter 6, pages 150-51 above), he may alternatively show that there was an agreed procedure, that his selection for redundancy contravened this and that there were no special reasons justifying a departure from the procedure.[27] An agreed procedure, under s. 6(3), is one that has been

23. As such, however, it would not enjoy the easier qualification requirements in s. 6(7) of the Unfair Dismissals Act. See *Hayes v. Sean Curtin & Sons Ltd.* UD 137/1979 where claimant refused to join any trade union which the employers (builders) acknowledged was 'his right' although they insisted on union membership to avoid being refused admission to certain 'sites'. This allegation is not dealt with in the Tribunal's determination.

24. *Ed. Co. of Ireland v. Fitzpatrick* [1961] IR 323.

25. Constitutional protection of freedom of association is discussed in chapter one, page 34, above.

26. See chapter six, page 150, *ante,* where individual employment aspects of unfair selection for redundancy are dealt with.

27. *Kavanagh v. Weartex Ltd.,* UD 256/1979; *Brown v. McInerney Construction Ltd.* UD 117/1981; *Hayes v. Duggan Bros. Contractors Ltd.* UD 50/1981; *Mooney v. Collen Bros.* UD 73/1980; *Moran v. Same* UD 71/1980; *Mallon v. McKone Estates Ltd.* UD 76/1979; *Friel v. John Sisk & Son Ltd.* UD 71/1978; and agreement in circumstances of receivership: *Smyth v. Irish Board Mills Ltd.* UD 9/1979.

Where an agreed procedure was breached and negotiations would not have produced an outcome any different from that arrived at by an employer, dismissal was held not to be unfair: *McElvany and McPhillips v. Irish Joinery Monaghan Ltd.* UD 26/1980. In general, see H.M.G. Concannon: 'Collective Agreements and Unfair Dismissal' (1978) 128 NLJ 900. Breach of an agreed procedure might have particular repercussions at common law, see chapter three, pages 63, 64, *ante.*

agreed by or on behalf of the employer and by the employee or a trade union or an excepted body under the Trade Union Acts, 1941 and 1971,[28] or which has been established by the custom and practice of the employment concerned. In practice the most important procedures will be those agreed between employers and trade unions, although such agreements may be incorporated into the contract of employment of individual employees.

If there is no agreed procedure there may be a custom and practice in the particular employment which has created expectations as to the criteria to be used in selection for redundancy. Custom or practice must be proved as a question of fact. In *Bessenden Properties Ltd. v. Corness,* [29] the NIRC suggested that the term 'customary arrangement' (the British equivalent of 'custom and practice', found in s. 59 (b) EPCA, 1978) referred to something which is so well known, so certain and so clear as to amount in effect to an implied agreed procedure, as contrasted with the express agreed procedure which is the alternative contemplated by the statutory provision in question (in this respect s. 6(3) of the Irish Act is similar to s. 59 of the EPCA). The EAT in Britain has somewhat softened this approach,[30] but it is clear that something more is needed to prove a customary arrangement than the fact that, on one or two occasions, a particular policy has been adopted. A single precedent, even if applicable to the circumstances before the Tribunal, is not sufficient by itself to constitute a custom and practice.[31] Moreover, custom and practice will vary between industries — to say nothing of parts of industries. It is usual in the manufacturing industry, both under agreed procedures and custom and practice, for the 'last in first out' rule to apply when selective redundancies occur, but this does not apply, e.g., in the building industry.[32] Here the 'custom and practice' is generally for the foreman to make the selection for whatever reasons seem justifiable.[33] Employers have a defence for not following a procedure where there is a special reason for departing from what is customary or agreed. A 'special reason' will depend on the circumstances of each case.[34] It may justify dismissal; equally it may justify retention of an employee in breach of procedure where another or others are

---

28. See chapter 7, page 187, fn. 40, *ante.*
29. [1973] IRLR 365.
30. *Kyle Stewart Contractors v. Stainrod* (1977) EAT 406/77.
31. *Moloney v. J. & F. Goodbody Ltd.* UD 6/1978; *Kennedy v. Same* UD 8/1978.
32. *Flanagan v. Collen Bros. (Dublin) Ltd.* UD 72/1980.
33. *James v. Western Contractors Ltd.* UD 132/1980; *Gould v. O'Shea's Ltd.* UD 323/1978.
34. See, *Kearney v. Standard (1938) Ltd.* UD 138/1978; *Watson v. Flanagan* UD 209/1978; *McLoughlin v. Cappincur Joinery Ltd.* UD 36-7/1977.

dismissed. The EAT is likely to place considerable importance on the need to keep a company running efficiently in times of crisis or redundancy.

Where there is no agreed procedure or custom and practice relating to employment, and selection for dismissal does not result wholly or mainly from one or more of the grounds deemed unfair in section 6(2) of the Unfair Dismissals Act, the EAT will ask whether the employer has acted reasonably in the light of all the circumstances.[35] Two aspects are likely to be considered: the reasonableness of selection and the reasonableness of the manner of dismissal. Clearly, the EAT should not be hasty to substitute another view for that of the employer. At the same time, the EAT is required to apply its own collective wisdom. Reasonableness should be judged:

> 'by the objective standard of the way in which a reasonable employer in these circumstances, in that line of business, would have behaved.'[36]

Employers will be required (where appropriate) to have thought about the problem of redundancy in good time so as to have formulated a policy.[37] They will be required to have identified factors crucial to selection in their particular circumstances, such as length of service, experience, age, ability,[38] attendance or disciplinary records. Factors such as better management potential, administrative ability, stronger personality, more drive and greater cost consciousness may all outweigh length of service, Counter-allegations (e.g., personal disagreement between the social partners)[39] may be put forward by an employee.

35. *Clehane v. Gouldings Chemicals Ltd.* UD 280/1978.
36. *Watling & Co. Ltd. v. Richardson* (1978) EAT 774/77. On the reluctance of the British EAT to interfere with the decisions of employers, see P. Elias: 'The Concept of Fairness in Unfair Dismissal' (1981) ILJ 201. See, too, chapter six, pages 159-160, *ante.*
37. Note the provisions on collective redundancies contained in the Protection of Employees Act, 1977. Breach of the statutory obligation to consult trade unions before collective redundancies are set out therein might influence the EAT in cases involving s. 6(3) of the UDA. The Protection of Employment Act will have to be revised if Ireland adopts what is probable to become the new ILO Convention on Termination of Employment, see chapter five, page 117, fn. 4, *ante.*
38. *Delaney v. Mather & Platt (Irl.) Ltd.* UD 73/1978; see, too, *Meade v. Talbot Ireland Ltd.* UD 69/1980; *Humphries v. Weartex Ltd.* UD 89/1979; *Hennessy v. SAFA (Ireland) Ltd.* UD 57/1978; *Clarke v. P. J. Hegarty & Sons Ltd.* UD 36/1978; *Sinclair v. Armstrong Autoparts (Ire.) Ltd.* UD 225/1978.
39. *Kinsella v. D.L. Rafter* UD 312/1978. Among the circumstances in Britain which have been held to render selection for dismissal on grounds of redundancy unfair are: failure to consult an employee or his union before selection: *Clarkson International Tools Ltd. v. Short* [1973] ICR 191; failure to give reasons for his selection for redundancy: *Rigby v. British Steel Corporation* [1973] ITR 191; failure to find the employee suitable alternative employment: *Modern Injection Moulds Ltd. v. Price* [1976] ICR 370; *Vokes Ltd. v. Bear* [1974] ITR 85.

(3) *Dismissal for participating in strike or other industrial action*[40]

Union bargaining power will generally ensure that there is no discrimination where workers are dismissed for participating in strike or other industrial action. Yet there is still a need for some *tabula in naufragio* to protect workers against loss of their jobs,[41] not least because of the common law's uncertainty as to the effect of industrial action on individual contracts of employment. Section 5(2) of the Unfair Dismissals Act provides that:

> 'the dismissal of an employee for taking part in a strike or other industrial action shall be deemed, for the purposes of this Act, to be an unfair dismissal, if;
>
> (a) one or more employees of the same employer who took part in the strike or other industrial action were not dismissed for so taking part, or
> (b) one or more of such employees who were dismissed for so taking part are subsequently offered reinstatement or re-engagement and the employee is not.'[42]

Prima facie, section 5 protects the freedom to strike. It is consonant with the theory that Ireland recognises a positive right to strike in domestic and international law.[43] The sub-section has been described

---

40. See, by the author: 'Dismissal for taking part in Strike or other Industrial Action' (1980) *Gazette of the Incorporated Law Society of Ireland*, 101, 119.

41. See, in general, O. Kahn-Freund and B. Hepple: *Laws Against Strikes*, 7.

42. Note that, unlike under s. 7, reinstatement under s. 5 can be by the original employer, a successor of his, or an associated employer.

43. In the constitutional sense, the right to strike would seem to be a personal right protected by Article 40, s. 3 sub-s. 1 although it has not been analysed in any depth and the recent Supreme Court decision in *Talbot (Ire.) Ltd. v. Merrigan & Others* (unreported, 1 May 1981) may render the right virtually meaningless in future. The right of workers 'to deal with and dispose of their . . . labour as they will without interference, unless such interference be made legitimate by law' was first referred to by Budd J. in *Brendan Dunne Ltd. v. Fitzpatrick and Others* [1958] IR 29, 34 but only by a generous extension of the words used could this right be taken to include a right to strike. More to the point were the *obiter dicta* of Kingsmill Moore J. in *Educational Co. of Ireland v. Fitzpatrick* [1961] IR 345, 397. He described the 'right to dispose of one's labour and to withdraw it' as a fundamental right. It was a right which the judge did not see to have been adversely affected by anything within the intendment of the Constitution. But a right to strike was doubted in *Crowley and Others v. Ireland and Others* (Supreme Court unreported, 1 October 1979). If such a right did exist, said O'Higgins C.J., 'it was not a right which could be exercised for the purpose of frustrating, infringing or destroying the constitutional rights of others'. These words apparently do not perceive as worthy of consideration the central point that strike action is used as an economic or political weapon. If it could not be so used, it would be a pointless phenomenon of industrial relations (see

as 'extremely obscure and technical'.[44] Its technicalities have not been explored on the very rare occasions section 5(2) has been invoked.[45]

During the Committee Stage of the Unfair Dismissals Bill in Dáil Éireann, the Minister for Labour explained the intention behind section 5(2):

> '. . . that no individual victimisation would result from a return to work after a trade dispute'

further

> '[the] section would cover a number of employees who would collectively feel themselves victims of unfair treatment at the hands of the employer.'[46]

Sir Fitzjames Stephen: *The History of the Criminal Law of England*, Vol. III, 219). The Chief Justice delivered a minority judgment in *Crowley* but it is clear from *Talbot, supra,* that the Court shares his view on the right to strike. The full implications of *Talbot* are not yet known (the Supreme Court judgment is not available to the parties) but from newspaper reports, and a transcript made available to the author, courtesy of ICTU, it seems the Court held that, notwithstanding the Trade Disputes Act, 1906, a striking body or bodies must operate within the constitutional framework and the constitutional guarantee in Article 40. Innocent persons cannot be damnified as a result of industrial action: a trade dispute will not be protected in so far as it affects dealers who have no dispute with anyone or the owners of vehicles not in dispute or who, because of an embargo, cannot get their vehicles serviced where they are entitled to such service under contract. Until the law is clearly stated, it is preferable, in the author's opinion, to regard Kingsmill Moore J.'s *dicta* above as authoritative. For what is necessarily a dated account, seeJ.C.B. McCartney: 'Strike Law and the Constitution of Eire' in *Labour Relations and the Law*, 154.

In relation to international law, the right to strike is found in the UN International Convention on Economic, Social and Cultural Rights adopted in 1966. In addition Ireland is a party to the European Social Charter which in Art. 6 recognises the right of workers to strike in cases of conflicts of interests. In 1955, as a member of the ILO, Ireland ratified ILO Convention No. 87 (1948) concerning Freedom of Association and Protection of the Right to Organise and Convention No. 98 (1949) concerning the Application of the Principles of the Right to Organise and to Bargain Collectively. The Governing Body's Committee on Freedom of Association has frequently reiterated that, although there is no express reference to strike action in the two Conventions, they impliedly guarantee a right to strike: *Freedom of Assembly: Digest of Decisions of the Freedom of Assembly Committee of the Governing Body of the ILO:* Geneva, 1972, paras. 240, 292. See the article by Dr. P. O'Higgins: 'The Right to Strike — Some International Reflections' in *Studies in Labour Law* (ed. J.R. Carby-Hall), 110, which contains some disturbing reflections on s. 62 of the EPCA, the equivalent of Ireland's s. 5 UDA.

44. N. Wayne: *Labour Law in Ireland*, 93.
45. E.g., *Tara Mines Ltd. v. Duffy* UD 50/1980.
46. *Dáil Debates*, Vol. 296 (25 Jan. 1977) Cols. 59 and 60. The philosophy behind the equivalent s. 62 of the British EPCA, 1978, may be contrasted. The section was prompted by the need to give the employer protection when his business

Contrary to the widely held belief, particularly on the part of trade unionists, that s. 5(2) concerns automatically unfair dismissal, s. 6(1) of the Act of 1977 applies, i.e., dismissal in the circumstances of s. 5(2) is deemed to be unfair unless, having regard to all the circumstances, there are substantial grounds justifying the dismissal. Employers, it is true, are no less vulnerable than employees to victimisation on account of industrial action. But the present law is unsatisfactory in as much as it calls upon the enforcing authorities to consider the merits of collective industrial disputes (contrast EPCA, s. 62, below). Moreover, freedom to strike, although it may be exercised in what amounts to a very complicated situation in law and in fact, should be distinguished from the various incidents or results which may accompany strike action. If section 5(2) were to embody a conclusive presumption of unfairness, that would not preclude the possibility of an employer dismissing workers because they used unlawful acts or methods in connection with strike action.

It has been argued that there is a contrary principle implied in s. 5(2), i.e., that non-selective or non-discriminatory dismissals in circumstances of strike or other industrial action are completely outside the jurisdiction of the Act. It is, once more, commonly but erroneously believed that the sub-section affords complete liberty for an employer to dismiss all of his workforce during a dispute and that the question of unfair dismissal arises only where work is resumed and the employer is selective in his treatment of the employees. The EPCA, s. 62, provides for an exclusion of jurisdiction where all the workforce have been dismissed. Its wording could not be more unequivocal, however: unless there is discrimination in dismissal or in the reinstatement or re-engagement of workers taking part in strike or other industrial action the Act declares that:

'an industrial tribunal shall not determine whether the dismissal was fair or unfair.'[47]

---

is faced with ruin by industrial action. As Sir Hugh Griffiths put it in *Heath v. Longman Ltd.* [1973] 2 All E.R. 1228 at 1230-'1: '[it provides] a measure of protection to an employer if his business is faced with ruin by a strike. It enables him in these circumstances, if he cannot carry on the business without a labour force, to dismiss the labour force on strike; to take on another labour force without the stigma of it being an unfair dismissal'. In *Thompson v. Eaton* [1976] 3 All E.R. 383, 388 Phillips J. expressed a similar view saying that, but for the legislation 'an employer must either submit to the demands of the strikers, go out of business, or pay compensation for unfair dismissal'. In reality it is unlikely that an employer will wish to dismiss all those on strike, or that many strikes threaten an employer with ruin.

47. Section 62 (1) and (2) of the EPCA, 1978, enacts that where an employee claims he has been unfairly dismissed and at the date of dismissal (a) the employer was conducting or instituting a lock-out, or (b) the employee was taking part in a strike or other industrial action, an industrial tribunal shall not determine whether the

The belief that section 5(2) of the Irish Act is similarly restrictive may spring in some measure from a mistaken assumption that section 5(2) re-echoes section 62 of the British Act. In fact there is a significant difference between the wording of the two provisions. Section 5(2) of the Unfair Dismissals Act deems it unfair for an employer selectively to dismiss in an industrial dispute situation — no more, no less. If one bears in mind, not only Ireland's obligations in international law, but also that by striking, a person may be exercising a fundamental constitutional right,[48] it would be *ultra vires* the Constitution to grant an immunity to employers who penalised their entire workforce by dismissing each and every employee who had taken part in strike action.[49] It is clear that s. 6(1) applies to non-selective dismissals, and that they come within the Act's jurisdiction.

The strike in s. 5 is solely the phenomenon of industrial relations. It retains its traditional link with the processes of collective bargaining. Consumer or political strikes are not covered. 'Strike' is defined in s. 1 to mean:

> 'the cessation of work by any number or body of employees acting in combination or a concerted refusal or a refusal under a common understanding of any number of employees to continue to work for an employer, in consequence of a dispute, done as a means of compelling the employer or any employee or body of employees, or to aid other employees in compelling their employer or any employee or body of employees to accept or not to accept terms or conditions of or affecting employment.'[50]

---

dismissal was fair or unfair unless it is shown (a) that one or more relevant employees of the same employer have not been dismissed or (b) that one or more such employees have been offered re-engagement, and that the employee concerned has not been offered re-engagement. The statute does not say the dismissal shall be deemed fair or unfair, rather the question shall not even be considered. See R. Kidner: 'Dismissing Strikers' (1978) Vol. 128. N.L.J. 203; J. McMullen: 'Unfair Dismissal and the Merits of an Industrial Dispute' (1980) 130 NLJ 670.

48. Fn. 43 *ante.*

49. Policy considerations are also relevant although they fall outside the present compass.

50. See a similar definition in section 6 of the Redundancy Payments Act, 1967. (Note that a strike is not defined for purposes of s. 62 of the EPCA.) The statutory protection for strikers in section 5 has rendered almost academic the lengthy arguments about whether the effect of strike notice at common law is to terminate the contract of employment or 'merely to suspend the contract' as suggested by Lord Denning in *Morgan v. Fry* [1968] 2 Q.B. 710, and supported by Walsh J. and the majority of the Irish Supreme Court in *Becton Dickinson Ltd. v. Lee* [1973] I.R. 1, 35. Before *Morgan v. Fry*, see Devlin and Donovan L. JJ. in *Rookes v. Barnard* [1963] 1 QB 623, 682-'83; [1964] AC 1204 (House of Lords); Denning L.J. in *Stratford v. Lindley* [1965] A.C. 307, 322. The doctrine of suspension has now been severely

If strike notice is expressed as notice to terminate the contract and is of sufficient length it will bring the contract to an end. A grave disadvantage of giving strike notice in this form is that the worker will not be protected by the Unfair Dismissals Act. The Act is inapplicable where an employee has effectively resigned (unless he is able to show that the employer has broken the contract and his resignation is in response to this breach). A strike starts from the moment an employee makes his intentions clear to his employer.[51]

'Industrial action' is defined in section 1 to mean:

> 'lawful action taken by any number or body of employees acting in combination or under a common understanding, in consequence of a dispute, as a means of compelling their employers or any employee or body of employees, or to aid other employees in compelling their employer or any employee or body of employees, to accept or not to accept terms or conditions of or affecting employment.'[52]

It is impossible to explain why 'lawfulness' should be required for industrial action and not for strikes. 'Lawfulness' may refer to the consequences of industrial action or to the acts *per se*. The Act is not explicit as to the sense which is intended. Several different branches of the law — criminal law, contract, constitutional law, tort — may be

---

doubted in Britain and a more reasonable approach adopted by the EAT in *Simmons v. Hoover Ltd.* [1977] I.C.R. 61.

See X. Blanc-Jouvan: 'The Effect of Industrial Action on the Status of the Individual Employee' in *Industrial Conflict — A Comparative Legal Survey* 176; P. O'Higgins: 'Strike Notices: Another Approach' (1973) 2 *Industrial Law Journal* 152-'7; Lord Denning: *The Discipline of Law*, 180-2.

51. *Winnet v. Seamark Bros. Ltd.* (1978) EAT 695/77.

52. In Britain, industrial action is not defined. It is generally held open to complainants to argue that 'lawful action' by employees is not encompassed by s. 62 of the EPCA. There, industrial action applies to action short of a strike, such as picketing within the works or a collective refusal to obey instructions to work on a particular machine: *Thompson v. Eaton Ltd.* [1976] 2 All E.R. 383; [1976] ICR 336. It also applies to an unlawful go-slow, work to rule, or ban on overtime: *Derving v. Kilvington* (1973) 8 ITR 266. The Industrial Relations Act, 1971, defined 'irregular industrial action short of a strike' as action involving a breach of contract; neither the phrase nor its definition were retained in TULRA. The fact that TULRA did not incorporate a similar definition for 'other industrial action' does not necessarily mean, according to some writers, that a similar distinction between lawful and unlawful action cannot be read into TULRA. The earlier definition was omitted; it was not replaced by a different definition. Until Parliament provides a positive definition of 'other industrial action', rejecting the former definition, it has been argued that complainants may contend that 'lawful action' by employees is not encompassed by s. 62: see S.D. Anderman: *The Law of Unfair Dismissal* 179.

involved in assessing lawfulness.[53] Statute law is frequently relevant.[54] Given the ambiguity of the definition in section 1, the sort of industrial action likely to be described as 'lawful' is very limited indeed. In *Power and Others v. National Corrugated Products,*[55] which is considered below, it was argued that the dismissed workers did not come within section 5 because their industrial action, namely, a sit-in, constituted unlawful action, but the EAT turned a blind eye to this argument.

British caselaw deals with a number of issues which could be germane to the operation of section 5(2) of the Irish Act.[56] On the question of selectiveness, for instance, the House of Lords in *Stock v. Frank Jones*[57] declared that, in deciding whether employers had picked and chosen, all those who 'had taken part in' the strike or industrial action, not just those still taking part at the date of dismissal, should be considered. It is irrelevant that some strikers may have been taken back before others.[58] If an employer warns strikers that they will be dismissed unless they return by a certain date, and if, say, two return but the rest remain on strike and are dismissed, section 5(2) could be invoked by the dismissed employees: the workers who were taken back were nevertheless workers who 'took part in' the strike. This may put an employer in a difficult position since, if he issues an ultimatum that the strikers must return or be dismissed, the ultimatum is valueless if even one of the strikers returns. It would then be impossible for him fairly to dismiss the remainder (within section 5(2)).[59]

The reasonableness of dismissal in circumstances involving strike action is likely to present interpretative problems. In the British case of *Cruikshank v. Hobbs*[60] for example, which arose out of the Newmarket Stable lads' strike of 1975, the overall reasonableness of the dismissal had to be determined in accordance with the then relevant legislative provision, schedule 1 of the Trade Union and Labour Relations Act, 1974. The employer dismissed five of the six strikers for redundancy and the question was whether it was unfair in accordance with the relevant legislation to select those strikers for redund-

53. See article by this author, page 212, fn. 40, *ante*, 121.

54. E.g., Conspiracy and Protection of Property Act, 1875; Electricity (Supply) Act, 1927; Offences against the State Act, 1939. For further detail see the article above.

55. UD 336/1980.

56. One must remember that s. 5(2) of the UDA, 1977, does not involve a conclusive presumption of unfairness. Contrast this with the stark exclusion of jurisdiction found in s. 62 of the EPCA, 1978.

57. [1978] ICR 347.

58. *Stock v. Frank Jones (Tipton) Ltd.* [1978] ICR 347.

59. Ways of neutralising the decision are suggested by H.G. Collins in (1979) ILJ 109-10.

60. [1977] ICR 725.

ancy. The EAT rejected the submission that striking was irrelevant to the issue of selection for redundancy on the grounds (i) that the strike might have contributed to the need for redundancies; and (ii) that if the strike had been long enough there might be technical or administrative difficulties in taking the men back; and (iii) that to take back strikers and dismiss those who had remained at work would cause friction, impairing the efficiency of the undertaking. Accordingly, by a majority, the Tribunal held the dismissals fair.[61] The Irish case of *Power and Others v. National Corrugated Products*[62] may be contrasted. There, one hundred and twenty-eight employees were dismissed for taking part in a sit-in. The EAT's decision is not specific in regard to the legislation. It held by a unanimous decision that the dismissals were unfair "within the meaning" of the Act. If, as seems reasonable, the EAT's determination was based on s. 5(2), then not only did it not operate a conclusive presumption of fairness within the contrary implied meaning of s. 5(2) (all employees taking part in the sit-in had been dismissed) but it interpreted reasonableness in the same broad way it has been interpreted in relation to individual dismissal. The tribunal took into account the fact that management made no serious effort to contact the chief claimant's union during the "sit-in"; that the employer's action in issuing dismissal notices prior to a union meeting to discuss the sit-in was 'inconsiderate and irresponsible'; that the decision to dismiss the claimants came from a person whom the EAT felt was not involved sufficiently to make such a decision without consultation. At the same time, the claimants' action in participating in the 'sit-in' without their union's advice, was found to be unjustified and they were held to have contributed to their own dismissals.

Lest there should be any doubt, the British EAT held in *Wilkins & Others v. Cantrell & Cochrane (Great Britain) Ltd.*[63] that the mere act of going on strike did not amount to a sufficient indication by an employee that he was treating the contract as having been terminated by the employer's repudiation. The following extract from *Wilkins* was cited with approval by Talbot J. in *Marsden & Others v. Fairey Stainless Ltd.*:[64]

61. *Cruikshank's* case is perhaps unique in that someone allegedly had to be dismissed and the choice was between strikers, returned strikers, and those who had stayed at work. It may not have been unreasonable to select strikers over workers who remained but this is no argument for suggesting that it is reasonable to dismiss a person who has been on strike.
62. Fn. 55 *ante.*
63. [1978] IRLR 483; cf. the earlier *Thompson v. Eaton Ltd.* [1976] ICR 336.
64. [1979] IRLR 103, 105 (EAT). On the facts before the EAT it was held that there was no evidence that the strike had been engineered by the employers in order to get rid of the employees.

'Even if the employers had been in fundamental breach of contract by requiring the employees to drive vehicles which were overloaded [which was alleged in the case before him] the act of going out on strike could not be held to be a sufficient indication by an employee that he is treating the contract not only as capable of being repudiated but as one which has been broken and which he, therefore, regards as at an end. The point of a strike is so that the existing contract can be put right, so that grievances can be remedied, so that management will agree to the demands. The law makes it plain that going on strike does not terminate the contract. Rather, as was established in *Simmons v. Hoover Ltd.*,[65] it gives the employer a right to regard the conduct of the employee as a breach of contract and to dismiss him.'

Although Irish law does not follow the approach in *Simmons'* case,[66] the reality of the parties' intentions supports Talbot J.s' view.

65. [1977] QB 284; [1977] ICR 61; [1976] 2 WLR 901; [1977] 1 All ER 775.
66. See fn. 50 *ante*.

CHAPTER NINE

A Final Drawing Together of Strands and Trends

A. The Three Jurisdictions Contrasted

'To men dependent for their daily existence on continuous employment, the protection of their means of livelihood from confiscation or encroachment appears as fundamental a basis of the social order as it does to owners of land. What both parties claim is security and continuity of livelihood – that maintenance of the "established expectation" which is the "condition precedent" of civilized life'.[1]

This study has attempted to discover how far, in the Webbs' terminology, Irish law maintains the 'established expectation', the 'condition precedent' of civilised life. It has sought to analyse and to compare the three avenues of redress available to a worker whose means of livelihood have been confiscated abruptly or without lawful cause by his employer.

As a first option, an aggrieved employee may seek redress under the Irish Constitution. This jurisdiction introduces fundamentally different considerations into the law on termination of employment as between Ireland and Britain. Beneath the surface of the Constitution lies a vast and untapped source of individual employment law. So far there is only one example of dismissal recorded in the *Irish Reports* where an employer's actions have been held to be in breach of an employee's constitutional rights. But there exists a sufficiently developed constitutional jurisprudence to enable the boundaries of this form of action to be drawn up or at least hazarded. Chapter two describes the sensitivity and flexibility of the constitutional jurisdiction. Throughout, it has been illustrated how, in the ultimate, the Constitution informs every aspect of Irish law, both enacted and received.

The common law is of particular significance in vindicating the rights of office-holders, of persons whose employment is regulated by statute, and of workers who are excluded from the protection of the Unfair Dismissals Act. These categories are not exclusive. Workers who are entitled to invoke the Act may prefer instead to seek redress before the civil courts. By far the most important remedy for ordinary

1. S. and B. Webb: *Industrial Democracy* 566.

workers is damages and, unlike its statutory equivalent, there is no limit on the amount of compensation that may be awarded. Office-holders and workers whose employment is regulated by statute may seek more far-reaching remedies, such as a declaration or one of the prerogative orders. The common law is therefore of considerable significance and the diminutive number of reported cases before the superior courts cannot detract from this. At most, two or three cases are reported each year concerning dismissal. Natural justice tends to be their dominant theme.

Various conceptual and doctrinal problems were outlined in chapters three and five deriving from the pivotal role of the contract model in the employment relationship. The move to a contract model may be congruent with economic theory but its assumptions and disregard of other factors such as the realities of hiring and firing, not to mention the inequality of bargaining power between the parties, render the model at odds with traditional contract notions. The contract model poses difficulties both for wrongful dismissal and for statutory unfair dismissal. It is further examined in the concluding section of this chapter.

The most vibrant source of litigation in Irish individual employment law is now the Unfair Dismissals Act. In recent times, several hundreds of claims have been decided annually by the Employment Appeals Tribunal. The literal explosion in the number of statutory claims proves dramatically how vital is the Act's protection. Before 1977, if a wrongfully dismissed worker sought redress, he had to contend with the cumbersome paraphanalia of common law proceedings, with the law's delays and the ineffectiveness, by and large, of its remedies. Above all he had to face the likelihood of very high costs. These were powerful deterrents and most employees took their grievances no further. The Unfair Dismissals Act introduced a remedial forum which was at once speedy,[2] informal and free. Under the Act — unlike at common law — much weight is attached to the casual and capacious element in an employer's decision to dismiss. An employer must have a reason for dismissal which is admissible under the Act. In addition, and more importantly, he must be capable of justifying his decision to dismiss, whatever the circumstances. Procedural justice is of the essence — it is finely balanced against substantive justice. If a worker is found to have been unfairly dismissed, he may be reinstated or re-engaged in his job or he may be awarded compensation.

The Unfair Dismissals Act is currently under review in the

---

2. The speed with which the Tribunal operates has been affected by the vast increase (75%) of cases referred to the Tribunal in 1980. It took approximately 18 weeks to hear an appeal on 31 December, 1980.

Department of Labour. Reforms to the Act, procedural,[3] substantive[4] and definitional,[5] have been suggested in the preceding chapters. Conceptually the Act is most defective when it attempts to define 'dismissal'. A second major weakness is to be found in its presumptions of fairness and unfairness. A re-assessment of the precise nature of these will open up a fresh and important debate on the policy of the Act. There are compelling reasons why some grounds for dismissal should be automatically unfair, e.g., where dismissal is for taking part in strike action or is connected with trade union membership or activities.

There are as yet no empirical studies as to the influence or effects

3. Some examples at random and bearing in mind the changes proposed by the ILO, (see *Report,* chapter five, fn. 4 *ante).* The effect of sections 2-4 is to exclude large numbers of employees from the Act's protection. A particular problem has emerged concerning temporary officers of a local authority who lie outside the scope of the Act and at the same time are not protected by Local Government Acts. Again, the statutory requirement of one year's continuous service for eligibility under the Act means that its operation is excluded for a large number of dismissals. A high proportion of dismissals occurs within the first few months of service. Insecurity of employment for some workers has actually increased on account of the Act. Firms tend to review staff records and 'tighten up' staff appraisal schemes as workers near the one-year mark. For those workers not excluded by the Act, the rigid time-limit for the initiation of proceedings in section 8 can be productive of injustice. The time-limit of six months might be retained but a 'let-out' provided in appropriate circumstances. The rather convoluted method of initiating a claim before the EAT in the first instance rather than before the Rights Commissioners might also be simplified.

4. Certain aspects of the remedies in section 7 involving procedure as well as substance require re-examination. For instance, a more precise method of computing compensation seems desirable. At the present time there is a discrepancy in approach between different divisions of the EAT. The same or similar items may be differently assessed or not assessed at all. In particular, pension and taxation issues need a more reasoned approach and the practice of deducting Social Welfare benefits operates unfairly to the advantage of an offending employer. The relationship between section 7(1) (c) and 7(2) (b), i.e., between compensation and deductions for contributory conduct, needs clearer elaboration in the Act. The EAT's decision in *McCabe's* case should be given statutory expression even though it has been upheld recently by the High Court. There is much, too, to be said for providing a basic award for all employees who have been adjudged unfairly dismissed and for whom compensation is held to be the appropriate remedy. *Inter alia,* this would avoid the so-called 100% deduction dilemma. More profoundly it would say something about the nature of an employee's interest in his job. Again, when ordering reinstatement the EAT in practice requires an employer to treat an employee as if he had benefited from any improvement in the terms and conditions of his employment from the date of dismissal. It would be preferable to spell this out in section 7. Lastly, the engagement of a 'permanent' replacement has not influenced the Tribunal against awarding reinstatement but it would be well to give statutory force to this in section 7.

5. Apart from a redefinition of dismissal referred to in the text, other redefinitions are desirable, e.g., of industrial action (section 5) and there is no reason why a uniform meaning should not be given to 'reinstatement' and 're-engagement' in sections 5 and 7.

of the Act in Ireland[6] but trends may be detected from the *Annual Reports* of the EAT. It would obviously be premature to draw conclusions, hard, fast or otherwise, from these. Nonetheless they merit brief attention.

(1) *Trends in EAT practice since 1977*

(i) *Resort to the EAT*

An interesting feature to emerge from the *Annual Reports* is that the Tribunal is being approached more and more as a 'court of first instance'. In the beginning the Rights Commissioners were frequently resorted to but in recent years this had not been the case. In 1977, 82 cases were heard (as opposed to decided) by the EAT under the Act; about 45% of these arose as a result of Rights Commissioners' recommendations. In 1978 approximately 10% of the cases submitted to the EAT were appeals by workers or employers against recommendations of Rights Commissioners. In about 1 out of every 10 appeals the EAT rejected or varied the Rights Commissioner's findings. The following years roughly the same percentage of appeals from Rights Commissioners' recommendations came before the EAT. The bulk of these were by employers. Very few were rejected or varied. These appeals represented between 30% and 40% of the total number of recommendations made by the Rights Commissioners. This figure compares most unfavourably with the number of Rights Commissioners' recommendations annually appealed to the Labour Court under the Industrial Relations Act 1969 (always below 10%).[7] The number of recommendations issued by each Commissioner under the Unfair Dismissals Act in the years 1977-'79 is shown in the following table:

---

6. Unlike in Britain. See, e.g., K. Williams and D. Lewis 'The aftermath of tribunal reinstatement and re-engagement' DES Research Paper No. 23 (June 1981). But Ireland is not totally devoid of studies concerning the Unfair Dismissals Act. In November, 1981, a *Review of the Unfair Dismissals Act* was published by the Analysis Section of the Department of Finance (T. Gaffney). The study examines the practical operation of the Act from mid-1977 to 1980. Summary data on claims and their outcomes are presented together with the results of a survey of the main characteristics of both claimants and respondents. The views of a small number of unions, individual employers and their representative organisations were also sought with regard to the administration, effects and desired (technical) amendments to the Act. The *Review* was published too late to enable reference to be made to it in the text.

7. See *Annual Reports* of the Labour Court, published by the Government Publications Office. For 1978 the percentage was c.8%; for 1979 it was c.7%

Year	Mr. C. Murphy	Mr. W. Farrell	Mr. T. Cahill
1977	60	14	11
1978	110	22	40
1979	95	10	31

(Reply to Dáil Question No. 306, 1980(22 April 1980) Minister for Labour.)

The relevant figures for the EAT during those years are 16, 151 and 331 respectively. There are no figures concerning the Rights Commissioners to compare with the EAT's number of claims for 1980 (754). It was suggested in an earlier chapter that one reason for the apparent unpopularity of the Rights Commissioner's justice may be the manner in which it is dispensed. The Commissioners operate behind closed doors, their recommendations are available only to the parties. In short, a claimant has little idea what to expect.

(ii) *Number of dismissals adjudged unfair*

From figures provided in *Trade Union Information*[8] it seems the number of dismissals adjudged unfair by the Rights Commissioners has been constantly just below fifty per cent. This may be contrasted with EAT figures since 1977. In the first half year of the Act's operation, the number of claims allowed for unfair dismissal represented 25% of the grand total of decided cases. In 1978 when the number of claims began to increase it rose to 44% and in 1979 it was just under fifty per cent. In 1980 it dropped to 37%.

(iii) *Legal representation*

The *Annual Reports* of the EAT express a fear, no doubt well founded, that increased legal representation will slow down proceedings under the Act and make cases generally more complex. In 1978, 81% of the claimants under the Act were represented, less than half by lawyers. The following year the total number of represented claimants fell to 64% (this must be seen against a steep rise in the number of cases overall) but among that percentage the number of claimants legally represented rose to 55%. One reason for the increase in legal representation is a growing awareness that legal issues may arise in the course of proceedings under the Act. A more important reason is because dismissal complaints, more often than not, come from work areas that are unorganised or poorly organised by trade unions. In any event, trade unions tend to be selective about the cases they take up — although the basis of their selectivity is not always clear. Because legal representation is becoming more frequent, it is regrettable that free legal aid is not available for claimants

8. Summer, 1980, 21.

before the EAT. Unavailability of legal representation is one of the major reasons why hearings of the EAT have to be postponed.[9]

(iv) *Withdrawal of claims*

The amount of cases withdrawn is increasing. In 1978 about one quarter of the cases listed for hearing under the Act was withdrawn, mostly prior to the hearing. The following year almost 28% were withdrawn, slightly more during rather than before the hearing. The EAT allows a minimum of half a day to each case. Withdrawals (as well as postponements at short notice and adjournments for lack of essential evidence) cause very serious disruptions in the schedule of the Tribunal and add to the workload of the Secretariat. Although booklets are available about the EAT and about the Act the evidence is that claimants are not always as informed as they might be about the Act's precise requirements. In addition, claims may be lodged under the Act which are intended only as a threat or warning to particular employers. Or workers may lack the necessary courage to present their grievance once a claim is actually listed for hearing. It would be worthwhile to analyse the causes of withdrawal. There may be a case to be made for the introduction of a screening process by the EAT (a pre-hearing assessment as in Britain)[10] or for additional staff to provide information for unrepresented claimants at every stage of the proceedings.

(v) *The parties*

Valuable items of statistical information are not found in the *Annual Reports* of the EAT. These relate to the type of claimant and respondent involved in cases under the Act. In the course of this work a random study was carried out of 400 determinations issued during the years 1978 and 1979. The study produced what is here proffered as no more than a crude indication of trends. First, concerning the occupations of claimants, white collar and manual employees were represented broadly as their proportion in the total population would suggest.[11] Certain characteristics of the sample, such as sex, proved

---

9. For representation at sittings in 1980 see Appendix VII.
10. Industrial Tribunals (Rules of Procedure) Regulations 1980 (S.I. 1980 no. 884), schedule 1, Rule 6. A tribunal may at any time before the hearing assess the contents of the originating 'application, and other papers, and if it considers the application unlikely to succeed, it may indicate that if the application is not withdrawn the party in question may have an order for costs made against him at the hearing.
11. See *Economic Review and Outlook* Summer 1980 and recent revised estimate of the workforce (published in December, 1980, by the Central Statistics Office, Dublin).

interesting. Women were adequately represented (30%) in EAT determinations.[12] This is significant as the main industries in which women work are not well organised from a trade union point of view. Women workers are concentrated in small industries: 70% are in three areas, textile, footwear and food processing — and the bulk of claims before the EAT comes from small firms or industries.

Small firms (i.e., those employing 50 employees or less) tended to be heavily represented. Almost 60% of the firms represented before the EAT in the sample selected fall into this category. This no doubt reflects the relative insecurity of the small firm where it is less likely that employees will be covered by formal joint dismissal procedures. Also it is a reflection of the fact that where unions are well organised there will be fewer applications of unfair dismissal.

(2) *The EAT: consistency or finality?*

Although it is true that:

'A tribunal must not pursue consistency at the expense of individual cases'[13]

at the same time such a body's discretion cannot and should not be totally without reins. Clearly, anything savouring of formalism in the narrow sense would be undesirable but the fact is that labour law — and particularly the subject under discussion — possesses all the major attributes of other law subjects, possibly in more dynamic form.[14] Irish unfair dismissal law has an accessible hierarchy of jurisdictions — albeit with unclear edges but the need to attend to these is quite another issue: it has a growing personnel, and, although not yet realised, a fertile source of complex legislative material. In this sense, in providing a service which is informal and comparatively free, the Rights Commissioners and the EAT do away with much of the procedural trappings of the law courts. But it would be unrealistic, undesirable and wrong to argue that the EAT is totally unlike a court. How else can it interpret the Unfair Dismissals Act except in legal fashion? Should it do so in any other way? The Act itself purports to consist of straightforward provisions and to a greater or lesser extent the Oireachtas may be taken to have made its

12. Women constitute approximately 28% of the total workforce in Ireland; footnote 11 above.
13. *Merchandise Transport Ltd. v. B.T.C.* [1962] 2 Q.B. 173, 193 *per* Devlin L.J.
14. R. Munday: 'Tribunal Lore: Legalism and the Industrial Tribunals' (1981) ILJ 146, 158.

intentions plain. But previous chapters have illustrated how the Act of 1977 contains many ambiguous provisions, many points calling for interpretation or construction. The Act is not without interpretative difficulties when it comes to complex legal matters concerning the contract of employment, frustration, breach of contract, repudiation, constructive dismissal and the like. Again, problems arise where its provisions correspond to but are not identical with those in the relevant British legislation. Equally, parts of the Act, although drafted and enacted in clear terms, could prove difficult to apply to the facts of individual cases. It is surely unacceptable that each case should depend solely upon its own facts.

At present the hallmark of EAT determinations is finality rather than consistency. This stamp needs to be resisted. When the absence of a code of practice is borne in mind, the case for clear and reasoned decisions of the EAT scarcely needs to be made. The EAT's *ad hoc* decision-making is rendered more vulnerable by the lack of an effective review mechanism for its determinations. The provision of such a mechanism must rank as a priority in any future reform of the Act. The Circuit Court could — indeed should — exercise a useful function in promoting consistency in much the same way as the British EAT does for industrial tribunals. Unfortunately, however, the Court has not done so to date. At the very least, the Act should be amended so as to enable the EAT, at any stage during its proceedings, to state a case for the opinion of the High Court on a point of law. Chapter five recorded serious criticisms of EAT practice, all of which contribute to the erroneous view, not uncommon in Ireland, that the Oireachtas in the Unfair Dismissals Act created a species of layman's law which can be safely administered by the EAT without guiding legal principle or precedent of any sort. The very concepts and language of the Act, the nature of the claims and the nature of lawyers all give the lie to that argument.

B. Whither the Contract Model?

Throughout this work, the contract of employment has been shown to underpin every major aspect of dismissal law. Its central role begs so many questions, and the area is so replete with confusion, that it would be difficult — if not remiss — to conclude this treatise without a brief attempt to signpost a way out of the morass. Anyone writing in or researching dismissal law sooner or later encounters a serious obstacle. Judicial and academic authorities alike have failed to examine at all fully the structure of the mutual obligations in the contract of employment.

It is not surprising, in the light of this, that some studies have rejected contract law altogether as a method for structuring employment relationships, based as it is on market theory and an assumption that the employment relationship is an exchange of a commodity, that is, labour, for compensation.[15] While it cannot be denied that many drawbacks exist in the contract model, the same pessimism is not adopted here. If analysed from a structural point of view, it is submitted that the contract model is capable of accounting both for transactional and relational aspects of employment. There is an increasing tendency in the courts to protect values other than freedom to bargain and to differentiate remedies according to the identity of the parties.

The basic problem is whether the law looks upon the contract of employment as more than an exchange of work for remuneration and, if so, what is the nature of this further element? In the United States Professor Corbin has written:

> 'That portion of the field of law that is classified and described as the law of contracts attempts the realisation of reasonable expectations that have been induced by the making of a promise ... [A]n understanding of many of the existing rules, and a determination of their effectiveness, require a lively consciousness of their underlying purpose.'[16]

The additional or further element referred to is intrinsically bound up with the parties' reasonable expectations.[17] It is necessary if the law is to protect an employee's interest in the continuance of his employment and remuneration and an employer's interest in the continuance of the employment contract.[18]

The additional element just mentioned, which of necessity enters the law of statutory unfair dismissal also, concerns the relationship as distinct from the contract of employment — the contract, that is, as traditionally understood. The 'relationship' is obviously something over and above the cluster of exchanges as to work and wages between the parties themselves.[19] It is not a solely personal,

---

15. E.g., D. M. Beatty: 'Labour is Not a Commodity' in *Studies in Contract Law* (B.J. Reiter and J. Swan, eds.) 313. Contrast K. Swinton: 'Contract Law and the Employment Relationship: The Proper Forum for Reform' *ibid.*, 358.

16. *Corbin on Contracts* Vol. 1, 1.

17. See Professors Swan and Reiter: 'Contracts and the Protection of Reasonable Expectations' *op. cit.*, fn. 15 *ante*, 1.

18. The application of general principles of contract tends to obscure this crucial element: M. R. Freedland: *The Contract of Employment*, 19-20.

19. 'Work' and 'wages' are equivocal concepts in themselves, deriving their substance and specificity in any one instance from the particular contract in which the so-called exchange takes place. Prof. Corbin points out that it was always misleading to refer to employment as 'a relation' or to a contract of employment as 'a relation' because this use involves the constant danger of an assumption that their

psychological, social or economic phenomenon — or any mixture of these — however much an assumption to that effect may have become common coin. It is capable of expression in legal terms.

The question, of course, is how? The short answer is: by a clearer, more precise understanding of the nature of the specific contract of employment, particularly its conditional implied promises. Further brief elucidation is called for.

Early contract law asserted that contracting parties, in the absence of an express condition, were bound to perform their part of the contract regardless of whether the other party had performed or would perform his part. Following the judgment of Lord Mansfield in *Kingston v. Preston*,[20] even where there was no express condition, it was possible to imply a condition into an agreement making the performance of one promise dependant upon the prior performance of the other 'where the sense and meaning of the parties demanded it'. In the contract of employment it is important to ascertain the nature of the breach that can be assigned on repudiation. It may be contended as a result of *Laird v. Pim*,[21] that the common understanding of the parties in a bilateral contract, such as the contract of employment, is that one party's promise to perform is conditional on that party having received the other party's promised performance, i.e., on the consideration becoming executed. In other words, an employer is bound to pay his employee's wages only if the employee has performed his services. The performance of one promise is a condition of the duty to perform the other. In the current state of the law the obligation to work precedes that to pay wages. But these are not the only obligation in the contract of employment.

Freedland sees the structural issue concerning the contract of employment as how far the contract protects each party's interest in the due occurrence of the exchange or series of exchanges which form the basis of the contract.[22] The contract, as he sees it, has a two-tiered structure. At the first level there is an exchange of work and

---

content is fixed and uniform, that the component factors are always identical, *op. cit.*, fn. 16 *ante*, 674. Contractual obligations can be and are modified or limited by the parties in any one or more of a variety of ways. Legally speaking they are interdependent. The scope of the cluster of obligations is determined by noting those terms which have been expressly agreed, modified or excluded between the parties and those terms which are implied as a matter of statute law or otherwise, or from custom and practice, or as a result of incorporation from collective agreements. The formulation of these is 'a dynamic and cumulative process': Freedland *op. cit.* fn. 18 *ante*, 12.

20. (1773) 2 Doug. 689; 99 E.R. 436. See F. Dawson: 'Metaphors and Anticipatory Breach of Contract' [1981] CLJ 83 for a fresh examination of the ideas that lie beneath the action for wrongful repudiation.

21. (1841) 7 M & W 474; 151 ER 852.

22. *Op. cit.*, fn. 18 *ante*, 19-20.

remuneration. At the second, there is an exchange of mutual obligations for future performance. The second tier concerns the relationship of employment. Here, the promises to employ and to be
employed provide the employment arrangement with its stability and
continuity as a contract. Each promise is conditional: performance
depends on the readiness and willingness of the other party to
perform his counter-promise. Freedland's analysis is most useful,
particularly his presentation of the contract as having a two-tiered
structure. If the employer's promise to pay wages is conditional on
the employee performing the work, it is submitted that the employer
must, impliedly, promise to undertake not to prevent the employee
from becoming entitled to wages by wrongfully sending him away. In
turn, this undertaking makes sense only if it is impliedly conditional
upon the employee making himself available for the work concerned.
Otherwise the promises to pay and to work would be illusory. The
employer (or employee) could prevent any obligation from arising by
simply refusing work (or refusing to turn up for work). The contract
of employment would approximate to a unilateral contract. It would
seem to follow, and to be the most crucial feature in the second level
of the contract of employment, that each party impliedly promises
not to hinder or to prevent the other from complying with the
performance of one promise which is the condition of the duty to
perform the other. The principle that contracting parties impliedly
promise not to hinder or prevent compliance in this way is reasonably well established.[23] There is no reason why it should not be
extended to the effect that a wrongful refusal to perform, i.e., a mere
renunciation, hinders or prevents compliance with performance in the
way already mentioned.[24]

Wrongful dismissal cannot be understood without an analysis of
this sort. When an employer dismisses an employee he does not break
his promise to pay wages. For wages to become payable the
employee must show an executed consideration. The employer breaks
a separate promise when he wrongfully repudiates his obligations.
The wrong committed is not a failure to pay wages but a deprivation
of the employee's right to claim them. An employer's refusal to proceed with the contract entitles the employee to treat himself as
excused — the employer as defaulting party cannot enforce the
contract — and the employer is prevented from complying with the
implied undertaking of his right to claim the counter-performance.
For this breach, the employee is entitled to claim damages (not
wages). To maintain an action for wrongful dismissal, the employee

23. See Halsbury's *Laws of England*, Vol. 9, paras. 359, 518; Chitty: *The Law
of Contracts*, Vol. 1, paras. 788, 1491; Williston: *A Treatise on the Law of
Contracts* para. 1293A.
24. Dawson, *art. cit.* fn. 20 above, 97.

need show only that he was willing to perform and that he would have performed but for the repudiation. Because of the complicated struc ture of the employment relationship, of its conditional implied promises, it is possible to accommodate a theory of automatic termination in this area of law. The consequences of wrongful repudiation are no doubt correctly set out in the House of Lords' decision in *Photo Productions Ltd.*[25] but, as earlier remarked, the common law boot cannot be applied to every foot without some measurement or analysis. An understanding of the two-tier nature of the contract of employment makes it apparent that where one party is in breach of the implied promise not to hinder or prevent the innocent party from complying with the 'condition precedent' to his right to claim the counter-performance, such wrongful repudiation terminates the contract without the need for acceptance by the injured party. The language of acceptance cannot be applied unreflectively to the contract of employment.

Understandably, the courts are reluctant to implement dramatic revisions in the law but a re-evaluation of the precise application of contract principles to the employment relationship in the manner here suggested would not savour of innovation or unduly offend against traditional judicial reluctance to create new law. Undeniably, the most immediate need for a rethinking of the employment contract arises in the area of statutory unfair dismissal. Here a response is needed from the Oireachtas. The legislated solution can tailor the remedial mechanism more speedily than the judicial, with a maximum of certainty and a minimum of fuss. Of course the unorganised worker, unlike the employer group, is without lobbying power. But the Unfair Dismissals Act was passed mainly with the unorganised or poorly organised blue-collar and lower-status collar worker in mind. Clarification of the definition of 'dismissal' is no mere academic *desideratum*. It pertains to the very core of the legislation and should rank as a first priority in the current review of the Act.

25. [1980] 2 WLR 283; [1980] 1 All E.R. 556.

Unfair Dismissals Act, 1977

ARRANGEMENT OF SECTIONS

Section

1. Definitions.
2. Exclusions.
3. Dismissal during probation or training.
4. Dismissal during apprenticeship.
5. Dismissal by way of lock-out or for taking part in strike.
6. Unfair dismissal.
7. Redress for unfair dismissal.
8. Determination of claims for unfair dismissal.
9. Appeal from recommendation of rights commissioner.
10. Proceedings in Circuit Court for redress under Act.
11. Service of documents on bodies.
12. Provisions relating to winding up and bankruptcy.
13. Voidance of certain provisions in agreements.
14. Notice to employees of procedure for, and grounds of, dismissal.
15. Alternative remedies of employee.
16. Amendment of Act by order of Minister.
17. Regulations.
18. Employment Appeals Tribunal.
19. Repayment of monies paid under Redundancy Payments Acts, 1967 and 1973.
20. Amendment of First Schedule to Minimum Notice and Terms of Employment Act, 1973.
21. Expenses.
22. Short title and commencement.

Acts Referred to

Agriculture Act, 1931	1931, No. 8
Anti-Discrimination (Pay) Act, 1974	1974, No. 15
Companies Act, 1963	1963, No. 33
Defence Act, 1954	1954, No. 18
Industrial Relations Act, 1946	1946, No. 26
Industrial Relations Act, 1969	1969, No. 1
Industrial Training Act, 1967	1967, No. 5
Local Government Act, 1941	1941, No. 23
Minimum Notice and Terms of Employment Act, 1973	1973, No. 4
Preferential Payments in Bankruptcy (Ireland) Act, 1889	1889, c. 60
Redundancy Payments Act, 1967	1967, No. 21
Redundancy Payments Act, 1971	1971, No. 20
Vocational Education Act, 1930	1930, No. 29

UNFAIR DISMISSALS ACT, 1977

AN ACT TO PROVIDE FOR REDRESS FOR
EMPLOYEES UNFAIRLY DISMISSED FROM
THEIR EMPLOYMENT, TO PROVIDE FOR
THE DETERMINATION OF CLAIMS FOR
SUCH REDRESS BY RIGHTS COM-
MISSIONERS AND BY THE TRIBUNAL
ESTABLISHED, FOR THE PURPOSE OF
DETERMINING CERTAIN APPEALS, BY THE
REDUNDANCY PAYMENTS ACT, 1967, TO
PROVIDE THAT THAT TRIBUNAL SHALL BE
KNOWN AS THE EMPLOYMENT APPEALS
TRIBUNAL, TO MAKE PROVISION FOR
OTHER MATTERS CONNECTED WITH THE
MATTERS AFORESAID AND TO AMEND THE
MINIMUM NOTICE AND TERMS OF
EMPLOYMENT ACT, 1973. [*6th April, 1977.*]

BE IT ENACTED BY THE OIREACHTAS AS
FOLLOWS:

1.—In this Act—   Definitions

"contract of employment" means a contract of service or
of apprenticeship, whether it is express or implied and (if
it is express) whether it is oral or in writing;

"date of dismissal" means—

(*a*) where prior notice of the termination of the
     contract of employment is given and it
     complies with the provisions of that contract
     and of the Minimum Notice and Terms of
     Employment Act, 1973, the date on which
     that notice expires,

(*b*) where either prior notice of such termination is not
     given or the notice given does not comply with
     the provisions of the contract of employment
     or the Minimum Notice and Terms of
     Employment Act, 1973, the date on which
     such a notice would have expired, if it had

been given on the date of such termination and had been expressed to expire on the later of the following dates—

    (i) the earliest date that would be in compliance with the provisions of the contract of employment,

    (ii) the earliest date that would be in compliance with the provisions of the Minimum Notice and Terms of Employment Act, 1973,

(c) where a contract of employment for a fixed term expires without its being renewed under the same contract or, in the case of a contract for a specified purpose (being a purpose of such a kind that the duration of the contract was limited, but was, at the time of its making, incapable of precise ascertainment), there is a cesser of the purpose, the date of the expiry or cesser;

"dismissal", in relation to an employee, means—

    (a) the termination by his employer of the employee's contract of employment with the employer, whether prior notice of the termination was or was not given to the employee,

    (b) the termination by the employee of his contract of employment with his employer, whether prior notice of the termination was or was not given to the employer, in circumstances in which, because of the conduct of the employer, the employee was or would have been entitled, or it was or would have been reasonable for the employee, to terminate the contract of employment without giving prior notice of the termination to the employer, or

    (c) the expiration of a contract of employment for a fixed term without its being renewed under the same contract or, in the case of a contract for a specified purpose (being a purpose of such a kind that the duration of the contract was limited but was, at the time of its making, incapable of precise ascertainment), the cesser of the purpose;

"employee" means an individual who has entered into or works under (or, where the employment has ceased, worked under) a contract of employment and, in relation to redress for a dismissal under this Act, includes, in the case of the death of the employee concerned at any time following the dismissal, his personal representative;

"employer", in relation to an employee, means the person by whom the employee is (or, in a case where the employment has ceased, was) employed under a contract of employment and an individual in the service of a local authority for the purposes of the Local Government Act, 1941, shall be deemed to be employed by the local authority;

"industrial action" means lawful action taken by any number or body of employees acting in combination or under a common understanding, in consequence of a dispute, as a means of compelling their employers or any employee or body of employees, or to aid other employees in compelling their employer or any employee or body of employees, to accept or not to accept terms or conditions of or affecting employment;

"the minister" means the Minister for Labour;

"redundancy" means any of the matters referred to in paragraphs (*a*) to (*e*) of section 7 (2) of the Redundancy Payments Act, 1967, as amended by the Redundancy Payments Act, 1971;

"statutory apprenticeship" means an apprenticeship in a designated industrial activity within the meaning of the Industrial Training Act, 1967, and includes any apprenticeship in a trade to which an order, rule or notice referred to in paragraph (*a*) or (*b*) of section 49 (1) of that Act applies;

"strike" means the cessation of work by any number or body of employees acting in combination or a concerted refusal or a refusal under a common understanding of any number of employees to continue to work for an employer, in consequence of a dispute, done as a means of compelling their employer or any employee or body of employees, or to aid other employees in compelling their employer or any employee or body of employees, to accept or not to accept terms or conditions of or affecting employment;

"trade union" means a trade union which is the holder of a negotiation licence granted under the Trade Union Acts, 1941 and 1971;

"the Tribunal" means the Employment Appeals Tribunal established by the Redundancy Payments Act, 1967.

2.—(1) This Act shall not apply in relation to any of the following persons; *Exclusions.*

  (*a*) an employee (other than a person referred to in section 4 of this Act) who is dismissed, who, at the date of his dismissal, had less than one year's continuous service with the employer who dismissed him and whose dismissal does not result wholly or mainly from the matters referred to in section 6 (2) (*f*) of this Act,

  (*b*) an employee who is dismissed and who, on or before the date of his dismissal, has reached the normal retiring age for employees of the same employer in similar employment or who on that date was a person to whom by reason of his age the Redundancy Payments Acts, 1967 to 1973, did not apply,

  (*c*) a person who is employed by his spouse, father, mother, grandfather, grandmother, step-father, step-mother, son, daughter, grandson, granddaughter, step-son, step-daughter, brother, sister, half-brother or half-sister, is a member of his employer's household and whose place of employment is a private dwellinghouse or a farm in or on which both the employee and the employer reside,

(d) a person in employment as a member of the Defence Forces, the Judge Advocate-General, the chairman of the Army Pensions Board or the ordinary member thereof who is not an officer of the Medical Corps of the Defence Forces,

(e) a member of the Garda Síochána,

(f) a person (other than a person employed under a contract of employment) who is receiving a training allowance from or undergoing instruction by An Chomhairle Oiliúna or is receiving a training allowance from and undergoing instruction by that body,

(g) a person who is employed by An Chomhairle Oiliúna under a contract of apprenticeship,

(h) a person employed by or under the State other than persons standing designated for the time being under section 17 of the Industrial Relations Act, 1969,

(i) officers of a local authority for the purposes of the Local Government Act, 1941,

(j) officers of a health board, a vocational education committee established by the Vocational Education Act, 1930, or a committee of agriculture established by the Agriculture Act, 1931.

(2) This Act shall not apply in relation to—

(a) dismissal where the employment was under a contract of employment for a fixed term made before the 16th day of September, 1976, and the dismissal consisted only of the expiry of the term without its being renewed under the same contract, or

(b) dismissal where the employment was under a contract of employment for a fixed term or for a specified purpose (being a purpose of such a kind that the duration of the contract was limited but was, at the time of its making, incapable of precise ascertainment) and the dismissal consisted only of the expiry of the term without its being renewed under the said contract or the cesser of the purpose and the contract is in writing, was signed by or on behalf of the employer and by the employee and provides that this Act shall not apply to a dismissal consisting only of the expiry or cesser aforesiad.

(3) (*a*) This Act shall not apply in relation to the dismissal of an employee who, under the relevant contract of employment, ordinarily worked outside the State unless—

    (i) he was ordinarily resident in the State during the term of the contract, or

    (ii) he was domiciled in the State during the term of the contract, and the employer—

        (I) in case the employer was an individual, was ordinarily resident in the State, during the term of the contract, or

        (II) in case the employer was a body corporate or an unincorporated body of persons, had its principal place of business in the State during the term of the contract.

    (*b*) In this subsection "term of the contract" means the whole of the period from the time of the commencement of work under the contract to the time of the relevant dismissal.

(4) The First Schedule to the Minimum Notice and Terms of Employment Act, 1973, as amended by section 20 of this Act, shall apply for the purpose of ascertaining for the purposes of this Act the period of service of an employee and whether that service has been continuous.

3.—(1) This Act shall not apply in relation to the dismissal of an employee during a period starting with the commencement of the employment when he is on probation or undergoing training—

    (*a*) if his contract of employment is in writing, the duration of the probation or training is 1 year or less and is specified in the contract, or

    (*b*) if his contract of employment was made before the commencement of this Act and was not in writing and the duration of the probation or training is 1 year or less.

(2) This Act shall not apply in relation to the dismissal of an employee during a period starting with the commencement of the employment when he is undergoing training for the purpose of becoming qualified or registered, as the case may be, as a nurse, pharmacist, health inspector, medical laboratory technician, occupational therapist, physiotherapist, speech therapist, radiographer or social worker.

4.—This Act shall not apply in relation to the dismissal of a person who is or was employed under a statutory apprenticeship if the dismissal takes place within 6 months after the commencement of the apprenticeship or within 1 month after the completion of the apprenticeship.

5.—(1) The dismissal of an employee by way of a lockout shall be deemed, for the purposes of this Act, not to be an unfair dismissal if the employee is offered re-instatement or re-engagement as from the date of resumption of work.

(2) The dismissal of an employee for taking part in a strike or other industrial action shall be deemed, for the purposes of this Act, to be an unfair dismissal, if—

    (*a*) one or more employees of the same employer who took part in the strike or other industrial action were not dismissed for so taking part, or

(b) one or more of such employees who were dismissed for so taking part are subsequently offered re-instatement or re-engagement and the employee is not.

(3) References in paragraphs (a), (b) and (c) of section 7 (1) of this Act to dismissals include, in the case of employees dismissed by way of lock-out or for taking part in a strike or other industrial action, references to failure to offer them re-instatement or re-engagement in accordance with any agreement by the employer and by or on behalf of the employees, or, in the absence of such agreement, from the earliest date for which re-instatement or re-engagement was offered to the other employees of the same employer who were locked out or took part in the strike or other industrial action or to a majority of such employees.

(4) In this section a reference to an offer of re-instatement or re-engagement, in relation to an employee, is a reference to an offer (made either by the original employer or by a successor of that employer or by an associated employer) to ·re-instate that employee in the position which he held immediately before his dismissal on the terms and conditions on which he was employed immediately before his dismissal together with a term that the re-instatement shall be deemed to have commenced on the day of the dismissal, or to re-engage him, either in the position which he held immediately before his dismissal or in a different position which would be reasonably suitable for him, on such terms and conditions as are reasonable having regard to all the circumstances.

(5) In this section—

"lock-out" means an action which, in contemplation or furtherance of a trade dispute (within the meaning of the Industrial Relations Act, 1946), is taken by one or more employers, whether parties to the dispute or not, and which consists of the exclusion of one or more employees from one or more factories, offices or other places of work or of the suspension of work in one or more such places or of the collective, simultaneous or otherwise connected termination or suspension of employment of a group of employees;

"the original employer" means, in relation to the employee, the employer who dismisses the employee.

6.—(1) Subject to the provisions of this section, the dismissal of an employee shall be deemed, for the purposes of this Act, to be an unfair dismissal unless, having regard to all the circumstances, there were substantial grounds justifying the dismissal.

Unfair dismissal.

(2) Without prejudice to the generality of subsection (1) of this section, the dismissal of an employee shall be deemed, for the purposes of this Act, to be an unfair dismissal if it results wholly or mainly from one or more of the following:

> (a) the employee's membership, or proposal that he or another person become a member, of, or his engaging in activities on behalf of, a trade union or excepted body under the Trade Union Acts, 1941 and 1971, where the times at which he engages in such activities are outside his hours of work or are times during his hours of work in which he is permitted pursuant to the contract of employment between him and his employer so to engage,

> (b) the religious or political opinions of the employee,

> (c) civil proceedings whether actual, threatened or proposed against the employer to which the employee is or will be a party or in which the employee was or is likely to be a witness,

> (d) criminal proceedings against the employer, whether actual, threatened or proposed, in relation to which the employee has made, proposed or threatened to make a complaint or statement to the prosecuting authority or to any other authority connected with or involved in the prosecution of the proceedings or in which the employee was or is likely to be a witness,

> (e) the race or colour of the employee,

(*f*) the pregnancy of the employee or matters connected therewith, unless—

    (i) the employee was unable, by reason of the pregnancy or matters connected therewith—

        (I) to do adequately the work for which she was employed, or

        (II) to continue to do such work without contravention by her or her employer of a provision of a statute or instrument made under statute, and

    (ii) (I) there was not, at the time of the dismissal, any other employment with her employer that was suitable for her and in relation to which there was a vacancy, or

        (II) the employee refused an offer by her employer of alternative employment on terms and conditions corresponding to those of the employment to which the dismissal related, being an offer made so as to enable her to be retained in the employment of her employer notwithstanding pregnancy.

(3) Without prejudice to the generality of subsection (1) of this section, if an employee was dismissed due to redundancy but the circumstances constituting the redundancy applied equally to one or more other employees in similar employment with the same employer who have not been dismissed, and either—

(*a*) the selection of that employee for dismissal resulted wholly or mainly from one or more of the matters specified in subsection (2) of this section or another matter that would not be a ground justifying dismissal, or

(*b*) he was selected for dismissal in contravention of a procedure (being a procedure that has been agreed upon by or on behalf of the employer and by the employee or a trade union, or an excepted body under the Trade Union Acts, 1941 and 1971, representing him or has been established by the custom and practice of the employment concerned) relating to redundancy and there were no special reasons justifying a departure from that procedure,

then the dismissal shall be deemed, for the purposes of this Act, to be an unfair dismissal.

(4) Without prejudice to the generality of subsection (1) of this section, the dismissal of an employee shall be deemed, for the purposes of this Act, not to be an unfair dismissal, if it results wholly or mainly from one or more of the following:

(*a*) the capability, competence or qualifications of the employee for performing work of the kind which he was employed by the employer to do,

(*b*) the conduct of the employee,

(*c*) the redundancy of the employee, and

(*d*) the employee being unable to work or continue to work in the position which he held without contravention (by him or by his employer) of a duty or restriction imposed by or under any statute or instrument made under statute.

(5) (a) Without prejudice to the generality of subsection (1) of this section, the dismissal by the Minister for Defence of a civilian employed with the Defence Forces under section 30 (1) (*g*) of the Defence Act, 1954, shall be deemed for the purposes of this Act not to be an unfair dismissal if it is shown that the dismissal was for the purpose of safeguarding national security.

(b) A certificate purporting to be signed by the Minister for Defence and stating that a dismissal by the Minister for Defence of a civilian named in the certificate from employment with the Defence Forces under section 30 (1) *(g)* of the Defence Act, 1954, was for the purpose of safeguarding national security shall be evidence, for the purposes of this Act, of the facts stated in the certificate without further proof.

(6) In determining for the purposes of this Act whether the dismissal of an employee was an unfair dismissal or not, it shall be for the employer to show that the dismissal resulted wholly or mainly from one or more of the matters specified in subsection (4) of this section or that there were other substantial grounds justifying the dismissal.

(7) Where it is shown that a dismissal of a person referred to in paragraph *(a)* or *(b)* of section 2 (1) or section 3 or 4 of this Act results wholly or mainly from one or more of the matters referred to in subsection (2) *(a)* of this section, then subsections (1) and (6) of this section and the said sections 2 (1), 3 and 4 shall not apply in relation to the dismissal.

7.—(1) Where an employee is dismissed and the dismissal is an unfair dismissal, the employee shall be entitled to redress consisting of whichever of the following the rights commissioner, the Tribunal or the Circuit Court, as the case may be, considers appropriate having regard to all the circumstances:

> Redress for
> unfair dismissal.

(*a*) re-instatement by the employer of the employee in the position which he held immediately before his dismissal on the terms and conditions on which he was employed immediately before his dismissal together with a term that the re-instatement shall be deemed to have commenced on the day of the dismissal, or

(*b*) re-engagement by the employer of the employee either in the position which he held immediately before his dismissal or in a different position which would be reasonably suitable for him on such terms and conditions as are reasonable having regard to all the circumstances, or (*c*) payment by the employer to the employee of such compensation (not exceeding in amount 104 weeks remuneration in respect of the employment from which he was dismissed calculated in accordance with regulations under section 17 of this Act) in respect of any financial loss incurred by him and attributable to the dismissal as is just and equitable having regard to all the circumstances.

(2) Without prejudice to the generality of subsection (1) of this section, in determining the amount of compensation payable under that subsection regard shall be had to—

(*a*) the extent (if any) to which the financial loss referred to in that subsection was attributable to an act, omission or conduct by or on behalf of the employer,

(*b*) the extent (if any) to which the said financial loss was attributable to an action, omission or conduct by or on behalf of the employee,

(*c*) the measures (if any) adopted by the employee or, as the case may be, his failure to adopt measures, to mitigate the loss aforesaid, and

(*d*) the extent (if any) of the compliance or failure to comply by the employer or employee with any procedure of the kind referred to in section 14 (3) of this Act or with the provisions of any code of practice relating to procedures regarding dismissal approved of by the Minister.

(3) In this section—

"financial loss", in relation to the dismissal of an employee, includes any actual loss and any estimated prospective loss of income attributable to the dismissal and the value of any loss or diminution, attributable to the dismissal, of the rights of the employee under the Redundancy Payments Acts, 1967 to 1973, or in relation to superannuation;

"remuneration" includes allowances in the nature of pay and benefits in lieu of or in addition to pay.

8.—(1) A claim by an employee against an employer for redress under this Act for unfair dismissal may be brought by the employee before a rights commissioner or the Tribunal and the commissioner or Tribunal shall hear the parties and any evidence relevant to the claim tendered by them and, in the case of a rights commissioner, shall make a recommendation in relation to the claim, and, in the case of the Tribunal, shall make a determination in relation to the claim.

Determination of claims for unfair dismissal.

(2) A claim for redress under this Act shall be initiated by giving a notice in writing (containing such particulars (if any) as may be specified in regulations under section 17 of this Act made for the purposes of subsection (8) of this section) to a rights commissioner or the Tribunal, as the case may be, within 6 months of the date of the relevant dismissal and a copy of the notice shall be given to the employer concerned within the same period.

(3) A rights commissioner shall not hear a claim for redress under this Act if—

(*a*) the Tribunal has made a determination in relation to the claim, or

(*b*) any party concerned notifies the commissioner in writing that he objects to the claim being heard by a rights commissioner.

(4)(*a*) Where a recommendation of a rights commissioner in relation to a claim for redress under this Act is not carried out by the employer in accordance with its terms, the employee concerned may bring the claim before the Tribunal under subsection (1) of this section.

(*b*) The bringing of a claim before the Tribunal by virtue of this subsection shall be effected by giving to the Tribunal a notice in writing containing such particulars (if any) as may be specified in regulations under section 17 of this Act made for the purposes of subsection (8) of this section.

(5) Subject to subsection (4) of this section, the Tribunal shall not hear a claim for redress under this Act (except by way of appeal from a recommendation of a rights commissioner)—

> (*a*) if a rights commissioner has made a recommendation in relation to the claim, or
>
> (*b*) unless one of the parties concerned notifies a rights commissioner in writing that he objects to the claim being heard by a rights commissioner.

(6) Proceedings under this section before a rights commissioner shall be conducted otherwise than in public.

(7) A rights commissioner shall notify the Tribunal of any recommendation he makes under this section.

(8) Regulations under section 17 of this Act may provide for all or any of the following matters and for anything consequential thereon or incidental or ancillary thereto—

> (*a*) the procedure to be followed regarding the bringing of claims under this section or appeals under section 9 of this Act before the Tribunal,
>
> (*b*) the times and places of hearings by the Tribunal,
>
> (*c*) the representation of parties attending hearings by the Tribunal,
>
> (*d*) procedure regarding the hearing of such claims and appeals as aforesaid by the Tribunal,
>
> (*e*) publication and notification of determinations of the Tribunal,
>
> (*f*) the particulars to be contained in the notices referred to in subsections (2) and (4) of this section and section 9 of this Act,

(g) the award by the Tribunal of costs and expenses in relation to such claims and appeals as aforesaid and the payment thereof.

(9) Section 21 (2) of the Industrial Relations Act, 1946, shall apply in relation to all proceedings before the Tribunal as if the references in that section to the Labour Court were references to the Tribunal and subsection (17) of section 39 of the Redundancy Payments Act, 1967, shall apply in relation to proceedings before the Tribunal under this Act as it applies to matters referred to it under the said section 39.

(10) A dispute in relation to a dismissal that is an unfair dismissal for the purposes of this Act shall not be referred to a rights commissioner under section 13 (2) of the Industrial Relations Act, 1969.

9.—(1) A party concerned may appeal to the Tribunal from a recommendation of a rights commissioner in relation to a claim for redress under this Act and the Tribunal shall hear the parties and any evidence relevant to the appeal tendered by them and shall make a determination in relation to the appeal.

Appeal from recommendation of rights commissioner.

(2) An appeal under this section shall be initiated by a party by giving, within 6 weeks of the date on which the recommendation to which it relates was given to the parties concerned, a notice in writing (containing such particulars (if any) as may be specified in regulations under section 17 of this Act for the purposes of section 8 (8) thereof) to the Tribunal and stating the intention of the party concerned to appeal against the recommendation and a copy of the notice shall be given to the other party concerned within the said period of 6 weeks.

10.—(1) If an employer fails to carry out in accordance with its terms a determination of the Tribunal in relation to a claim for redress under this Act within 6 weeks from the date on which the determination is communicated to the parties the Minister may, if he thinks it appropriate, having regard to all the circumstances, to do so, institute and carry on proceedings in the Circuit Court in his name on behalf of the employee against the employer for redress under this Act.

Proceedings in Circuit Court for redress under Act.

(2) Where, in proceedings under this section, the Circuit Court finds that an employee is entitled to redress under this Act, it shall order the employer concerned to make to the employee concerned the appropriate redress.

(3) Any costs—

  (*a*) incurred by the Minister in relation to proceedings under this section, or

  (*b*) incurred by the employer concerned in any such proceedings,

and required by the Circuit Court to be borne by the Minister shall be paid by the Minister, and the employee concerned shall be under no liability in relation to any such costs.

(4) A party concerned may appeal to the Circuit Court from any determination of the Tribunal in relation to a claim for redress under this Act within 6 weeks from the date on which the determination is communicated to the parties.

(5) Proceedings under this section shall be heard in the county where the employer concerned ordinarily resides or carries on any profession, business or occupation.

(6) The reference in subsection (1) of this section to a determination of the Tribunal is a reference to such a determination in relation to which, at the expiration of the time for bringing an appeal against the determination, no such appeal has been brought.

11.—Any summons or other document required to be served for the purpose or in the course of any proceedings under this Act on a body corporate or an unincorporated body of persons may be served by leaving it at or sending it by post to the registered office for the purpose of the Companies Act, 1963, of that body or, if there is no such office, by leaving it at or sending it by post to any place in the State at which that body conducts its business.

Service of documents on bodies.

12.—(1) There shall be included among the debts which, under section 285 of the Companies Act, 1963, are, in the distribution of the assets of a company being wound up, to be paid in priority to all other debts, all compensation payable under this Act by the company to an employee, and that Act shall have effect accordingly, and formal proof of the debts to which priority is given under this subsection shall not be required except in cases where it may otherwise be provided by rules made under that Act.

Provisions relating to winding up and bankruptcy.

(2) There shall be included among the debts which, under section 4 of the Preferential Payments in Bankruptcy (Ireland) Act, 1889, are, in the distribution of the property of a bankrupt or arranging debtor, to be paid in priority to all other debts, all compensation payable under this Act by the bankrupt or arranging debtor, as the case may be, to an employee, and that Act shall have effect accordingly, and formal proof of the debts to which priority is given under this subsection shall not be required except in cases where it may otherwise be provided by general orders made under the said Act.

13.—A provision in an agreement (whether a contract of employment or not and whether made before or after the commencement of this Act) shall be void in so far as it purports to exclude or limit the application of, or is inconsistent with, any provision of this Act.

Voidance of certain provisions in agreements.

14.—(1) An employer shall, not later than 28 days after he enters into a contract of employment with an employee, give to the employee a notice in writing setting out the procedure which the employer will observe before and for the purpose of dismissing the employee.

Notice to employees of procedure for, and grounds of, dismissal.

(2) Where there is an alteration in the procedure referred to in subsection (1) of this section, the employer concerned shall, within 28 days after the alteration takes effect, give to any employee concerned a notice in writing setting out the procedure as so altered.

(3) The reference in subsection (1) of this section to a procedure is a reference to a procedure that has been agreed upon by or on behalf of the employer concerned and by the employee concerned or a trade union, or an

excepted body under the Trade Union Acts, 1941 and 1971, representing him or has been established by the custom and practice of the employment concerned, and the references in subsection (2) of this section to an alteration in the said procedure are references to an alteration that has been agreed upon by the employer concerned or a person representing him and by a trade union, or an excepted body under the Trade Union Acts, 1941 and 1971, representing the employee concerned.

(4) Where an employee is dismissed, the employer shall, if so requested, furnish to the employee within 14 days of the request, particulars in writing of the grounds for the dismissal, but in determining for the purposes of this Act whether the dismissal was unfair there may be taken into account any other grounds which are substantial grounds and which would have justified the dismissal.

15.—(1) Nothing in this Act, apart from this section, shall prejudice the right of a person to recover damages at common law for wrongful dismissal.

Alternative remedies of employee.

(2) Where an employee gives a notice in writing under section 8 (2) of this Act in respect of a dismissal to a rights commissioner or the Tribunal, he shall not be entitled to recover damages at common law for wrongful dismissal in respect of that dismissal.

(3) Where proceedings for damages at common law for wrongful dismissal are initiated by or on behalf of an employee, the employee shall not be entitled to redress under this Act in respect of the dismissal to which the proceedings relate.

(4) A person who accepts redress awarded under section 9 or 10 of the Anti-Discrimination (Pay) Act, 1974, in respect of any dismissal shall not be entitled to accept redress awarded under section 7 of this Act in respect of that dismissal and a person who accepts redress awarded under the said section 7 in respect of any dismissal shall not be entitled to accept redress awarded under the said section 9 or 10 in respect of that dismissal.

16.—(1) The Minister may by order amend section 2 (1) of this Act so as to extend the application of the Act to

Amendment of Act by order of Minister.

any class of employee specified in that section or part (defined in such manner and by reference to such matters as the Minister considers appropriate) of any such class.

(2) The Minister may by order amend paragraph (*c*) of section 7 (1) of this Act so as to vary the maximum amount of compensation referred to in the said paragraph (*c*).

(3) The Minister may by order amend section 2 (2), 3 or 4 of this Act so as to vary—

    (*a*) the application of this Act in relation to dismissals where the employment was under a contract of employment for a fixed term or a specified purpose.

    (*b*) the periods of 1 year specified in the said section 3, or

    (*c*) the periods of 6 months and 1 month specified in the said section 4 or either of them.

(4) The Minister may, by order, made with the consent of the Minister for Health, amend subsection (2) of section 3 of this Act so as to extend the application of the subsection to other employments connected with medicine or health.

(5) The Minister may by order amend any provision of this Act so as to comply with any international obligations in relation to dismissals that the State has decided to assume.

(6) An order under this section may contain such supplementary and ancillary provisions as the Minister considers necessary or expedient.

(7) The Minister may by order revoke or amend an order under this section including an order under this subsection.

(8) Where an order is proposed to be made under this section, a draft thereof shall be laid before both Houses of the Oireachtas and the order shall not be made until a

resolution approving of the draft has been passed by each such House.

17.—(1) The Minister may make regulations for the purposes of sections 7 (1) (*c*) and 8 (8) of this Act and for the purpose of enabling any other provisions of this Act to have full effect.

(2) Regulations under this section may contain such incidental, supplementary and consequential provisions as appear to the Minister to be necessary for the purposes of the regulations.

(3) Every regulation made under this section shall be laid before each House of the Oireachtas as soon as may be after it is made, and if a resolution annulling the regulation is passed by either such House within the next 21 days on which that House has sat after the regulation is laid before it, the regulation shall be annulled accordingly, but without prejudice to the validity of anything previously done thereunder.

18.—The tribunal established by section 39 of the Redundancy Payments Act, 1967, shall be known as the Employment Appeals Tribunal and references in that Act and any other Act of the Oireachtas and any instrument made under any Act of the Oireachtas to the Redundancy Appeals Tribunal shall be construed as references to the Employment Appeals Tribunal.

19.—Where an employee is re-instated or re-engaged by an employer in pursuance of a determination or order under this Act in relation to the dismissal of the employee by the employer, any payments made under the Redundancy Payments Acts, 1967 and 1973, in relation to the dismissal shall be repaid by the person to whom they were made to the person by whom they were made and may be recovered by the latter from the former as a simple contract debt in any court of competent jurisdiction and any moneys due and owing to any person under those Acts in relation to the dismissal shall cease to be due or owing.

20.—The First Schedule to the Minimum Notice and Terms of Employment Act, 1973, is hereby amended by the substitution of the following paragraphs for paragraphs 5 and 7:

Amendment of First Schedule to Minimum Notice and Terms of Employment Act, 1973.

"5. An employee who claims and receives redundancy payment in respect of lay-off or short time shall be deemed to have voluntarily left his employment.

7. Where the whole or part of a trade, business or undertaking was or is transferred to another person either before or after the passing of this Act, the service of an employee in the trade, business or undertaking, or the part thereof, so transferred shall be reckoned as part of the service of the employee with the transferee and the transfer shall not operate to break the continuity of the service of the employee."

21.—The expenses incurred by the Minister in the administration of this Act shall, to such extent as may be sanctioned by the Minister for Finance, be paid out of moneys provided by the Oireachtas.

Expenses.

22.—(1) This Act may be cited as the Unfair Dismissals Act, 1977.

Short title and commencement.

(2) This Act shall come into operation on such day as the Minister may appoint by order.

APPENDIX II

S.I. No. 286 of 1977

UNFAIR DISMISSALS (CLAIMS AND APPEALS) REGULATIONS, 1977

I, GENE FITZGERALD, Minister for Labour, in exercise of the powers conferred on me by section 17 of the Unfair Dismissals Act, 1977 (No. 10 of 1977), hereby make the following regulations:

1. (1) These Regulations may be cited as the Unfair Dismissals (Claims and Appeals) Regulations, 1977.

(2) These Regulations shall come into operation on the 14th day of September, 1977.

2. In these Regulations—

"the Act" means the Unfair Dismissals Act, 1977 (No. 10 of 1977);

"appeal" means an appeal under section 9 of the Act;

"claim" means a claim under section 8 (1) or section 8 (4) (*a*) of the Act;

"the Minister" means the Minister for Labour;

"the Tribunal" means the Employment Appeals Tribunal established by the Redundancy Payments Act, 1967.

3. A notice under subsection (2) of section 8 of the Act to the Tribunal or under subsection (4) of the said section 8 or section 9 (2) of the Act shall specify—

    (*a*) the name and address of the person bringing the claim or appeal,

    (*b*) the name and address of the employer or the employee, as the case may be, concerned,

    (*c*) the date of the commencement of the employment to which the notice relates,

    (*d*) the date of the dismissal to which the notice relates, and

Notice of the making of this Statutory Instrument was published in "Iris Oifigiúil" of 13th September, 1977.

256

(*e*) the amount claimed by the said person to be the weekly remuneration of the said person in respect of the said employment calculated in accordance with regulations under section 17 of the Act.

4. A claim or appeal may be withdrawn by sending a notification in writing signifying such withdrawal to the tribunal.

5. (1) A party to a claim or appeal who receives notice thereof under section 8 or 9, as the case may be, of the Act and who intends to oppose the claim or appeal shall enter an appearance to the claim or appeal by giving to the Tribunal, within 14 days of the receipt by him of the said notice, a notice in writing stating that he intends to oppose the claim or appeal, as the case may be, and containing the facts and contentions on which he will ground such opposition.

(2) A party to a claim or appeal who does not enter an appearance to the claim or appeal in pursuance of this Regulation shall not be entitled to take part in or be present or represented at any proceedings before the Tribunal in relation to the claim or appeal.

(3) A party to a claim or appeal may, before the expiration of the period referred to in paragraph (1) of this Regulation, apply, by giving to the Tribunal a notice in writing containing the facts and contentions on which he grounds the application, for an extension of the said period and the Tribunal may make such order in relation to the application as it thinks just.

6. On receipt by the Tribunal of a notice referred to in Regulation 3 or 5 of these Regulations or a notification under Regulation 4 of these Regulations, the Tribunal shall cause a copy of the notice or notification, as the case may be, to be given to the other party concerned.

7. The chairman of the Tribunal may, by certificate under his hand, correct any mistake (including an omission) of a verbal or formal nature in a determination of the Tribunal.

8. (1) The Tribunal shall maintain a register, to be known as the Register of Unfair Dismissals Determinations (referred to subsequently in this Regulation as "the Register"), and shall cause to be entered in the Register particulars of every determination by the Tribunal under section 8 or 9 of the Act.

(2) The Register may be inspected free of charge by any person during normal office hours.

(3) Where the chairman of the Tribunal makes a correction, pursuant to Regulation 7 of these Regulations, particulars thereof shall be entered in the Register.

(4) A copy of an entry in the Register shall be sent to the parties concerned.

9. (1) A notice required by subsection (2) or (4) of section 8 or section 9 (2) of the Act or by these Regulations to be given to the Tribunal may be sent by registered post addressed to the Secretary, Employment Appeals Tribunal, Dublin 4, and a document required by these Regulations to be given to a party to proceedings before the Tribunal may be sent by registered post addressed to the party—

  (*a*)   in case his address is specified in a notice referred to in Regulation 3 of these Regulations, at that address, and

  (*b*)   in the case of a body corporate (being a case to which paragraph (*a*) of this Regulation does not apply) at its registered office, and

  (*c*)   in any other case, at his known place of residence or at a place where he works or carries on business.

(2) Any such notice of notification as aforesaid that is sent or given to a person authorised to receive it by the person to whom it is required by these Regulations to be given shall be deemed to have been sent to the latter person.

10. Regulations 10 to 17 (2), 19, 20, 20A (inserted by the Redundancy (Redundancy Appeals Tribunal) (Amendment) Regulations, 1969 (S.I. No. 26 of 1969)), 23 and 24 of the Redundancy (Redundancy Appeals Tribunal) Regulations, 1968 (S.I. No. 24 of 1968), shall, with any necessary modifications, and in the case of the said Regulations 20 and 20A, with the modification that a sum awarded by the Tribunal under either such Regulation shall, in lieu of being paid out of the fund referred to therein, be paid by the Minister for Labour with the consent of the Minister for Finance, apply in relation to a claim under Section 8 of the Act, an appeal under section 9 of the Act and proceedings in relation to such a claim or appeal as they apply in relation to appeals provided for by section 39 of the Redundancy Payments Act, 1967 (No. 21 of 1967).

GIVEN under my Official Seal, this 7th day of September, 1977.

GENE FITZGERALD,
Minister for Labour.

EXPLANATORY NOTE

(This note is not part of the Instrument and does not purport to be a legal interpretation.)

These regulations prescribe the procedure to be followed in relation to the submission and hearing of claims and appeals before the Employment Appeals Tribunal under the Unfair Dismissals Act, 1977.

S.I. No. 287 of 1977

UNFAIR DISMISSALS (CALCULATION OF WEEKLY REMUNERATION) REGULATIONS, 1977

I, GENE FITZGERALD, Minister for Labour, in exercise of the powers conferred on me by section 17 of the Unfair Dismissals Act, 1977 (No. 10 of 1977), hereby make the following Regulations:

1. (1) These Regulations may be cited as the Unfair Dismissals (Calculation of Weekly Remuneration) Regulations, 1977.

2. In these Regulations—

"the Act" means the Unfair Dismissals Act, 1977 (No. 10 of 1977);

"date of dismissal" has the meaning assigned to it by section 1 of the Act, and "date", in relation to a dismissal, shall be construed accordingly;

"relevant employment", in relation to an employee, means the employment in respect of which the weekly remuneration of the employee is calculated for the purposes of section 7 (1) (c) of the Act;

"week", in relation to an employee whose remuneration is calculated by reference to a week ending on a day other than a Saturday, means a week ending on that other day and, in relation to any other employee, means a week ending on a Saturday, and "weekly" shall be construed accordingly.

3. (a) A week's remuneration of an employee in respect of an employment shall be calculated for the purposes of section 7 (1) (c) of the Act in accordance with these Regulations.

   (b) Where, at the date of his dismissal from an employment, an employee had less than 52 weeks' continuous service in the employment, a week's remuneration of the employee in respect of the employment shall be calculated, for the purposes of the said section 7 (1) (c), in the manner that in the opinion of the Tribunal corresponds most closely with that specified in these Regulations.

Notice of the making of this Statutory Instrument was published in "Iris Oifigiúil" of 13th September, 1977.

4. In the case of an employee who is wholly remunerated in respect of the relevant employment at an hourly time rate or by a fixed wage or salary, and in the case of any other employee whose remuneration in respect of the relevant employment does not vary by reference to the amount of work done by him, his weekly remuneration in respect of the relevant employment shall be his earnings in respect of that employment (including any regular bonus or allowance which does not vary having regard to the amount of work done and any payment in kind) in the latest week before the date of the relevant dismissal in which he worked for the number of hours that was normal for the employment together with, if he was normally required to work overtime in the relevant employment, his average weekly overtime earnings in the relevant employment as determined in accordance with Regulation 5 of these Regulations.

5. For the purpose of Regulation 4 of these Regulations, the average weekly overtime earnings of an employee in the relevant employment shall be the amount obtained by dividing by 26 the total amount of his overtime earnings in that employment in the period of 26 weeks ending 13 weeks before the date of the dismissal of the employee.

6. For the purpose of Regulations 5 and 7 (*b*) of these Regulations, any week during which the employee concerned did not work shall be disregarded and the latest week before the period of 26 weeks mentioned in the said Regulation 5 or 7 (*b*), as the case may be, of these Regulations or before a week taken into account under this Regulation, as may be appropriate, shall be taken into account instead of a week during which the employee did not work as aforesaid.

7. (*a*) In the case of an employee who is paid remuneration in respect of the relevant employment wholly or partly at piece rates, or whose remuneration includes commissions (being piece rates or commissions related directly to his output at work) or bonuses, and in the case of any other employee whose remuneration in respect of the relevant employment varies in relation to the amount of work done by him, his weekly remuneration shall be the amount obtained by dividing the amount of the remuneration to be taken into account in accordance with paragraph (*b*) of this Regulation by the number of hours worked in the period of 26 weeks mentioned in the said paragraph (*b*) and multiplying the resulting amount by the normal number of hours for which, at the date of the dismissal of the employee, an employee in the relevant employment was required to work in each week.

(*b*) The remuneration to be taken into account for the purposes of paragraph (*a*) of this Regulation shall be the total remuneration paid to the employee concerned in respect of the employment concerned for all the hours worked by the employee in the employment in the period of 26 weeks that ended 13 weeks before the date on which the employee was dismissed, adjusted in respect of any variations in the rates of pay which became operative during the period of 13 weeks ending on the date of dismissal of the employee.

(*c*) For the purposes of paragraph (*b*) of this Regulation, any week worked in another employment shall be taken into account if it would not have operated, for the purposes of the First Schedule to the Minimum Notice and Terms of Employment Act, 1973 (No. 4 of 1973), to break the continuity of service of the employee concerned in the employment from which he was dismissed.

8. (1) Where, under his contract of employment, an employee is required to work for more hours than the number of hours that is normal for the employment, the hours for which he is so required to work shall be taken, for the purposes of Regulations 4 and 7 (*b*) of these Regulations, to be, in the case of that employee, the number of hours that is normal for the employment.

(2) Where, under his contract of employment, an employee is entitled to additional remuneration for working for more than a specified number of hours per week—

(*a*) in case the employee is required under the said contract to work for more than the said specified number of hours per week, the number of hours per week for which he is so required to work shall, for the purposes of Regulations 4 and 7 (*b*) of these Regulations, be taken to be, in his case, the number of hours of work per week that is normal for the employment, and

(*b*) in any other case, the specified number of hours shall be taken, for the purposes of the said Regulations 4 and 7 (*b*), to be, in the case of that employee, the number of hours of work per week that is normal for the employment.

9. Where, in a particular week, an employee qualifies for a payment of a bonus, pay allowance or commission which relates to work the whole or part of which was not done in that particular week, the whole or the appropriate proportionate part of the payment as the case may be, shall, for the purposes of Regulations 4 and 7 (*b*) of these Regulations, be disregarded in

relation to that particular week and shall for those purposes, be taken into account in relation to any week in which any of the work was done.

10. An employee who is normally employed on a shift cycle and whose remuneration in respect of the employment varies having regard to the particular shift on which he is employed, and an employee whose remuneration for working for the number of hours that is normal for the employment varies having regard to the days of the week or the times of the day on or at which he works, shall each be taken, for the purposes of these Regulations, to be an employee who is paid wholly or partly by piece rates.

11. Where, in respect of the relevant employment, there is no number of hours for which employees work in each week that is normal for the employment, the weekly remuneration of each such employee shall be taken, for the purposes of these Regulations, to be the average amount of the remuneration paid to each such employee in the 52 weeks in each of which he was working in the employment immediately before the date of the relevant dismissal.

12. Where under these Regulations account is to be taken of remuneration paid in a period which does not coincide with the periods for which the remuneration is calculated, the remuneration shall be apportioned in such manner as may be just.

13. For the purposes of Regulations 4 and 7 of these Regulations, account shall not be taken of any sums paid to an employee by way of recoupment of expenses incurred by him in the discharge of the duties of his employment.

GIVEN under my Official Seal, this 7th day of September, 1977.

GENE FITZGERALD, Minister for Labour.

EXPLANATORY NOTE

(This note is not part of the Instrument and does not purport to be a legal interpretation.)

These regulations prescribe the method of calculating weekly remuneration for the purpose of redress in the form of compensation under the Unfair Dismissals Act, 1977.

Extracts from S.I. No. 24 of 1968

REDUNDANCY (REDUNDANCY APPEALS TRIBUNAL) REGULATIONS, 1968

Hearings by the Tribunal

10. The chairman of the Tribunal shall from time to time fix dates, times and places for the hearing of appeals by the Tribunal and notice thereof shall be given by the Secretary to the Tribunal to all persons appearing to the chairman to be concerned.

11. The hearing of an appeal by the Tribunal shall take place in public unless the Tribunal decides at the request of either party to the appeal to hear the appeal in private.

12. Parties summoned to attend a hearing of the Tribunal may appear and be heard in person or may be represented by counsel or solicitor or by a representative of a trade union or of an employers' association or, with the leave of the Tribunal, by any other person.

Procedure at Hearings

13. A party to an appeal heard by the Tribunal may—

   (a) make an opening statement,

   (b) call witnesses,

   (c) cross-examine any witnesses called by any other party,

   (d) give evidence on his own behalf, and

   (e) address the Tribunal at the close of the evidence.

14. The Tribunal may postpone or adjourn the hearing of an appeal from time to time.

15. The Tribunal may admit any duly authenticated written statement as prima facie evidence of any fact whenever it thinks it just and proper so to do.

16. If, after notice of a hearing has been duly given, any of the parties fails to appear at the hearing, the Tribunal may determine the question under appeal or may adjourn the hearing to a later date: provided that before determining the question under appeal the Tribunal shall consider all the evidence before it at the time of the hearing.

17. (1) A decision of the Tribunal may be taken by a majority of the members thereof.

(2) A decision of the Tribunal shall be recorded in a document signed by the chairman and sealed with the seal of the Tribunal.

Costs and Expenses

19. (1) Subject to subparagraph (2), the Tribunal shall not award costs against any party to an appeal.

(2) Where in the opinion of the Tribunal a party to the proceedings (and, if he is a respondent, whether or not he has entered an appearance) has acted frivolously or vexatiously, the Tribunal may make an order that that party shall pay to another party a specified amount in respect of travelling expenses and any other costs or expenses reasonably incurred by that other party in connection with the hearing.

(3) Notwithstanding subparagraph (2), costs shall not be awarded in respect of the costs or expenses in respect of the attendance of counsel, solicitors, officials of a trade union or of an employers' association appearing before the Tribunal in a representative capacity.

(4) Where the Tribunal has made an order under subparagraph (2), the amount referred to in the order shall be recoverable as a simple contract debt.

20. (1) The Tribunal may award to a person appearing before it a sum in respect of travelling expenses and subsistence allowances in accordance with such scale as the Minister, with the consent of the Minister for Finance, may from time to time determine.

(2) A sum awarded under subparagraph (1) shall be paid out of the Redundancy Fund.

20A. (1) Subject to subparagraph (2), the Tribunal may, at its discretion, award to a person appearing before it and whose attendance is deemed essential by the Tribunal such sum in respect of expenses for loss of remunerative time as it considers reasonable.

(2) The Tribunal shall not make an award under subparagraph (1) in respect of the attendance before the Tribunal of—

(a) appellants or respondents,

(b) any of the following persons appearing in a representative capacity—counsel, solicitors, officials of a trade union, officials of an employers' association.

(3) A sum awarded under subparagraph (1) shall be paid out of the Redundancy Fund.

Miscellaneous

23. The Tribunal may consider and decide any question duly referred to it for consideration and determination, notwithstanding the failure or neglect of any person to comply with any requirement of these Regulations.

24. The Tribunal may require any party to an appeal to furnish in writing further particulars with regard to the facts and contentions contained in either the notice of appeal or the notice of appearance and when the required particulars have been received by the Secretary of the Tribunal he shall furnish the other party to the appeal with a copy of the particulars provided.

APPENDIX V

Form RP51A and Notes

APPLICATION TO EMPLOYMENT APPEALS TRIBUNAL UNDER:

(i)   REDUNDANCY PAYMENTS ACTS, 1967/79 AND/OR

(ii) MINIMUM NOTICE AND TERMS OF EMPLOYMENT ACT, 1973 AND/OR

(iii) UNFAIR DISMISSALS ACT, 1977 '

(iv) MATERNITY PROTECTION OF EMPLOYEES ACT, 1981

Notes for Persons Making Application

I. **TIME LIMITS OR OTHER CONSTRAINTS WHICH APPLY TO APPLICATIONS MADE TO THE TRIBUNAL**

A. **Redundancy Payments Acts — Time Limits**

(i)   A claim for a redundancy lump sum payment must be

   (a) made to the employer

   or

   (b) referred to the Employment Appeals Tribunal

   within **52** weeks from

   (a) date of dismissal

   or

   (b) date of ending of contract of employment.

   (Section 24 of the 1967 Act as amended by Section 12 of the 1971 Act refers).

(ii) In certain cases and for good cause the Tribunal may allow claims made within 104 weeks. (Section 24 of the 1967 Act as amended by Section 12 of the 1971 Act refers).

(iii) Where an employer **rejects** an employee's claim it must normally be referred to the Tribunal within **21** days of such rejection. (The Tribunal **may** allow claims made outside this period). (S.I. No. 24 of 1968 refers).

B. **Minimum Notice and Terms of Employment Act 1973 — Time Limits**

   No expressed time limit

   but

   Disputes which cannot be resolved should be **referred promptly** to the Tribunal.

C. **Unfair Dismissals Act 1977 — Time Limits**

(i)   **Claims** must be made **within 6 months** of date of dismissal.

   N.B. A copy of the claim must be served on the employer within the same 6 months.

   (Section 8(2) of the Act refers).

(ii) **Appeals** against a recommendation of a Rights Commissioner must be brought **within 6 weeks** of the date of the issue of the recommendation. (Section 9(2) of the Act refers).

(iii) Appeals against a determination of the Tribunal must be brought to the Circuit Court **within 6 weeks** of the date determination is notified to the parties. (Section 10(4) of the Act refers).

D. Maternity Protection of Employees Act, 1981 — Time Limits

(i) Disputes arising within 156 weeks of the date of the relevant confinement may be referred to the Tribunal within 6 months of the commencement of the dispute. (A copy of the notice of referral should be sent or given to the other party concerned as soon as practicable).

(ii) Appeals against a recommendation of a Rights Commissioner must be brought within 6 weeks of the date of issue of the recommendation.

N.B.   The above time-limits may be waived by the Tribunal when it receives evidence it considers sufficient as to the reason(s) why the time-limits were not observed. (S.I. No. 357 of 1981 refers).

(iii) Appeals against a determination of the Tribunal must be brought to the Circuit Court within 6 weeks of the date on which the determination is notified to the parties.
(S. 27(3) of the Act refers).

II NOTES ON COMPLETING FORM RP51A (ATTACHED)

(N.B.   In a case under the Unfair Dismissals Act 1977 or the Maternity Protection of Employees Act 1981 **first** read Part II of the form, **then** fill in the form.)

(1) Box 1 — If you change your address after lodging this form, be sure to notify the Secretary to the Tribunal (see address at end of form).

(2) Box 2 — NAME AND ADDRESS OF EMPLOYER: If possible give the name of your employer as it appears on printed stationery, invoices, pay-slips etc. If you fail to designate your employer correctly, your application may have to be returned to you to establish this. If your employer is a Company or Corporation, give its registered address if you know it.

(3) Box 3 — REPRESENTATIVE OF PERSON MAKING THE APPEAL: If you have arranged for a representative, such as a Trade Union Official, etc. to attend on your behalf at the Tribunal, notification of the hearing of your appeal will be sent to him as well as to yourself. In no circumstances should you name a representative without consulting him in advance about your appeal and obtaining his consent to represent you.

(4) Box 6 — NORMAL WEEKLY PAY:

Basic Weekly Pay. This means the basic pay before any deductions are made.

Average Weekly Overtime. In redundancy and unfair dismissals cases this is normally pay for the average weekly overtime worked during the six months preceding the last three months of employment. In minimum notice cases, overtime is disregarded unless it is a normal feature of work. If it is a normal feature of work inasmuch as you are normally expected to work it, overtime pay is included in your normal weekly pay and overtime is included in normal weekly working hours.

Payment in Kind. These would include the value of meals or board, use of company house or car etc.

(5) Box 7 — BASIS OF EMPLOYMENT: Applicants should state the type of employment contract e.g. permanent, temporary, short-term contract (if short-term contract please give date of expiry of contract).

(6) Box 8 — GROUNDS OF APPLICATION:

Keep explanations as short as possible. The following are examples:

"Lump sum wrongly calculated — excludes service prior to change of ownership".

"Employer not conceding redundancy".

"Received only two weeks notice of dismissal instead of   weeks".

"Dismissed without explanation".

"Dismissed wrongfully for alleged misconduct".

"Employer not granting maternity leave".

"Unsuitable job offered on return to work from maternity leave".

(7) Box 9 — REDRESS SOUGHT

APPLICANTS should state type of redress sought — e.g. Reinstatement; Re-engagement; Compensation. If compensation, state how much is claimed and how it is made up.

(8) ACKNOWLEDGEMENT OF APPLICATION: If you do not get an acknowledgement of your application within fourteen days of sending it to the Tribunal you should contact the Secretary to the Tribunal by letter or telephone.

(9) HEARING OF APPEAL: Once you have received an acknowledgement your case will be listed for hearing as soon as possible at the nearest town to place of employment. You will be notified in advance. Meantime please assist the Tribunal by refraining from all but essential correspondence.

(10) **ADJOURNMENTS**

Adjournments are only granted in exceptional circumstances. A party seeking an adjournment must make a formal application to any sitting division of the Tribunal. Good cause must be shown and the consent of the other party sought before any application for an adjournment will be considered by the Tribunal.

(11) N.B.   (i)   **Withdrawal of Applications.** If you are seeking to withdraw your application, the Secretary to the Tribunal should be notified at once.

(ii)   **Caution.** The Tribunal has power to award costs in the case of frivolous or vexatious applications.

(12) **LEAFLET: TRIBUNAL — An explanatory leaflet on the Employment Appeals Tribunal** is available from the Department of Labour. A copy of this leaflet is automatically sent to each person making an application to the Tribunal and to the respondent as well.

LABOUR LEGISLATION — **Explanatory leaflets** on the various items of legislation mentioned in these notes are available from the Department of Labour, Davitt House, Mespil Road, Dublin 4 (Phone: 765861, Inquiry Office). In addition, a Guide to the Redundancy Payments Acts is available from any Employment Exchange/Office and from National Manpower Service Offices.

FORM RP 51A
(Part II is overleaf)

DETACH THIS PAGE
FROM THE NOTES

FOR OFFICIAL USE		
Case No.		

NOTICE OF APPEAL TO EMPLOYMENT APPEALS TRIBUNAL UNDER

    (i)   Redundancy Payments Acts 1967-79. ☐

    (ii) Minimum Notice and Terms of Employment
        Act, 1973. ☐

    (iii) Unfair Dismissals Act, 1977 (see overleaf). ☐

    (iv) Maternity Protection of Employees Act,
        1981. (see overleaf) ☐

*Tick the appropriate box(es)
to show under which Legislation
the appeal is being made.*

IMPORTANT Please read the notes supplied then complete this form in BLOCK CAPITALS

PART I

1. NAME AND ADDRESS OF PERSON MAKING APPEAL

'Phone No.:	
Occupation	
RSI No.	

2. NAME AND ADDRESS OF EMPLOYER

'Phone No.:

3. NAME, ADDRESS OF REPRESENTATIVE (UNION OFFICIAL, ETC.) OF PERSON MAKING THIS APPEAL

'Phone No.:

4. TOWN OR NEAREST TOWN TO PLACE OF EMPLOYMENT

5. GIVE THE FOLLOWING DATES:

	Day	Month	Year
Birth			
Employment began			
Dismissal notice recd.			
Employment ended			
Date or expected date of confinement		.	

6. NORMAL WEEKLY PAY

	£	p
Basic weekly pay		
Regular Bonus or allowances		
Average weekly overtime		
Any other payments including payments in kind — specify:		
Weekly Total		
	NUMBER	
Normal weekly working hours		

7. BASIS OF EMPLOYMENT (PERMANENT, TEMPORARY, ETC. — SEE NOTES)

8. THE GROUNDS OF MY APPLICATION ARE AS FOLLOWS:

9. REDRESS SOUGHT

Signed:

Date:

Send this form to: Secretary,
                      Employment Appeals Tribunal,
                      Davitt House,
                      Mespil Road,
                      Dublin 4.

PART II

IF YOU WISH A CLAIM UNDER THE UNFAIR DISMISSALS ACT 1977 OR A DISPUTE UNDER THE MATERNITY PROTECTION OF EMPLOYEES ACT 1981 TO BE HEARD BY THE EMPLOYMENT APPEALS TRIBUNAL, ANSWER ANY OF THE FOLLOWING QUESTIONS WHICH ARE RELEVANT TO YOU.

Claim under Unfair Dismissals Act

Insert "Yes" or "No" in each box

Have you sued your employer under Common Law procedures in the matter of your claim on unfair dismissal?

Have you a claim currently with a Rights Commissioner on unfair dismissal?

Do you object to a claim on unfair dismissal being heard by a Rights Commissioner?

Has your employer objected to a claim on unfair dismissal being heard by a Rights Commissioner?

Are you appealing a recommendation of a Rights Commissioner in regard to your claim on unfair dismissal? If so, state:—

name of Rights Commissioner: _____

date of his recommendation: _____ .

Are you referring your claim to the Tribunal following the failure of your employer to implement (within six weeks) a recommendation of a Rights Commissioner on unfair dismissal? If so, state:—

name of Rights Commissioner: _____

date of his recommendation: _____

Dispute under the Maternity Protection of Employees Act

Have you a dispute currently with a Rights Commissioner about maternity entitlement (other than unfair dismissal)?

Do you object to a dispute under the Maternity Protection of Employees Act being heard by a Rights Commissioner?

Has your employer objected to a dispute under the Maternity Protection of Employees Act being heard by a Rights Commissioner?

Are you appealing a recommendation of a Rights Commissioner in regard to a dispute about maternity entitlement? If so, state:—

name of Rights Commissioner: _____

date of his recommendation: _____

Are you referring your case to the Tribunal following the failure of your employer to implement a recommendation of a Rights Commissioner on maternity entitlement? If so, state:—

name of Rights Commissioner: _____

date of recommendation: _____

[Supplied by the Department of Labour.]

APPENDIX VI

Distribution of compensation awarded by the Employment Appeals Tribunal in determinations of Unfair Dismissal

£
Total Awarded (150,706.00)
Average Award (1732.25)

Compensation Award £	Number	Compensation Award £	Number
£1 to £100	13	£1,000 to £2,000	9
£100 to £200	8	£2,000 to £3,000	2
£200 to £300	13	£3,000 to £4,000	2
£300 to £400	9	£4,000 to £5,000	—
£400 to £500	7	£5,000 to £6,000	—
£500 to £600	5	£6,000 t0 £7,000	1
£600 to £700	3	£7,000 to £8,000	1
£700 to £800	5	£8,000 to £9,000	—
£800 to £900	1	£9,000 to £10,000	1
£900 to £1,000	2	£10,000 to £11,000	2
		£11,000 to £12,000	1
		£21,000 to £22,000	1
		£24,000 to £25,000	1

Source: *Annual Report of the EAT*, 1980.

APPENDIX VII

Representation at Sittings of the Employment Appeals Tribunal in 1980

Relevant Act	Year	Employee			Employer				Total of parties represented
		Representation by Trade Union	Representation by Solicitor or Counsel	Total	Representation by Employer organisations	Representation by Solicitor or Counsel	Total	
Redundancy Payments Acts and Minimum Notice and Terms of Employment Act, 1973	1980	591	207	798	140	516	656	1,454
Unfair Dismissals Act, 1977.	1980	210	180	390	118	260	378	768
Total		801	387	1,188	258	776	1,034	2,222

Source: Annual Report of the EAT, 1980.

273

BIBLIOGRAPHY

Aaron, B. and Wedderburn, K. W.: *Industrial Conflict — A Comparative Legal Survey* (London, 1972).

Anderman, S.: *The Law of Unfair Dismissal* (London, 1978).

Atiyah, P.: *The Rise and Fall of Freedom of Contract* (Oxford, 1979).

Ball: *Irish Legislative Systems* (London, 1888).

Bartholomew, P.: *The Irish Judiciary* (Dublin, 1971).

Beckett, J.C.: *The Making of Modern Ireland 1603-1923* (Faber, 1966).

Best, G.: *Mid-Victorian Britain 1851-'70* (Fontana, 1979).

Bichens, J.E.: *Ireland and its Economy* (London, 1830).

Blackstone, Sir W.: *Commentaries on the Laws of England* (London, 1876).

Bradshaw, B.: *The Irish Constitutional Revolution of the Sixteenth Century* (Cambridge, 1979).

Brittan, S.: *The Economic Consequences of Democracy* (Temple Smith, 1977).

Carby-Hall, J.R. (ed.): *Studies in Labour Law* (MCB Books, 1976).

Chart, D.A.: *The Economic History of Ireland* (Dublin, 1920).

Cheshire & Fifoot: *The Law of Contract* (London, 1977).

Chitty, J.: *The Law of Contracts* (London, 1977).

Chubb, B.: *The Constitution and Constitutional Change in Ireland* (Dublin, 1979).

Clancy, J.J.: *Ireland: As she is, As she has been and As she ought to be* (New York, 1877).

Commons, J.R.: *Legal Foundations of Capitalism* (Wisconsin, 1961).

Corbin on Contracts (West Publishing Co. 1950).

Coyne, W.P.(ed.): *Ireland: Industrial and Agricultural* (Dublin, 1902).

Cronin & Grime: *Labour Law* (London, 1974).

Davies, P. and Freedland, M.R.: *Labour Law Texts and Materials* (London, 1979).

Davis, J. E.: *The Master and Servant Act, 1867, with an introduction, notes and forms, and table of offences* (London, 1868).

Denning, Lord: *The Discipline of Law* (London, 1979).

de Smith, S.A.: *Judicial Review of Administrative Action* (4th ed., London, 1980).

——*Administrative Law* (London, 1980).

——*Constitutional and Administrative Law* (London, 1978).

Dix and Crump: *Contracts of Employment* (London, 1980).

Donaldson, A.G.: *Some Comparative Aspects of Irish Law* (London, 1957).
Drake, C. and Bercusson, B.: *The Employment Acts 1974-1980* (London, 1981).
Dutton, M.: *The Law of Masters and Servants in Ireland* (Dublin, 1723).
Dworkin, R.: *Taking Rights Seriously* (London, 1977).

Elias, P., Napier, B. and Wallington, P.: *Labour Law: Cases and Materials* (London, 1980).

Falconer, A. (ed.): *Understanding Human Rights* (Dublin, 1980).
Figgis, D.: *The Irish Constitution explained* (Dublin, 1922).
Fitzjames Stephen, Sir J.: *History of the Criminal Law of England* (London, 1877).
Fox, A.: *Beyond Contract: Work, Power and Trust Relations* (London, 1974).
Freedland, M.R.: *The Contract of Employment* (Oxford, 1976).
Friedmann, W.G.: *Government Enterprise* (London, 1970).

Ganz, G.: *Administrative Procedures* (London, 1974).
Gwynn, D.: *The Irish Free State Constitution 1922-1927* (London, 1928).
Gwynn, S.: *The History of Ireland* (Dublin, 1924).

Halsburys Laws of England 4th edition.
Hand, G.J.: *English Law in Ireland 1290-1324* (Cambridge, 1967).
Harvey: *Industrial Relations and Employment Law* (ed. P. Elias London, 1981).
Hepple, B.A. & O'Higgins, P.: *Individual Employment Law* (London, 1979).
Hepple, B.A., Neeson, J.M., O'Higgins, P.: *A Bibliography of the Literature on British and Irish Law* (London, 1975).
Hunter, W.A.: *The Master and Servant Act, 1867, and the first report of the Royal Commission, 1874* (London, 1875, LSE).
Hyman, R. and Brough, I.: *Social Values and Industrial Relations* (Oxford, 1975).

Jackson, D.: *Unfair Dismissal* (Cambridge, 1975).
Jackson, P.: *Natural Justice* (London, 1979).

Kahn-Freund, O. (ed.): *Labour Relations and the Law* (London, 1965).
——*Labour Law: Old Traditions and New Developments* (Toronto, 1967).
——*Labour and the Law* (London, 1977).

——(and Hepple, B. eds.): *Laws Against Strikes* (Fabian Research Series, no. 305, 1972).

MacCarthy, C.: *Trade Unions in Ireland 1894-1960* (Dublin, 1977).
McGlyne, J.E.: *Unfair Dismissal Cases* (London, 1979).
McGregor on Damages (14 ed., London, 1980).
Maine, Sir H.: *Ancient Law* (ed. F. Pollock, J. Murray, London, 1930).
Mansergh, N.: *The Irish Free State Constitution, its Government and Politics* (London, 1934).
Marx, K.: *Capital, The Communist Manifesto and Other Writings* (ed. M. Eastman, New York, 1932).
Meyers, F. *Ownership in Jobs* (California, 1964).
Murphy, J.N.: *Ireland, Industrial, Political and Social* (London, 1870).
Murray, A.: *Commercial Relations between England and Ireland* (London, 1903).
Murray, J.: *The Irish Economy since 1922* (Liverpool, 1970).

Napier, B.: *The Contract of Service: The Concept and its Application* (unpublished doctoral thesis for the University of Cambridge, 1976).
Nevin, D. (ed.): *Trade Unions and Change in Irish Society* (Dublin, 1980).
Newman, J.: *Studies in Political Morality* (Dublin, 1962).

O'Brien, G.: *Economic History of Ireland from the Union to the Famine* (London, 1921).
——*The Economic History of Ireland in the Eighteenth Century* (Dublin & London, 1918).
——*The Economic History of Ireland in the Seventeenth Century* (Dublin & London, 1919).
Ogus, A.I.: *The Law on Damages* (London, 1973).
O'Higgins, P.: *A Bibliography of Periodical Literature relating to Irish Law* (Belfast, 1966).
——First Supplement (Belfast, 1973).
O'Mahony, D.: *The Irish Economy* (Cork, 1967).
O'Reilly J. and Redmond, M.: *Cases and Materials on the Irish Constitution* (Dublin, 1980).

Petty, Sir W.: *Economic Writings* (Cambridge, 1899).
Pollock, H.M. (ed.): *Industrial Relations in Practice* (Dublin, 1981).

Redmond, M. & O'Reilly, J.: *Cases and Materials on the Irish Constitution* (Dublin, 1980).

Richardson & Sayles: *The Irish Parliament in the Middle Ages* (Philadelphia, 1952).
Rideout, R.: *Principles of Labour Law* (3rd ed., London, 1979).

Saville, J.: *Democracy and the Labour Movement* (Lawrence and Wishart, 1954).
Selznick, P.: *Law, Society and Industrial Justice* (New York, 1969).
Simon's Taxes (3rd ed., London, looseleaf).
Smith, C.M. on *Master and Servant* (London, 1860).
Street, H.: *Principles of the Law of Damages* (London, 1962).
Swift MacNeill, J.G.: *Studies in the Constitution of the Irish Free State* (Dublin, 1925).

Unger, R.M.: *Law in Modern Society* (London, 1976).

Wade and Phillips: *Constitutional and Administrative Law* (London, 1977).
Wayne, N.: *Labour Law in Ireland* (Dublin, 1980).
Webb, S. & B.: *Industrial Democracy* (London, 1899).
Williston: *A Treatise on the Law of Contracts* Rev. ed.

Zamir, I.: *The Declaratory Judgment* (London, 1962).

ARTICLES

Abrahamson, M.: 'Trade Disputes Act — Strict Interpretation in Ireland' (1961) 24 MLR 596.

Anon: 'Notice of Termination of a Contract of Service' (1941) 75 ILTSJ 59.

Anon: 'Wrongful Dismissal' (1919) 53 ILTSJ 75

Anon: 'Dismissal — Wrongful or Otherwise' (1959) 93 ILTSJ 23.

Anon: 'Master and Servant' (1866-'7) S.J. 11.

Bale, G.: 'British Transport Commission v. Gourley Reconsidered' (1966) 44 *Can. B.R.* 66.

Ballantine, D.G.: 'Assessment of Pensions Loss on Unfair Dismissal' (1980) 130 NLJ 576.

Beatty. D.M.: 'Labour is not a Commodity' in *Studies in Labour Law* (eds. B.J. Reiter and J. Swan) 313.

Blaghd, E.P. de.: 'How closed can my shop be?' (1972) 106 ILTSJ 67.

Blair, L.: 'The Civil Servant — A Status Relationship?' 21 MLR 265.

Blanc-Jouvan, X.: 'The Effect of Industrial Action on the Status of the Individual Employee' in *Industrial Conflict — A Comparative Legal Survey* (eds. B. Aaron and K. W. Wedderburn, London, 1972) 176.

Bowers, T. and Clarke A.: 'Unfair Dismissal and Managerial Prerogative: A study of "Other Substantial Reasons" ' (1981) ILJ 34.

Capstick, B.: 'Constructive Dismissal' (1979) 129 NLJ 499.

Carby-Hall, J.R.: 'Termination Aspects of Modern Employment' in *Studies in Labour Law* (ed., same, MCB Books, 1976).

Carr, C.: 'Unfair Dismissal — Exclusion of Subsequent Evidence' (1977) 127 NLJ 128.

Casey, J.: 'Judicial Power under Irish Constitutional Law' (1975) 24 ICLQ 305.

——'Some Implications of Freedom of Association in Labour Law: a comparative study with special reference to Ireland' (1972) 21 ICLQ 699.

Clampett, C.J.T.: 'The Economic Life of Ireland' (1928) JIBI 139.

Clark, de N.G.: 'Remedies for Unfair Dismissal: a European Comparison (1971) 20 ICLQ 397.

——'Unfair Dismissal and Reinstatement' (1969) 32 MLR 532.

——'Remedies for Unjust Dismissal' (1970) PEP Broadsheet 518.

Clark, D.H.: 'Natural Justice — Shadow or Substance?' (1975) *Public Law* 20.

Concannon, H.M.G.: 'Collective Agreements and Unfair Dismissal' (1978) 128 NLJ 900.

Connolly, P.: 'Damage in Tort and in Breach of Contract' (1975) Society of Young Solicitors Lecture no. 87.

Cook, Sir R.: 'Remoteness of Damage and Judicial Discretion' [1978] CLJ 288.

Costello, D.: 'Aspects of a Judicially Developed Jurisprudence of Human Rights in Ireland' in *Understanding Human Rights* (ed. A.D. Falconer, Dublin, 1980).

——'Measuring Damages in Breach of Contract Cases — some recent Irish decisions' (1978) Society of Young Solicitors Lecture no. 112.

Crowe, M.: 'Human Rights, The Irish Constitution and the Courts' (1971) 47 *Notre Dame Lawyer* 281.

Dawson, F.: 'Metaphors and Anticipatory Breach of Contract' [1981] CLJ 83.

Dickens, L. and others: 'Re-employment of Unfairly Dismissed Workers: The Lost Remedy' (1981) ILJ 160.

Dworkin, G.: 'Damages and Tax, a Comparative Survey' [1967] *British Tax Review* 315.

Elias, P.: 'The Concept of Fairness in Unfair Dismissal' — unpublished article to appear in (1981) ILJ, December.

——'Unravelling the Concept of Dismissal' (1978) ILJ 16, 100.

Farrell, B.: 'The Drafting of the Irish Free State Constitution' (1970) *Irish Jurist* 115.

Forrest, H.: 'Political Values in Individual Employment Law' (1980) 43 MLR 361.

Foster, K.: 'Strike Notice: Section 147' (1973) 2 ILJ 28.

——'From Status to Contract: Legal Form and Works Relations 1750-1850' Warwick Law Working Papers Vol. 3, no. 1 (1979).

Franzen, H.: 'Irland und Grossbrittanien seit 1919' in *Jahrbuch des offentlichen Rechts* (1938).

Fridman, H.L.: 'Termination of the Contract of Employment' (1966) 116 NLJ 551.

Fuller, L.L. & Perdue, W.R.: 'The Reliance Interest in Contract Damages' (1936) 46 YLJ 52.

Ganz, G.: 'Public Law Principles Applicable to Dismissal from Employment' (1967) 30 MLR 288.

Geary, R.C.: 'Irish Economic Development since the Treaty' (1951) *Studies* 399.

Goodhart, A.L.: 'Ridge v. Baldwin: Administration and Natural Justice' (1964) 80 LQR 105.

Hall, J.S.: "Taxation of Compensation for Loss of Income' (1959) 73 LQR 212.

Hart, H.M.: 'The Relations between State and Federal Law' (1954) 54 *Col. L. Rev.* 489.

Hart, H.M: and Wechsler, H.: 'The Federal Courts and the Federal System' (1954) 54 *Col. L. Rev.* 650.

Hepple, B.: 'A Right to Work' (1981) ILJ 65.

Herz, E.: 'The Protection of Employees on the Termination of Contracts of Employment' 69 *Int. L. R.* 215.

Heuston, R.F.V.: 'Personal Rights under the Irish Constitution' (1976) XI *Irish Jurist* 205.

——'Trade Unions and the Law' (1969) IV *Irish Jurist* 10.

Hill, A.: 'Constitutional Remedies' (1969) 69 *Col. L. Rev.* 1109.

Hiller, A.: 'Compensation for Stress in Unfair Dismissal' (1978) 128 NLJ 1212.

Holmes, R.: 'The Ownership of Work: A Psychological Approach' (1967) 5 BJIR 19.

Jackson, J.: 'The Right to Work' (1959) 13 *Christus Rex* 203.

Jeffers, V.: 'Fixed-Term Contracts' (1978) 128 NLJ 180.

Jolowicz, A.J.: 'Damages and Income Tax' [1959] CLJ 86.

Kahn-Freund, O.: 'Uses and Misuses of Comparative Law' (1974) 37 MLR 1.

——'Blackstone's Neglected Child' (1977) 93 LQR 508.

——'A note on Status and Contract in British Labour Law' (1967) 30 MLR 635.

Katz, A.: 'The Jurisprudence of Remedies: Constitutional Legality and the Law of Torts in Bell v. Hood' (1968) 117 *U. Penn L. Rev.* 1.

Keigher, S.D.: 'Unfair Dismissals Awards and Taxation' (1979) 113 ILTSJ 301.

Kelly, J.M.: 'Audi Alteram Partem' (1964) 9 *Natural Law Forum* 103.

Lawson, R.G.: 'Damages — Some Recent Developments' (1978) 128 NLJ 600, 627.

——'Mitigation of Damages: Recent Developments' (1978) 128 NLJ 1185.

Lee, J.: 'The Role of the Worker in Irish Society since 1945' in *Trade Unions and Change in Irish Society* (ed. D. Nevin, Dublin, 1980) 11.

Lehain, P.: 'Calculating the question of Damages for Wrongful Dismissal' (1979) 129 NLJ 887.

Levy, H.M.: 'The Role of the Law in the US and England in Protecting the Worker from Discharge and Discrimination' (1968) 18 ICLQ 558.

McCartney, J.C.B.: 'Strike Law and the Constitution of Éire' in *Labour Relations and the Law* (ed. O. Kahn-Freund, London, 1965).

McGregor, H.: 'Compensation versus Punishment in Damages Awards' (1965) 28 MLR 629.

McMullen, J.: 'Unfair Dismissal and the Merits of an Industrial Dispute' (1980) 130 NLJ 670.

McWhinney: 'The Courts and the Constitution in Catholic Ireland' (1954) 29 *Tul. L. Rev.* 69.

Manchester, C.: 'Frustration or Dismissal' (1978) 128 NLJ 674.

——'Remoteness of Damage — Contract and Tort reconciled?' (1978) 128 NLJ 113.

Markson, H.E.: 'Commercial Contracts: Damages for Distress?' (1979) 129 NLJ 359.

Mathews, M.: 'The Tort of Conspiracy in Irish Labour Law' (1973) VIII *Irish Jurist* 252.

Mellish M. and Collis-Squire, N.: 'Legal and Social Norms in Discipline and Dismissal' (1976) 5 ILJ 164.

Melville, L.: 'The Nature of Fundamental Breach' (1980) 130 NLJ 307.

Messineo, F.: 'La Nuova Constituzione Irlandese' 88 *Civiltà Cattolica* 239.

Munday, R.: 'Tribunal Lore: Legalism and the Industrial Tribunals' (1981) ILJ 146.

Napier, B.: 'Judicial Attitudes towards the Employment Relationship — Some Recent Developments' (1977) 6 ILJ 1.

Newark, F.N.: 'Notes on Irish Legal History' (1947) 7 NILQ 121.

Norris, A.E.: 'Fixed Term Contracts: The Continuing Problems' (1979) 129 NLJ 1195.

O'Brien, G.: 'The Economic Progress of Ireland 1912-'62' (1960) JIBI 251.

O'Driscoll, J.: 'The Effect of Recent Case and Statute Law in the Common Law Employer/Employee Relationship' Society of Young Solicitors Lecture no. 101, April 1977.

O'Higgins, P.: 'The Right to Strike — Some International Reflections' in *Studies in Labour Law* (ed. J.R. Carby-Hall, MCB Books, 1976).

——'Strike Notices: Another Approach' (1973) 2 ILJ 152.

O'Mahony, D.: 'Economic Theory and the Irish Economy' (1960) JIBI 251.

Park, P.: 'The Combination Acts in Ireland, 1727-1825' (1979) 14 *Irish Jurist,* 340.

Redmond, M.: 'Waiver of Constitutional Rights' (1979-'80) DULR 104.

——'Justifying his decision to dismiss: the Employer's Role under the Unfair Dismissals Act 1979' (1980) IBAR 58.

——'Dismissal for taking part in Strike or other industrial action' (1980) *Gazette of the Incorporated Law Society of Ireland* 101, 119.

——'The Law and Workers Rights' in *Trade Unions and Change in Irish Society* (ed. D. Nevin, Dublin, 1980) 82.

——'Section 7: Primary Remedies for Unfair Dismissal' (1977) 111 ILTSJ 245.

——(unsigned): 'The System of Rights Commissioners in Ireland' (1974) 108 ILTSJ 252.

Roach, P.M.: 'Damages for loss of earnings in personal injury claims' (1959) 33 ALJ 11.

Robinson, M. and Temple Lang, J.: 'The Constitution and the Right to Reinstatement after Wrongful Dismissal' (1977) *Gazette of the Incorporated Law Society of Ireland* 78.

Samuels, A.: 'Summary or instant dismissal of an employee' (1967) 111 *Sol. J.* 709.

——'Gourley Revisited and Rejected' (1967) 30 MLR 83.

——'Safety and Dismissal: Dismissal and Safety' (1980) 130 NLJ 395.

——'Jurisdiction of Employment Appeal Tribunal: The Need to Widen the Scope' (1981) 131 NLJ 931.

Shrubsall, V.: 'Some Rulings by the EAT on Unfair Dismissal' (1977) 127 NLJ 506.

Simon, D.: 'Master and Servant' in *Democracy and the Labour Movement* (ed. J. Saville, Lawrence & Wishart, 1954).

Steiber, J.: 'Protection against Unfair Dismissal: A Comparative View', paper presented to International Industrial Relations Association (Paris) 1979.

Swan, J. and Reiter, B.J.: 'Contracts and the Protection of Reasonable Expectations' in *Studies in Contract Law* (eds. B.J. Reiter and J. Swan) 1.

Swinton, K.: 'Contract Law and the Employment Relationship: The Proper Forum for Reform' in *Studies in Contract Law* (eds. B.J. Reiter and J. Swan) 358.

——'Forseeability: Where Should The Award of Contract Damages Cease?' *ibid.,* 61.

Temple Lang, J.: 'Private Law Aspects of the Irish Constitution' (1971) VI *Irish Jurist* 237.

Townshend-Smith, R.: 'Recognising a Contract of Employment' (1979) 129 NLJ 993.

Valticos, N.: 'The future prospects for international labour standards' (1979) 118 *Int. Lab. Rev.* 679.

Weisbard, S.: 'Termination of contract of service' (1968) 118 NLJ 412.

White, F.: 'Terminating the Contract of Employment' (1964) JBL 314.

Williams, K.: 'Job Security and Unfair Dismissal' (1975) 38 MLR 292.

Williams, K. and Lewis, D.: 'The aftermath of tribunal reinstatement and re-engagement' DES Research Paper no. 23, 1981.

Woods, J.C.: 'The Disobedient Servant' (1959) 22 MLR 526.

Wylie, J. and McGlyne, J.: 'Taxation, Damages and Compensation for Unfair Dismissal' (1978) 128 NLJ 550.

OFFICIAL PUBLICATIONS

Publications of the Stationery Office, Dublin, and of Government Departments

Tenth Annual Report of the EAT, 1977 (Stationery Office, Dublin, Prl. 7272).

Eleventh Annual Report of the EAT, 1978 (Prl. 8373).

Twelfth Annual Report of the EAT, 1979 (Prl. 9233).

Reports of Important Decisions by the EAT under the Unfair Dismissals Act 1977: years 1977 and 1978 (Stationery Office, Dublin, Prl. 8765).

Thirty-Third Annual Report of the Labour Court, 1979 (Stationery Office, Dublin, Prl. 8932).

Economic Review and Outlook, Summer 1980, Stationery Office, Dublin, Prl. 8967.

Debates of *Dáil* and *Seanad Éireann*

Irish Statistical Bulletin.

British and other Reports

The Journals of the House of Commons of the Kingdom of Ireland.

Seventh Report of the English Law Reform Committee on the Taxation of Damages Cmnd. 501 (1958).

Report of the Royal Commission on Trade Unions and Employer's Associations (Donovan Report) 1968, Cmnd. 3623.

ILO: *Record of Proceedings,* Int. Lab. Conference 33rd Sess., (1950).

ILO: *Termination of Employment (dismissal and lay-off) Report VII (1),* International Labour Conference, 46th sess., 1962.

Freedom of Assembly: Digest of Decisions of the Freedom of Assembly Committee of the Governing Body of the ILO (Geneva, 1972).

ILO: *Report III: Termination of Employment* Int. Lab. Conf. 59th sess., 1974.

ILO: *Report VIII (2) on Termination of Employment at the Initiative of the Employer* (67th session, 1981).

Department of Employment Gazette.

INDEX

Note: The method of alphabetisation used is *word-by-word*.
Abbreviations: EAT: Employment Appeals Tribunal
UDA: Unfair Dismissals Act

ABSENTEEISM
dismissal for, 148
ABUSIVE BEHAVIOUR
employer, of, 173
AGE-LIMIT
applications under UDA, for, 130
AGREEMENT
discharging statutory claims 201-02
excluding or limiting application of
UDA, 121, 142*n*
ALTERNATIVE EMPLOYMENT
refusal of,
duty to mitigate and, 108, 200-01
pregnant employee 155
what constitutes 155-6
APPEAL
Circuit Court, to, 122-3
form 270
High Court, to, 123, 123*n*-24*n*
legal aid 122*n*, 125
regulations 256-9
Rights Commissioner, from, 124,
223
time for bringing 134
APPRENTICE
restrictions in UDA concerning, 131,
132-3
ASSOCIATION, FREEDOM OF, 34-
5
dismissal for exercise of, 32-3
dissociation, includes right of, 35-7
employer's right to,
reinstatement or re-engagement
and, 176-7
limit on, 36*n*
regulation of, by UDA, 177
AUDI ALTERAM PARTEM 69
fair hearing 76-7
employees governed by Statute 70-4
offices held at will or pleasure 74-6
principle 70
scope of, 76-8
tribunals, hearings before, 76-7
AUTOMATIC THEORY OF
TERMINATION
unfair dismissal 135-40, 143-4
wrongful dismissal 83, 84, 231

BLACKSTONE, SIR WILLIAM
Commentaries 6, 9-10

BOLTON, SIR RICHARD, 9
BONUS PAYMENTS
damages for loss of, 103

CAPABILITY
dismissal for, 147
warning: need for, 163
CERTIORARI 109, 111*n*
CIRCUIT COURT
appeals to, under UDA, 122-3
legal aid 122*n*
time for bringing 134
CIVIL SERVANT
nature of employment 51
termination of services 51
notice of, 57
see also Public Employee
CLOSED SHOP 109*n*
pre-entry, 38-9
right of dissociation and, 35
right to work and, 37-8
CODE OF PRACTICE
need for, 203*n*
COLLECTIVE AGREEMENT
disciplinary and dismissal procedures
in, 26, 63*n*
legal enforceability of, 26
COLLECTIVE ISSUES
individualisation of, in UDA, 203-04
COMMISSION PAYMENTS
damages for loss of, 103
COMMON LAW
Constitution superior to, 33, 41
dismissal at, 45-86, 220-1
abuse of Constitution 32-33
contract, importance of, 45-6, 221
damages, *see* Damages for
Wrongful Dismissal
employee, definition of, 46-7
lawful, *see* Lawful Dismissal
office-holder, definition 47-51
wrongful 19-20, 23-5 *and see*
Wrongful Dismissal
master-servant relationship,
development of, 18-23
COMPENSATION FOR UNFAIR
DISMISSAL 176, 184-202
actual loss 188-90
deductions 191
expenses 189-90

illness, where, 189
legal costs 190
manner of dismissal, loss relating
    to, 190
mitigate, duty to, 189, 199-201
agreed settlements 202
assessment of, principles for, 186*n*
average award 185, 272
basic award, need for, 222*n*
Britain, in, 185*n*-86*n*
calculation of loss 185-6
    need for improvement 222*n*
contributory action 191, 197-9, 201,
    222*n*
costs 189-90
deductions
    contribution to loss 191, 197-9,
        222*n*
    income tax 192, 222*n*
    mitigate, failure to, 200, 201
    notice period, payment during, 189
    redundancy payments 150*n*
    social welfare benefits 188, 191,
        222*n*
definition 186
determination of, 187
deterrent effect 184-5
Employment Appeals Tribunal,
    approach of, 184-6, 222*n*
ex-gratia payments 187-8, 201-02
expenses, loss of, 189*n*-90*n*
financial loss: meaning 186-7
future loss, *see* prospective loss
    (infra)
maximum limit 186, 188
mitigate, duty to, 189, 199
    general principles 200
    reasonableness test 201
    re-engagement or reinstatement
        and, 201
    refusal of offer of employment
        200-01
nil award 188
pension rights, loss of, 195-6, 222*n*
proof of loss 187
property right in job 176, 186*n*
prospective loss 188, 192-4
    disability benefit, receipt of, 193
    statutory rights, loss of protection
        of, 188, 194
reforms suggested 222*n*
regulations, 260-3
remedy of, 186-8
severance payments and, 187-8, 201-
    02

statutory rights
    loss or diminution of, 188, 194
taxation of, 192, 222*n*
unfair dismissal finding necessary
    for, 187-8
COMPETENCE
    dismissal for reasons of, 147, 148
    reasonableness of, 167
    summary dismissal 58-9
    warning 163
COMPULSORY LABOUR 6, 7-8
CONDUCT, *see* Misconduct
CONSTITUTION OF IRELAND
    actions *inter partes* 30-1
        locus standi 31
    constitutional justice 68-9
    Directive Principles of Social Policy 3
    dismissal, and, 4, 28-44, 220
        abuse of rights 33
        damages for, 42
        express rights in relation to, 33-4
        infringement of rights 32-40
        remedies 40-4
    fundamental rights, *see* personal
        rights *(infra)*
    judicial review 28*n*, 29-30, 29*n*
    legislation:
        presumption of constitutionality
            29*n*, 71-2
    natural justice and, 68-9, 71-2, 75
    office-holder at will or pleasure
        dismissal of, 75
    personal rights, 3-4, 29, 31-2
        abuse of, 33
        access to courts 126*n*
        association, freedom of, 34-5
            employer, of, 176-8
        breach of remedies for, 40-4
        dissociation, freedom of, 35-7
        emuneration of, 3*n*, 31-2
        fair procedures 39-40, 65, 76
        infringement of, 30, 32-3
        property rights, distinguished from,
            32*n*
        protection of, 30
        strike, right to, 32, 212*n*-13*n*
        unspecified 31-2
        waiver of, 38-9
        work, right to, 32, 37-9
    Preamble 2-3
    remedies for breach of, 40-4
    separation of powers, 29*n*
    sources of inspiration for, 33*n*
    supreme position of, 4, 33, 41, 75

CONSTITUTION OF THE IRISH
FREE STATE
fundamental rights 28-9
CONSTITUTIONAL JUSTICE
natural justice, and, 68-9
CONSTITUTIONAL REMEDIES 40
damages 41-3
declaration 41
injunction 41
reinstatement 43-4
CONSTRUCTIVE DISMISSAL 136,
137, 140-2, 145, 154, 169-74
abusive behaviour 173
contract test 140, 145, 169-70
contractual repudiation by employer
change in obligations, insistence
on, 154, 170-1
definition 134, 136
demotion 170n-71n
employee repudiation 138, 142
flexibility clause 174
hours of work, change in, 171
mobility clause 174
onus of proof 170
place of work, change in, 171
reasonableness test 140, 141-2, 145,
170
remuneration, reduction in 170
resignation by employee 170n
unreasonable treatment 173
variation of contract 174
CONTINUOUS SERVICE 129-30,
222n
calculation of, 129n
re-engagement and, 180
CONTRACT FOR SERVICES
self-employed person bound by, 47
CONTRACT OF EMPLOYMENT
breach of condition 85
central role of, 221, 227
change in terms
employer's insistence on, 82, 154,
170-1
refusal of employee to accept 153-
4
common law:
development of doctrine at, 18-20,
23
contract for services, and, 47
dismissal
in accordance with, *see* Lawful
Dismissal
in breach of, *see* Wrongful Dismissal
procedures 63-4

duties 229
employee, of, 58-9, 150n
employer, of, 171-2
equality and domination, dual feature
of, 19, 45
fixed-term, for, *see* Fixed-term
Contract
flexibility clause 153, 174
frustration of, 52n-53n, 148, 169
fundamental breach 85
implied terms
breach of, 64-6, 170n, 171-3
examples of, 171-2
fair procedures 40, 64-6
notice of termination, as to, 52, 53
importance of, 45-6
life, for, 55
mobility clause 153, 174
nature of, 228-30
civil servant 51
employee 46-7
office-holder 47-9
public employee 50-1
status 49-50
two-tiered structure 229-30, 231
notice of termination, *see* Notice of
Termination
obligations 229
office-holder, and, 48, 49
permanent employment, meaning 54-
5
procedural fairness, breach of, 64-6
procedural limitations, breach of, 63-
4, 94-5
repudiation of, *see* Repudiation of
Contract
specific performance of,
unavailability of, 83, 87-90
specified purpose contract 55, 132,
134
statute law, recognition in, 6, 9-10,
15-16
strike: effect of, 215n, 216, 218-19
structure of, 229-30
substantive limitations, breach of, 66-
7, 94
termination of, *see* Termination
Unfair Dismissals Act
based on, 128
excluding or limiting application
of, 121, 142n
variation of, 174
CONTRIBUTORY ACTION,
see under Compensation

COSTS
  award of, 126, 190
  expenses, as, 190
CRIMINAL OFFENCE 158n, 165-6
  involvement of Gardai in, 166
  jail sentence:
    frustration of contract by, 169
  outside employment 169
  representation, right to, 165-6

DAMAGES FOR WRONGFUL DIS-
    MISSAL 87, 91-109
  assessment of,
    general principles 91-4
  bonus payments, loss of, 103
  breach of contract, for, 87, 230
  claim: time for bringing 87
  commission payments, loss of, 103
  constitutional right, breach of, 41-2
  deductions
    income tax 104-06, 192n
    redundancy payments 103-04
    social welfare benefits 107
  demotion 100-01
  disappointment 98, 100-01
  earnings in kind, loss of, 103
  elective theory of repudiatory breach
      and, 95-8
  exemplary 115
  ex-gratia payments, loss of, 103
  feelings, injury to, 98, 99
  fixed-term contract 93
  limit, absence of, 221
  mental distress 98, 100-01
  mitigation of loss 107-09
  office-holders and pubic employees:
    additional remedy, as, 111-12
    alternative remedy, as, 110-11
    exemplary 115
    quantum of, 113-15
  overtime, loss of, 103
  pension rights, loss of, 101-03
  procedural limitations, breach of, 94-
      5
  publicity, loss of, 99-100
  redundancy payments, deductability
      of, 103-04
  reputation, loss of, 98, 99
  statutory seniority rights, loss of, 103
  substantive limitations, breach of, 94
  taxation of, 104-06
  unconstitutional dismissal 41-3
DEATH
  employee, of, 129n, 130
  employer, of, 130

DECLARATORY RELIEF 109-10
  employees, for, 90-1
  unconstitutional dismissal
    as remedy for, 41
DEFENCE FORCES
  discharge of member of, 72
  excluded from UDA provisions 131
  officers 51
DEFINITIONS
  date of dismissal 143
  dismissal 134
  employee
    common law, at, 46-7
    UDA, in, 129n, 130
  employer, 130
  industrial action 216-17
  office-holder 47-50
  redundancy, dismissal for, 151n
  re-engagement and reinstatement
      178-80
  repudiation of contract 82
  self-employed person 47
  strike 215
  trade dispute 18, 205
  workmen 205
  wrongful dismissal 45
DISABILITY BENEFITS, RECEIPT
    OF, 193
DISAPPOINTMENT
  damages for, 98, 100-01
DISCIPLINARY AND DISMISSAL
    PROCEDURES
  collective agreement, inclusion in,
      26-7, 63n
  contract, incorporation in, 63
  dismissal in breach of, 63
    damages for, 94-5
  duty of employer to furnish details of,
      63-4
  example of, 162n
  terms of employment, inclusion in, 64
DISHONESTY, DISMISSAL FOR,
    168-9
DISMISSAL
  Constitution and, *see* Constitution of
    Ireland
  constructive, *see* Constructive Dis-
    missal
  common law, at, *see:* Lawful Dis-
    missal; Wrongful Dismissal
  definition of, 134
    need for clarification 222, 231
  disputes relating to, *see under* Trade
    Dispute
  summary, *see* Summary Dismissal

unconstitutional 33-4, 40-4
unfair, *see* Unfair Dismissal
wrongful, *see* Wrongful Dismissal
DISMISSAL LAW
British influences 1-2
collective agreements
legal enforceability of, 26
Constitution, influence of, 2-4
contract model 4
recognition of, 6, 9-10, 15-16,
17-18, 19-20
historical development of, 4-23
DISMISSAL PROCEDURES
see Disciplinary and Dismissal Procedures
DISOBEDIENCE, DISMISSAL FOR,
154
reasonableness test 167-8
DISPUTE, *see* Trade Dispute
DISSOCIATION, RIGHT OF, 35-7,
35n
dismissal for insistence on, 33, 36-7
limit on, 36n
DUTTON, MATTHEW, 5n, 8-11,
12n, 13

EARNINGS IN KIND, LOSS OF,
damages for, 103
ELECTIVE THEORY OF TERMINA-
TION
damages and, 95-8
unfair dismissal context, in, 136, 137
wrongful dismissal context, in, 82-6
ELIAS, P., 136
EMPLOYEE
constructive dismissal, *see* Constructive Dismissal
death of, 129n, 130
definition of,
common law, at, 46-7
UDA, in, 129n, 130
dismissal, *see* Dismissal
duties of, 150n
mitigation of loss, *see* Mitigation
office-holder, distinguished from, 46,
47-8
repudiation of contract 83, 136, 138,
142
summary dismissal for, 58-9
rights of, 171-2
Constitutional, *see under*
Constitution
EMPLOYER
abusive behaviour 173
death of, 130

definition 130
duties towards employee 171-2
freedom of association, right to,
reinstatement and, 176-7
reasonableness of, *see* Reasonableness of Decision to Dismiss
repudiation of contract *see* Repudiation of contract
EMPLOYER LABOUR
CONFERENCE
Codes of Fair Employment, Report
on, 27
EMPLOYMENT APPEALS
TRIBUNAL 121-7, 223-7
Annual Reports 223, 224
appeals *see* Appeal
attendance, notice requiring 125n
chairman 124
claim, time for bringing 133
compensation, approach to, 184-6
see also Compensation
composition of, 124-5
costs, award of, 126, 190
expenses, as, 190
determinations 121-2, 125n
consistency: need for, 226-7
failure to carry out 122
precedent 125n
review mechanism 227
documents, production of, 125n
establishment of, 124
evidence before, 125n
excluded claims 125-6
expenses 126, 190
hearing
legal representation at, 125, 224-5
non-attendance by employer 153n
postponement of, 225
legal aid, unavailability of, 125,
224-5
legal representation before, 125,
224-5, 273
legislation, interpretation of, 226-7
parties and claims, study of, 225-6
penalties 125n
practice
generally, 122, 227
trends in, 223-6
principles, generally, 122
procedure 125-6
reasonableness of employers decision
determination of, 159-60
reinstatement or re-engagement
determination of appropriateness
of, 181-4

Reports of Important Decisions
  1977-1978, 121-2
representation before 125, 224-5
resort to, 223-4
review of decisions 227
Rights Commissioner Recommendation appeals 124, 134, 223
speed of operation 221*n*
statistics
  cases decided, 126
  dismissals judged unfair 224
time-limits for claims and appeals
  133-4, 222*n*
vexatious or frivolous applications
  126, 190
withdrawal of claims 225
witnesses 125*n*
EMPLOYMENT REGULATED BY
  STATUTE
see Public employee
EUROPEAN COMMISSION
individual dismissals, report on,
  (1976) 119
EXPENSES
award of, 126, 190
compensation for loss of, 189*n*-90*n*
legal costs as, 190
EX-GRATIA PAYMENTS
agreed settlements, in, 201-02
damages for loss of, 103

FAIR DISMISSAL
categories of, 147
FAIR HEARING, RIGHT TO, 76-7,
  164-5
FAIR PROCEDURES, RIGHT TO,
  39-40, 65, 76
breach of, 64-6
contract, implied in, 40, 64-6
enforcement of, 44
FEELINGS, INJURY TO,
compensation for, 190
damages for, 98, 99
FIGHTING 163-4, 168
FIXED-PURPOSE CONTRACT
see Specified Purpose Contract
FIXED — TERM CONTRACT
damages for breach of, 93
date of dismissal 143
expiry of, without renewal 132
  dismissal, as, 134, 135
termination before time 55
FLEXIBILITY CLAUSE 153, 174
FREEDOM OF ASSOCIATION, *see*
  Association, Freedom of,

FRUSTRATION OF CONTRACT
illness or incapacity, through, 148
  notice, whether necessary 52*n*-53*n*
jail sentence, by, 169

GARDA SIOCHANA, MEMBER OF,
dismissal of, 73-4
excluded from UDA, 131
natural justice, right to, 73-4
office-holder, as, 51
GROSS MISCONDUCT 149-50
see also Misconduct

HEALTH BOARD, OFFICER OF,
excluded from UDA, 131, 131*n*-32*n*
HEARING
appeal procedures 80-1
criminal conduct, where, 165-6
EAT, before, *see under* Employment
  Appeals Tribunal
employees governed by Statute 70-4
fair, right to, 76-7, 164-5
  denial of, 77-8
misconduct, where, 166
natural justice, requirements of, 69,
  76-80
  failure to comply with, 81
notice to employee 70
procedures 77
representation, right to, 165
HIGH COURT
appeal to, under UDA, 123, 123*n*-
  24*n*
HISTORICAL DEVELOPMENT
  OF DISMISSAL LAW, 4-23
HOURS OF WORK
change in, 171

ILLNESS, *see* Sickness
INCAPACITY 147
frustration of contract 52*n*-53*n*
INCOME TAX, LIABILITY TO,
compensation, 192, 222*n*
damages, 104-06, 192*n*
INCOMPETENCE *see* Competence
INDUSTRIAL ACTION
definition 216-17
dismissal for participation in, 206,
  212
immunity under Trade Disputes Act
  205
pressure on employer to dismiss 158
reinstatement or re-engagement,
  where, 183
selective dismissals 217
see also Strike

INJUNCTION RESTRAINING
DISMISSAL
office-holders 109
ordinary employees 89-90
unconstitutional dismissals 41
INSTANT DISMISSAL, *see* Summary
Dismissal
INTERNATIONAL LABOUR
ORGANISATION
Conventions and Recommendations
116n
Recommendation no. 119, 116
excluded categories 129n
standards 117-18
summary dismissal 149n
under review 128
Report (VIII) on Termination (1981),
117n, 129n, 150n

JOB, PROPERTY INTEREST IN,
175-6, 186n
JUDICIAL REVIEW 28n, 29-30

LABOUR, MINISTER FOR,
appellate proceedings in Circuit
Court 122
LABOUR FORCE SURVEY, 1979,
45n
LANGUAGE, ABUSIVE, 173
LAWFUL DISMISSAL 51-62
definition 51
fixed-term contract 55
notice of termination 52-4, 54-5
statutory notice 56-7
summary, 57-62, *see also* Summary
Dismissal
LEGAL AID
Circuit Court proceedings, 122n
unavailability of, in EAT cases, 125,
224-5
LEGAL COSTS 126, 190
LEGAL REPRESENTATION 124n,
125, 224-5, 273
LITIGATE, RIGHT TO, 126n
LOCAL AUTHORITY
dismissal of servants 50
officer of,
excluded from UDA, 131, 222n
temporary 131n-32n, 222n

MAINE, SIR HENRY 5
MANAGEMENT-UNION AGREE-
MENT
dismissal in accordance with, 160n

MANNER OF DISMISSAL, LOSS
DUE TO,
compensation for, 190
damages for, 98-9
MASTER-SERVANT RELATION-
SHIP
contractual basis of,
recognition of, 9-10, 15-16, 18-20,
23
development of,
common law, at, 18-23
statute law, at, 4-18
termination of, 11, 12-14, 20-3
wrongful dismissal, action for, 19-20,
23-5
MATERNITY LEAVE
remedies for unfair dismissal 156
replacement, dismissal of, 133
return to work, right to, 156
MINIMUM NOTICE 56-7
MISCONDUCT
criminal 158n, 165-6, 168-9
dismissal for, 147, 149-50
delay in, 166
fair, 147
procedure 163-4, 165, 166
reasonableness of decision 158,
168
fighting or violence 163-4, 168
gross 149
first offence 149
what constitutes 149-50
reinstatement 183
subsequently discovered evidence
157, 197n
summary dismissal 57n, 59-61, 62,
149n
MITIGATION OF DAMAGES
applicable to compensation claim 199
burden of proof 199
principles 200
refusal of other employment
200-01
reasonableness test 108-09
rules of, 107
MOBILITY CLAUSE 153, 174

NATURAL JUSTICE, RULES OF,
68-81
appeal procedures 80-1
audi alteram partem 69-78
constitutional justice, and, 68-9
employees governed by statute 70-4
fair hearings 76-8
industrial due process 161

nemo judex in re sua 78-81
offices held at will or pleasure 74-6
unfair dismissal cases, 160-1
NEMO JUDEX IN RE SUA, 78-81
NOTICE OF TERMINATION
  common law, at, 52-4
  dismissal without, *see* Summary Dismissal
  fixed term contract 55
  frustration of contract, where, 52n-53n
  inadequate 62
  period 143
    payment during, 189
    time-off 120n
  permanent employment and, 54-5
  revocation of, 143n
  statutory minimum notice 56-7
OFFICE-HOLDER
  civil servant, whether, 51
  definition 47-50
  employee, distinguished from, 47
  exclusion from UDA, 131
  natural justice, *see* Natural Justice
  notice of termination 57
  status-holder 49-50
  statute, employment regulated by, 50-1, 70-4
  temporary officer 131n-32n
  will or pleasure, at, 74-6
  wrongful dismissal 67-8
    damages for, 110-12, 113-15
    declaratory relief 109-10
    injunction 109
    protection against, 67-8,
    and see Natural Justice
OIREACHTAS, ACT OF,
  judicial review of, 29
  office-holder under, 48n
  presumption of constitutionality 29n
OVERTIME, LOSS OF,
  damages for, 103

PARLIAMENT OF IRELAND
  compulsory labour , Act effecting 7-8
  extent of application of Acts 7
PENAL LAWS, 5n-6n
PENSION RIGHTS, LOSS OF,
  compensation for, 195-6, 222n
  damages for, 101-03
PERMANENT EMPLOYMENT 54-5
PLACE OF WORK
  change in, 171
PREGNANCY, DISMISSAL FOR,
  130, 133

  alternative employment, offer of, 155-6
  compensation 193n
  failure to disclose pregnancy 155
  reinstatement, right to, 156
  return to work 156
  unfair dismissal, as, 154-5
  see also Maternity Leave
PROBATIONARY WORKER 132
  office-holder 109n
PROCEDURAL FAIRNESS, *see* Fair Procedures
PROCEDURAL JUSTICE
  definition 158-9
  substantive justice and, 159, 161-2
PROCEDURES, DISMISSAL
  see Disciplinary and Dismissal Procedures
PROPERTY RIGHT IN JOB 175-6, 186n
PUBLIC EMPLOYEE
  dismissal of, 50-1
    natural justice, right to, 70-4
  wrongful dismissal 67-8
    remedies for, 109-15
PUBLICITY, LOSS OF,
  damages for, 99-100

QUALIFICATIONS, DISMISSAL FOR, 147

REASON FOR DISMISSAL
  absenteeism 148
  bad example 153
  burden of proof 147
  capability 147, 148, 163
  competence 147, 148, 163, 167
  conduct, *see* Misconduct
  contractual terms
    refusal to accept change in, 153
  evidence of, 156-8
    subsequent, 156-7
  fair dismissal 147
    other substantial grounds 153-4
  identification of, 145-6
  industrial action, participation in, 206, 212, 216-17
  industrial pressure on employer 158
  maternity leave, refusal to permit return 156
  misconduct, *see* Misconduct
  potentially valid 147
  pregnancy 154-6
  qualifications 147, 148
  real reason, 157-8
  reasonableness of decision, *see*

Reasonableness of decision to
dismiss
redundancy
see Redundancy
strike, participation in, *see* Strike
subsequent evidence 156-7, 197*n*
summary dismissal, justifying, 57-61
theft 158*n*, 165-6
trade union membership or activities
206, 207-09
unfair, reasons deemed to be, 154-6
written statement of, 146-7
REASONABLE NOTICE 53
REASONABLENESS OF DECISION
TO DISMISS 158-69
EAT, role of, 159-60, 167
employer's enquiry, nature of, 160-6
adequate hearing 164-6
fair procedures 161
natural justice, requirements of,
160-1
representation 165
warning, *see* Warning
in light of all circumstances 166-9
objective standard of fairness 160
test of reasonableness 159
REDUNDANCY
collective, 211*n*
dismissal for, 147, 150-3
burden of proof 151-2
fair 147
unfair 152
meaning 151
payments: compensation reduced by,
150*n*
proof of, 152-3
Redundancy Appeals Tribunal
regulations 264-6
selection for,
agreed procedure, contravention
of, 209-10
custom or practice, breach of,
210-11
reasonableness of, 211
striking workers 217-18
unfair 150-1, 209
REDUNDANCY PAYMENTS
compensation reduced by, 150*n*
damages, whether deductible from,
103-04
refund of, on reinstatement 183
tax-free 192*n*
RE-ENGAGEMENT, *see* Reinstatement and Re-Engagement

REFERENCE
refusal to provide 200
REINSTATEMENT AND RE-
ENGAGEMENT 87-9, 176-84
application of, in Britain 178*n*-79*n*
appropriateness of, 181-4
closure of factory, where, 182
constitutional right, for breach of,
43-4
continuous service and, 180
contributory conduct 182-3
definition 178-80, 222*n*
employee, wishes of, 181
employer's right to freedom of
association, and, 176-8
maternity leave, after, 156
opposition to, 181, 183
order for,
enforcement of, 91, 123*n*
non-compliance with, 179*n*
practicality of compliance 181-2,
183-4
redundancy payments, refund of, 183
replacement, after appointment of,
181-2, 222*n*
rights and privileges 180
salary 179-80
social welfare benefits 179
statistics 184
strike, after dismissal for, 212*n*
unconstitutional dismissal, after, 43-4
wrongful dismissal, refusal for, 87-9,
91
REMEDIES
see under: Constitution; Unfair Dismissal; Wrongful Dismissal
REPLACEMENT EMPLOYEE
maternity leave, where, 133
reinstatement or re-engagement and,
181-2, 222*n*
REPUDIATION OF CONTRACT
breach of express terms 170
change in performance or obligations
insistence on, 82, 154, 170-1
effect of,
automatic theory of termination
83, 84, 135-40, 143-4
elective theory 82-6, 136, 137
employee, by, 83, 136, 138, 142
summary dismissal for, 58-9
REPUTATION, LOSS OF,
damages for, 98,99
RESTITUTIO IN INTEGRUM
91-3

RETIRING AGE, EMPLOYEE
OVER, 130
RIGHTS COMMISSIONER 121, 124
appeal from 124, 223
time limit for, 134
appointment of, 27, 124
dispute dismissals
reference of, 127
excluded claims 125
objections to hearings before, 124*n*,
125
procedure 124
proceedings before, 121
recommendations
failure to carry out 124
statistics 1977-9: 223, 224
resort to, 126, 223
time-limit for claims, 120

SELECTION FOR REDUNDANCY,
see under Redundancy
SELF-EMPLOYED PERSON 47
SEMI-STATE EMPLOYEE
inclusion in UDA, 131*n*
SEVERANCE PAYMENTS 201-02
SICKNESS, ABSENCE DUE TO,
frustration of contract by, 52*n*-53*n*,
148
ground for dismissal 148
SMALL EMPLOYMENTS 130
SOCIAL WELFARE BENEFITS
deduction of,
compensation, from, 188, 191
damages, from, 107
reinstated employee 179
SPECIFIC PERFORMANCE 21*n*
unavailability of, 87-90
SPECIFIED PURPOSE CONTRACT
55
completion of, 132, 134
date of dismissal 143
STATE EMPLOYEE 131
see also Civil Servant; Public
Employee
STATUS-HOLDER
office-holder, as, 49-50
STATUTE
employee governed by, *see* Public
Employee
STATUTORY AUTHORITY
dismissal of servants, 50-1
STRIKE
contract:
whether terminated by, 215*n*, 216,
218-19

definition 215
dismissal for participation in, 206,
212-19
non-selective, 214-15
reasonableness of, 217-18
redundancy, selection for, 217-18
reinstatement or re-engagement
212
unfair 212
immunities 205
notice of, 216
right to, 32, 212-4
Constitution, under, 212*n*-13*n*
international law, 213*n*
unlawful acts in connection with, 214
SUMMARY DISMISSAL 27, 57-62
grounds existing at time of dismissal
57-61
lawful, when, 57-62
reasons justifying 58-9
subsequent evidence 61-2
unlawful, 62
damages for, 94
SUPERANNUATION, *see* Pension
Rights
SUPREME COURT
judicial review 29-30

TAX, *see* Income Tax
TEMPORARY EMPLOYEE 130*n*
TEMPORARY OFFICER
civil servant 51
local authority, of, 131*n*-32*n*, 222*n*
TERMINATION OF CONTRACT
common law, at, *see* Common Law
meaning 85-6
repudiatory breach, effect of, on,
unfair dismissal context, 134-40
wrongful dismissal context 81-6,
230-1
wrongful, *see* Wrongful Dismissal
TERMS OF EMPLOYMENT
dismissal procedures, inclusion of, 64
written statement 63
THEFT, DISMISSAL FOR, 149,
158*n*, 165-6, 166*n*
reasonableness test 168-9
TIME LIMITS
unfair dismissal claims and appeals
133-4
wrongful dismissal claims 87
TRADE DISPUTE
definition of, 18, 205
dismissal, relating to, 18, 27*n*,
205-06

reference to Rights Commr. 127
statistics, 116, 204
immunities 205
industrial action
definition 216-17
dismissal for, 206, 212, 217
strike, *see* Strike
unofficial disputes
analysis of causes, 1977-9, 204*n*
wrongful dismissal, cases concerning
206*n*
TRADE UNION
closed shop agreement 109*n*
pre-entry 38-9
right of dissociation and, 35
right to work and, 37-8
collective agreements
dismissal procedures in, 26-7, 63*n*
enforceability of, 26
freedom of association 34-5, 209
freedom of dissociation 35, 209
membership and activities, dismissal
for, 130, 208
burden of proof 208
Constitution and, 209
unfair, 206-09
non-membership of, dismissal for,
207*n*, 208-09
TRAINING, DISMISSAL DURING,
132
TRIBUNALS 76-81
fair procedures, right to, 39-40
hearings, *see* Hearing

UNCONSTITUTIONAL DISMISSAL
33
remedies for, 40-4
rights in relation to, 33-4
UNESTABLISHED CIVIL
SERVANT 51
UNFAIR DISMISSAL
agreements
excluding or limiting application of
Act, 121, 142*n*
alternative remedies, regulation of,
126-7
appeals *see* Appeal
basic principles of Act, 120-1
claims
applications, 267-9
costs of, 126
determination of, *see:* Employment Appeals Tribunal; Rights
Commissioner
procedure 125-6, 222*n*

regulations 256-9
time for bringing 133-4, 222*n*
withdrawal of, 225
code of practice, need for, 203*n*
collective aspects 203-19
compensation, *see* Compensation for
Unfair Dismissal
constructive dismissal *see* Constructive dismissal
contract of employment, based on,
128
date of dismissal 137, 143-4
defects in Act 128
dismissal
conflict of evidence as to, 142
constructive, *see* Constructive Dismissal
definition 134, 222, 231
employee repudiation 138-9, 142
fact of, 134-40, 142
fixed term contract, expiry of, 134,
135
theories of termination 136-40,
143-4
dispute dismissals 127
employee, definition 129*n*, 130
employer, definition 130
Employment Appeals Tribunal, *see*
Employment Appeals Tribunal
enforcing authorities 121-7
exclusions and qualifications 128-33
age-limit 130
continuous service 129-30, 222*n*
excluded categories 130-2
fixed-term contract 132
hours of employment 129*n*-30*n*
replacement employee 133
small employments 130
fairness, specific conception of, 120-1
fixed term contract, non-renewal of,
132, 134, 135
legal aid 122*n*, 125, 224-5
legislation
common law, contrast with, 221
defects in, 222
history of, 116-20
international influences 116-19
interpretation of, by EAT 226-7
preliminary requirements 128-33
principles 120-1
reforms suggested 128, 222, 227
review of, 221-2, 231
text of Act, 233-55
managerial prerogative,
limitations on, 206-07

maternity protection provisions 133
presumption of unfairness 207
property right in job 175-6
reason for dismissal, *see* Reason for
   Dismissal
reasonableness of employer,
   see Reasonableness of Decision to
   Dismiss
re-engagement, *see* Reinstatement
   and Re-engagement
remedies for, 175-202
   see: Compensation; Reinstatement
   and Re-engagement
replacement worker, dismissal of,
   133
temporary employee 130n
time-limits for claims and appeals
   133-4
wrongful dismissal action, exclusion
   of, 126-7
union *see* Trade Union
UNION-MANAGEMENT AGREE-
   MENT
dismissal in accordance with, 160n
UNION MEMBERSHIP AGREE-
   MENT, *see* Closed Shop

WARNING 162-4
adequate communication necessary
   163, 164
agreed procedure, example of, 162n
omission to give, 162-3
WORK, RIGHT TO, 32, 37-9
closed shop and, 37-8
WRONGFUL DISMISSAL
action for, 19-20, 23-5, 45, 62-81

development of caselaw 23-5
excludes redress under UDA
   126-7
time for bringing 87
constitutional right, infringement of,
   32-40
contract, effect on, 45, 62, 81-6,
   230-1
damages for, *see* Damages
employee, 62-8
   definition 46-7
   implied term of fairness, breach of,
      64-6
   procedural limitations 63-4, 94-5
   remedies 87-91, *and see* Damages
   substantive limitations, breach of,
      66-7, 94
employer's defence 45
office-holders and public employees
   67-86
   definition 47-51
   natural justice 69-81, *see also*
      Natural Justice
   remedies 109-15
remedies for, 87-115
   damages, *see* Damages
   declaratory relief 90, 109-10
   equitable remedies, refusal of, for
      employees 87-91
   injunctions 89-90, 109
   specific performance, refusal of,
      87-90
special category employees 67-8
summary dismissal 62

YEARLY HIRING 21-2, 53, 54